The Myth of 1648

Class, Geopolitics, and the Making of
Modern International Relations

BENNO TESCHKE

VERSO

London • New York

First published by Verso 2003
© Benno Teschke 2003
All rights reserved

The moral rights of the author have been asserted

1 3 5 7 9 10 8 6 4 2

Verso
UK: 6 Meard Street, London W1F 0EG
USA: 180 Varick Street, New York, NY 10014–4606
www.versobooks.com

Verso is the imprint of New Left Books

ISBN 1–85984–693–9

British Library Cataloguing in Publication Data
A catalogue record for this book is available from the British Library

Library of Congress Cataloging-in-Publication Data
A catalog record for this book is available from the Library of Congress

Typeset in 11 on 13.5 Bembo by
SetSystems Ltd, Saffron Walden, Essex
Printed in the UK by Bath Press

Für meinen Vater

Contents

Acknowledgements

This book is a revised version of a doctoral thesis researched at the Department of International Relations, London School of Economics and Political Science, under the supervision of Justin Rosenberg, to whom I am grateful for his inspirational intellectual companionship and unfailing moral support. In an academic climate that militates against large-scale and long-term critical social science projects whose economic benefits and user communities are not readily identifiable, such support cannot be taken for granted. His 'Modernity and IR' and 'Historical Materialism and IR' seminars at the LSE provided the principal context for developing and testing many of the ideas offered in this book. I am equally indebted to Robert Brenner, who gave the project a new impetus and direction while I was a fellow at his Center for Social Theory and Comparative History at the University of California, Los Angeles. The argument benefited considerably from probing questions by Simon Bromley during the doctoral examination and Peter Gowan's discerning written comments on the manuscript. In a very different sense, I am grateful for years of intense intellectual debate with Christian Heine and Hannes Lacher at the LSE. Some of the ideas presented here were developed collectively by us and are further elaborated in Lacher's forthcoming monograph on globalization. The thesis also benefited from the sympathetic advice offered by Herfried Münkler during a research period at the Institut für Politische Theorie at the Humboldt-Universität zu Berlin. I am also grateful to the LSE's Department of International Relations for award of an R.J. Vincent Memorial Scholarship and to the Center for Social Theory and Comparative History at the University of California, Los Angeles for the award of an Andrew Mellon Fellowship. Further thanks are due to Perry Anderson, Gopal Balakrishnan, Sebastian Budgen, Alejandro Colas, Alan Finlayson, Fred Halliday, Hajo Krombach, Tom Mertes, Dylan Riley, Henning

Teschke, Kees van der Pijl, Achin Vanaik, Ellen Meiksins Wood, and fellow graduate participants at LSE and UCLA seminars. I would also like to acknowledge the effective guidance and patience of my editor, Tim Clark at Verso, and the superbly conscientious editing of James Ingram from the New School in New York and Miranda Chaytor in London. My final thanks go to my wife, Maryam, for her years of encouragement, support, and innumerable improvements to the manuscript.

An earlier version of chapter 2 was published under the title 'Geopolitical Relations in the European Middle Ages: History and Theory', in *International Organization*, 52 (2), 1998, pp. 325–58. Parts of chapters 7 and 8 were published as 'Theorising the Westphalian System of States: International Relations from Absolutism to Capitalism', in the *European Journal of International Relations*, 8 (1), 2002, pp. 5–48. I am grateful to MIT Press and Sage Publications for permission to republish the articles in adapted form. *Habent sua fata libelli.*

This book is about fundamental socio-political and geopolitical transformations. For some transformations, the time is yet to come.

New Delhi, October 2002

Introduction

The Myth of 1648

Empire, neo-medievalism, multi-level global governance, republican peace – these are some of the concepts and metaphors invoked in contemporary International Relations (IR) and International Political Economy (IPE) to make sense of recent changes in the structure of the international system. The causes, nature, and extent of these changes are, of course, widely debated among the defenders of competing theoretical approaches within these two disciplines. While Realists insist on a mere reconfiguration of the balance of power, premised on changes in the distribution of power across the system's units, affecting only the polarity within an unaltered anarchical system of states, the near-unanimous verdict in the non-Realist camp is that traditional state sovereignty is under attack. The classical Westphalian system, rooted in the primacy of the modern, territorially bounded sovereign state, is being replaced by a post-territorial, postmodern global order. The old logic of geopolitical security is being subordinated to geo-economics, multi-level global governance, or the demands of a multi-actor international civil society. A fundamental transformation in the structure of the international system and its rules of conflict and co-operation is unfolding before our eyes. However, while Realists and non-Realists diverge in their assessments of the contemporary world-historical conjuncture, IR and IPE scholars are united in invoking the Westphalian states-system as the benchmark for measuring the present-day structure of world politics.

Uncertainty over the direction and consequences of contemporary trends has forced the IR community to readdress the wider problem of the general nature of transformations between and within international systems by appealing to history as a surer guide to theory-building. The historical turn in IR has produced a new set of questions. If modern sovereignty and the modern states-system are in decline, how did they come about? If we are on the threshold of a new international order, what lessons can we learn from earlier geopolitical transformations? If this new order threatens to undermine state sovereignty rooted in exclusive territoriality as the fundamental building-block of inter-state relations, does the discipline lose its status as an independent social science, justified by the existence of a discrete sphere of the 'international'?

Conventionally, the question of the rise of the modern international order is associated with the peace treaties of Westphalia that ended the Thirty Years' War. From American political science via British IR to German social philosophy, the shared conviction is that the Westphalian settlement organized the European order on the basis of sovereign states adhering to distinctly modern principles of conflict and co-operation. Cross-disciplinary and cross-paradigmatic convergence on 1648 as the origin of modern international relations has given the discipline of IR a sense of theoretical direction, thematic unity, and historical legitimacy. A line of tacit acceptance runs through the literature, passed down unexamined from IR generation to IR generation. Dates cannot lie, and the more distant the dates, the less the willingness to uncover their social content, context, and significance. But periodization is no innocent exercise, no mere pedagogical and heuristic device to plant markers in the uncharted flow of history. It entails assumptions about the duration and identity of specific epochs and geopolitical orders, as it implicates IR theories with respect to the adequacy of criteria adduced to theorize the continuity or discontinuity of international orders. Consequently, agreement on 1648's modernity implies further claims about the persistence of the Westphalian order from the mid-seventeenth century to the present. While few IR scholars would argue that seventeenth-century European politics can be directly compared with twentieth-century international politics, most do agree that the fundamental principles of geopolitical order have not changed in the last 340 years, and may only have been challenged in the course of the last decade or two.[1]

According to this conventional account, shared by Realists, members of the English school, and Constructivists alike, the Westphalian treaties were a decisive turning point in the history of international relations. After 1648, formalized relations between modern sovereign states superseded the criss-crossing relations between heterogeneous feudal actors capped by the hierarchical claims of the Empire and the Church. The consolidation of exclusive sovereignty, resting on the internal monopolization of the means of violence, translated into rulers' exclusive control of the instruments of foreign policy – the army, diplomacy, and treaty-making. By the mid-seventeenth century, only rulers holding these prerogatives were subjects of international law, based on mutual recognition to the exclusion of rival power centres. With the arrogation of the means of violence by multiple sovereigns and the concomitant establishment of bounded territoriality, the field of politics was formally differentiated into distinct domestic and international spheres, based on internal political hierarchy and external geopolitical anarchy. After the Westphalian settlement, non-territorial political actors, city-states, city-leagues, feudal lords, and other corporate actors 'dropped out' of international politics. International relations were institutionalized in permanent embassies, co-ordinating international affairs through regular diplomatic intercourse governed by codified and binding diplomatic protocols and culminating in the regular convocation of multi-lateral congresses. At the same time, political sovereignty and the discourse of *raison d'État* secularized international relations by undermining religion as a mode of legitimacy, curtailing the universalizing ambitions of the Roman Catholic Church. The separation of politics and religion and the concomitant idea of self-determination entailed the principle of peaceful coexistence among legally equal members of international society. This was embodied in a code of international law that acknowledged mutual recognition, non-intervention, and religious toleration. Universal conceptions of empire and papal aspirations to moral primacy in the context of the *res publica christiana* gave way to the balance of power as the natural regulator of competitive international relations in a multipolar, anarchical environment. In the period between the Peace of Westphalia (1648) and the Peace of Utrecht (1713), the international states-system started to approximate to modern international relations.

This interpretation of the Westphalian settlement has over time become a constitutive foundation myth within IR. In contrast, this book argues that 1648, far from signalling a breakthrough to modern inter-state relations, was the culmination of the epoch of absolutist state formation; it marked the recognition and regulation of the international – or, to be more precise, inter-dynastic – relations of absolutist, dynastic polities. But any substantiation of this thesis cannot merely point to the external properties of political phenomena – sovereignty, bounded territoriality, multiple states – or to 'anarchy' as the systemic structuring principle of international order. It has to unpack the *social relations of sovereignty* that underwrote the Westphalian order to reveal its non-modern nature. This demands a social and historical approach. The Neorealist 'logic of anarchy' says next to nothing about the generative sources and substantive practices – wars of succession, political marriages, dynastic unions, mercantilist trade wars, and eliminatory equilibrium – of early modern international relations. However, it is one thing to read contemporary historiography that rectifies empirical shortcomings, and quite another to develop an alternative theoretical framework that provides an original reconstruction of the meaning of 1648 in the wider historical continuum of the evolution of the European states-system. This study seeks to demystify Westphalia by offering a revisionist interpretation of the development and dynamics of the European states-system between the eighth and eighteenth centuries, rooted in a dialectical historical-materialist approach. My interpretation revolves around five axes of inquiry.

1. A *comparative historical sociology* that seeks to specify the differences between varying geopolitical orders. If there is a growing consensus that international politics across the centuries does not abide by one transhistorical 'covering law', then we need to identify differentiated sets of international 'rules of the game'. To what degree do international relations vary across different historical periods, be they the classical, medieval, renaissance, early modern, modern, or contemporary eras? What was the nature and meaning of geopolitical core institutions such as political authority and public power, peace and war, territoriality and borders, legitimation and coercion, empire-building and geopolitical fragmentation, alliance formation and the resolution of conflicts across these different historical periods?

2. A *causal inquiry* that examines the fundamental determinants of these systemic variations. How should we understand the nexus between geopolitics, political authority, and social forces? While complex, large-scale and macrohistorical phenomena do not easily comply with the social-scientific demands of causal rigour and systematicity, the flight into narrative and description is not an uncontested option either. This poses again the challenge of identifying causalities and/ or the reasons – and maybe even the reasons behind the reasons – that actors, collective and individual, give themselves for justifying their actions. This calls for an elaboration and clarification of the core explanatory variables within the Realist, Constructivist and Critical strands of IR theory.

3. A *dynamic perspective* that attempts to identify and theorize the major agents and processes of systemic geopolitical transformations. Is geopolitical change a function of the rise and fall of great powers and

their hegemonic projects and the uneven distribution of power across the system's conflict units, or is it driven by the deeper and organic structures and conjunctures of social and economic history? Does it spring from learning processes within the diplomatic community and from ingenious statecraft, or is it determined by collective changes in the mentality and self-understandings of collective actors and the transfer of ideas? Do transformations follow changes in the balance of class forces that lead to major regime changes and the restructuration of international orders, or do changes in class structures and political regimes follow geopolitical pressures and transformations? Are these processes of change gradual, evolutionary, and almost imperceptible, or do they manifest themselves abruptly and violently during major periods of systemic crisis?

4. An inquiry into the *chronological and geographical origins of modern international relations*. Should we assume that the origins of the contemporary international system can be adequately conceptualized in terms of one 'medieval-to-modern shift', or should we refine this simplified perspective by arguing the case for a series of transitions between and among distinct geopolitical orders, whose cumulative effect was the contemporary geopolitical configuration? If we have to deal with several major transitions, what are the implications for determining the origins of the modern order? If it does not fall, as generally assumed, in the seventeenth century after the Westphalian peace settlement, can we identify a later system-wide caesura, be it the Treaties of Rastatt–Utrecht, the Congress of Vienna, or even, the peace treaty of Versailles? What was the connection between the development of the modern state – and, *a fortiori*, plurality of states – and capitalism? When was modernity in international relations?

5. A *re-evaluation and refinement of IR theories* in terms of their internal logical stringency, political implications, and explanatory power, as measured against the historical evidence. While it is possible for didactic purposes to group very diverse scholars together under convenient labels, differences within competing schools of thought are often as pronounced as differences between them. Even if cross-paradigmatic agreement is hardly possible, and perhaps not even desirable in a pluralist scientific community, the objective is to bring out divergences and convergences in perspectives as clearly as possible to allow for constructive criticism at the levels of empirical accuracy, immanent logic, explanatory reach, and epistemological assumptions.

I combine two modes of exposition. First, I proceed comparatively and chronologically by elaborating and contrasting different historical logics of 'international' relations, exemplified by the medieval, early modern, and modern geopolitical systems. This *comparative perspective* allows us to identify fundamental differences in their respective patterns of co-operation and conflict. Second, I adopt a developmental perspective with a more narrative, yet theoretically controlled, exposition of the domestic and international dynamics that drove systemic transformations. This *processual perspective* enables us also to address the crucial question of the causes of passages from one geopolitical order to another. However, the conception of history as a process also reveals that these transformations were never system-wide occurrences that justify the representation of world history as a clear succession of different geopolitical orders. Since changes in state forms were regionally and chronologically highly uneven, we need to theorize the international relations of diverse co-existing political actors in 'mixed-actor' systems.

IR theory is ideally placed to combine comparative studies with developmental explanations, given that one of its disciplinary axioms is that political communities are never self-contained entities, but that their forms and development are always already co-determined by numerous interactions within a wider geopolitical environment. However, the relative paucity of IR contributions to a historical sociology of international relations requires mobilizing non-IR literatures on general historical development. In historical sociology, the key problem is defined by long-standing debates on the rise of the modern state. This includes the body of thought on medieval and early modern state-building, as well as that on the rise of modern economic relations, including the literature on pre-capitalist economic systems and the origins of capitalism. This involves an extensive engagement with neo-Weberian historical sociology, which has provided during the last two decades the most influential accounts of the impact of military competition in a multipolar states-system on state formation, social revolutions, and general historical development. The objective is not to provide an exhaustive exegesis of Karl Marx's 'sacred' texts, but to think through the latest results of contemporary historiography in their relevance for the discipline of IR, informed by a dialectical understanding of historical development.

The Core Theoretical Argument

Any encounter between IR as a social science and history will have to start from the assumption that there is no universal covering law that explains international conduct across the centuries, as there is no one general explanatory theory of history. However, this proposition does not warrant the call for methodological pluralism, the intellectual abdication to contingency, and the retreat to thick narrative descriptions. The task is to identify a social praxis whose construction, destruction, and reconstruction mediates humanity's metabolism with nature, while centrally implicating politics and geopolitics: social property relations. My core theoretical argument, developed by elaborating the principles of political Marxism, is that the constitution, operation, and transformation of geopolitical orders are predicated on the changing identities of their constitutive units.[2] Social property relations, mediating the relations between the major classes, primarily define the *constitution* and identity of these political units. The time-bound balances of social forces find expression in politically constituted institutions – petrified praxes – that set the parameters for class-specific, and therefore antagonistic, rules of reproduction. Political institutions fix social property regimes, providing rules and norms, as well as force and sanctions, for the reproduction of historically specific class relations. Strategies of reproduction, in turn, define domestic and international relations, accounting for the *modes of operation* of diverse geopolitical orders. While politically constituted property regimes institutionalize social conflicts and set the limits of class-specific strategies, they may themselves be contested in times of general crisis.

Yet no transhistorical theory of general crisis can be superimposed upon the historical evidence. On the contrary, the conditions, general course, and outcomes of these crises can only be established through historical inquiry. History is not teleological, but it is retrospectively intelligible. *Geopolitical transformations* are governed by the variable, but not contingent, resolution of these social conflicts, which generate new property regimes and authority relations, fixing the new status quo by providing new rules and norms for its reproduction. Changes in property regimes restructure the identity of political communities and their distinct forms of conflict and co-operation. Rule maintenance and rule negotiation – violent or not – are active and conscious processes, both domestically and internationally.

This elementary theoretical argument will be referred to throughout the text as *the theory of social property relations*. This alternative point of departure generates a series of substantive results that challenge central assumptions of IR theory and historical sociology.

Structure of the Argument

The implications of the theory of social property relations for IR and historical sociology are developed over eight chapters. The first chapter surveys six influential IR interpretations of the historical development of the European states-system. It begins by briefly examining the ahistorical assumptions of Neorealism and its inability to comprehend systemic geopolitical transformations and variations in international behaviour. It then critically reviews two innovative Constructivist accounts that start from the assumption that international systems cannot be dissociated from history, locating the core problematique of IR theory in the emergence and possible supersession of the modern international system. The chapter then moves on to assess the strengths and weaknesses of a recent neo-Marxist interpretation. It concludes by offering an outline of how to reframe our theoretical perspective in order to address the question of the long-term and large-scale transformation of geopolitical orders. The objective is to contribute to the historical turn in IR by providing a critical theory of international relations.

Chapter 2 begins with a reconstruction of the origins and development of the European states-system by critically intervening into the ongoing IR debate on the Middle Ages. It develops the theory of social property relations by contrasting and comparing Max Weber's and Karl Marx's positions on the relation between the political and the economic, and reconceptualizes Marx's thought on pre-capitalist societies by drawing on the work of Robert Brenner. It then reinterprets medieval geopolitical order on this basis. The argument is that conditional feudal property relations governed the contradictory strategies of reproduction of the two dominant classes (lords and peasants). These strategies determined the territorial and administrative properties of the medieval polity as an ensemble of lordships, explain economic non-development, and reveal the character of medieval geopolitics as a culture of war driven by systematic reinvestment in the means of coercion and (geo)political accumulation. Neither system-structure (anarchy/hierarchy) nor modes of territoriality but social property relations explain feudal geopolitics.

Chapter 3 turns to the history of the social relations of lordship. It starts by outlining the proprietary basis of the Carolingian Empire, theorizes the transition from imperial hierarchy to feudal fragmentation during the crisis of the millennium, as a result of changes in class relations and explains the fourfold outward movement of the eleventh century (the Norman Conquest, the German *Ostsiedlung*, the Spanish *Reconquista*, and the Crusades) as an outcome of the land hunger of ex-Frankish knights after the introduction of primogeniture that restricted noble access to the political means of appropriation. It then shows how the twelfth-century urban revival was connected to feudal class relations and why growing inter-urban commerce was neither a capitalist phenomenon, nor the motor behind a European 'economic take-off'. The chapter concludes by theorizing the reconsolidation of feudal kingdoms during the high Middle Ages as processes of geopolitical accumulation and traces the medieval beginnings of the divergent trajectories of state/society formation in France and England – developments that laid down the territorial parameters for Europe as a multi-actor system of states.

Chapter 4 interrupts the historical reconstruction for some fundamental theoretical clarifications. It starts by re-examining three influential histori-cal-sociological theories of the transition to modernity: the neo-Weberian geopolitical competition model, the neo-Malthusian demographic model, and the neo-Marxist commercialization model, contending that all three models fail on theoretical as well as empirical grounds. Drawing on the work of political Marxists, I then develop an alternative conception of capitalism that shows the link between capitalist social property relations and the specifically modern state. But I also stress that while the modern state is internal to the capital relation, the modern states-system (multiple territories) in which capitalism later emerged was the legacy of inter-ruling class conflict among pre-capitalist rulers. The conception of capitalism adopted here breaks with the conventional view that its development was a system-wide and simultaneous European occurrence driven by the urban revival and the expansion of trade (either in the twelfth or sixteenth century). By rejecting the neo-Smithean assumptions that underlie much of the literature on the expansion of capitalism, I argue that economic and political development in medieval and early modern Europe was highly regionally divergent, especially in France and England, leading to very different state/society complexes that are central to understanding the nature and dynamics of the early modern and modern states-systems. This set of theses provides a new starting point for rethinking the uneven transition to economic and (geo)political modernity.

Against this background, chapter 5 resumes the historical reconstruction by investigating the development and nature of absolutism in France – the dominant signatory of the Peace of Westphalia. I start by retracing the regionally specific transition from feudalism to absolutism and explore the nexus between the persistence of pre-capitalist social property relations, economic non-development, and the logic of personalized dynastic sovereignty. I then show the distinctly pre-modern nature of core absolutist institutions – office venality, a standing army, taxation, the legal system, and the nature of warfare – and conclude that the bellicose nature of absolutist states was the external expression of political strategies of accumulation rooted in a social property regime characterized by a tax/office state taking coerced rents from a peasantry in possession of its means of subsistence. Far from preparing the transition to capitalism, absolutism entrenched pre-capitalist agrarian property regimes through excessive levels of taxation that penalized productivity and technological progress. The nexus between a pre-capitalist property regime and punitive taxation cyclically subverted and finally exhausted the performance of the French agrarian economy that remained governed throughout the early modern period by typically pre-capitalist eco-demographic cycles. Simultaneously, absolutism entailed the hypertrophic growth of a dysfunctional, non-bureaucratic state apparatus geared towards external war and coercive internal surplus extraction. The absolutist state was not modern, rationalized, or 'efficient'. The chapter concludes that *Ancien Régime* France was not only distinctly non-modern, but that its social property regime hindered a transition to both capitalism and a rationalized state. In the long run, the breakdown of the absolutist-patrimonial 'tax/office' state was 'externally' induced, deriving primarily from the economic and military pressures exerted by capitalist Britain.

Chapter 6 explores the nature and dynamics of the early modern international political economy against the claim that the 'long sixteenth century' inaugurated the modern world-system. The argument is that both the trading empires of the Italian city-states and the mercantilist empires of early modern dynastic states depended upon the territorial projection of political and military power for the generation of commercial profits. This generated a zero-sum logic of militarized international trading monopolies that prevented sustained economic growth. Economic empire-building and power-political reach were coextensive and thus incommensurable with the capitalist logic of economic competition, regulated by the price mechanism, through free trade in open markets. The social logic of mercantilism was rooted in a 'backward-looking' class-alliance between rights-dispensing monarchs and privileged merchants, both reaping and sharing the profits of unequal exchange. The chapter concludes that the rise of capitalism was not an outcome of the expansion of trade promoted by either commercial capitalism or mercantilism, and that the sixteenth-century international economy remained tied to the age-old commercial practices of buying cheap and selling dear.

Chapter 7 challenges the core IR myth that the Westphalian settlement inaugurated the era of modern international relations. Building on the argument for the non-modern nature of dynastic sovereignty, the chapter advances an account of inter-dynastic relations during the Age of Westphalia. It shows why and how dynastic sovereignty translated into a series of 'peculiar' practices of geopolitical conflict and co-operation specific to the early modern geopolitical order. The logic of international relations was characterized by dynastic unions welded together through royal and aristocratic political marriages, and torn asunder by wars of succession. Territories remained an adjunct of royal marriage policies and inter-dynastic wars of succession. The predatory logic of dynastic equilibrium was incompatible with the Realist balance of power. The chapter concludes with a textual reinterpretation of the Westphalian peace treaties' provisions that demonstrates how 1648 expressed and codified the social and geopolitical relations of absolutist sovereignty.

The final chapter argues that the origins of modern international relations were bound up with the rise of capitalism in early modern England. But rather than assuming a sudden 'structural break' in the logic of international relations – from early modern to modern geopolitics – I stress the peculiar combination of different state/society complexes in early modern Europe, which have to be theorized as a 'mixed-case' scenario. I first set out the effects of the establishment of agrarian capitalism in England on the transformation of the seventeenth-century English state as a shift from dynastic to parliamentary sovereignty, sealed in the Glorious Revolution of 1688. I then show how the adoption of a new post-revolutionary and parliamentary foreign policy – the 'blue-water' policy – was linked to the reorganization of economic and political power in Britain, and how it broke with pre-capitalist imperatives of geopolitical accumulation. I then draw out its consequences for eighteenth-century European geopolitics. The argument is that British power-balancing occurred in a 'mixed' states-system still fundamentally constituted by pre-capitalist, geopolitically accumulating states. Active power-balancing had the side-effect of playing states off against each other until they were militarily and financially exhausted. While the endogenous development of capitalism was unique to England, its expansion was not a transnational but a *geopolitically mediated* process that transformed the dynastic states on the continent into modern states in a long-term process of geopolitically combined and socio-politically uneven development. In this process, international relations in nineteenth-century Europe were largely about the management of the modernizing pressure created by the new British state/society complex, which put its European neighbours at a *competitive and economic comparative disadvantage*. This forced state classes to design counter-strategies that led to a series of 'revolutions from above' – the introduction of capitalism. This long period of transformation lasted from 1688 to the First World War for Europe, and beyond for the rest of the world. International relations during this period were not modern, but *modernizing*. However, while the expansion of capitalism had a profound impact on European class and regime changes (from absolutism to capitalism and from dynastic to modern sovereignty), it could not alter Europe's territorially divided nature as a geopolitical pluriverse. Plural territories were a determinate outcome of conflicts among pre-capitalist ruling classes. But it is precisely this pre-capitalist legacy that may today be threatened by globalization and global governance, whether in a more unilateral-imperialist or in a multilateral guise.

The conclusion summarizes the results and draws out their broader implications for IR theory and historical sociology, sketching a historical and theoretical research programme that follows from the dynamic approach developed in the previous chapters. It reflects on the politically and intellectually deleterious effects of IR 'rationalism' and advocates dialectic as the appropriate meta-theory for thinking about international relations.

Notes

1 In the absence of a more accurate term, I use the term geopolitics generically for all relations between public carriers of political power. For the specific meaning of the German inter-war tradition of *Geopolitik*, see Teschke 2001.
2 Core texts of this paradigm include Brenner 1977, 1985a, 1985b, 1986, 1989, 1993, 2001; Wood 1991, 1995, 2002; Comninel 1987. See also Anderson 1974a, 1974b; Gerstenberger 1990; Rosenberg 1994. Meta-theoretically, the theory of social property relations is compatible with dialectical thinking; see Heine and Teschke 1996, 1997; Teschke and Heine 2002. Core reference texts on dialectic are Kosík 1976; Bernstein 1972; Schmidt 1981.

Origins and Evolution of the Modern States-System:

The Debate in International Relations Theory

1. Introduction: From Structure to History

Attempts to reintroduce a historical dimension into IR theory are for the better part still locked into the methodological parameters of Neorealism and bear the marks of its peculiar idiom. I begin by showing the ahistorical nature of Neorealism and criticizing the self-referential logic of its theoretical closure. I then seek to show how the subsequent intellectual trajectory of historicizing IR theories is marked by a successive theoretical emancipation from the conceptual strictures of Neorealism. The inverse relation between intellectual faithfulness to IR's major theory and explanatory power is exemplified by Robert Gilpin's historicizing Realism, Stephen Krasner's rereading of the Westphalian peace treaties, John Gerard Ruggie's historicizing Constructivism, Hendrik Spruyt's neo-evolutionary historical sociology, and Justin Rosenberg's Marxist account. The first four authors – representative of broader strands within contemporary IR theory – either belong to or struggle with the Realist/Neorealist tradition. While Gilpin seeks to reaffirm the richness of Realism by incorporating a rational-choice theory of social action and change into an essentially systemic framework, Stephen Krasner dissolves the Westphalian order into a series of historical accidents that resist theorization. He thus reinstates Realism as the only meaningful IR theory. While Ruggie undertakes a progressive shift towards Social Constructivism, Spruyt embraces a post-Neorealist Constructivist framework from the outset. The intellectual filiation ends with Justin Rosenberg's powerful Marxist account, a direct attack on Realism's explanatory utility and ideological complicity. Confronted with concrete historical questions, IR theory is forced to diversify and widen its methodological stances.

By critically retracing this process of paradigmatic reorientation, we will see how the terrain of IR theory shifted from a narrowly defined positivism that privileged structure to a wider social, and finally critical theory of macro-historical processes. In the process, academic IR underwent a profound methodological self-examination reconnecting with contemporary social science. Yet this restructuring ran into theoretical and empirical problems. While the historical turn in IR discarded the positivist certainties of Neorealism, no convincing long-term and large-scale account emerged that combined a comparative perspective with a systematic inquiry into systemic transformations.

But why was history, in spite of the 'International Society' literature associated with the 'English school', cleansed from contemporary IR theory? Why did IR theory, under the shadow of Neorealism's intellectual hegemony, turn into a discipline without history?

2. Structural Neorealism

Kenneth Waltz: History as Perennial Structure

In a decisive step away from the pre-scientific moralizing premises of classical Realism, Kenneth Waltz pegged the absolute limits of international politics to the overriding imperatives of anarchy, the fundamental structural principle of the international system. From this perspective, qualitative transformations of the system shrank to an alternation between two structural principles: anarchy and hierarchy (Waltz 1979: 114–16). This had the doubtful advantage of subsuming history under two rubrics. As long as the states-system comprises a multiplicity of functionally undifferentiated actors, anarchy prevails; as soon as empires or other forms of central authority are identifiable, hierarchy reigns. Although Waltz allowed for alteration within a system due to changes in the distribution of power among its units, they were relevant only to switches from multipolarity to bipolarity, leaving the deep logic of anarchy untouched. In such a system of survival, units are forced to behave according to the tenets of self-help and power maximization. Power-balancing and alliance-building bring stability, security, and order.[1] Strong behavioural regularities are inferred from the overriding logic of anarchy. Balancing, not bandwagoning, should occur in the case of marked power asymmetries between states. Although acknowledging the domestic causes of variations in power capabilities, Waltz's structuralist model – with the exception of the persistence of anarchy itself – is completely indeterminate in its predictive and retrospective, that is, historically explanatory, capacities. It depends upon 'exogenous variables' to explain why an actor opted for alliance-building in a specific situation while another took to war (Waltz 1988: 620). Both extreme potentialities (and an infinity of intermediate solutions) are covered as long as the systemic end of equilibrium is preserved by the balance of power. The survival of the system overrides the survival of any of its components.

On these premises, history turns into a non-problem. Anarchy shrinks causally to a permissive cause, hierarchy eclipses the need for IR theory, and variations in unit-level causes do not entail variations in observable outcomes. Laconically, Waltz maintains that 'the logic of anarchy does not vary with its content. . . . The logic of anarchy obtains whether the system is composed of tribes, nations, oligopolistic firms, or street gangs' (Waltz 1990: 37). The case for history as perennial anarchical structure seems to be established.

The immanent coherence of Waltz's argumentation seems impeccable. Critique is strategically pre-empted by the definition of the type of theory formation embraced by Waltz: 'Theories must be evaluated in terms of what they claim to explain' (Waltz 1979: 118). The effect of this immunization strategy is that questions which address problems that do not fall within the ambit of Neorealism's explanatory reach are externalized and invalidated (Halliday and Rosenberg 1998: 379). Thus, critique has to proceed first and foremost on the meta-theoretical level. The key to unlocking the Waltzian theoretical tower lies in questioning Neorealism's hermetic, self-referential, and self-sufficient epistemological nature, which is predicated upon an *a priori* definition of legitimate IR theory. Waltz specifies his appropriate field of inquiry (the international system) by marking it off from all other spheres of human action, introduces one macro-*explanans* (anarchy), deduces international politics from the constraints it imposes, and faults all other approaches for not conforming to his definition of 'scientific' IR.[2] The eviction of human volition (consciousness, choice, policy) and the negation of the very possibility of variable outcomes constitute the criterion for Neorealism's status as a science. On this basis, Waltz's often-cited comment that 'the enduring character of international politics accounts for the striking sameness in the quality of international life through the millennia' (Waltz 1986: 53) appears less the result of historical observation than the consequence of a theorem superimposed on, but not checked by, historical evidence. Since human behaviour is deduced from the anarchical logic of the system, imposing a rational-choice problem, non-compliance does not falsify Neorealism; it is rather branded non-systemic, non-rational, and therefore extra-theoretical behaviour.[3] The system penalizes deviance, but deviance does not penalize the theory. This, of course, inverts the scientific protocols of validation and logic. 'Behavioural anomalies' do not prompt Waltz to reformulate Neo-realism so as to accommodate 'irrational' but purposive behaviour; they rather fall outside its scope, leaving its validity intact. No number of empirical cases could ever refute or validate its theorems; the whole argument becomes circular, self-referential, and self-validating. International politics is objectified, history is frozen, and theory is reified: *mors immortalis!*[4]

The fundamental fallacy of Neorealism is its affirmation of anarchy (in the absence of world government) as a transhistorical given. Anarchy poses as the unexamined historical condition for its transformation into a theoretical principle. Anarchy as history and anarchy as theory are conflated, leaving only tautology: anarchy prevails wherever the conditions for its existence are met. Consequently, the natural starting point for a critique of Neorealism is a shift to the historical conditions of anarchy, i.e., a theory of the formation of the modern system of states. This research-organizing shift readmits history as a legitimate and necessary field of inquiry for IR theory. Simultaneously, it destroys Neorealism's rationale as a 'non-reductionist' theory in which the burden of causality for state behaviour falls exclusively on the system as the primary level of determination. Anarchy must be historicized.

3. Historicizing Realism

1. Robert Gilpin: Systems Change as Rational Choice

Robert Gilpin advances a Realist theory of international change which, from the first, neither succumbs to Waltz's theorem of the causal primacy of systemic structure and his axiomatic acceptance of the transhistoricity of anarchy, nor retreats into ahistorical parsimony. Combining a rational choice approach with a structuralist systems theory, the problem of international change becomes the central focus of his *War and Change in World Politics*. Yet, despite this shift, Gilpin converges in the final analysis with Waltz by concluding that 'the nature of international relations has not changed fundamentally over the millennia' (Gilpin 1981: 211).

How is this claim justified? Gilpin distinguishes between three types of change arranged by ascending frequency and descending structural impact. *Systems change* is 'a change in the nature of the actors or diverse entities that compose an international system'. *Systemic change* refers to 'a change in the form of control or governance of an international system'. *Interaction change* is a change 'in the form of regular interactions or processes among the entities in an ongoing international system' (Gilpin 1981: 39–40). The first denotes a change of the system itself, the second a change within the system, the third a change in the modes of interaction within a given system. In *War and Change in World Politics*, Gilpin focuses on the first two types of transformation.

World history is divided into a pre-modern cycle of empires and a modern system of power-balancing among nation-states characterized by a succession of hegemonies, *Pax Britannica* and *Pax Americana*. The break comes in the seventeenth century. Gilpin claims to have a universal theory to explain the dynamic that drives the cycle of empires, the late medieval rise of the modern nation-state, and the modern succession of hegemonies. Despite some cautionary provisos, he suggests a strict rational-choice model with reference to both systems change and systemic change (Gilpin 1981: 74–5). In the first case, collective actors strive to optimize their political organization once they perceive a discrepancy between returns and costs in maintaining the status quo. In the second case, 'states' seek to alter the governance of the system until equilibrium is reached between the expected costs and benefits of further change (Gilpin 1981: 10–11). The initial incentive behind their disequilibrating ambitions is provided by the differential growth of power capabilities, a function of changing environmental (technological, military, and economic) and domestic factors. A disjuncture between a new distribution of power and the system-maintaining interests of the dominant power generates a geopolitical crisis, which is generally resolved by hegemonic war. These wars restore equilibrium on the basis of a new status quo, regulated by a new hegemon.

How does this model of change on the basis of an interest-driven cost–benefit calculation translate into a historical explanation of imperial cyclical change (systemic change) and the transformation of medieval geopolitics into modern international relations (systems change)?

Let us turn first to the cycle of empires. Gilpin starts off by tying the rise and fall of empires directly to their economic underpinnings. 'The principal determinant of this cycle of empires was the underlying agriculture-based social formation. During this imperial era . . . the wealth of societies and the power of states rested on the exploitation of peasant and slave agriculture' (Gilpin 1981: 111). He proceeds to deduce the dominant dynamic of imperial expansion from this economic basis:

A fundamental feature of the era of empires was the relatively static nature of wealth. In the absence of significant technological advances, agricultural productivity remained at a low level, and the primary determinant of economic growth and wealth was the availability of land and the man/ land ratio. For this reason, the growth of wealth and power of the state was primarily a function of its control over territory that could generate an economic surplus. With only limited and intermittent periods of real economic growth, the dynamics of international relations were provided by the continuous division and redivision of territory and the conquest of slaves (or a docile peasantry) to till the land. Thus, when agriculture was the basis of wealth and power, growth in power and wealth was nearly synonymous with conquest of territory. (Gilpin 1981: 112)

Thus, serf- or slave-based agriculture generates a systematic need for horizontal-territorial expansion, governing the dynamic of pre-modern imperial international relations.

Yet Gilpin draws no further conclusions from this nexus between surplus maximization and territorial expansion. The causal determination of international relations does not run from a specific economic structure to a specific state form, translating into a specific geopolitical dynamic. On the contrary, imperial territorial expansion is the corollary of the nature of imperial command economies, which prioritize public security over private economic interests:

Because empires are created by warriors, bureaucracies, and autocracies in their own interests, the primary function of the imperial economy is to advance the wealth and power of these dominant elites. The economy and economic activities are subordinate to the perceived security and economic interests of the state and the ruling elite. A major function of economic exchange is to enhance the war-making capability of the state. (Gilpin 1981: 112)

Here, the lack of agrarian productivity growth and technological advances are not necessary consequences of labour-intensive, serf- or slave-based modes of production, which prevent systematic reinvestment into production while favouring territorial expansion. Rather, economic development is a function of the security interests of military elites. Thus, the very existence of imperial command economies and strategies of territorial expansion seems to be the solution to contingent economic and technological absences, seized upon by warring elites. By dint of this inversion of cause and effect, the Realist primacy of the political and the military is reinstated.

How, then, do pre-modern empires rise and fall? Instead of finally putting his model to the test by studying a case of imperial decline, Gilpin merely reasserts his basic 'military overstretch' thesis: the costs of military security increase at a faster rate than the economic surplus generated by territorial expansion (Gilpin 1981: 115). At this level of generality, Gilpin is unable to explain the timing, circumstances, and outcome of any concrete case of imperial rise and decline.

Let us turn to the logic of systems change. The replacement of the pre-modern cycle of empires by a system of modern states occurred as the result of three 'interrelated' and mutually 'reinforcing' developments: the triumph of the nation-state, the advent of sustained economic growth, and the emergence of a world market. Nation-states grew because they were 'the most efficient form of political organization for the set of environmental conditions that developed in early modern Europe' (Gilpin 1981: 116). In turn, the politically fragmented feudal system was made possible by a series of absences; Gilpin singles out the lack of long-distance trade and the weakness of central political authority – a perfectly circular argument. When these absences were rectified 'between 900 and 1700' (Gilpin 1981: 118), rulers responded to the incentives provided by the revival of trade and the 'Military Revolution' by setting off rising military costs with broader fiscal bases, creating an 'optimum size' in terms of military and economic efficiency. Simultaneously, a competition among scale-optimizing units set in, in which sub-optimal actors – feudal lords, city-states, and empires – were crowded out. By the seventeenth century, the modern state was born, characterized by its classical Weberian properties: a strong central authority, operated by a bureaucracy on the basis of a uniform set of laws, exercises exclusive control over a well-defined and contiguous territory, enjoying a monopoly over the legitimate use of force (Gilpin 1981: 121–2).[5]

How convincing is this account of the origins of the modern states-system and how does it square with Gilpin's public-choice approach? First, Gilpin's account of systems change commences with a highly contentious assertion:

> there are the localized social formations of the primitive-communal, feudal, and simple petty-commodity types. These economies are characterized by inability of the society to generate a sufficiently large economic surplus to invest in political or economic expansion; frequently these economies do not operate much beyond the subsistence level. This is the situation, for example, with most tribal societies; it was the condition in feudal Europe prior to the revival of long-distance trade in the twelfth

and thirteenth centuries. Because these localized types of society seldom play important roles in international political change, they will not be considered in detail here. (Gilpin 1981: 108–9)

This hypothesis contradicts Gilpin's earlier association of economic surplus and territorial conquest within serf-based agrarian empires. The historical record is replete with examples of relentless feudal geopolitical expansion – the Carolingian Empire, the Angevin Empire, and the German Empire under the Ottonians, the Salians, and the Stauffer. The recurrence of feudal expansion was, however, no accident; as will be shown below, it was built into the social property regime of feudal polities, expressing their very *raison d'être* as cultures of war. These feudal empires did not expand because their economic surplus was great enough to invest in the military, but because the limits of productivity growth in labour-intensive, peasant-based agrarian economies made territorial conquest, next to the intensification of domestic exploitation, the most 'rational' way of expanding lordly income.

Furthermore, while the class contradictions of feudal societies produced a systematic drive for horizontal territorial expansion, medieval social property regimes tended to generate cyclical neo-Malthusian crises mediated by changing land/labour ratios. The best known was the general crisis of the fourteenth century, which Gilpin later acknowledges as having been crucial to 'modern' state formation. By dismissing feudalism as inconsequential for international political change, Gilpin is unable to show how the emergence of an early modern states-system was related to the underlying crisis-ridden dynamic of the feudal system, culminating in the fourteenth-century crisis.

This lack of attention to the feudal case does not go unpunished. For the necessary background conditions for the triumph of the nation-state – the crisis of feudalism, the revival of trade, the growth of a money economy, the 'Military Revolution' – remain theoretically divorced from the nature of the feudal economy. They are introduced as a 'set of environmental conditions', which interfere from outside. This theoretical expulsion of conditions internal to the process of early modern state formation jars with Gilpin's ambitious research agenda:

the character of the international system is largely determined by the type of state-actor: city-states, empires, nation-states, etc. A fundamental task of a theory of international political change is to inquire into the factors that influence the type of state characteristic of a particular era and international system. (Gilpin 1981: 26–7)

Yet this inquiry is missing. These 'factors' simply enter the historical stage like proverbial thunderbolts out of a clear blue sky.

Gilpin also fails to note that the rulers who transformed themselves into territorial kings between the fourteenth and the seventeenth centuries began as feudal lords: 'The changing of economic and political arrangements is a costly affair as individuals must be forced to alter their behaviour in ways contrary to what they regard as their interests. This task of organizational innovation was beyond the military and financial capabilities of the feudal lords' (Gilpin 1981: 119). This statement reveals three problems. First, if Gilpin was faithful to his public-choice approach, feudal lords would not be forced to act contrary to their interests, since they would have opted for a new set of institutions on the basis of a rational insight into the diminishing returns and growing costs of the dominant 'public institution' – lordship. Second, who then was able to perform the task of organizational innovation? For Gilpin, it was late medieval kings. And yet feudal kings were nothing but *primi inter pares*, facing the same mismatch between income and military expenses as non-royal lords. How, then, did they muster the organizational means to turn themselves into something else? This points to the third and central weakness of Gilpin's account: feudal kings did not transform their territories into modern nation-states, but – at least in western continental Europe – into absolutist kingdoms based on unproductive agrarian economies, which aimed at territorial conquests as sources of royal income. In the process, they competed with and generally won out over subaltern feudal lords over the issue of peasant taxation. Thus, the logic of public choice collapses; Gilpin's imputed result, the triumph of the nation-state, turns out to be a mirage. On the basis of this misconceptualization and misperiodization of the early modern state, Gilpin joins the mainstream IR community, which interprets the Westphalian peace treaties as the constitutional charter of the modern system of sovereign states.

This verdict can be substantiated by looking more closely at the logic of the rise of the nation-state. 'The nation-state triumphed over other forms of political organization because it solved the fiscal crisis of feudalism' (Gilpin 1981: 123). Irrespective of the unaddressed problem of the causes of this crisis, Gilpin's sketch imputes a uniformity of post-crisis outcomes of state formation that is hard to reconcile with the historical record. If the success of the nation-state rested upon the achievement of an optimum size, matching fiscal income with military costs and efficiency, then one would expect similar states of similar size to emerge at around the same time. Yet the Age of Absolutism witnessed the coexistence not only of absolutist polities with widely diverging territorial bases and war-making capabilities, but also of widely diverging political regimes – the Dutch oligarchic merchant republic, the post-1688 British constitutional monarchy, the Swiss Confederation, the German confederate Empire, and the Polish aristocratic republic may suffice to prove this point. Furthermore, a truly comprehensive theory of state formation in early modern Europe would also have to explain the failure of certain polities, like Burgundy, to survive, while smaller polities, like the western German mini-absolutisms, endured. A general theory of public choice coupled to a neo-evolutionary theory of competitive selection is unable to account for these 'dysfunctional anomalies'. In short, Gilpin's model is unable to explain why the resolution of the fourteenth-century crisis resulted in diverging political outcomes in different European regions.

This historical problem requires reassessing the public-choice theory of public-institution building. Where the economic theory of public institutions assumes a unity of interests and a functionality and uniformity of outcomes, different responses to identical conditions suggest that the social formation of collective social actors and the interaction among them mediates identical incentives or pressures to different effect. Apart from the minor problem of whether the rational calculus of individual actors – anticipating costs and benefits, while having some knowledge of alternative strategies of action – can actually be empirically shown, the public-choice approach requires an examination of the processes whereby individuals see their interests promoted by collective actors. Variations in policy formation on the basis of uneven bargains determine variations in the institutionalization of aggregated private interests. This Gilpin signally fails to show. The 'choice' of lords is simply inferred from the later existence of more 'efficient' institutions. In this case, there is no choice, but sheer determination. The circularity of this kind of argument and its functionalist and determinist bias has been aptly criticized as the *post hoc, ergo propter hoc* fallacy (Spruyt 1994a: 26). For Gilpin, the causal nexus between interest and outcome remains unproblematic, because his focus is *a priori* reduced to the ruling feudal class, as if it were operating in a frictionless socio-historical vacuum. By failing to set the logic of collective action into a wider social context, and by turning a blind eye to divergences in early modern institutional outcomes, Gilpin's public-choice approach assumes only a perfunctory plausibility.

How, then, does Gilpin weave the two other macro-factors of systems change – the onset of economic growth and the emergence of a world market – into his scheme? He starts by stressing the unique character of modern economic organization: 'The market system (or what today we call international economic interdependence) runs so counter to the great bulk of human experience that only extraordinary changes and novel circumstances could have led to its innovation and triumph over other means of economic exchange.' These novel circumstances are then listed as 'dramatic and rapid improvements in communications and transportation; the political success of the rising middle class, the discovery of the New World', as well as 'the monetarization of economic relations, the "innovation" of private property, the structure of the European state system' (Gilpin 1981: 130). Gilpin spares himself the trouble of showing how the three great environmental changes – the triumph of the nation-state, the onset of sustained economic growth, and the emergence of a world market – and the auxiliary sub-factors are logically and historically connected. His loose pluralist framework leads him to assume a mutually reinforcing, but essentially exogenous, interrelation between these three independent macro-phenomena. This interrelation is described rather than theorized. The narrative logic of addition assumes the function of the theoretical logic of social relations.

This points to a deeper epistemological issue. Although Gilpin's mobilization of a whole array of factors nurtures the impression that he is engaged in 'total history' – simultaneously vindicating the richness of Realism – these factors are cut loose from their social preconditions. As socially disembodied phenomena, they are assigned the task of explaining change, developing a dynamic of their own, while inflecting the course of history. But what are the social conditions of sustained economic growth? What are the social conditions for the imputed rise of the middle class? What are the social conditions for the monetarization of economic relations? Why was the early modern structure of the European states-system multipolar rather than unipolar? These pressing questions expose a broader dilemma. Although Gilpin has to be credited with trying to 'integrate the study of international economics with the study of international politics to deepen our comprehension of the forces at work in the world' (Gilpin 1987: 3), he consistently assumes that the political (state) and the economic (market) are two transhistorically separate spheres: 'States and markets, whatever their respective origins, have independent existences, have logics of their own, and interact with one another' (Gilpin 1987: 10 fn.). Theoretical integration is then limited to the *ex post* clarification of the changing linkages between these hypostasized spheres of determination, establishing a pluralist field of multiple non-reductionist causalities. 'Political economy', Gilpin professes, 'indicates a set of questions to be examined by means of an eclectic mixture of analytical methods and theoretical perspectives' (Gilpin 1987: 9). We are left with the impression that systems change was the result of a coincidental conjuncture of an expandable list of contingencies.[6] While everything can change any time, nothing changes for any determinate reason. The retreat to pluralism absolves the social scientist from the labour of theorization.

Gilpin's theoretical indeterminacy leads him to miss the chronologically uneven character and geographically uneven distribution of institutional innovations. At one stage, he maintains that:

> the relationship between wealth and power began to change in the late medieval period. It was then that Europe began to surpass its rival civilization in economic growth. The supremacy of Europe was based on its technological mastery of sea power, its perfection of artillery, and its social organization, as well as its overall economic superiority. (Gilpin 1981: 125)

Two paragraphs later, he asserts that 'the initial creation of an efficient economic organization and the breakthrough to sustained economic/ technological development took place in the Netherlands and shortly thereafter in Great Britain' (Gilpin 1981: 126). The apparent paradox is resolved by presenting early modern mercantilism and modern economic liberalism as two stages of one and the same process – the creation of the world market:

> In the modern period, the failure of the several efforts to unify Europe politically permitted the expansion of a market-type international economy. The absence of an imperial power to organize and control production and exchange gave free rein to market forces. As a consequence, the market system has come to encompass more and more of the globe since its beginning in the seventeenth century. The first phase of this emerging world market economy was the mercantilist era of the seventeenth and eighteenth centuries. (Gilpin 1981: 133)

The assumption that mercantilism implied the free rein of market forces, however, stretches the economic imagination. If mercantilism really implied economic competition regulated by the price mechanism on the basis of demand and supply, how do we explain the intensifying inter-mercantilist geopolitical struggles over political control of trading empires? If mercantilism really promoted production and was instrumental for the onset of sustained economic growth, how do we explain the resurgence of Malthusian crises during the seventeenth century in continental Europe and the low agrarian productivity levels in non-British Europe up to the mid-nineteenth century? Gilpin states that

> a primary objective of British foreign policy became the creation of a world market economy based on free trade, freedom of capital movements, and a unified international monetary system. The achievement of this objective required primarily the creation and enforcement of a set of international rules protecting private property rights rather than the more costly and less beneficial task of conquering an empire. (Gilpin 1981: 138)

If so, would this not call for an inquiry into the qualitative change in British economic organization? And if this radical break in the structure of economic organization fundamentally altered the nature of international relations in the course of the nineteenth century, what implications are to be drawn for the conventional periodization of the origins of the modern states-system in the seventeenth century?

While Gilpin identifies this disjuncture between Britain and France and its associated tensions, he shrinks from theorizing their social rationale. Precisely because he fails to see Anglo-French differences as rooted in the disjuncture between a pre-capitalist agrarian property regime in France and a capitalist property regime in Britain, his account of the timing of the onset of modern international relations oscillates continuously between the seventeenth and the nineteenth century.

Independent of the vices and virtues of Gilpin's account of systemic change and systems change, how do we assess his general conclusions for IR theory? Let us recall that Gilpin suggests that 'the fundamental nature of international politics has not changed over the millennia'. This thesis is then qualified by noting that 'one of the sub-themes of this book, in fact, is that modern statecraft and pre-modern statecraft differ in significant respects', only to finally revert to his original Realist thesis that 'nevertheless we contend that the fundamentals have not been altered' (Gilpin 1981: 7). To the extent that these fundamentals are the 'recurring struggle for wealth and power among independent actors in a state of anarchy' (Gilpin 1981: 7), and to the extent that hegemonic war is the principal mechanism of these struggles realigning the position of ascending powers in the international system, his 'no-fundamental-change' claim is sustained only at the price of failing to bring the acknowledged differences and specificities of historical communities and their respective international relations to bear for IR theory. Since these differences do not alter the age-old overriding logic of international anarchy and the associated neo-Rankean theme of the rise and fall of Great Powers, Realism seems to be vindicated. However, at this level of abstraction, theoretical conclusions are either trivial or meaningless. After Gilpin's stimulating foray into world history, it is rather counter-intuitive to find that the more it changes, the more it remains the same.

2. Stephen Krasner: Undermining Westphalia, Reinstating Anarchy

This position of 'no deep change' is affirmed by Stephen Krasner from a more classical Realist perspective. According to Krasner, the Treaties of Westphalia did not mark the beginning of the sovereign system of states. The constitution of sovereign rule in different parts of Europe was essentially contingent and regionally diachronic; it resists theorization. Forms of modern sovereignty predated Westphalia and pre-modern forms of rule outlasted it (Krasner 1993, 1995). But when a sovereign states-system eventually came into being, its ground rules (exclusive territorial authority, etc.) were frequently violated and compromised. The realist 'logic of consequences' (rational and power-political state behaviour) trumps the 'logic of appropriateness' (state behaviour in accord with intersubjective norms) due to the fundamental logic of anarchy. This leads Krasner to conclude that sovereignty is organized hypocrisy and to the wider claim that rulers – independent of the specific make-up of their polities – want to rule (Krasner 1999). This universal statement also implies that theories of systemic change remain irrelevant, since geopolitical orders are always configured by anarchy, power asymmetries, and power politics.

However, Krasner fails to draw out the theoretical implications of his empirical corrections. He dissolves IR theory into history. His observation that 'modern' institutions of state sovereignty antedated, and feudal institutions outlasted, the Westphalian settlement does not absolve him from explaining these regional differences. They are too easily ascribed to the 'untidiness' of history and the diachronic temporalities of regionally diverse state formation. To make sense of these differences, we must ask three questions. What was the generative grammar of feudal forms of political authority? What was the generative grammar of modern sovereignty? And how can we understand the regionally diverging and diachronic trajectories of European state formation? As with pre-modern forms of political authority,[7] Krasner fails to identify the generative grammar of modern sovereignty. In the period of the transition to a modern states-system, 'heterogeneity and irregular change, rather than the working out of some deep generative grammar, have characterized institutional developments in Europe' (Krasner 1993: 247).

This neglect goes hand in hand with a denial that regionally specific transitions from medieval to early modern to modern ways of organizing international political authority and geopolitical space can be accounted for: 'Chance and power, *fortuna* and *virtù*, launched local historical trajectories, especially in England and northern Italy, that led in practice to political entities that could assert practical control over a given territory' (Krasner 1993: 257). Although allusions are made to the two grand macro-sociological paradigms of the emergence of the modern state – the military techno-determinism thesis and the commercial-development thesis – Krasner sees four largely undifferentiated centuries of contestation and counter-contestation in the development of modern sovereignty, so that the setting up of the European Community, for example, obeys virtually the same logic as earlier historical attempts to transcend the principle of state sovereignty through international conventions, contracts, coercion, and imposition (Krasner 1993: 246, 261). Consequently, Krasner calls for the abandonment of a large-scale theorization of systems change and a retreat into historical contingency: 'No deep structure is evident in the heterogeneous and fluid character of political order from the Middle Ages to the present' (Krasner 1993: 261).

4. Historicizing Constructivism

Mainly on methodological grounds, Neorealism and Realism have been powerfully criticized by scholars from different intellectual traditions (Cox 1981; Ashley 1984; Walker 1987; Bromley 1991: ch. 1; Rosenberg 1994: ch. 1; Agnew and Corbridge 1995; for empirical critiques, see Schroeder 1994a, 1994b). Their survival arguably owes less to theoretical stringency or explanatory power than to what philosophers of science call diverging 'knowledge-guiding interests' (Habermas 1987) and the theoretical inertia of institutionalized paradigms, which socialize young scholars and gratify repetition while penalizing critique (Kuhn 1962). However, even within the Realist tradition, objections emerged, based less on meta-theoretical questions than on substantive issues.

John Gerard Ruggie: Property Rights, Epistemes, Contingency

John Gerard Ruggie raises two fundamental objections to Kenneth Waltz's Neorealist theory of international politics (Ruggie 1986, 1993, 1998). First, he argues that while Neorealism might be able to theorize the operation of the modern system of states, it fails to account for the specificity of pre-Westphalian geopolitical orders. And second, he objects that Neorealism contains only a 'reproductive', not a 'transformative logic', i.e., it fails to provide a theory of large-scale systemic change to explain 'the most important contextual change in international politics in this *millennium*: the shift from the medieval to the modern international system' (Ruggie 1986: 141).

Ruggie's critique can be reformulated as follows. If anarchy is the defining feature of diverse geopolitical systems, it cannot suffice to explain radically different patterns of international conflict and co-operation. However, if we accept the causal indeterminacy of anarchy, then we are forced to develop a non-systemic IR theory to explain these variations. This implies that we shift our attention away from a narrowly defined political science to a wider social science that identifies the broader social forces that constitute and reproduce political communities and geopolitical systems. Given the existence of profound geopolitical variations, we need a macro-theory of systemic change that does not hide massive transformations in the prevailing forms of political authority and territorial order, but starts from the assumption that these domestic changes are bound up with long-term, large-scale transitions from one system to another. This means looking to the social sources of political transformations. In short, we need a historical sociology of the formation of the modern system of states.

Agreeing with Ruggie's basic objections to Neorealism does not mean, however, accepting his Constructivist alternative. Overall, Ruggie's critique of Waltz falls short on its own Constructivist terms. The empirical and theoretical shortcomings of Ruggie's proposal show the inadequacy of Constructivist accounts and the need for an alternative theoretical framework.

Ruggie argues that differences in geopolitical systems can be explained in terms of property rights. While the medieval system was defined by conditional property, generating heterogeneous forms of territoriality, the modern system is defined by exclusive, absolute private property rights, generating homogeneous forms of territoriality. 'The early modern redefinition of property rights and reorganization of political space unleashed both interstate political relations and capitalist property relations' (Ruggie 1986: 148). He goes on to argue that the shift from medieval conditional to modern private property can be explained as a contingent confluence of three 'irreducible' dimensions of collective experience:

> These domains included material environments (eco-demographics, relations of production, relations of force); the matrix of constraints and opportunities within which social actors interacted (the structure of property rights, divergences between private and social rates of return, coalitional possibilities among major social actors); and social epistemes (political doctrines, political metaphysics, spatial constructs). Each was undergoing change in accordance with its own endogenous logic. (Ruggie 1993: 168–9)

While the relation between these phenomena is causally indeterminate, Ruggie emphasizes the implications of profound changes in early modern social epistemes, collectively shared assumptions about the self and social reality (Ruggie 1993: 169). Ruggie singles out the emergence of the modern notion of subjectivity as the decisive epistemic innovation of early modern (self-)consciousness. The modern self and the concentration of political power in an indivisible notion of sovereignty over a spatially demarcated territory are historically parallel phenomena. Whether or not Ruggie's pluralist sketch of the nexus between the rise of a private property regime, modern subjectivity, and modern territorial sovereignty is theoretically persuasive, he fails to identify those social agents that sustained, lived out, and changed property titles – not merely as formal institutions, but as politically maintained and actively negotiated social relations. This desocialization and depoliticization of property rights translates into a failure to recognize their inherently conflictual character and consider the social conflicts that transformed them.

On the basis of this undertheorization of the social character of property relations, Ruggie's historical-sociological incursions into the processes that generated the private property regime, its historical timing, its geographically uneven expansion, and its implications for absolutist sovereignty, remain suggestive intimations. Ruggie is circumspect enough to desist from establishing any clear-cut causalities between changes in material environments, strategic behaviour, and social epistemes. While he insists that these three spheres are irreducible and relatively autonomous, he merely allows for contingent interactions between them: 'But these changes also interacted, sometimes sequentially, sometimes functionally, sometimes simply via the mechanism of diffusion, that is, of conscious and unconscious borrowing'

(Ruggie 1993: 169). In other words, they coincided in time and space. Any attempt to challenge this soft, additive account of systemic transformation would mean a relapse into the temptations of 'grand theory', incurring the censure of totalization (Ruggie 1993: 169). Modernity is thus essentially contingent – a curious confluence of logically separate phenomena.

Ruggie's favoured epistemological posture, which emphasizes 'the local and contingent', is however only meaningful on the basis of a prior recognition of their antonyms: the total/global and the structural/determinate (Ruggie 1993: 171). His conception of history as a series of geographically uneven contingencies requires the chronicle as mode of exposition. Yet he claims to theorize, not to narrate. Thus, in their loose juxtaposition, Ruggie's three relatively autonomous spheres fail to account for what he set out to explain – the co-determination of private property and modern sovereignty. This failure to advance beyond temporal and spatial contingency was already implicit in the historiographical protocols he adopted from the *Annales* school. It subdivided the historical process into three levels of historical time – immutable structures, cyclical conjunctures, contingent events – connected to concrete spheres of history with separate velocities and autonomous developmental logics (Ruggie 1989; cf. Braudel 1972a, 1972b). However, what was an analytical and heuristic distinction in the original Braudelian framework becomes for Ruggie an ontological divide between independent spheres of determination, never to be reunited in concrete historical explanations (for critiques see Hexter 1972; Groh 1973: 79–91; Gerstenberger 1987).

While causality is trumped by contingency, Ruggie clearly situates the medieval-to-modern shift between the Renaissance and the Reformation, reaching its terminus during the Age of Absolutism. That this transformation was not brought about by early modern England but seventeenth-century France is made clear by Ruggie's citation of Perry Anderson: 'The age in which "Absolutist" public authority was imposed was also simultaneously the age in which "absolute" private property was progressively consolidated' (Ruggie 1986: 143). For Ruggie, early modern France was a modern state with exclusive territoriality and a domestic hierarchy. Here Ruggie's account converges with the mainstream consensus in the IR community by suggesting that the origins of modern inter-state relations are bound up with the Peace of Westphalia, which expressed and codified this prior political transformation.[8] Although 1648 is not elevated to the cataclysmic denouement of outdated medieval international practices, it is acknowledged as 'the usual marker of the inception of modern international relations' (Ruggie 1993: 167). In his narrative, the transformation in the organization of political space is clearly situated in the Renaissance, sometimes even earlier, e.g., after the end of the Hundred Years' War (Ruggie 1993: 147). The modern state, in Ruggie's words, 'was invented by the early modern Europeans. Indeed, it was invented by them twice, once in the leading cities of the Italian Renaissance and once again in the Kingdoms north of the Alps sometime thereafter' (Ruggie 1993: 166).

By conflating absolutist with modern sovereignty, Ruggie identifies only one major systemic shift from the medieval to the modern. He thus fails to recognize, first, that the medieval geopolitical system itself underwent major transformations, and, second, that it initially gave way to the early modern absolutist-dynastic system, which itself underwent a further massive transformation before it developed recognizably modern attributes. This reduction of two systemic transformations to one misrecognizes the *sui generis* character of the early modern system of dynastic states, conflating the Westphalian with the modern states-system and failing to specify and explain the social processes that led to the emergence of the latter.

Irrespective of whether capitalist private property regimes were first established in England or France, the mere existence of private property rights is insufficient to account for the plurality of states within the modern geopolitical order. While private property rights do underlie the separation of modern political authority from capitalist private ownership, i.e., the horizontal separation between state and civil society/economy, it does not account *eo ipso* for the vertical fragmentation of a plurality of mutually exclusive units of authority. Private property cannot explain the territorial differentiation between functionally similar states. It is perfectly possible to imagine one universal state on the basis of a generalized private property regime.

Empirical misjudgements and theoretical failures cannot be dissociated from Ruggie's Constructivist approach. It is not sufficient to conceive property rights or sovereignty exclusively in terms of intersubjective and thus non-coercive and consensus-based conventions or constitutive rules, since they are based on asymmetrical social relations involving force and coercion, i.e., conflict and imposition. We cannot simply read changes in system-structure, innovations in regime formation, or the very formation of the sovereign modern state off a series of intersubjective negotiations and agreements among political elites, be they domestic in origin or the result of a chain of international peace congresses. We must instead identify broader social forces with antagonistic interests that drive political and geopolitical change in conflictual, often violent, domestic and international processes. Constructivism's depoliticized theoretical grasp and explanatory scope do not exhaust the empirical and theoretical issues at stake. To address these issues, we need to abandon Neorealism, Realism and Constructivism and turn instead to a theoretical tradition in which property – conceived not as an abstract juridical category but as a social relation – is at the heart of social inquiry.

5. Neo-Evolutionary Historical Sociology

Hendrik Spruyt: Social Coalitions, Institutional Variations, and Neo-Evolutionary Selection

If Ruggie's answers are insufficient, his critique modifies the Neorealist framework beyond recognition. Hendrik Spruyt, in turn, renders it obsolete by drawing out the radical theoretical conclusions of Ruggie's new research agenda. Spruyt's macro-theoretical account of systems change posits from the first that 'a change in the constitutive elements of the system means a change in the structure of the system' (Spruyt 1994a: 5). By accepting exclusive territoriality and internal hierarchy as the defining traits of the units of the modern states-system, the new central *explanandum* of IR theory is clearly identified: 'At the end of the Middle Ages, the international system went through a dramatic transformation in which the crosscutting jurisdictions of feudal lords, emperors, kings, and popes started to give way to territorially defined authorities. The feudal order was gradually replaced by a system of sovereign states.' At the same time, Spruyt leaves no doubt that the late medieval sovereign state was conceptually identical to the modern state:

> The new element introduced by the late medieval state was the notion of sovereignty. This was the critical turn in the political organization of the Late Middle Ages, not the particular level of monarchical administration or royal revenue, nor the physical size of the state. Instead it was the concept of sovereignty that altered the structure of the international system by basing political authority on the principle of territorial exclusivity. The modern state is based on these two key elements, internal hierarchy and external autonomy, which emerged for the first time in the Late Middle Ages. (Spruyt 1994a: 3)

Given this epochal transformation, how can we understand the formation and generalization of the sovereign territorial state in early modern Europe? Changes in unit types, according to Spruyt, are extremely rare since the institutional structure expresses a set of vested interests defended by a dominant coalition of social forces. Given this system-maintaining bias, a 'broad exogenous change – punctuation' is needed to create a new structure of action-altering, and thus institution-altering, incentives (Spruyt 1994a: 24). Spruyt significantly refines the problem of the 'medieval-to-modern shift' by arguing – implicitly against Gilpin – that 'the expansion of trade was the critical external change that set this process in motion during the High Middle Ages' (Spruyt 1994a: 25). The trade-driven dissolution of non-exclusive feudal territoriality generated regionally *divergent social coalitions* among kings, nobles, burghers, and the Church. These resulted in three competing late medieval conflict units: sovereign territorial states, city-states, and city-leagues. Rejecting any unilinear and functional explanation of state formation and arguing instead for institutional variation, his focus shifts to the mechanism that generated these institutional variations and the mechanism which secured the modern state's victory over its rivals. Drawing on Stephen Jay Gould's reformulation of Darwinian theory, Spruyt proposes a two-step model in which the origins of the modern state and its subsequent *systemic selection* among a field of alternative competitors are differentiated.

Exemplified by France, the rise of the modern state was, according to Spruyt, the result of a coalition between burghers and the monarch, generating a coherent legal and institutional framework for the late medieval expansion of town-based commerce, while providing new fiscal resources for the monarchy. On the basis of generalized taxation and rational administration, the territorial state replaced feudal modes of social organization by reducing transaction costs, diminishing free riding, and more credibly committing its constituents. French state formation resulted in an efficient, rationalized, and superior mode of economic, political, and military organization. Coalitional patterns in Germany and Italy varied. In Germany, towns were extra-territorialized by a *rapprochement* between the nobility and the monarchy, allowing urban self-organization in city-leagues. Political power remained territorially fragmented. In Italy, due to the weakness of territorial rulers and the German emperor's failed Italian imperial policy, urban elites, while integrating nobles into mercantile activities, organized themselves on a territorial basis, giving rise to a system of city-states. Once these internal organizational variations were established, a process of institutional competitive selection set in between the three dominant forms of early modern political community, in which the survival of the modern territorial state and its rise to universality resulted from its economic and military superiority, the unique legitimacy provided by international mutual recognition, and defections and institutional imitation by its rivals.

Spruyt's two-step model of geopolitical transformation – divergent class alliances followed by state-selecting competition – further radicalizes the parameters of IR theory by retrieving the nexus between agency and variations in institutional outcomes on the basis of interest-driven choices by and bargains between differently situated social actors. In this respect, Spruyt significantly refines the unilinear conclusions of Gilpin's public-choice model. Yet there are several theoretical and empirical problems with Spruyt's theory of international transformation.

While Spruyt rightly insists on the qualitative difference in the geopolitics of the European Middle Ages and the modern inter-state system, his analysis of feudalism does not advance beyond an institutional description of medieval order revolving around interpersonal ties of vassalage. He thus fails to explore the causes and consequences of feudal conditional property, which Ruggie rightly stressed as the principle of territorial non-differentiation. Spruyt's description of feudalism as a system of non-territorial rule is purely comparative. In other words, while Spruyt perceptively elaborates *how* the feudal geopolitical system differed from the modern one, he fails to specify *why* this was the case. He thus fails not only to explain the structure of the medieval geopolitical system, but also to theorize its violence-driven mode of operation, i.e., the patterns of inter-unit behaviour. Consequently, the war-prone specificity and socio-political dynamic of feudal geopolitics remain unexplained.

This neglect leads directly to his misinterpretation of late medieval commercialization as the driving force behind the demise of feudal social organization. The rise of towns and its corollaries, expanding market exchange, increasing division of labour – in short, the conventional 'commercialization model' – is the unaccounted demiurge, the 'exogenous' and 'independent variable', which created those economic transformations that translated directly into new political demands on the side of municipal burghers for a more efficient reorganization of political space (Spruyt 1994a: 6). Spruyt's account shares all the shortcomings of the commercialization model, which, as will be shown in greater detail in chapter 4, in itself cannot explain the demise of feudalism, the origin of capitalism, or the rise of the modern state.

To begin with, it is intellectually spurious to introduce the expansion of trade as an external, independent variable, while declaring at the same time that 'the causes of this economic upswing need not concern us here' (Spruyt 1994a: 61), when the central question concerning the post-millennial economic revival is precisely whether it was internal to the economic dynamic of feudalism or not (Sweezy, Dobb et al. 1976; Aston and Philpin 1985; Katz 1989). There are, indeed, good arguments to support the view that this general upswing was internal to the feudal economy. But if the high medieval economic revival was internal to feudalism, then Spruyt's neo-evolutionary model of change as 'punctuated equilibrium', relying on massive external shocks, explains nothing.

Furthermore, in the French case Spruyt assumes a long-term clash of interests between rising urban burghers and falling feudal lords, but fails to show how and why the growth of towns was antithetical to the feudal mode of economic and political organization: 'I have suggested in this chapter that towns were basically antagonistic to the feudal aristocracy. What is puzzling is that neo-Marxist accounts admit this but nevertheless wish to place towns within feudalism' (Spruyt 1994a: 107). Irrespective of whether such a monolithic neo-Marxist account actually exists, Spruyt seems to misunderstand the argument. John Merrington clarifies the issue by showing that towns were indeed economically internal to feudalism – meaning primarily dependent upon the agrarian rhythms of supply and demand – and at the same time politically external to the control of feudal lords (Merrington 1976). This combination of political emancipation from and economic embeddedness within the agrarian feudal economy united feudal lords and municipal communes in the common exploitation of a dependent peasantry; both profited from direct extra-economic rents and politically imposed monopoly prices. Simultaneously, the two classes were divided over their relative shares of the peasant-produced surplus. Their antagonism was not over the nature of the economic system – a conflict between an ascending bourgeoisie presiding over a nascent capitalist urban market and a declining nobility defending a decaying feudal economy – but over the distribution of peasant output.

Irrespective of whether the medieval economic revival was internal or external to feudalism, Spruyt's explanation of institutional variations in France, Germany, and Italy is incomplete without a prior analysis of the *wider class relations* between the monarchy, the nobility, the burghers, and, crucially, the peasantry. The regionally specific coalitions between the monarchy, the nobility, and the towns were in all three cases decisively co-determined by the struggle of the peasantry over its regionally differentiated legal status, i.e., by class conflict. Spruyt argues that the French burgher–king alliance held, because the nobility was weak. Yet the weakness of the nobility cannot be understood apart from the French peasantry's successful struggle against serfdom assisted by royal policies of peasant protection to out-compete local lords over access to peasant surplus – this clash between a noble rent regime and a royal tax regime was a development specific to France. In this process, the French monarchy sought to gain control over the revenues generated by the towns – not so much creating a coalition between commercial burghers and the king as violently imposing royal power over previously semi-independent urban communes. There was thus neither a convergence of preferences nor an affinity of interests nor a mutually accommodating bargain, but intra-ruling class conflict over the politically constituted proceeds of circulation, which was won by the king.[9]

In other words, the central motive behind early modern French state formation was not the town-driven establishment of a national market, but the establishment of an expanded tax base for the monarchy. Nor did this highly conflictual process of urban incorporation establish the administratively centralized and legally rationalized level playing field allegedly favoured by merchants (Spruyt 1994a: 86–94, 99–108). It rather led to an intractable political economy defined by regionally diverse laws, highly uneven levels of taxation, a welter of internal customs and duties, currencies, privileges, non-bureaucratic and venal officers, and privately negotiated monopolies sold by the king. The French absolutist state remained decisively non-modern in its institutions and highly inefficient in terms of economic performance.

Spruyt describes but does not explain the expansion and consolidation of the French state from the Capetians to the Bourbons (Spruyt 1994a: 77–108). While he rightly rejects the functionalist assumption that military-technological advances determined the size and organization of political units, merely pointing to a burgher–royal alliance does not even broach the question of why and how the French monarchy expanded and consolidated its sphere of influence over the centuries. Due to this omission, royal state-making appears as the natural growth of the state. As will be demonstrated later, the decisive dynamic in the French case was not so much a political bargain between town dwellers and the king, but the struggle between a rent regime operated by independent feudal lords and a generalized tax regime operated by the monarchy and its patrimonial officers.

But since Spruyt, like Ruggie, clings to the idea of the modernizing potential of trading burghers, and since he identifies exclusive territoriality and internal hierarchy as the decisive criteria of modern statehood, he erroneously defines late medieval and early modern kingdoms as modern states: 'It would be too much to suggest that we find modern France in the 1300s. There was still a protracted war with England to come, years of religious turmoil, and domestic opposition by cities, nobility, and clergy.

Nevertheless, we do already find the essential traits of modern statehood' (Spruyt 1994a: 79). Such an equation not only runs counter to Max Weber's ideal type of the modern state, which revolves around its impersonal character and rational bureaucracy, it thoroughly misinterprets the personalized nature of late medieval and early modern royal sovereignty. While the logic of feudal political and territorial fragmentation was indeed broken after the fourteenth-century crisis, the nascent absolutist state merely tried to centralize rents as a 'gigantic landlord' (Rosenberg 1994: 135), imposing, according to Heide Gerstenberger, a regime of 'generalized personal domination [*verallgemeinerte personale Gewalt*]' (Gerstenberger 1990: 510–22). Territoriality, in turn, became a function of patrimonial dynasticism. It was neither bounded in the modern sense nor administered by a clear domestic hierarchy. By misreading absolutist sovereignty, Spruyt radically misperiodizes the medieval-to-modern shift. Following Gilpin and Ruggie, he thus contributes to the myth that the Peace of Westphalia constituted the founding charter of a modern system of sovereign states.[10]

While, according to Spruyt, commercialization led to three divergent regional responses in Europe (the sovereign territorial state, city-states, and city-leagues), Spruyt's tripartite distinction does not exhaust the full range of political alternatives in early modern Europe. The reduction of institutional variations to two basic alternatives, territorial and non-territorial, does not do justice to the highly uneven and variegated, i.e., temporally synchronous yet qualitatively diachronous development of early modern European political communities. This is not a plea for historical completeness, but an argument that seriously weakens Spruyt's thesis of competitive selection on the basis of institutional efficiency.

How does the Holy Roman Empire, which combined decentralized semi-autonomous actors under an imperial umbrella and survived until 1806, fit this model of institutional selection? It neither succumbed to the allegedly greater economic, military, and political efficiency of classical territorial states, nor did it 'mimic' their institutions, nor was it delegitimized as an actor by international conventions. On the contrary, the Westphalian treaties recognized its unique confederal-imperial constitution and enshrined its status in international law. How do we explain the proliferation of territorial states, like the Dutch oligarchic merchant republic, the Swiss peasant confederation, and the Polish aristocratic republic, which not only did not conform to the classical 'Western' pattern of territorial state formation, but survived – with the exception of Poland – the competitive onslaught and institutional lure of their 'more efficient' Western neighbours? Even within the framework of absolutist states, it should matter that

the Eastern absolutisms based on the 'second serfdom' evinced institutional
peculiarities at stark variance with the 'Western' model and were only
structurally transformed in the late nineteenth and early twentieth centuries
(Anderson 1974b). In other words, the criterion 'bounded territoriality plus
domestic hierarchy' neither exhausts the variations in European state-
building, nor explains why some early modern states, territorial but with
widely varying political regimes, successfully competed and coexisted with
France and England without emulating them. The logic of neo-evolutionary selection thus stands in need of serious refinement.

This explanatory weakness is best exemplified with regard to early
modern France and England. Since Spruyt is primarily interested in
sovereignty and bounded territoriality *per se*, and not in variations in regime
formation, he subsumes early modern France and England under one type
of successful sovereign territorial state. But these two polities were radically
distinct entities with highly divergent long-term trajectories and non-
equivalencies in all dimensions of society, economy, and political organization. Spruyt's remarks on England are sporadic and cursory: 'Sovereign
territorial states contained a final locus of authority. Although my main
emphasis has been on France, the same was true for other states such as
England. Sovereignty need not imply absolutism' (Spruyt 1994a: 153).
True, sovereignty need not imply absolutism, but nor need absolutism
imply modern sovereignty. Sovereignty *per se* is too indeterminate a
concept to distinguish between early modern France and England. Crucially, while seventeenth-century England turned into a parliamentary-
constitutional state based on an expanding capitalist economy in which
sovereignty came to lie with Parliament, France started to perfect its
patrimonial-dynastic absolutist state form based on a non-capitalist agrarian
economy while sovereignty came to be personalized by the king. Again,
'bounded territoriality' or 'sovereignty' obscure more than they reveal. The
assumption of just one fundamental transformation in system structure does
not do justice to the radical geopolitical discontinuity between the Middle
Ages and modernity. What we need is a theory of international change
that addresses *both* the transition from medieval to early modern
(geo)political organization *and* the subsequent transition from early modern
to distinctly modern international relations. The second shift requires
understanding the English case. Yet, like the peasantry, England is mysteri-
ously absent from Spruyt's study.

Finally, if we examine more closely the empirical basis of Spruyt's claim
that the early modern territorial state, exemplified by France, featured
efficient modern institutions which privileged its selection over non-

territorial alternatives, the neo-evolutionary logic of competitive institutional selection collapses. If, as was in fact the case, early modern France lacked a centralized rational bureaucracy, standardized national taxation, administration, and adjudication, the logic of France's relative predominance in the seventeenth century and its subsequent relative decline against post-1688 Britain has to be reassessed on a different theoretical basis. Moreover, the process whereby the first modern state – England – came to universalize its state form and logic of international relations has to be retheorized and reperiodized according to an entirely different social rationale and politico-economic dynamic.

6. Neo-Marxist IR Theory

Justin Rosenberg: Modernity as 'Structural Discontinuity' and Modernity as Process

Critical IR scholars suggest that variations in international patterns of conflict and co-operation are bound up with changing modes of production. The structural discontinuity between pre-modern and modern international relations is rooted in the development of capitalism and a series of revolutionary regime changes. The establishment of capitalism brought about a differentiation between politics, generating a system of states, and economics, generating a transnational 'empire of civil society'. Only after processes of surplus extraction were depoliticized could sovereignty be pooled in a public state over and above a self-regulating capitalist economy and a citizen-based civil society. This, then, would be the starting point for the discourse and practice of *Realpolitik*, concealing a second level of private power – an inherently universalizing world market.

Justin Rosenberg's work is pioneering in this respect. He demonstrates how specific geopolitical systems – the classical Greek polis system, the Italian Renaissance city-state systems, early modern empires, and the modern system of sovereign states – were structurally tied to different modes of production. 'Geopolitical systems are not constituted independently of, and cannot be understood in isolation from, the wider structures of the production and reproduction of social life' (Rosenberg 1994: 6). Rosenberg further argues that although most geopolitical orders are characterized by anarchy, a 'structural discontinuity' separates all pre-capitalist systems from the modern capitalist international order. This fundamental break is predicated on the distinction between personalized domination

under pre-capitalist relations of production, and impersonal modern sovereignty, premised on the separation between the economic and the political.
For Rosenberg, this structural discontinuity explains the co-genesis and
compatibility of a system of bordered (but porous) sovereign states and a
transnational international economy. The capitalist anarchy of the market
is replicated in the international anarchy of the states-system. He further
concludes that this is why the modern balance of power is not simply
analogous to Adam Smith's invisible hand of the market; it 'is its other
half', the mechanical and superficially desocialized regulator of an abstract
notion of the political (Rosenberg 1994: 139, 155). Equally, the conjunction of capitalism, the modern state, and the modern states-system is the
condition of possibility for modern power politics and its Realist discourse.
And since modern capitalist sovereignty is not equivalent to absolutist
sovereignty, the significance of the Westphalian settlement as the starting
point for modern international relations is fundamentally undermined.

Rosenberg's study is an enormous advance for IR theory on several
levels of method and substance. However, it is marked by a certain tension
between a residual structuralist understanding of Marxism and its attention
to historical development. The structuralist overtones come to the fore in
Rosenberg's reconstruction of European history as essentially a series of
successive, discrete, and self-contained geopolitical orders. He thus neglects
to theorize the transitions between them, including the social conflicts,
crises, and wars that underwrote these transformations. Agency is under-
represented. While this omission is of less concern for pre-capitalist
geopolitical orders for the purposes of IR theory (though not for Marxism),
it becomes more problematic with respect to the question of the social,
geographical, and chronological origins of capitalism, its relation to the
states-system, and the definition of *modern* international relations. While
Rosenberg argues persuasively, but primarily analytically, for the structural
interrelation and functional compatibility between a territorially divided
states-system and a private, transnational world market, he does not provide
a dynamic account of the co-development of capitalism, the modern state,
and the modern states-system. The latter two phenomena are analytically
derived from the first, while all three are regarded as structurally and
temporally coeval aspects of modernity. This thesis overplays the explanatory power of capitalism, leaving the complex historical co-development
(but not co-genesis) of capitalism, state, and states-system underexplored.
This gap between theoretical assertion and historical demonstration
becomes evident only towards the end of his account. Rosenberg's remarks
on the origins of capitalism are exploratory and point to the need to retrace

the highly uneven processes through which the twin processes of 'primitive accumulation' and the consolidation of modern sovereignty spread across Europe during the nineteenth and twentieth centuries.

Two problems emerge. First, a chasm opens up between Rosenberg's statement that a 'structural discontinuity' divided pre-modern from modern geopolitics, and his recognition, spelt out in his research programme, that the arrival of inter-state modernity was not system-wide and simultaneous, somehow coeval with the onset of capitalist anarchy in the private sphere, but rather a long-term, large-scale process that is, in many ways, still under way. Modern international relations did not simply succeed pre-modern geopolitics, but coexisted with it and tried to transcend it without completely destroying all of its attributes, especially multiple territories. Conversely, pre-capitalist states under international pressure to modernize devised counter-strategies that reacted back on capitalist Britain, so as to 'soil' the assumption of its pristine capitalist-liberal culture. Modernity is not a structure but a process.

Second, this dilemma raises a series of questions. When, where, and how did capitalism first emerge? What was its impact on modern state formation? Given that capitalism emerged unevenly over the course of three centuries in various regions of Europe, how do we understand the coexistence of heterogeneous political communities in a 'mixed-case scenario' international order? How do we theorize this long transition? Given that the balance of power was operated first by Britain in the context of a pre-capitalist geopolitical system, to what degree is it an abstract capitalist mechanism of international regulation? If capitalism emerged in early modern England in the context of a states-system that was, by Rosenberg's own admission, no longer imperial but already constituted as a system of territorially defined absolutist states, how do we account for the formation of this pre-capitalist states-system (Rosenberg 1994: 130, 137)? And if a system of territorial states preceded the nexus between capitalism and modern sovereignty, can we still maintain that the modern system of divided political authority is a function and continuous product of capitalism?

In short, the assumption of a clear structural break, although conceptually compelling, has to be historically relaxed if we want to reconstruct the making of the modern states-system.

7. Conclusion: Towards a New Theory of the Making of Modern International Relations

Recent developments in IR theory have significantly restructured its research agenda. After Waltz's purging of history from the field, a new set of questions gave rise to novel theoretical and meta-theoretical approaches. While the critiques of Waltz's ahistorical structuralism reunited IR scholars in a quest to rehistoricize the discipline, they pursued different tracks for understanding large-scale and long-term geopolitical transformations.

Gilpin's typology of change considerably refines Waltz's binary distinction between anarchy and hierarchy, focusing on the rise of the modern states-system and the rise and fall of powers within it. However, his combination of a rational public-choice model with the structuralist precepts of Neorealism is grafted on to a historical process that defies its utilitarian premises and functionalist conclusions. Historical diversity is pressed into a public-choice model that remains tied to a distinctly modern notion of instrumental rationality. Once this sanitized concept of rationality is assumed as a timeless principle of social action, unanticipated consequences and 'dysfunctional anomalies' disappear from view. By first externalizing action-changing incentives to exogenous factors and then inferring institutional outcomes from collective choices based on a rational calculation of expected costs and returns, international change follows a universal and unilinear pattern. However, while Gilpin fails to demonstrate this process of collective rational choice in any concrete case, the historical record shows strong variations in early modern state formation, which he never addresses. Once the modern system of states is in place, the history of international relations shrinks to a mechanical, functionalist account of shifting rank orders among rising and declining powers mediated by hegemonic rivalry – a finding subsequently transformed into a law-like theorem.

Krasner's rereading of the Westphalian peace treaties downgrades their importance as a watershed in international relations. But rather than explore the uneven development of the political communities that composed the Westphalian society of states, Krasner merely asserts that, with or without sovereignty as an international ground rule, rulers act according to their rational interests, which are fundamentally governed by anarchy and power politics.

Ruggie's Constructivist account retrieves the nexus between property rights as principles of territorial differentiation and varying forms of political and geopolitical order. While the emphasis on the social character of changing forms of international relations highlights the medieval-to-modern shift, his account fails to move beyond an indeterminate, multi-dimensional pluralism. This retreat to contingency follows from his unwillingness to interpret property as anything more than a legal institution or a constitutive rule. The invocation of Weberian themes comes, however, at a price: the transformation of medieval conditional property into modern private property is not seen as bound up with regionalized social conflicts over access to land and labour, but rather as part of a general Europe-wide epistemic revolution. These theoretical weaknesses translate directly into an empirical misjudgement. Since the nature of early modern European international relations is largely extrapolated from the allegedly archetypical French case, Ruggie seriously misidentifies the temporal and geographical origins of geopolitical modernity, conflating French absolutist and English capitalist soverignty. His emphasis on the local and contingent is diametrically opposed to what he sees as the universality of absolute individuation and bounded territoriality – *coincidentia oppositorum*?

Spruyt further historicizes IR theory by reversing the Neorealist logic in the gradation of policy-determining 'images'. Yet no sooner is the causal primacy of international change attributed to the system-constituting units and the social forces prevailing within them, than Spruyt finds himself forced to revert to commercialization as an 'external shock'. While avoiding Gilpin's functionalism and Ruggie's causal indeterminacy by explaining early modern variation as the result of regionally divergent social coalitions, the nature of these social alliances remains undertheorized in abstraction of wider class relations. His tacit appeal to a largely outdated Marxist interpretation of a coalition between French burghers and the Valois and Bourbon monarchies leads him to exaggerate the efficiency and modernity of the early modern French state. When the case for the organizational superiority of the *Ancien Régime* is called into question, his theory of subsequent selective competition among qualitatively different conflict units collapses.

Finally, Rosenberg's study presents a breakthrough in IR theory on a number of levels, but faces difficulties in translating a conceptual abstraction, 'capitalism', into a historical reconstruction of its origins in and impact on an already territorially defined states-system. His structuralist interpretation emphasizes a radical discontinuity between pre-modern and modern geopolitics – a rupture which neglects the very complex dynamic of international relations between 1688 and the First World War and beyond in the long transition to modern international relations.

★

In order to move beyond these incomplete attempts to account for the origins and development of the modern states-system, we must develop a comprehensive and coherent, historically informed and theoretically controlled interpretation which is able to (a) theorize the nature of the medieval geopolitical order and the systemic transformations within it; (b) specify the dynamics which caused the rise of diverging and plural polities in the early modern states-system; (c) establish in spite of these variations the principles of Westphalian international relations; and (d) explain the rise of capitalism and the first modern state, and how it came to universalize its logic of political organization and international relations in the pluriverse created by absolutist state formation. This is the task of the chapters that follow.

Notes

1 Waltz's systems theory is, of course, predicated on a micro-economic theory of rational choice under free-market conditions. Although classical political economy and Neorealism both have roots in liberal traditions of thought, harmony qua balance operates on the built-in assumption that entire nation-states might vanish in processes of 'dynamic adjustment', just as entire firms do. And, indeed, Waltz concludes that the security optimum is achieved in a bipolar condition – a historical conjuncture that converges not unsurprisingly with the duopolistic state of US–Soviet relations at the time of the book's publication, giving it a Panglossian gloss.

2 Whereas Neorealism constitutes a *science*, other theories that address the same questions are devalued as *philosophy*, or *historical interpretation* (Halliday and Rosenberg 1998: 381–2 and 386).

3 Mearsheimer commits the same inversion of evidence and validity when noting that state behaviour not conforming to structural Realism is 'foolish' and therewith a theoretical 'anomaly' (Mearsheimer 2001: 10–12).

4 Marx quipped that 'there is a continual movement of growth in the productive forces, of destruction in social relations, of formation in ideas; the only immutable thing is the abstraction of movement – *mors immortalis*' (Marx 1976d: 166).

5 In Gilpin 1987: 4, the nation-state emerged in the sixteenth century.

6 '[T]he modern state and the nation-state system arose due to a peculiar set of economic, technological, and other circumstances' (Gilpin 1986: 314). If these were circumstances, what then was the stance?

7 The medieval world did not possess 'a deep generative grammar' (Krasner 1993: 257).

8 Similarly, two other Constructivist accounts conflate early modern French and English state formation. Rodney Bruce Hall suggests that eighteenth-

century France and Britain are two variants of the same 'territorial–sovereign' identity (Hall 1999: 100). With respect to Westphalia, he asserts first that post-1648 collective identity equated the state with its dynasty. Later, he affirms that the Settlement sparked a dynastic legitimation crisis by replacing dynastic with territorial legitimacy, *raison d'État*, and the 'institution of the modern state' (Hall 1999: 60–63, 99). Kurt Burch, in turn, provides a Constructivist account of modern sovereignty in seventeenth-century England that revolves around the discourse of private property rights. He maintains that similar processes occurred in seventeenth-century France. This leads him to concur with the standard IR account that 'the Thirty Years' War effectively marks this transition [i.e., from dynastic authority to the sovereign state] on the continent' (Burch 1998: 89).

9 David Parker, for example, argues that 'where mercantilist policies did have some effect it is doubtful that this was with the support, or to the benefit, of the bourgeoisie. On the contrary, the autonomy of French towns was one of the obvious victims of the assertion of royal authority' (Parker 1996: 28–9). The autonomy of cities (in France and elsewhere) remained intact as long as monarchs were not yet unchallenged rulers (1100–1450), but was lost thereafter to centralizing kings. The town–king relation was thus not conducive to capitalist rationalization, but burghers 'saw the profits to be derived from playing the game under submission to the crown: The sale of offices, tax privileges, and the rents of public debts were the cornerstones of their mutual interest' (Blockmans 1994: 237).

10 'My discussion ends at about the time of the Peace of Westphalia (1648), which formally acknowledged a system of sovereign states' (Spruyt 1994a: 27).

2

A Theory of Geopolitical Relations in the European Middle Ages

One thing is clear: the Middle Ages could not live on Catholicism, nor could the ancient world on politics. On the contrary, it is the manner in which they gained their livelihood which explains why in one case politics, in the other case Catholicism, played the chief part. (Marx 1976b: 176)

1. Introduction

This chapter offers a distinct approach to theorizing changing geopolitical orders. The central thesis is that the nature and dynamics of international systems are governed by the character of their constitutive units, which, in turn, rests on the specific property relations prevailing within them. Medieval 'international' relations and their changes over the centuries before the rise of capitalism have to be interpreted on the basis of changing social property relations. The dynamics of medieval change, however, were bound up with contradictory strategies of reproduction between and within the two major classes, the lords and the peasantry.

The argument is that due to peasant possession of the means of subsistence, the feudal nobility enforced access to peasant produce by political and military means. Since every lord reproduced himself not only politically but also individually on the basis of his lordship, control over the means of violence was not monopolized by the state, but oligopolistically dispersed among a landed nobility. The medieval 'state' consisted of a political community of lords with the right to armed resistance. Relations among lords were inherently non-pacified and competitive. Forced redistribution of peasant surplus and competition over land occurred along three axes: (1) between peasants and lords, (2) among lords, and (3) between the collectivity of lords (the feudal 'state') and external actors. Consequently, the geopolitical system was characterized by constant military rivalry over territory and labour between lords, and within and between their 'states'. The geopolitical dynamic of medieval Europe followed the zero-sum logic of territorial conquest. The form and dynamic of the 'international' system arose directly from the structure of social property relations.

The implications of the social-property approach for the discipline of IR extend far beyond the Middle Ages. It is applicable to all geopolitical orders, be they tribal, feudal, absolutist, or capitalist. In each case, a definite set of property relations generates specific geopolitical authority relations governing and setting limits to inter-actor rationalities. I thus aspire not simply to trace the correspondence between property relations and international systems, but to uncover the dynamics of these systems in class strategies of reproduction, both within polities and between them. Property relations explain institutional structures, conditioning the conflictual relations of appropriation that explain change. 'Internal' changes in property relations, themselves subject to 'external' pressures, alter geopolitical behaviour. This perspective combines a substantive theory of social and international interaction with a theory of socio-political structure. This is achieved by a historical account of the interplay between the constraining structures of property and authority and their consequences for the goal-orientated yet bounded and antagonistic practices which animate and change these social relations.[1] Thus, I propose a starting point for a theory of large-scale geopolitical transformation.

This understanding of social change seeks to recast the debate over whether economics 'determines' politics, the domestic 'determines' the international, or vice versa. The problem is that reflection on the interrelation between these spheres or 'levels' typically only begins after their historical constitution, that is, after they have become differentiated in capitalist societies. The common methodological temptation is to play one reified sphere off against another – archetypically in either an economistic Marxist or a politicist Weberian account – without asking how they emerged in the first place and how they flow back into the reproduction of society as a whole. Similarly, analyses of pre-capitalist geopolitical systems tend to project the familiar vocabulary of states and markets, the domestic and the international, on to differently structured pasts.

The medieval social order exhibited neither the demarcation between the domestic and the international spheres nor the separation of politics and economics characteristic of the modern international system. These differentiations are reproduced by the modern state, which, based on its monopoly over the means of violence, conducts domestic politics through law and international politics through power politics. They underlie the Realist concepts of international anarchy and domestic hierarchy and the corresponding behavioural expectations of balancing and bandwagoning. For a medieval world without this double differentiation, the fundamental problem is to determine the nature of the (geo)political and to specify the actors qualified to conduct 'international' relations. Medieval (geo)politics was neither purely anarchical nor purely hierarchical, but contained both vertical and horizontal relations of subordination and co-ordination among highly differentiated bearers of political power. It is therefore misleading to subsume these diverse political authorities – pope, emperor, kings, dukes, counts, bishops, cities, lords – under the generic term 'conflict unit', since none of them enjoyed a monopoly over the means of violence guaranteeing exclusive control over a bounded territory. The Realist strategy of applying timeless categories to a stateless society produces conceptual anachronisms that translate into erroneous analyses (Fischer 1992; for critiques see Hall and Kratochwil 1993 and Teschke 1998: 328–36). To avoid these pitfalls, we need to inquire into the nature and social determinants of feudal political power. In short, we must make sense of medieval (geo)politics in its own terms.

The chapter is divided into four sections. Section 2 compares Max Weber's and Karl Marx's theories of feudalism and re-examines the concept of the 'relations of production' in the context of pre-capitalist societies. Section 3 offers an account of how the agency and structure problem can be addressed in medieval society by demonstrating the dialectical nexus between medieval conditional property and the resulting contradictory strategies of reproduction among the two major classes. Section 4 outlines a phenomenology of medieval 'international' institutions (state and domination, territory and frontiers, war and peace) by systematically relating their *political form* to their *social content*. The final section clarifies diverging structuring principles of geopolitical organization in the early, high, and late Middle Ages and argues that while these shifts in system structure can be explained on the basis of changes in social property relations, they are irrelevant for determining feudal geopolitical behaviour.

2. The Relation between the Economic and the Political in Feudal Society

1. Weber versus Marx: Type of Domination versus Extra-Economic Compulsion

One way to approach the controversies surrounding feudalism is by theorizing the relation between 'the economic' and 'the political' in medieval society. A dominant line of thinking running through the literature – essentially inspired by the work of Max Weber and Otto Hintze – identifies feudalism as a political phenomenon (Weber 1968a: 255–66, 1070–110, esp. 1090–92; Hintze 1968). Especially Weber, analogously to the significance Marx attributed to possessing the means of production, elaborates on the political significance of possessing the means of administration for the decentralized patrimonial state:

> All states may be classified according to whether they rest on the principle that the staff of men themselves *own* the administrative means, or whether the staff is 'separated' from these means of administration. . . . These political associations in which the material means of administration are autonomously controlled, wholly or partly, by the dependent administrative staff may be called associations organized in '*estates*'. The vassal in the feudal association, for instance, paid out of his own pocket for the administration and judicature of the district enfeoffed to him. He supplied his own equipment and provisions for war, and his subvassals did likewise. Of course, this had consequences for the lord's position of power, which only rested upon a relation of personal faith and upon the fact that the legitimacy of his possession of the fief and the social honour of the vassal were derived from the overlord. (Weber 1946: 81)

As a specific system of government or a hierarchical-military relationship between bearers of political power, feudalism falls within the confines of political science, constitutional history, or the sociology of types of domination. '[Occidental] feudalism [*Lehensfeudalität*] is a marginal case of patrimonialism that tends toward stereotyped and fixed relationships between lord and vassal' (Weber 1968a: 1070; see also Axtmann 1990: 296–8).[2] For all their erudition and meticulous conceptual differentiation, these accounts tend to abstract from the agrarian social basis of feudal political power. While Weber was, of course, not blind to the economic implications of feudalism,[3] economic issues, and in particular the legal status and conscious agency of the peasantry, remain theoretically epiphenomenal.

In particular, the Weber–Hintze tradition dissociates forms of government and domination from the processes of lordly reproduction with which they were obviously connected. This observation does not imply a plea for an equally abstract consideration of 'the economy'. It rather serves as a reminder that beneath the political 'level' of relations between lords, feudal society exhibited a second 'level' of political relations between lords and peasants, which governed the specific modes of surplus appropriation.

The broader epistemological crux of these issues is that Weber's method of ideal-type formation is, on a strict methodological reading, not only barred from exploring the social content of feudal domination, it is inherently incapable of even thinking the broader problem of historical change. Ideal types are constructed by surveying the historical evidence and choosing on the basis of an *a priori* subjective value-orientation (*Wertbezug*) – which cannot be inferred from the material itself – a culturally significant (*Kulturbedeutung*) social macro-phenomenon. Its most distinctive typological traits are then interpolated and regrouped through a process of abstraction into a purified ideal type (Weber 1949a, 1968b, 1949b). Its 'ideality' bears no normative significance. For practical research purposes, these distilled ideal types serve the heuristic function of being employed either to measure the distance between a concrete empirical case and its pure 'ideal', or to compare ideal type A with ideal type B (say, the feudal patrimonial and the modern bureaucratic modes of administration) so as to sharpen their differences. Yet the problem of social change remains excluded from this procedure. Theodor Adorno, among many others, noted that:

> if I handle the concept of ideal-type as strictly as it was articulated by Max Weber in his essay on categories (*Kategorienaufsatz*) in his theory of social science, then it is devoid of any tendency to transform itself into another, since it is an *ad hoc* invention, construed as something completely monadological, in order to subsume certain phenomena. (Adorno 1993: 207)[4]

Weber's analysis of feudalism merely presents an ideal type of domination, by definition both static and non-causal, within a sociology of administrative organization abstracted from society and history.[5]

In other words, Weber's historical sociology first and foremost serves comparison by constructing ideal types under which the most diverse historical and geographical cases can be subsumed and stored away. This is, of course, not without scientific value, but it implies the transformation of history as an open process into history as a database furnishing evidentiary material for a series of systematized taxonomies. This is the death of history as becoming. Certainly, Weber, the historian (Weber 1927), did not always comply with the self-imposed methodological rules of Weber the social scientist. In the historical sections of *Economy and Society*, we find many allusions to and remarks on transitional tendencies from one type of domination to another. But these passing remarks have no systematic place in his theory of social science, and thus lack a meta-theoretical foundation which spells out the principles of historical and social change. This leads Weber to maintain that structures of social action follow 'laws of their own' (*Eigengesetzlichkeit*) (Weber 1949a: 70, 1968a: 341) Any reconstruction of European history will therefore have to retrace the *independent developmental logics* of different social spheres (political, economic, legal, religious, etc.) that never stand in any necessary relation of co-constitution, but may or may not form 'elective affinities'.[6] Historical development takes then the form of an unlimited multiplication and combination of externally interacting social dimensions of an empirical whole with no underlying unity. Consequently, Weber cannot provide an encompassing conception of feudalism – genetically, substantively, and reproductively – understood as a dialectical and contradictory totality in motion. It is this blindness to the underlying deficiencies of Weber's methodology that turns so many Anglo-American, neo-Weberian historical sociologies of universal history into exercises in undertheorized eclecticism (Poggi 1978; Giddens 1985; Collins 1986; Mann 1986).

Conversely, some strands of Marxism interpret feudalism economistically as a static agrarian mode of production. The lack of sustained economic growth is explained in terms of underdeveloped forces of production, inefficient use of land, and negligible trade. However, such a one-sided focus on economic issues, e.g., in the form of a long-term tendency of the rate of lordly rents to decline (Bois 1984; Kula 1976), sits uneasily with the political and military aspects of medieval society, which decisively disrupted this tendency. Thus, some Althusserian Marxists have revised the undue pre-eminence of economic considerations, arguing for 'treating the state as an independent social force' in feudal societies (Gintis and Bowles 1984: 19; Haldon 1993). Whether the stress is on 'the economic' or the 'political' in Marxist traditions of thought, this simplified polarization has led many to question the capacity of Marxism to unify 'the political' and 'the economic' in a coherent theory of feudal society as a totality (Poggi 1988: 212).

In the wake of the Anglo-American Weber renaissance, some contemporary Weberian sociologists have drawn the wider conclusion that Marx may have correctly located the primary source of social power in capitalist societies in the ownership of the means of production (Giddens 1985). In traditional societies, however, the locus of social power lay in possession of the means of violence. This finding goes typically hand in hand with a typology of sources of social power – usually political/military, economic, ideological/normative, and cultural. Historical processes are then explained by a pluralist, multi-causal account based on this typology (Mann 1986: 379–99; Poggi 1978: ch. 2; Collins 1986). The neo-Weberians concur, then, in stressing the primacy of political, administrative, and military aspects in feudal society. In contrast, Marxian analyses are held to be reductionist, determinist, monocausal, and functionalist, or simply dismissed as irrelevant, deficient, or incommensurable in their concern with 'the economy'.

Against this alleged incommensurability, during the debate on the transition from feudalism to capitalism attention was redirected to Marx's writings on pre-capitalist societies (Sweezy, Dobb et al. 1976). Here, Marx specified the constitutive role of political power as expressed in various forms of 'extra-economic surplus appropriation' where the means of subsistence are possessed by the immediate producer:

> It is clear, too, that in all forms where the actual worker himself remains the 'possessor' of the means of production and the conditions of labour needed for the production of his own means of subsistence, the property relationship must appear at the same time as a direct relationship of domination and servitude, and the direct producer therefore as an unfree person – an unfreedom which may undergo a progressive attenuation from serfdom with statute-labour down to a mere tribute obligation. The direct producer in this case is by our assumption in possession of his own means of production, the objective conditions of labour needed for the realization of his labour and the production of his means of subsistence; he pursues his agriculture independently, as well as the rural-domestic industry associated with it. . . . Under these conditions, the surplus labour for the nominal landowner can only be extorted from them by extra-economic compulsion, whatever the form this might assume. . . . Relations of personal dependence are therefore necessary, in other words personal unfreedom, to whatever degree, and being chained to the land as its accessory – bondage in the true sense. (Marx 1981: 926–7)

This passage identifies the crucial nexus, mediated by extra-economic compulsion, with which the feudal relation between 'the economic' and 'the political' – indeed, their actual fusion – can be understood. It stands in sharp contrast to the configuration of the political and the economic – now differentiated as the state and the market – in capitalist societies:

> The abstraction of the *state as such* belongs only to modern times, because
> the abstraction of private life belongs only to modern times. The abstrac-
> tion of the *political state* is a modern product. In the Middle Ages there
> were serfs, feudal estates, merchant and trade guilds, corporations of
> scholars, etc.: that is to say, in the Middle Ages property, trade, society,
> man are *political*; the material content of the state is given by its form;
> every private sphere has a political character or is a political sphere; that
> is, politics is a characteristic of the private spheres too. In the Middle Ages
> the political constitution is the constitution of private property, but only
> because the constitution of private property is a political constitution. In
> the Middle Ages the life of the nation and the life of the state are identical.
> (Marx 1975: 32)

In feudal society, property relations are such that the noble class reproduces
itself primarily by forced appropriation of peasant surplus by administrative,
military, and political means. Seen from this angle, the primacy the Weber–
Hintze tradition concedes to the political sphere rests on an abstraction in
which the political form is emptied of its economic content and granted
autonomous causal or typological status. Yet it is precisely this political
sphere in which the struggles over surplus are played out.

The incommensurability thesis thus turns out to rest on an illusion.
Theorizing the identity of the political and economic within a conception
of totality does not simply offer an alternative to Weberian ideal-typical
and pluralist accounts. It presents a real advance in explanatory power and
epistemological rigour vis-à-vis one-sided abstractions. 'Extra-economic
compulsion' in the form of specific political modes of surplus appropriation
is the central analytical principle for understanding feudal societies.

2. From the Logic of Production to the Logic of Exploitation

Retrieving the idea of extra-economic compulsion requires further clarification of one of Marx's master-concepts, the relations of production, and
its place in a theory of the state. In a seminal passage, Perry Anderson
systematically develops the implications of extra-economic coercion as the
differentia specifica distinguishing non-capitalist from capitalist societies:

> *all* modes of production in class societies prior to capitalism extract surplus
> labour from the immediate producers by means of extra-economic coer-
> cion. Capitalism is the first mode of production in history in which the
> means whereby the surplus is pumped out of the direct producer is
> 'purely' economic in form – the wage contract: the equal exchange
> between free agents which reproduces, hourly and daily, inequality and

oppression. All other previous modes of exploitation operate through *extra-economic* sanctions – kin, customary, religious, legal or political. It is therefore on principle always impossible to read them off from economic relations as such. The 'superstructures' of kinship, religion, law or the state necessarily enter into the constitutive structure of the mode of production in pre-capitalist social formations. They intervene *directly* in the 'internal' nexus of surplus-extraction, where in capitalist social formations, the first in history to separate the economy as a formally self-contained order, they provide by contrast its 'external' preconditions. In consequence, pre-capitalist modes of production cannot be defined *except* via their political, legal and ideological superstructures, since these are what determine the type of extra-economic coercion that specifies them. The precise forms of juridical dependence, property and sovereignty that characterize a pre-capitalist social formation, far from being merely accessory or contingent epiphenomena, compose on the contrary the central indices of the determinate mode of production dominant within it. A scrupulous and exact taxonomy of these legal and political configurations is thus a pre-condition of establishing any comprehensive typology of pre-capitalist modes of production. It is evident, in fact, that the complex *imbrications* of economic exploitation with extra-economic institutions and ideologies creates a much wider gamut of possible modes of production prior to capitalism. . . . (Anderson 1974b: 403–4)

This extraordinary passage engendered a theoretical *volte-face* in Marxist thinking on pre-capitalist social formations, which was as liberating as it was fraught with unresolved theoretical implications.

On the one hand, Anderson's retheorization turns on its head the orthodox Marxist theorem – vulgar, trivialized, or dogmatically distorted as it may have been – that economic structures determine political superstructures. In one bold stroke, it thereby renders the entire political history of medieval societies amenable to a Marxist interpretation, both institutionally and developmentally. Institutionally, property now becomes the *principium medium* between the economic and the political, or rather, the institutional expression of the political construction of the economic:

The immediate producers and the means of production – comprising both the tools of labour and the objects of labour, e.g. land – are always dominated by the exploiting class through the prevalent property system, the nodal intersection between law and economy: but because property relations are themselves directly articulated on the political and ideological order, which indeed often expressly governs their distribution (confining landownership to aristocrats, for example, or excluding nobles from trade), the total apparatus of exploitation always extends upwards into the sphere of the superstructures themselves. (Anderson 1974b: 404)

Developmentally, Anderson recalls that 'secular struggle between classes is ultimately resolved at the political – not at the economic or cultural – level of society. In other words, it is the construction and destruction of states which seal the basic shifts in the relations of production, so long as classes subsist' (Anderson 1974b: 11).

On the other hand, if feudal societies were really characterized by a fusion of the political and the economic mediated through social property relations, it would follow that the entire vocabulary of base and superstructure, relations of production and modes of production, itself becomes questionable.[7] Given these unresolved issues, a further conceptual shift from the 'relations of production' to the 'relations of exploitation' can yield greater analytical precision while avoiding an overly 'politicist' reading of Europe's pre-capitalist history. Class relations in pre-capitalist society are never economic relations (they are economic only in capitalism). They are best defined in terms of property in the means of violence that structure the relations of exploitation. Any attempt to rescue the term 'relations of production' for pre-capitalist societies faces severe difficulties in 'deriving' the form of the state from existing relations of production, for the pre-capitalist 'state' maintains them.[8] The following quotation exemplifies the dilemma:

> The specific economic form in which unpaid surplus labour is pumped out of the direct producers determines the relationship of domination and servitude, as this grows directly out of production itself and reacts back on it in turn as a determinant. On this is based the entire configuration of the economic community arising from the actual relations of production, and hence also its specific political form. It is in each case the direct relationship of the owners of the conditions of production to the immediate producers – a relationship whose particular form naturally corresponds always to a certain level of development of the type and manner of labour, and hence to its social productive power – in which we find the innermost secret, the hidden basis of the entire social edifice, and hence also the political form of the relationship of sovereignty and dependence, in short, the specific form of state in each case. (Marx 1981: 927)

This passage, often adduced to show an embryonic Marxian theory of the state (Comninel 1987: 168; Rosenberg 1994: 84), is not unequivocal. Apart from the questionable techno-determinist 'correspondence' of social relations to 'methods of labour', relations of domination cannot grow out of 'production itself' understood as a pre-political or pre-social activity – a metabolic process between man and nature mediated by the forces of production.[9] It is difficult to conceive of feudal relations between lords and direct producers, who possess their means of production, as a relation between the 'owners of the conditions of production to the direct producers'. It was a relation between the owners of the conditions of exploitation to the direct producers.

Still, it is no exaggeration to suggest that Marx sketches here the essential contours of the nexus between the forms of surplus appropriation and the form of the political. Here, the political is not external to the property relation, i.e., the process of exploitation, but co-constitutes and reproduces it, provided that we understand the 'state' as a class relation. A focus on the logic of exploitation overcomes the danger of conceiving the pre-capitalist 'state' and 'economy' as two separate institutional spheres and foregrounds the class-mediated nexus between political force and economic appropriation. By insisting that the 'state' never conclusively fixes or institutionalizes a given set of class relations, it implies that property is always a contested social relation, defined, defended, and renegotiated by the 'state' in the face of pressures from direct producers. In other words, a shift to the relations of exploitation and the associated social contradictions between exploiters and exploited, rather than the 'dialectic' between forces and relations of production, rejects the teleological tendencies inherent in the 'modes of production' paradigm and preserves the moment of historical openness and change which is always latent in the unpredictable resolutions of class conflicts. While this reformulation cannot in itself resolve the long-standing dispute over structure and agency, a dialectical *via media* would remain sensitive to the historical processes by which determinate relations of exploitation generate social discontent. During periods of general crisis, transcendence, i.e., institutional or structural change, is itself never a necessary, but always a possible outcome, depending on the degree of class organization and the unpredictable resolution of social conflicts. Thus, the historical process appears neither as a necessitous succession of 'modes of production', nor as a contingent succession of 'types of domination', but remains suspended as an open conflict between possible alternatives. In short, a shift towards the relations of exploitation prevents conceptual reification, economic reductionism, teleological and functionalist tendencies, and historical closure.[10]

In sum, I propose a theoretical framework for feudal societies centred on the logic of exploitation as mediated by determinate social property relations. While class conflict remains the *primum mobile* of history, its logic revolves essentially around four conflicts: (1) between peasants and lords (class conflict); (2) among lords (intra-ruling-class conflict); (3) between the collectivity of lords (the feudal 'state') and 'external' lordly communities (inter-ruling-class conflict); and (4) among the peasantry (intra-producing-class conflict). Together, these horizontal and vertical lines of conflict proceed from and generate definite balances of class forces, which themselves govern and filter the rhythms of war and peace. In other words, political organization, conscious social activity, remains the strategic locus of institution-altering forms of agency. From this angle, the argument that intra-ruling-class conflict constitutes a separate order of reality – the sphere of politics proper, understood in Weberian terms as the status-driven competition for power – collapses. Equally, geopolitical relations do not occupy an independent, self-enclosed sphere of reality (the geopolitical), as Neorealists and neo-Weberians maintain (Mann 1986; Hobson 1998). In feudal societies, intra-ruling-class conflicts, both domestic and geopolitical, are not conflicts over the maximization of power, but conflicts between and among politically accumulating classes over their relative share in the means of extra-economic coercion. Finally, we must reject the proposition that peasant life can be confined to a distinct, self-contained sphere, the object of 'history from below', divorced from political history. These spheres of social action do not follow 'laws of their own' but are the *disiecta membra* of one contradictory totality. It remains to translate this model of property and collective social agency into a series of more concrete propositions.

3. The Structure–Agent Problem in Feudal Terms

We now have to specify the basic political and economic unit of feudal society. On this basis, we can demonstrate how this unit governs specific forms of social action that pervade, animate, and possibly change structural relations. This will help us show how the structure–agent problem can be conceptualized in feudal society (Wendt 1987, 1992).

1. Lordship as Conditional Property (Structure)

The basic unit of the feudal fusion of the economic and the political was the institution of lordship. It is essential to recall that lordship was not simply an agrarian economic enterprise, but a 'unit of authority' in which ties between men were not mediated via 'freely' entered contracts between private persons, but stipulated through political power, i.e., domination (Bloch

1966b: 236). The 'economic' was inscribed into the 'political'. Men were ascribed to a lord. The striking peculiarity of medieval property, then, resides in the fact that property rights were political rights of governance as much as economic rights of tenure; in fact, the two were inseparable. This non-separation is captured by the Latin term *potestas et utilitas* (Kuchenbuch 1997). Mere property rights to land were meaningless if they did not include authority over the people who cultivated it, because peasants possessed their means of subsistence and were therefore under no internal compulsion to rent from or work for the lord. This contrasts to capitalist property, where ownership of land is 'real' because it constitutes a value, precisely because cultivators no longer possess their means of subsistence and are compelled to rent from or work for landlords (Marx 1976b: 873–907, 1981: 917–50).

Yet, although lords wielded political power, they did not as a rule constitute sovereign mini-states. Classically, they held their land in tenure as a fief that carried, along with specific rights to exploit the peasantry, military and administrative duties to the land-granting overlord: 'Land, in fact, was not "owned" by anyone; it was "held" by superiors in a ladder of "tenures" leading to the king or other supreme lord' (Berman 1983: 312). The specific legal status of land has thus been variously described by jurisprudence as conditional property or usufruct (*dominium utile*), while the overlord nominally retained the overlordship (*dominium directum*). This meant that the fiefholder could not freely dispose of 'his' land, but only enjoy its exploitation for definite purposes. Property was conditional.

This brings us back to the question of how the pretension to lordship was asserted against overlords, rival lords, and a subjected peasantry. Otto Brunner classically distinguished lordship from great estates through an interpretation of the medieval concept of *Gewere* (domain). *Gewere* refers to 'the actual possession and use of a thing, with the presumption of a property right in it' (Brunner 1992: 209). Decisively, the lord exercised politically legitimate violence by enforcing these rights over and against non-complying peasants and rival lords – in contentious cases, even against his own overlord. In the last instance, his arms-bearing status secured his political lordship. *Gewere*

> presupposed the 'lawful force' – namely the protection and safeguard that a lord exercised in defence of his domain, not simply as an owner of property, but literally as the lord of his lands. . . . We see here a constitutional structure that recognized the use of force by members of the legal community against each other, with no state of the modern sort to claim a monopoly of legitimate force, and with every member of the legal community having a measure of executive power. (Brunner 1992: 210)

It is crucial to recognize that 'domestic' resistance was not criminalized but inscribed in the feudal constitution. It was legitimate and lawful if the overlord failed to comply with his obligations vis-à-vis his feoffee and vice versa. This dispersion of legitimate violence had profound consequences for the nature of the medieval state, its form of territoriality, the meaning of war as feud, and the entire structure of political power and 'international' organization. Here we begin to see why medieval property relations are central to understanding the institutions central to IR.[11]

2. Contradictory Strategies of Reproduction (Agency)

We can now outline the dominant forms of medieval agency. Let me rehearse the preconditions for class-specific and thus conflicting feudal strategies of reproduction. Medieval society constituted a system of agrarian production for use value and simple commodity production based on peasant labour. Its fundamental sources of wealth were land and labour. The means of production (land, tools, livestock, dwellings) were possessed by the direct producers, so that peasant communities formed subsistence communities. In this context, what were the main forms of social action?

Let us first turn to the noble class (Brenner 1985b; 1986: 27–32; 1987: 173–8; see also Duby 1974; Gerstenberger 1990: 503–7). The arms-bearing lord stood between a subjected peasantry tilling 'his' estate and competing rival lords vying for land and labour. To survive in this competitive situation, lords developed the following strategies of reproduction:

1. They maximized rents by squeezing the peasantry – the intensification of labour.
2. They expanded their land internally through land reclamation.
3. They colonized and settled land externally, usually in connection with warfare and conquest.
4. They conquered neighbouring regions, established client states, or exercised suzerainty over such regions without direct occupation but by annual tribute payments.
5. They engaged in direct internecine warfare, either by direct conquest and annexation or by cavalcades, plunder, pillage, and ransom.
6. Finally, they used dynastic marriage policies to amass lands and to increase their income bases.

These lordly strategies of reproduction are set out analytically. Historically, not every single lord engaged 'rationally' in such strategies. Yet the ruling class as a whole reproduced itself by conforming to such 'systemic' pressures of domination. Such bounded rationality tells us something about the limits of social action under specific property relations.[12] In times of crisis and social struggle, of course, the very institutions of surplus extraction were at stake. Depending on the resolution of these conflicts, new forms of bounded rationality sprang into existence. What all six feudal strategies implied, however, was investment in the means of violence. Robert Brenner subsumes such strategies under the general concept of 'political accumulation' (Brenner 1985b: 236–42).

The success of lordly strategies of reproduction was suspended between the internal cohesion of the members of the non-producing class and the collective resistance of the producing class. As a rule, peasant strategies of reproduction irreconcilably contradicted the interests of the lords. By integrating peasant rationality into the overall equation, a general picture emerges of clashing forms of collective agency in medieval society.

Living in subsistence communities, the peasantry was economically independent, i.e., it did not depend on the market for survival. Peasants had no need to sell their labour-power or to rent out or invest in agriculture. Since the peasantry was under no economic compulsion to render dues, it developed a specific form of economic rationality that should not be dismissed as irrational, but corresponded precisely to feudal conditions of social action:

1. Being self-sufficient and given that food formed the main part of total consumption (yet was in uncertain supply), peasants minimized risk by diversifying their agricultural products. In marked contrast to capitalist rationality, rural produce was not specialized.
2. Non-market dependency translated into reduced labour-time, which meant striking a balance between the lord's demands and the socio-cultural needs of the peasant and his family. Again, non-profit-orientated economic rationality was the essence of everyday life.
3. Risk minimization led to early marriages, a high rate of peasant reproduction, and division of land upon inheritance.
4. Against lordly demands, peasants organized in communities, developed forms of collective class organization to resist lordly encroachments, or withdrew their labour power through flight.

3. A 'Culture of War' based upon Political Accumulation

The fortunes of reproduction depended on the collective ability of both peasants and lords to redistribute peasant-produced surplus as circumscribed by the balance of class forces. Whereas peasant reproduction as a rule generated economic stagnation, the class of lords was under pressure to build up military power. Unsurprisingly, the development of agricultural technology was relatively lethargic, whereas military innovations based upon systematic investment in the means of violence were spectacular throughout the Middle Ages and beyond.[13] Military might was necessary to maintain the established aristocratic way of life. Violence was the *raison d'être* of the nobility, war-making its dominant form of rationality. Characteristically, lordly expanded reproduction took the form of system-wide, 'extensive-territorial' conquest (Merrington 1976: 179). *Contra* Gilpin, horizontal political expansion over territories and labour as sources of income *does* define the essence of feudal geopolitical expansion (Gilpin 1981: 108–9). 'Political accumulation' drove the socio-political dynamic of feudal society, revealing the hidden meaning of the Middle Ages as a 'culture of war'. At the same time, 'international' inter-lordly relations did not follow a transhistorical systemic logic in abstraction from the social relations of lordship. Feudal property structures and dominant forms of social action were dialectically mediated.[14]

4. A Phenomenology of Medieval 'International' Institutions

1. The Parcellized Sovereignty of the 'Medieval State'

The sovereign state was unknown in the Middle Ages. Political rule was simply domination. Since every lord appropriated individually, medieval polities faced the problem of squaring noble geographical particularism with the needs for central self-organization for collective aggression and self-defence.

What are the implications of individualized lordship for the form of medieval states? With the exception of the tenth and eleventh centuries, not every lordship constituted a 'mini-state'. Lordships were generally linked via vassalic relations in the classical feudal pyramid to an overlord. This relation was established through a synallagmatic 'contract' between lord and vassal.

Its decisive characteristic was its interpersonal and reciprocal nature, specifying personal, proprietary rights and obligations between the two 'contracting' parties. Among these obligations *auxilium et consilium* – military assistance and political advice – were the most prominent. Thus, medieval 'states' rested on a series of interpersonal bonds between the members of the landholding class. They were essentially ensembles of lordships.

Crucially, however, the fiefholder was not a mere functionary or official of the 'state' but a fully fledged political lord. He did not represent the 'state' and his status was not delegated by or derived from one. The 'state' was the sum-total of the class of lords – the self-organization of the ruling nobility. While a strict historical semantic would avoid the terms sovereignty or state in this context, for comparative purposes it is acceptable to say that sovereignty was 'parcellized' or 'divided', in the sense that each lord was a 'fragment of the state' (Anderson 1974a: 148, 1974b: 15; Brenner 1985b: 229; Wood 1995a: 39). But since the feudal 'state' was neither a corporate entity nor a 'legal person', since it lacked an abstract institutional existence beyond the life-spans of individual rulers, it is more precise to define the political in terms of a concrete praxis of personalized domination (*'personale Herrschaftspraxis'*) (Gerstenberger 1990: 500ff). Weber commented that 'feudalism is a "separation of powers", but unlike Montesquieu's scheme, which constitutes a qualitative division of labour, it is simply a quantitative division of authority' (Weber 1968a: 1082). German constitutional historians (Mayer 1963: 290; Mitteis 1975: 5) term this phenomenon a *Personenverbandsstaat* (a state of associated persons) in order to clearly demarcate it from the Weberian rationalized state (*rationale Staatsanstalt*) and the institutional-territorial state (*institutioneller Flächenstaat*). It follows that since the medieval world lacked a 'state', it also lacked an 'economy' and a 'society' as separate institutions with autonomous mechanisms of social integration and developmental logics. These three institutions, as Hegel and Marx suggested, are specific to the age of capitalism.

Further corollaries follow from the interpersonal character of medieval domination for determining the sphere of the political. Since domination was personal, noble families – dynasties – were perforce the 'natural' transmitters of political power. Consequently, dynastic family politics – noble marriages, problems of inheritance, laws of succession – were a general *politicum* of the first order, directly structuring inter-lordly and geopolitical relations. By implication, the biological accidents of noble sexual reproduction were tantamount to the reproduction of the political.

Given the purely interpersonal relationships among politically independent actors who were not answerable to a codified set of administrative laws, notions of fealty were at a premium. The well-documented corporeal rites of homage, the act of investment, and the highly refined code of honour were testimony to this precarious 'non-rationalized' mediation between plural, land-based, independent political wills. The inter-vasallic ethos of fealty and honour expressed the absence of a depoliticized bureaucracy. 'The result was to generate an aristocratic ideology which rendered compatible pride of rank and humility of homage, legal fixity of obligations and personal fidelity of allegiance' (Anderson 1974b: 410–11). The doctrine of the king's two bodies captured precisely the dual identity of the king's physical body with its theocratic and divine character (Kantorowicz 1957). *Contra* Constructivism, we cannot stress this discourse, *mentalité*, or mode of legitimation in dissociation from the socio-economic content of feudal relations (Hall and Kratochwil 1993). In sum, within these interpersonal relations of domination, public power was territorially fragmented, decentralized, personalized, and only loosely held together through bonds of vassalage (Hintze 1968: 24–5).

This configuration of power was not static. To the extent that localized noble appropriation required policing by armed retainers, lords found themselves simultaneously competing with their own overlords and other rival lords. Based on this underlying contradiction, an ebb and flow of feudal centralization and decentralization can be observed throughout the history of the European Middle Ages (Weber 1968a: 1038–44; Anderson 1974a: 151–2; Le Patourel 1976: 279–318; Brenner 1985b: 239; Haldon 1993: 213; Elias 1994: 275–86).

Strong unifying forces emerged wherever a competent warlord led his co-ruling nobles into successive cycles of campaigning, redistributing the conquered land and other spoils of war (slaves, women, hostages, treasure, tributes, armaments) among his contented warriors. These cycles of conquest and redistribution were self-reinforcing, for they fostered loyalty to the supreme warlord and simultaneously provided the means and manpower for further campaigning. The standing of Charles Martel, Henry Plantagenet, and Otto I, to name but a few, and the relative stability of their respective polities, were directly predicated upon such dynamic mechanisms of political accumulation. Dialectically, however, military success always contained the seeds of fragmentation. Those nobles who had flocked to a supreme warlord in order to generate a tightly knit military unit and who received large estates for their services turned into potential rivals. As long as their erstwhile leader could prove his military prowess, strategic competence, and ability to punish rebellious magnates, the nobles would continue to peg their fortunes to him. Otherwise, they used their newly acquired power base either to establish their independence or to challenge him directly.

In this case, an inverse cycle of intra-ruling-class altercations set in, inviting intervention by foreign tribes. Corroding central power led to regionalization and the end of ruling-class solidarity. This usually went hand in hand with the usurpation of public offices – as, for example, under Louis the Pious and his even weaker successors. Internal redistribution of land and rights of jurisdiction became the logical alternative to external conquest. In other words, central government always rested on a compromise – a fragile alliance for mutual gain – between the members of the lordly class. The perennially brittle medieval 'state' rested on organizing power in the force field between centrifugal tendencies of localized appropriation and centripetal tendencies of political consolidation and noble self-organization against the peasantry and for purposes of external defence or conquest.

Domination was, of course, not asserted on a day-to-day basis by the sharpness of the lord's sword. The sub-discipline of historical semantics has carefully distinguished domination from other notions of political power (Moraw 1982). Domination refers to practices of rule inseparable from the body of the incumbent. It therefore includes all those social practices which kept dependants in a subordinate position and demonstrated a lord's ability to rule to his co-rulers. Theocratic privileges, miraculous healing powers, and charismatic gestures of leadership were part and parcel of domination (Kantorowicz 1957; Bloch 1973; Duby 1974: 48–57). Rule was also mediated by a peculiar sphere of noble representation: conspicuous consumption, largesse, the maintenance of luxurious households, and the lavish display of symbols of power are not to be dissociated from the business of domination. Medievalists have elaborated at length on the significance of imagery for the rites of medieval power. The circulation of gifts especially was an essential part of inter-noble class consciousness and a clear indicator of social might (Ganshof 1970: 43). Far from being signs of irrational extravagance, subjective prodigality, or medieval mysticism, the political economy of symbolic reproduction reveals how ostentation and conspicuous consumption communicated to both noble peers and dependent peasants the lord's social power and extractive capacities (Habermas 1989: 5–9). To this extent, there is nothing mysterious about symbolic representation, even for 'the structuralist hardened by a more materialist historiography' (Hall and Kratochwil 1993: 485).[15]

2. The Political Economy of Medieval Territory and Frontiers

We have come to think of states as exercising sovereignty over a clearly bounded territory. Modern territoriality is exclusive and uniformly administered. The diplomatic institution of 'extra-territoriality' and the principle of non-intervention are the classical expressions of this form of international organization. The Middle Ages confront us with an inverse image. As a rule, medieval territory was coextensive with the ruler's ability to enforce his claims. Thus, we have to turn to the techniques of exercising political power under conditional property relations in order to understand the constitution of medieval territoriality.

The first thing to note is that within feudal Europe no clear distinction could be drawn between internal and external. Wherever the fief constituted the basic cell of political territory, authority claims by respective overlords to this territory were mediated – in medievalist parlance: mediatized – through the vassal. The vassal could not be bureaucratically sanctioned through written procedures because he possessed independent political power. Personal loyalty had to be maintained on a day-to-day basis by the paraphernalia of medieval patronage. The problem was compounded when the feudo-vassalic chain stretched over more than two links, so that the rear-vassal owed his primary allegiance to his direct overlord and only secondary or no allegiance to whoever occupied the apex of the feudal pyramid. In this instance, part of the territory was completely removed from the royal reach yet formed neither an exclave nor a part of another state.

Where territoriality stands on shifting ground, its assertion requires the lord's physical presence. In this respect, the peripatetic nature of royal households indicates the structural difficulty of maintaining effective authority over territory. Ceaseless royal mobility was shadowed on a smaller scale by the ceaseless movement of lesser lords. Few enjoyed lordship over a compact area. Most estates were scattered over far-flung territories, reflecting the vicissitudes of military acquisition and the politics of land partition on inheritance. Consider, for example, the Franco-Norman knights who followed William the Conqueror to England. After the conquest, the eradication of the Anglo-Saxon landholding class, and the redistribution of dispossessed land among the invading barons, many lords found themselves masters over an incongruous body of estates. In addition to their ancestral homelands in northern France, they now had to run their new lands in England, and, in the course of the conquest of the British

Isles, in Wales, Ireland, or Scotland (Given 1990: 91–152; Bartlett 1993: 57). Thus, William's incessant maritime voyages were mirrored by the peregrinations of his greater barons. Anglo-Norman lords were essentially 'cross-Channel lords' (Frame 1990: 53). State territory was coterminous with the landholding patterns of the ruling class.

The organization of political power over medieval territory was not uniform. Whereas there is, as a rule, no real administrative distinction between centre and periphery within modern states, frontier regions in medieval states – the marches – were quite distinct (Mitteis 1975: 66; Smith 1995). Ethnic, religious, natural-topographical, or linguistic differences were secondary in determining the 'demarcation' of frontier regions. Instead, the extension of medieval territory followed the patterns of conquest, that is, political accumulation. The administration of the periphery reflected a careful balancing act between the eradication, accommodation, or co-optation of the conquered local nobility, the needs of newly established conquest-lordships, and the wider security interests of the 'state'. This created another dilemma for feudal overlords: since marcher lords had to be invested with special military powers of command in order to deal effectively with unruly neighbours, they became semi-autonomous (Werner 1980). More often than not, they abused their privileges to build up regional strongholds. For example, the liberties enjoyed by the Anglo-Norman lords of the March of Wales, which lay between native-controlled Wales and the English kingdom, persisted well into the sixteenth century, even though the victorious Edwardian campaigns (1282–83) had undermined their *raison d'être* centuries earlier. In the Welsh Marches, the king's writ was idle (Davies 1989, 1990). Under these conditions, where did state territory start and where did it end? (Smith 1995: 179) Thus, modern linear borders were preceded in Europe by zonal frontier regions contested by semi-independent lords. This does not mean that lines were not drawn on the geopolitical map. The Treaty of Verdun (843) divided the Carolingian Empire into three clearly demarcated territories. Although this gave the respective rulers' claims on 'their' local lords some degree of legitimacy, it had to be practically negotiated and enforced from case to case.

Feudal territoriality can thus best be visualized in terms of concentric circles of power projection. Only the sporadic assertion of royal overlordship over semi-autonomous peripheral lords periodically reconstituted a sense of bounded territoriality. As a rule, central claims to authority petered out in frontier zones constantly on the verge of secession and busily engaged in their own 'foreign policies' vis-à-vis adjacent regions. Amorphous medieval territoriality cannot simply be explained in terms of a

mismatch between insufficient central administrative capacities (communication and enforcement) and spatial extension (Weber 1968a: 1091). It was
deeply engrained in the land-based political economy of lordships. Feudal
decentralization should thus not be understood as the contingent solution
to a series of economic, technological, and institutional absences, but rather
as the definite expression of a determinate social property regime. This, in
turn, explains why the means of communication and administration were
not developed: feudal relations of exploitation did not exert a systematic
pressure to invest in and thus to develop them. Medieval political geography is the story of the cohesion between and fragmentation of feudal
lordships – a phenomenon of ruling-class organization.

3. War and Peace: Mediaeval Feuding as Legal Redress

Given that medieval political power was dispersed amongst a multiplicity
of political actors, and that a political actor was primarily defined militarily,
the problematique of war and peace can only be understood in terms of a
diffuse oligopoly over the means of violence. Against this background, the
lines between pacified domestic politics and essentially hostile international
relations, between criminal law and international law, were blurred – in
fact, impossible to draw. What are the implications of this organization of
political power for modes of conflict resolution – for questions of war and
peace – in the Middle Ages?

The answer to this question lies in an interpretation of the feud (Geary
1986; Brunner 1992). The feud mediated the 'internal economic' contradictions of the ruling class into 'external political' conflicts by way of inter-
noble competition. This focus on the feud does not imply, of course, that
all medieval wars were inter-lordly feuds. Only conflicts among feudal
actors took the form of feuds. What is central here is that peace always
stood on the shaky ground of the noble right to armed resistance. Since
the right to resort to arms was part and parcel of conditional property,
legitimate feuding was exclusively restricted to the nobility. Although
monarchs attempted time and again to outlaw feuding in letter, they
seldom succeeded (England was the partial exception) in enforcing the
peace of the land in practice.

Noble 'self-help' was not a state of emergency, a civil war, or the
sudden re-emergence of a pre-contractual Hobbesian state of nature. Nor
was it a Waltzian form of reactive power maximization to be inferred from
international anarchy. Rather, it was a generally acknowledged form of

jurisdictional redress wielded by an aggrieved party. All secular nobles had the right to settle their disputes by force of arms, in cases of both failed arbitration and, ironically, successful arbitration – since in the absence of an overarching executive the execution of the sentence was the responsibility of the vindicated party.

Can we then distinguish meaningfully between feud and war in the European Middle Ages? Brunner suggests that within Christian Europe contemporaries distinguished between feuds and wars only by the magnitude of the conflict, not by the underlying principle (Brunner 1992: 33–5). He supports this interpretation by pointing out that warfare (legal feuding), both between minor lords and between powerful monarchs, was conducted according to the same formal proceedings. Notwithstanding the frequent transgression of these prerequisites and limits, we see here a mode of conflict resolution that (1) was exercised within 'states' as well as between 'states'; (2) was regarded as legitimate form of redress; (3) was not covered by some incipient international law; and (4) can only be adequately interpreted against the background of decentralized political power based on the necessity of localized appropriation. To be sure, these modes of conflict resolution might seem to constitute a self-help system in which might generates right, but only by abstracting from their social rationale and thus crudely equating modern inter-state wars with medieval feuds.[16]

Just as there was no 'international' concept of war, there was no 'international' concept of peace. Within 'states' and between 'states', lords stood principally in non-pacified relations. They were agents of war and peace. Since the authorities who sponsored peace were 'functionally differentiated', those efforts reflected the hierarchy of peacemakers (the king's peace, the peace of God, the peace of the land, the peace of towns, the peace of lords) and were geared towards pacifying inherently bellicose inter-noble relations. The vocabulary of anarchy and hierarchy does not suffice to grasp this state of affairs. The mechanisms of peacemaking, in turn, were as variegated as the diversity of feudal public actors. Let me illustrate this diversity of peacemaking under feudal property relations by looking at the activities of the bishops in the tenth century.

Efforts to establish peace during the tenth-century 'Feudal Revolution' (Wickham 1997) were everywhere initiated and orchestrated by regional bishops. The episcopal peace movements were not motivated by abstract considerations of non-violence or moral theology, nor even of compassion for a hard-hit peasantry that bore the brunt of lordly marauding: instead, they were a direct reaction to lordly encroachments on Church land and treasure (Duby 1980; Flori 1992a: 455–6; Brunner 1992: 15). In the absence of royal protection, the immunities granted to the Church lacked legal and military protection. In this precarious situation, the clergy, the only part of the non-producing class that did not bear arms, developed a long-term secular interest in establishing modalities of peace to maintain their socio-economic basis. Alternatively, the bishops began to arm themselves. However, the most effective means in their hands was privileged access to the means of spiritual reproduction. More drastically, the monopoly over the means of salvation provided the preferred lever of ecclesiastical interference in worldly affairs for the pre-Gregorian Church: excommunication (Poly and Bournazel 1991: 154). We should not be misled by its spiritual connotations: it was not simply the moral capital of the praying class, but an effective means of exclusion from the legal community, usually with devastating social and material consequences. Excommunication was analogous to loss of citizenship today (Berman 1983: 114; Geary 1986: 1119–20).

What, then, did the *pax dei* and the *treuga dei* entail? The bishop-led peace movements did not intend to, nor were they in a position to, outlaw feuding, since demilitarization would have undermined the very *raison d'être* of the knightly mode of life. Rather, they aimed to restrict and regulate the law of the fist by specifying exemptions to warring, first in terms of persons and objects (peace of God), and later in terms of time and space (truce of God). In sum, the peace movements were a conscious strategy of appeasement on the part of the unarmed clergy and an attempt to contain the feudal crisis of the tenth to twelfth centuries by those most afflicted before newly consolidated monarchies set to work restoring peace by public means.

5. Feudal 'International Systems': Beyond Anarchy and Hierarchy

What was the structuring principle of 'international' organization in the European Middle Ages? As we saw in chapter 1, Waltz, Krasner, Ruggie, and Spruyt agree on the anarchic nature of the Middle Ages. We can now qualify this assertion and fine-tune the anarchy/hierarchy problematique by historicizing structures of lordship. By focusing on the changing forms of lordship that defined differentiated access to property, we gain a criterion for drawing out differences in the political constitution of medieval geopolitical orders without losing sight of their essential identity. For these alterations in lordly property rights flowed from the social relations that underlay changing geopolitical contexts: feudal empires (650–950), feudal anarchy (950–1150), and the feudal states-system (1150–1450). In other words, the degree to which political powers of extraction were wielded by the landholding class decisively conditioned feudal geopolitical orders. However, while changes in property relations explain differences in structuring principles, these principles do not determine geopolitical behaviour, but only mediate the logic of geopolitical accumulation.

1. Banal, Domestic, and Landlordship

The literature distinguishes between three dominant forms of lordship in the European Middle Ages (Duby 1974, 174–7).[17] *Banal lordship* refers to what could most readily claim medieval public authority, namely royal powers of command, taxation, punishment, adjudication, and decree. Being authorized to wield the powers of the ban conferred the most encompassing form of domination and exploitation, constituting what Duby called the 'master class' within the medieval ruling class (Duby 1974: 176). *Domestic lordship* was the prevalent form of domination on the classical bipartite manor of Carolingian times. Here, the lord's land was divided into a seigneurial demesne tilled by slave labour and specified peasant services, and surrounding peasant plots cultivated independently by tenured peasants. The 'lord's men' had no access to public courts, nor did they have to pay public taxes. They were exclusively subject to manorial control (Bloch 1966a: 70). *Landlordship* emerged in various regions of Western Europe from the late twelfth to the late fourteenth century. Here, the personal character – both between lord and vassal and between lord and peasantry – gave way to the proprietary character of the holding. The continental West European peasantry was enfranchised (the end of serfdom) and managed to fix its rents and dues in peasant charters (Brenner 1996). Lords forfeited their power of command and taxation. The demesne, and with it labour services, lost importance in relation to rents in kind and increasingly in cash (monetarization).

2. Conditional Hierarchy, Personalized Anarchy, Territorial Anarchy

How did specific constellations of lordship translate into the diverging structuring principles of the early, high, and late medieval 'international' systems?

The Carolingian Empire was built upon a combination of banal lordship wielded by the emperor and his officials (*missi*, counts), domestic lordship wielded by lesser lords in the exploitation of their estates, and free and arms-bearing peasant proprietors. Within the Empire, there was a weak presumption of hierarchy. The emperor handed out all noble land, fiefs were not hereditary, the Church was still politically integrated into the Empire, and the power of the ban overrode lordly rights. Despite this, the assumption of hierarchy must be relaxed because the emperor was not head of state; he was the supreme vassalic lord, and thus bound by the reciprocal terms of the vassalic contract. The hierarchy of authority claims was further eroded by the spreading immunity of ecclesiastical estates from imperial interference. *Conditional hierarchy* reigned. Although a variety of competing autonomous sources of law coexisted with royal law, conditional hierarchy flowed from the emperor's overriding politico-military and theocratic authority over his imperial aristocracy and lesser lords. Talk of conditional hierarchy rests, of course, on the assumption that the Empire can be conceived as an 'international system' in the first place. This is justifiable to the extent that it was made up of multiple semi-independent political actors whose *ultima ratio* was the lawful recourse to arms and who were bound together by interpersonal contracts.

This brings us to the problem of 'external sovereignty', defined as the exclusive capacity to conclude treaties, declare war, and have diplomatic representation. Although only the emperor could perform these functions in the name of the Empire, Carolingian magnates engaged in these forms of international relations, not only with 'foreign political actors', but also among themselves (Ganshof 1970; Mattingly 1988: 23). Finally, we have to inquire into the relation of the Empire to the surrounding polities and powers. A string of neighbouring polities were bound to the Franks by either vassalage or tribute payments, without being at any time incorporated into the Empire. They were subject to Carolingian suzerainty. Some polities, however, were outside the sphere of Frankish influence (the Byzantine Empire, the Califat of Córdoba, and the kingdoms of the British Isles). In this wider geopolitical perspective, there was neither hierarchy nor anarchy. Within its domain, the Frankish Empire was hegemonial.

After the cessation of Frankish expansion, the Empire disintegrated from the mid-ninth century onwards into its constituent building-blocks: lordships. Local lords began to usurp the kingly power of the ban. They 'privatized' high justice, taxed their 'subjects', territorialized their fiefs, patrimonialized their lands by introducing heredity, and subjected the remaining free peasantry to serfdom (Bonnassie 1991b). The merger of banal lordship and domestic lordship during the Feudal Revolution converted the estate into a fully independent *seigneurie*. This chronologically and territorially uneven process culminated in the eleventh century, but was confined to the western kingdom due to the persistent opportunities for conquest on the eastern frontier. What was once an internally consolidated polity turned into a multiplicity of petty conflict units. Widespread feuding and the militarization of the countryside unleashed 'feudal anarchy'. The castellans and knights rose to power. The French king became one actor among many. This configuration has led medievalists to talk of the 'second feudal age' and 'parcellization of sovereignty' (Bloch 1961; Mitteis 1975). If we consider this political constellation an 'international system', then we have to call it an anarchy of 'functionally differentiated' actors – an anarchy based on changes in the proprietary patterns of the landholding class. Since, however, the fragmentation of political power cascaded down the ladder of territories to the smallest possible conflict unit, the castellan or even the knight, I will call it a *personalized anarchy*. Every lord was his own conflict unit.

Finally, a new separation of banal and domestic lordly power emerged during the reconsolidation of feudal states beginning in the late twelfth century. While banal lordship was reappropriated by greater magnates and eventually monopolized by a few kings, landlordship became the basis of reproduction for nobles on the land. 'Bastard feudalism' transformed lordly military services into money payments to the overlord. In France, lords were increasingly drawn into the service of greater magnates. The reconstitution of higher royal courts, in turn, was a result of competition between feuding lords. By the thirteenth century, competition had given rise to a reterritorialization of banal powers in the hands of a dozen competing principalities, among which the Capetians eventually emerged victorious in France (Hallam 1980). Although vassalic relations among the bigger conflict units (even the king of England nominally remained a vassal to the king of France until the fifteenth century) continued to compromise an exclusive notion of territoriality, their significance receded as feudal services were successively replaced by the tax/office structure in more centralized states. This meant the emergence of feudal *non-exclusive territorial anarchy* in the late Middle Ages. The non-exclusivity of this form of territoriality must be stressed, since landlords retained substantial political powers over their peasants; emergent towns, based upon urban law, freed themselves from seigneurial control; and the reformed papacy now asserted its authority claims through transnational canon law.

★

In sum, domestic lordship in connection with a kingly monopoly of the ban underwrote early-medieval empire-building, which endured as long as the Franks conquered surrounding tribes. Its structuring principle was *conditional hierarchy* (internal conditional hierarchy, external limited hegemony). Next, the heyday of 'feudal anarchy' was based on strongly personalized banal lordships. *Personalized anarchy* brought to the fore the inherently fragile basis of feudal state formation under localized conditions of appropriation (internal hierarchy, external personalized anarchy). Finally, the separation of banal lordship and landlordship allowed public power to be reterritorialized. *Non-exclusive territorial anarchy* emerged between the units of the feudal state system (internal conditional hierarchy, external heteronomous anarchy).

6. Conclusion: Geopolitical Systems as Social Systems

This chapter started from the assumption that the character of international systems expresses the nature of their constitutive units, which are themselves predicated on determinate social property relations. The medieval geopolitical order lacked both the differentiation between the domestic and the international and the differentiation between the economic and the political. This double absence can be explained on the basis of the specific relations of exploitation between lords and peasants institutionalized in lordship – the constitutive unit of feudal order – establishing political access to peasant produce. Responding to collective peasant resistance and the need for external conquest and defence, lords organized into a 'state of associated persons'. The 'state' guaranteed noble property and lordly survival. Lordly reproduction followed the logic of political accumulation, being both an 'economic' (lord–peasant) and a 'geopolitical' (lord–lord) process. However, the nexus between individual noble appropriation and the right to resist, fixed in the noble right to bear arms, precluded a state monopoly of the means of violence. Inter-lordly relations were therefore by definition neither 'international' and hence anarchic, nor domestic and hence hierarchic. 'Sovereignty' was parcellized among politically appropriating lords.

The theory of social property relations not only vindicates the common objection to Neorealism's lack of a generative grammar and transformative logic, it questions its very assumption that there was a distinct international level in medieval Europe that can be theorized in abstraction from the reproductive logic of feudal society. The state and the market, the domestic and the international, were not yet differentiated into separate spheres. How, then, did the twofold differentiation between the domestic/international and the economic/political come about? The *differentia specifica* of the European experience resides precisely in the formation of a plurality of states. The prior question that therefore has to be addressed is how political communities emerged in Europe in the plural. To answer it, we have to turn to the logic behind the decomposition of the last pan-European empire: the Carolingian Empire. I suggest that plural state formation, creating the distinction between the domestic and the international, and capitalism, creating the distinction between the political and the economic, were not geographically and temporally co-constitutive. Multiple state formations came first.

Notes

1 For the epistemological issues involved, see Heine and Teschke 1996, 1997; Teschke and Heine, 2002.

2 Weber famously distinguishes between traditional, legal-bureaucratic, and charismatic types of domination. Feudalism and patrimonialism are sub-types of traditional domination.

3 'The full fief is always a *rent-producing* complex of rights whose ownership can and should maintain a lord in a manner appropriate to his style of life. Primarily seigneurial rights and income-yielding political powers, that is, rent-producing rights, are conferred upon the warrior. In the feudal Middle Ages the *gewere* of a piece of land belonged to the recipient of the rent' (Weber 1968a: 1072–3).

4 See Mommsen 1974, 1989. Ideal types stand in stark contrast to the principles of dialectical concept formation that yield *Bewegungsbegriffe* (concepts of movement), which, precisely because they contain dynamic contradictions, point to their own transcendence. See Heine and Teschke 1996.

5 Max Breuer suggested that Weber's conception of modern bureaucracy is 'organization-, not society-centred; it does not proceed from a theory of social structures and processes, but from a closed and determinate administrative system, which is compared with other less closed systems' (Breuer 1991: 25).

6 Roland Axtmann demonstrates this methodological stance for Weber's account of modern state formation (Axtmann 1990).

7 Some problems of adopting an Althusserian understanding of Marxism are explored in Wood 1995b. I draw out the problems of Anderson's analysis of French absolutism in chapter 5.

8 For example, feudal social relations in tenth-century Burgundy and twelfth-century Anglo-Norman England were both defined by serf–lord relations. Yet it would be difficult, if not impossible, to 'derive' their different state forms from existing 'relations of production'. In the first case, serf–lord

relations were compatible with extreme political fragmentation expressed in banal lordships; in the second, the serf–lord relation was compatible with a tightly integrated, centralized feudal pyramid culminating in the king. In other words, without a dynamic account of the formation of specific, politically constituted social property relations on the basis of the resolutions of preceding class conflicts, temporarily institutionalized in political and legal forms, a given state form cannot be deduced from the existing relations of production.

9   In feudal societies where direct producers possess the means of production, the economic process of production precedes the political process of exploitation, defined by rents in kind or in cash. The moment of exploitation is not economically built into the relation of production. In fact, with the partial exception of *corvée* labour – i.e., peasant labour on the lord's demesne – there is virtually no production relation between the lord and the dependent peasant.

10 The primacy of the 'relations of exploitation' therefore does not approximate to Weber's 'mode of domination'. It rather 'contains' the political substance of the Weberian approach, provides its social contents, undermines its theoretical rationale – political ideal types – and provides a more encompassing explanation of socio-political relations and their changes.

11 I therefore disagree with Krasner, who maintains that the medieval world did not possess 'a deep generative grammar' (Krasner 1993: 257).

12 In contrast, rational-choice theory makes propositions about efficient means but remains silent on the ends, which appear as given. If we historicize rationality and set it within specific property relations, we can also analyse preferences themselves and see as rational behaviour which in a contemporary perspective would seem irrational; e.g., noble conspicuous consumption becomes meaningful only when embedded in definite social structures (Godelier 1972: 7–30).

13 A whole literature takes this epiphenomenon as the point of departure to argue for a military techno-determinism towards either the modern territorial state, capitalism, or 'the rise of the West' (Parker 1988; Downing 1992). Although the 'Military Revolution' has been situated in early modernity, it has been argued that continuous military innovation stretches back to the high Middle Ages (Ayton and Price 1995).

14 Constructivists tend to base their structure–agency accounts on Giddens's structuration theory (Giddens 1984). The Hegelian–Marxist dialectical idiom, in contrast, conceptualizes the problem of action-in-structure (or praxis-in-concretion) in a more coherent way (Heine and Teschke 1996, 1997).

15 NB: Neorealism is here the villain!

16 From a Neorealist perspective, it indeed does not matter whether the object of inquiry is urban gang warfare or the European Concert of Powers. In the dark night of Neorealism, all cows appear to be grey.

17 German terminology distinguishes *Leibherrschaft*, *Banngrundherrschaft*, and *Abgabengrundherrschaft* (Rösener 1992: 10–13).

3

The Medieval Making of a Multi-Actor Europe

The feudal mode of production, itself wholly 'pre-national' in character, objectively prepared the possibility of a multi-national state system in the epoch of its subsequent transition to capitalism. (Anderson 1974b: 412)

1. Introduction: From Hierarchy to Anarchy

In the tenth century, the European geopolitical order shifted from imperial hierarchy via feudal anarchy to royal anarchy. This shift was synonymous with the transition from the early to the high Middle Ages. The course of these transformations in system-structure can be divided into four major phases. The break-up of the Carolingian Empire in the ninth century (1) gave rise to the politically highly fragmented banal regime during the crisis of the year 1000 (2). This new property settlement conditioned a massive fourfold geopolitical expansion during the eleventh century, introducing feudal relations of exploitation into the European periphery (3). In the course of the post-crisis centuries, the banal regime was itself transformed through the regional reconsolidation of public authority by feudal kings (4). The outcome was an anarchic system composed of plural feudal kingdoms that were no longer geographically confined to the narrow old Carolingian heartlands, but covered the entire European continent – a system of feudal 'states'. These polities were organized by interpersonal bonds, not exclusive territorial jurisdictions, and characterized the European geopolitical order until the fourteenth-century crisis, laying the basic contours of the European states-system, which was consolidated during the early modern period as a political pluriverse. The origins of a multi-actor Europe are to be found in the class conflicts around the year 1000.

The Carolingian Empire was the last political community to successfully claim universal domination in Latin Europe. Although Arab Spain, the British Isles, Scandinavia, and eastern Europe remained outside its sphere of influence, the Frankish polity comprised the lands of western and central Europe under one political authority. It regarded itself as Rome's legitimate successor, blending religious and political might in a theocratic conception of imperial power. The process of its dissolution and the subsequent reconsolidation of political authority in plural and altered forms confronts IR theory with a series of challenges regarding its rationale, origins, timing, form, dynamics, and consequences.

Theoretically, the polycentric character of the modern system of states cannot be posited as a transhistorical given, as Neorealism assumes; nor can it be tautologically derived from international competition *per se*. It cannot be explained as the result of a series of international peace treaties or changes in the collective identity of political communities, as Constructivism submits – nor, indeed, can it be deduced from the 'logic of capital', as some Marxists aver. In order to demonstrate that the basis for a multi-actor Europe was already laid in the period between the ninth and the eleventh centuries, this chapter, informed by the theory of social property relations, inquires into the nature of the Carolingian Empire and the reasons for its collapse. For it is around the millennium that a new type of lordship spread throughout the Frankish heartlands. The new pattern of social relations it brought was decisive for the long-term social and political development of Europe. The 'Feudal Revolution' established a new mode of political domination and economic exploitation, spawning a series of closely inter-related innovations. Socially, it changed the status of the direct producers from slaves and free peasants to serfs. Politically, it ushered in a prolonged crisis of public governance resulting in the feudalization of political power. Militarily, it gave rise to an internal differentiation within the nobility associated with the emergence of the knightly class. Geopolitically, it marked the point of departure for a wave of noble 'political accumulation', resulting in four expansionary movements driving the late Frankish lords beyond the borders of the Carolingian core. Within eighty years, the post-Frankish knights sated their land hunger by conquering the British Isles (Norman Conquest, 1066), southern Italy (1061), the eastern Mediterranean (First Crusade, 1096–99), the Iberian peninsula (*Reconquista*, 1035), and large stretches of land east of the Elbe-Saale line (*Deutsche Ostsiedlung*, 1110). Out of the millennial crucible of the Feudal Revolution, lordship-based political communities spread throughout Europe with lasting implications for regional state formation in late medieval and early modern times. This knight-led expansion was not completed until the fifteenth century and established the institutional and geographical parameters for the international organization of the early modern states-system.

The relevance of this shift from imperial hierarchy to royal anarchy is not only an example of fundamental structural change. Its implications for the making of the Westphalian and modern states-systems are much wider. The break-up of the Frankish Empire not only had profound long-term implications for the spatial configuration of the modern states-system, it also conditioned regional trajectories of state formation. In later chapters, I shall demonstrate these divergences with respect to Europe's two core countries – France and England. *In nuce*, while England transformed itself in the course of the seventeenth century into a parliamentary constitutional monarchy (the first modern state) under the impact of an endogenously generated capitalist agrarian property regime, France remained an absolutist state, based on a non-capitalist agrarian economy. And yet it was *Ancien Régime* France that defined the character of the Westphalian settlement, which IR tends erroneously to interpret as the beginning of modern international relations. The implication is that while French state formation resulted in absolutist sovereignty, the cornerstone of the Westphalian states-system, English state formation resulted in capitalist sovereignty, the cornerstone of the post-Westphalian, i.e., modern, system. These diverging trajectories are rooted in different starting points of feudal state formation, themselves based on regionally different resolutions of the tenth-century crisis. Thus, the medieval-to-modern shift was not only preceded by a geopolitical transformation of a similar historical magnitude and theoretical importance, it took place in an international context that was already decisively prefigured by this prior epochal change from imperial hierarchy to royal anarchy.

In order to trace this process, this chapter shifts methodological gears. In the preceding chapter, I showed the *sui generis* meanings of a number of key medieval concepts. This analytical exposition captured the specificity of these macro-phenomena within the generality of the feudal order. This chapter, in contrast, seeks to translate or dissolve these medieval forms into the flow of history. This change in perspective, from a comparative-systematic to a developmental approach, mandates a stylistic shift from a conceptual to a more narrative mode of exposition – without, however, sacrificing the rigour of social-scientific inquiry. It will reconstruct the *history of the social relations of lordship*.

In the last chapter I argued that the apparent flux of history is animated by contradictory strategies of lordly and peasantry reproduction. Medieval rules of class reproduction were, of course, not simply free-floating modes of securing material reproduction in the social metabolism with nature. They could not be changed at will. Rather, these modes of action flowed from, were embedded in, and re-entered into particular structures of domination and exploitation: the institutions of lordship. It was within the varying forms of lordship that the antagonistic interests of direct producers and non-producers were negotiated, played out, and temporarily resolved. The range of social action within the institutions of lordship was therefore limited. Conversely, these structures of lordship did not impose absolute, timeless, or unalterable limits on social action. Although they were constantly and consciously reproduced, they were not immune to dispute and should thus not be 'frozen' or reified into insuperable 'iron cages of obedience' – ideal-types. People enter involuntarily into relations not of their own choosing or making, grasp and appropriate them subjectively, yet seek to either consolidate or transcend them – the pulse of dialectic. Bounded voluntary action and action-defining social institutions form a dialectical nexus, open to qualitative transformation. Whereas everyday social conflict in the European Middle Ages assumed routine quantitative alterations in the levels of rents – be they in kind, labour, or cash – in times of heightened conflict over the distribution of income, the very institutions of extraction were at stake. In other words, while the routine form of social interaction is competition and negotiation on the basis of tacitly accepted or openly recognized rules, rule maintenance can give way to rule contestation. The conditions of structural change are general social crises; it is then that qualitative alterations occur in the structural relations. Institutional change arises out of the competitive and precarious force field of contradictory social interests.

The timing and direction of historical change is unpredictable and only retrospectively intelligible. But the balance of class forces in time and space, as well as the degree of cohesion and solidarity within each class, are decisive in accounting for the establishment of new institutions of reproduction and domination: political communities. It is only when structural, 'desubjectified' long-term influences – be they demographic, technological, geopolitical, or commercial – are understood as a product of definite social property relations, and when their impact on human action is refracted through the decisions of historical agents, that the course of history acquires a definite direction and thus a discoverable meaning. History is therefore neither accidental and contingent nor teleologically determined or preordained, but nevertheless susceptible to rational understanding and critique.[1] This chapter, then, seeks to set out how contradictory class strategies of reproduction changed the course of European history, and especially the geopolitical configuration of power in the period between 800 and 1350. This dynamic history shows why this period cannot be understood as a succession of abstract international systems, but only as a crisis-ridden process in which geopolitical relations arose out of and flowed back into the reproduction of concrete but changing societies.

2. The Carolingian Empire

In order to comprehend the significance of the epochal shift that set in around the year 1000 and to specify its main agents, we must first briefly outline the nature of the Carolingian Empire.

1. The Patrimonial Nature of the Frankish State

At its zenith, the Carolingian Empire of the eight and ninth centuries embraced the whole of Gaul (including Septimania and Brittany), western and southern Germany (including Saxony, Frisia, and parts of the middle Danube region), the northeastern Iberian peninsula, and Lombardian Italy. Institutionally, it rested on a peculiar combination of public, 'Roman' elements and feudal, interpersonal, 'Germanic' elements (Anderson 1974a; Mitteis 1975: 7–23; Tabacco 1989: 109–24). In its post-coronation heyday, it evinced a pronounced public office structure – operated by counts and vice-counts – which overarched nascent feudo-vassalic inter-lordly relations (Ganshof 1971a; Mitteis 1975: 53–72; Nelson 1995). Appointed officials drawn from the Frankish imperial aristocracy or co-opted from conquered nobles staffed the 'offices' of the state – counts, bishops, abbots, or royal vassals. Their terms of office ceased on imperial deposition or on their death. Counts presided over courts, supervised royal estates, collected taxes, and enforced royal levies (Nelson 1995: 410–14). The office of the *missus*, the gem in the Carolingian state, supplemented the count system (Werner 1980: 220). *Missi* were temporary but plenipotentiary royal inspectors originally entrusted with the judicial, fiscal, and military supervision of landed counts, empowered to override comital decisions and to penalize comital public abuses and miscarriages. Shuttling between the peripatetic imperial court and their local districts, these landless *missi* formed the main pillar of imperial public governance, central control, and 'statehood' around 800. Although Frankish officers reproduced themselves like later vassals from the profits of public jurisdiction and the rents from their granted lands (*comitatus*), their offices were initially revocable and non-hereditary, allowing for a relatively high degree of centralized power.

This office structure depended upon strong kingship, epitomized by the king's monopoly of the ban – the power to tax, command, decree, and adjudicate. Kingship was dynastic, hereditary, and personal, i.e., patrimonial, in character. The kingdom was regarded as the king's private property. At the same time, the pre-Gregorian papacy remained politically subordinate to the emperor, while Church lands were integrated into the realm. Ecclesiastical organization lay in the hands of the reigning dynasty and was systematically employed to build up the imperial Church system (*Reichskirchensystem*). Its offices were normally staffed with royal favourites and dependants. Crucially, and in decisive contrast to post-millennial feudal polities, the Carolingian monarchy was a theocracy. The institutions of the political sphere were not independent of those of the religious sphere. The temporal and the spiritual were one.

Strictly speaking, political centralization is an anachronism in the medieval context. As in most medieval 'states', the Empire had virtually no central administration, no centralized judiciary, and no centrally administered fiscal system (Ganshof 1971a). Medieval kings did not govern or administer via well-entrenched bureaucracies; they reigned. The practice of domination was inseparable from the physical body of the lord. Medieval rule was personalized rule. In this respect, the peripatetic nature of the emperor and his entourage, perambulating between various palatinates and enjoying rights of residence at the courts of the higher nobility, is itself indicative of the structural difficulty of exercising effective and permanent transpersonal authority under conditions of localized political appropriation in the absence of a monopoly on the means of violence.

2. Frankish Dual Social Property Relations

The extraordinary degree of stability, internal peace, and public order during Charlemagne's reign – the *Pax Carolina* – was predicated on a distinct social property regime. This regime fostered the conditions for successful external aggression, which in turn sanctioned the internal institutions of the Empire.

Domestically, the coexistence of a hierarchical command structure culminating in the king with more reciprocal feudo-vassalic relations was based on a distinct, two-tiered social property regime. On one level, the classical Carolingian bipartite manor gave local lords absolute authority over their dependants. The manor was divided into the noble demesne worked by slaves and serfs personally bound to the domestic lord, and tenements cultivated by the same peasants for their own subsistence (Duby 1968: 28–58; Verhulst 1995: 488–99). At a second level, a substantial though decreasing number of free, arms-bearing peasants was exclusively subject to and taxed by royal counts recruited from the privileged imperial Frankish aristocracy (Duby 1974: 31–47; Goetz 1995: 451–80). The result of this dual property structure was a distinct division of political competencies and powers of exploitation between the monarch-cum-imperial aristocracy and the local noble class, dampening inter-noble competition in the exploitation of a differentiated peasantry. Schematically, we have a king/emperor directly taxing a free, allodial peasantry via his counts, as well as a local noble class extracting rents in labour and kind from slaves and serfs on their manors. This divided exploitation of the peasantry generated a viable system of class alliances. The free peasantry remained protected from the ambitions of local lords by kingly institutions, while the king had a permanent source of income which left the estates of local lords and their bonded labour untouched. Thus, the tensions between the imperial aristocracy and the local nobility remained latent.

Nevertheless, this class constellation was labile and contained the seeds of intra-ruling-class conflict. Public officials were not remunerated out of the public purse through salaries, but had to secure their reproduction by the political profits accruing from their public functions, notably through the collection of fines. In this respect, Carolingian officers were never state functionaries, but full-blown physical representatives of the king wielding the power of the ban by proxy. In addition, the grant of an office went along with a landed endowment, so that 'public' agents were simultaneously 'private' lords, drawing on independent sources of income and thus being in a position to maintain armed retinues. In order to counter the threat of secession, Carolingian rulers increasingly demanded a feudal oath of fidelity and service in return for land, which was thus held only conditionally. These personal and informal ties (vassalage) added another layer of central control, but could not remove the basic problem: the office holder had an independent power base. Decisively, then, the removal of a disloyal count depended *in concretu* on the overlord's power to separate the office holder from his lordship (*comitatus*) in a feud. The official was never separated from the means of administration – for Weber the essence of modern bureaucracy. This constitutive and precarious nexus between office and land was to underwrite much of the internal and external power struggles of feudalism.

3. Frankish 'Political Accumulation'

The relative stability of the Carolingian polity cannot be dissociated from the state-consolidating implications of Frankish strategies of political accumulation within the wider system of geopolitical relations. Externally, the latent conflict between the imperial aristocracy and lesser lords – and thus the very persistence of the powerful Frankish polity – was cushioned by the relentless Merovingian and Carolingian cycles of conquest (Haldon 1993: 213), pegging the landholding class to a supreme warlord continuously engaged in the systematic redistribution of conquered land and the wider spoils of war (Duby 1974: 72–6; Reuter 1985; Bonnassie 1991a).[2] The Empire was a conquest state, its economy to a large degree a 'war economy'. The authority of the royal ban remained unchallenged as long as the king or emperor succeeded in providing his aristocratic followers with opportunities for personal enrichment. Every spring the Frankish kings gathered their vassalic host to set out for summer-long campaigns driven by the collective aggressiveness of the Frankish ruling class. A self-regenerating cycle of campaigning, redistribution, and ruling-class solidarity was thereby kept in motion. The fortunes of the Frankish ruling class – and thus the Frankish state – rested to a large extent upon the political economy of war. At the same time, punitive expeditions had to be undertaken by the Frankish aristocracy against subjugated but rebellious peoples, ruled by ethnically diverse and sometimes pagan aristocracies in deadly battle with the Frankish invaders even after their incorporation into the Empire. Consequently, large stretches of the Carolingian polity resembled zones of military occupation rather than truly integrated regions (especially in Saxony, Brittany, and Acquitaine). However, so long as the Empire was itself successfully conquering and expanding – i.e., until about the Treaty of Verdun (843), which sealed the partition of the Empire – and so long as intra-ruling-class solidarity was cemented through the circulation of war-generated 'gifts', a relatively stable pattern of public governance prevailed. This was the 'Carolingian Renaissance': the alliance of a conniving aristocracy and an emperor who was competent, broad-minded, and generous in victory, yet unrelenting and harsh in the face of insubordination (James 1982: 158).[3]

Thus, the interface between the internal social property settlement and the expansionary strategy of (geo)political accumulation provided the social rationale of the Carolingian state. Within the confines of the Empire, conditional hierarchy reigned among the members of the ruling class.

Smaller adjacent polities like Bohemia, Pannonia, Croatia, the Benevento, or Brittany had to yield to Frankish hegemony through regular tribute (Ganshof 1970: 19–55). Only the greater polities – the Byzantine Empire, the Caliphate of Córdoba, the Anglo-Saxon and Scandinavian kingdoms, and the Abbasid caliphs of Baghdad – remained outside Frankish control. It was symptomatic of the absence of bounded territoriality under feudal property relations that 'the ambassador employed on a foreign mission, and the royal or imperial commissioner [the *missus*] dispatched on a mission inside the realm, were two species of the same genre' (Ganshof 1971b: 164). While the Carolingian Empire never enjoyed the centralization of its Roman predecessor, Latin Europe remained politically unified in one expanding feudal empire until the ninth century.

3. Explaining the Transition from Imperial Hierarchy to Feudal Anarchy

1. The Demise of the Carolingian Empire

Around 850, however, the opportunities for external conquest dried up (Reuter 1985 and 1995). Offensive campaigns turned into defensive wars. Vikings, Hungarians, and Saracens made deep inroads into the Carolingian heartlands, turning the logic of plunder against the Frankish lords. This turnabout in Carolingian fortunes was partly due to what may be called an early version of imperial overstretch – a mismatch between geopolitical ambitions and available resources for the enforcement of the *Pax Carolina* further restrained by difficult logistics of long-distance campaigning (Delbrück 1982: 24). But it was also due to the recovery of the neighbouring peoples, itself not to be dissociated from changes in their own internal modes of social organization and domination.

Under conditions of weakened imperial authority, a profound crisis of intra-ruling-class solidarity led to the gradual disintegration of the imperial state. Dissatisfied lords started to usurp public offices to offset lost income; they built up personal entourages of warriors by distributing land, and began to patrimonialize 'their' fiefs. Following the end of victorious expansion, the itinerant *missi* inspectors became sedentary and their functions were often delegated to or appropriated by land-based counts and margraves. Administrative districts gradually lost their public character and turned into territorial principalities, i.e., non-revocable hereditary fiefs. Temporary royal posts held *ex officio* became family property, handed down from generation to generation. The imperial aristocracy of service turned into a feudal aristocracy in its own right.

These developments caught the imperial state in a pincer movement. On the one hand, faced with the imminent threat of barbarian incursions, Charles the Bald and Louis I reacted by conceding greater autonomy and flexibility to counties in the financing and self-organization of defence measures against the invaders (Bloch 1961: 395). These concessions laid the foundations for the great principalities of the late ninth and tenth centuries. Furthermore, late Carolingian kings found themselves under pressure to grant immunities to the great abbeys, dioceses, and secular royal vassals, exempting them from taxes and public duties. This move was motivated by a concern to place effective power into the most reliable, i.e., non-secular, hands. The granting of immunities effectively offered tax exemption in return for informal support and loyalty – a policy that turned out to be thoroughly counterproductive. For here, in ecclesiastical lordships as in lay lordships, the same pattern emerged. In the Western Kingdom, immunities granted to bishops were arrogated as non-alienable rights by territorial princes and counts; in the Eastern Kingdom, the bishops disconnected themselves from imperial suzerainty and, under the growing antagonism between emperor and pope, came to see themselves at most as mere vassals of the emperor.

On the other hand, to the degree that the spoils of war dwindled and the Franks themselves now had to pay tribute to the Normans, the nobility relied more and more on land and the native peasantry as primary sources of profit. This land had to be protected not only against foreign aggression but also against public exactions. Furthermore, a steady stream of captured slaves no longer replenished the Frankish nobility's labour-force. In this context, the discontented local nobility developed a long-term interest in 'privatizing' public political powers in order to strengthen its political hold on the peasantry. Regional lords entered into a period of open conflict with their nominal overlords, the post-imperial states. Internal redistribution of titles to wealth became the logical alternative to external conquest. The conversion of landholding rights effected a decisive shift in the balance of power to the disadvantage of the king. The fief was no longer seen as a reward for loyal services; once 'privatized', it became the independent material basis for and precondition of the lord's claim to participate in public affairs. The paralysis of central power that followed the collapse of intra-ruling-class solidarity, was, of course, itself conducive to Norse success. They penetrated the continent by pushing up navigable rivers, looting towns and laying waste the countryside (Delbrück 1982: 86). This

inverse cycle of domestic ruling-class strife, invasion, and further internal
corrosion marked the latter half of the ninth century. Torn between
pressures from below and pressures from outside, the late Frankish kings
willy-nilly continued to alienate and thus deterritorialize public authority
until their own power was eventually completely eroded and reduced to
an empty nominal claim.

2. The 'Feudal Revolution' of the Year 1000 and the Rise of the Banal Regime

The dissolution of monarchical power and the rise of the principalities
were but one step in the slide towards political and territorial fragmentation,
for the Frankish magnates found their rights contested in turn by minor
lords, further eroding public governance. Similar patterns prevailed: what
had been delegated as office or prebend by a territorial lord was usurped
by the local incumbent as a patrimonial right. In a chronologically
sequential and geographically uneven process from roughly 900 to 1050,
public power cascaded down the ladder of political units – from dukes, to
margraves, counts, and vice-counts – until even the smallest landed lord,
the castellan, had appropriated the erstwhile regalian power of the ban
(Duby 1953; Bloch 1966a: 79; Fourquin 1975: 378–9; for Italy see Tabacco
1989: 144–66, 194ff).[4] Castellans, often exercising control over a few
villages and half a dozen small lordships, transformed their banal lordships
into quasi-sovereign mini-states, independent of royal or comital sanction
and control. 'Counts, castellans, knights were not merely landowners with
tenants but sovereigns‹with subjects' (Hilton 1990: 160). This meant the
'privatization' of public justice, the territorialization of fiefs, wilful taxation,
and the general subjection of the remaining free peasantry to serfdom
(Bonnassie 1991a, 1991b). Towards the end of the tenth century, the rise
of individualized banal lordships began and the 'Feudal Revolution' came
into its own (Duby 1980: 150ff.; Poly and Bournazel 1991; Bisson 1994).[5]
The castellans' usurpation of the regalian powers of the ban thus constituted
the end-point of a protracted political devolution to ever-smaller territorial
units. 'The commander of the castle garrison would take upon himself
responsibility for peace and justice over the whole territory – in other
words, the precise functions of kingship' (Duby 1974: 172). Castellanies
grew at the expense of the state.

Castellans became for two centuries (950–1150) the prime actors in
medieval political life, benefiting from the general crisis of governance and

forming the territorial nuclei of the geostrategic map. Once public power was completely individualized, castellans turned upon themselves in fierce inter-lordly competition over lucrative, formerly public rights, unleashing general anarchy and violence. Ecclesiastical lordships especially, which had derived their immunities from royal grants, found themselves attacked by lay banal lords, who contested their rights to agrarian profits and commercial monopolies (Duby 1968: 189). The Feudal Revolution sealed the demise of Carolingian public power. Conditional hierarchy gave way to 'feudal anarchy'. Generalized feuding resulted in a thorough redistribution of arable land and the consolidation of new dynasties, some growing out of old Frankish families, some with more humble knightly origins. The former empire-wide dual property structure, based on a general public tax regime in combination with a lord-centred rent regime, was transformed into a single, geographically fragmented property settlement, based on wilful surplus extraction in numerous independent banal lordships.

The story of the rise and fall of Carolingian state formation can be told, as by John Haldon, in terms of its inability to establish and maintain impersonal bureaucracies in Weber's sense – the failure to deprivatize the means of administration and coercion, i.e., to physically and legally separate the office from the incumbent (Haldon 1993: 215). Yet the deeper reasons for this failure cannot be understood within the parameters of Weberian political sociology. The short flowering of the *missi* and the public comital office was a conjunctural, not a permanent, phenomenon, based on the proprietary regime and the war fortunes of the Carolingians. The possibility of central government always rested on a compromise – a short-term alliance for mutual gain – between the members of the Frankish ruling class. It was based less on the leader's charismatic appeal than on his ability to provide his co-rulers with the wherewithal for expanded personal reproduction and to permanently assert his superiority and leadership by displays of power and largesse. Because the political appropriation of agrarian surplus depended on at least a modicum of armed force at the point of production, lords had to bear arms and control land and labour – the two essential prerequisites of medieval power. This constellation rendered the medieval state inherently fragile, non-bureaucratic, territorially dispersed, and prone to disintegration.

The dissolution of the Carolingian Empire should therefore be understood as a struggle among the lords for land and labour in times of reproductive crisis. It brought to the fore the inherent fragility of one of the most powerful medieval states under conditions of individualized, localized lordly appropriation, given peasant possession of the means of subsistence. The self-organization of the ruling, arms-bearing class – the form of the 'state' – should thus be understood in the light of definite property regimes governing inter-lordly redistributional struggles in response to the deeper cycles of land and labour scarcity. In this respect, the fate of the Carolingian Empire is but another instance of the contradictory logic of medieval state-building.

4. A New Mode of Exploitation

While the tenth century is often portrayed as the nadir of medieval political order, the late eleventh century ushered in a period of knight-led geopolitical expansion that drove the post-Carolingian lords into the non-Frankish European periphery, establishing feudal structures of domination and exploitation. The Norman Conquest, the Spanish *Reconquista*, the German *Ostsiedlung* (Eastern Settlement), and the Crusades express paradigmatically the form and dynamics of feudal geopolitical expansion in times of individualized lordship. Before exploring these four spectacular outward movements in more detail, however, we have to inquire into their social preconditions. They were, following my thesis, grounded in profound changes in noble social property relations after the Feudal Revolution. In particular, the ascent of banal lordships triggered a range of important and interconnected changes in agrarian labour relations, the internal composition and military outlook of the landholding class, and noble family structures and inheritance laws.

1. Predatory Lordship and the Rise of Serfdom

During the critical period of general political disintegration around the millennium, the protective link between a hitherto free, allodial peasantry and royal public power was cut, delivering the peasantry to the mercy of their immediate castellans. High and low justice, hitherto divided between clearly distinguishable courts, collapsed into a monopoly of justice held by countless – in both senses! – minor lords. Justice without appeal is justice denied: 'This almost unrestricted exercise of rights of jurisdiction armed lords with a weapon of economic exploitation whose potentialities seem limitless' (Bloch 1966a: 79). Since all three forms of lordship – domestic, land, and banal – were now amalgamated in the hands of one lord, those

peasants tilling his lands, whether slave, servile, or free, were indiscriminately subjected to the encastled banal lord. They became serfs.[6] The
usurpation of banal rights translated into a weighty apparatus of exploitation
based on the formerly royal right of confiscation. Formerly public taxes,
now arbitrarily set and collected by one and the same lord, involved such
exactions as tallage (*taille*) – a tax levied on personal protection nominally
offered by lords; the lord's right to shelter, board, and lodging (*gîte*) – a
pretext for arbitrary feasting and pillaging at the expense of the peasantry;
obligatory carting duties and ploughing services; and judicial fines, levied
especially on the transfer of property. Additionally, lords began to force
peasants to pay for the use of seigneurial facilities (*banalités*). These commercial monopolies forced the peasants to grind their corn at the lord's
mill, to bake in his ovens, to store grain in his barn, to press grapes and
apples in his press, and to buy his wines before the new vintage (*banvin*)
(Fourquin 1975: 386–94). Lay lords even began to monopolize tithes,
antagonizing bishops and abbots, who developed counterstrategies to
protect their income, such as peace movements. In sum, the right to judge
was tantamount to the right to command and the right to command
became the foremost source of noble income. All these essentially wilful
exactions, unchecked by superordinate authorities, bore down on the
peasantry alongside conventional rents. What had some measure of legitimacy when applied within customary limits degenerated into predatory
lordship – the pure imposition of the lord's will, backed up by sheer force.

2. Military Innovations and the Origins of the Knightly Class

This crisis-ridden political constellation went hand in hand with innovations in military technology and organization during the tenth and eleventh
centuries.[7] The old Carolingian light cavalry and free peasant armies gave
way to heavy knightly cavalry, the demilitarization of the formerly free
peasantry, and the widespread appearance of new, small but high stone
castles designed for local power protection. These castles, dotted in a dense
pattern – often within sight of one another – over the post-Carolingian
heartlands, symbolized the power of the defiant castellans. Embedded in
this new military topography, random violence – hostage-taking, plunder,
and looting – became the order of the day. Castellans and other banal lords
asserted their authority with the help of retinues of armed and mounted
men, forming what Bisson calls a 'terrorist police force' (Bisson 1994: 16).

These marauding bands were the armed executors of the lord's will, riding cavalcades against a helpless peasantry, policing the countryside, sharing booty, and smashing peasant resistance:

> Armed, pretentious and poor, the knights clung to their stoned-off space, talking of weapons and deeds, of strikes, of demands; of lucrative strata-gems more than of management or incomes. Ransom was a device of the keep from the outset; notoriously exemplified in the coups of the Vikings and Saracens, it became a seigneurial as well as a military technique, readily convertible into protection money. (Bisson 1994: 17–18)

These lordly practices came to be known as 'bad customs' (*mala consuetudi-nes*): 'They are no longer the expression of a more or less legitimate power, but they constitute the elements of a patrimony and the opportunity for profit' (Poly and Bournazel 1991: 33).

At the same time, the mounted war-bands that gathered around banal lords were compensated for their services by land grants or treasure.[8] Recruited from rather humble backgrounds, these retainers and body-guards, who served as the accomplices and executives of the predatory nobility, crystallized into the knightly class and came to form the lower nobility. The very appearance of the knights – heavily armed and fully armoured fighters on horseback, forming virtually self-sufficient moving castles – reflected the fragmentation and individualization of political power during this period. Their later exaltation as the bearers of the code of chivalry conceals their this-worldly origins and purposes. These knights, the most dynamic element in the new political order, came to dominate the militarized countryside during this intensive period of inter-noble feuding. They thus emerged out of the crucible of 'feudal anarchy' and the general crisis of early medieval governance (Duby 1977c). We shall see later how instrumental they were in translating and resolving its internal contradictions into external orientations.

3. Changes in Noble Proprietary Consciousness and the Making of Noble Excess Cadets

Although the patrimonialization of fiefs and the concomitant encastellation of central Europe were geographically and chronologically uneven, they engendered profound changes in noble proprietary consciousness, inheri-tance law, and family patterns. In the standard version of post-millennial expansion, demographic growth is singled out as its main cause. This growth, however, had rather specific social preconditions and dynamics. We have seen the formation of the knightly class in relation to the usurpation of banal powers by ever lower-ranking nobles. Let us now trace how demographic growth was refracted through changes in the political economy of aristocratic kinship structures, most notably in the rules of succession after the privatization of the ban. How did the nobility react to the territorialization of family power and the multiplication of its peers?

As a rule, these proprietary changes triggered radical reorientations in family consciousness and inheritance law. Previously, the concept of a clearly demarcated noble family with vertical genealogies, whether matrilineal or patrilineal, had scarcely existed. The kindred or the aristocratic kin group with horizontal rather than vertical lineages was the main frame of reference. This reflected the pragmatics of living off the patronage of a greater lord or king in relatively free-floating attachment to his 'house' (*Königsnähe*) (Tellenbach 1978: 208; Goetz 1995: 470). The non-hereditary character of noble landholding during Carolingian times prevented the formation of tighter family structures. When power was territorialized after the usurpation of the ban, family patterns changed from loose collateral kindreds to clearly defined agnatic (patrilineal) descent groups.[9] Changing property titles heightened aristocratic family consciousness of inheritance, culminating in a tightening of lineage in favour of agnatic primogeniture.[10] This assured the indivisibility of territorial property and the integrity of ancestral family seats. Inheritable lordships and fiefs brought constrictions in the rules of land succession and wider family law. Kindreds turned into dynasties. Henceforth, we find the particle of origin – '*de*', '*von*', and '*of*' – in dynastic family names as well as the adoption of toponymic surnames and heraldic emblems even among the lower nobility. The social identity of the noble class was henceforth rooted in ancestral family seats. However, primogeniture created the problem of landless nobles, excess cadets, who were to play a crucial role in the process of feudal expansion.

4. Conquest of Nature – Conquest of People

In the context of demographic recovery in the eleventh century, primogeniture and growing land scarcity in the post-Carolingian heartlands led to two typical responses: internal expansion, the conquest of nature, and external expansion, the conquest of people.

On the one hand, Frankish Europe entered an important phase of internal colonization and large-scale land reclamation. The extension of arable land typically correlates with labour-intensive agrarian economies. It is an upshot of limited pressures for innovation in productive technology and the need for higher productivity under pre-capitalist, coercive labour relations (Brenner 1986: 27–32). Although there were random advances in agrarian techniques in post-millennial Europe – the iron plough, the water mill, improved harnessing techniques, and field rotation – these innovations did not arise from systematic investment in the means of production. They thus did not evolve into a self-perpetuating cycle of agrarian technological revolution. These innovations were in themselves unable to keep up with the demand of a growing population. Mostly on the initiative of lords eager to broaden their rural income bases or to establish themselves as independent landed nobles, woods, marches, swamps, wastelands, alluvial lowlands, and even lakes and parts of the sea – e.g., by polder-making in Flanders – vanished to make room for ploughland. Bloch describes this period of unprecedented large-scale land clearance as 'the most considerable addition to the total area under cultivation in this country [i.e., France] since prehistoric times' (Bloch 1966a; see also Fourquin 1975). Internal colonization changed the rural landscape of feudal Europe, pushed on in a mutually reinforcing cycle by a growing population.

On the other hand, since the scope for land reclamation within the borders of the old Frankish Empire was finite, internal colonization was supplemented by external colonization, the conquest of foreign peoples (Wickham 1994: 140). For the closure of lineage in favour of the oldest son immediately posed the chronic problem of providing for noble cadets. It was precisely these younger sons, the 'youths', who most 'naturally' began to look beyond the narrow confines of their homelands:[11]

> Companies of youths . . . formed the spearhead of feudal aggression. Always on the lookout for adventure from which 'honour' and 'reward' could be gained and aiming, if possible, 'to come back rich', they were mobile and ready for action with their emotions at a pitch of war-like frenzy. In an unstable milieu they stirred up turbulence and provided manpower for any distant expedition. (Duby 1977a: 115)

The densely populated and cultivated area between the Loire and the Rhine in particular produced aristocratic supernumeraries who sought independent landed resources to found and support a dynasty: 'Younger sons and daughters were ejected from the paternal household and patrimony: unmarried daughters were placed in convents, while cadets entered the Church, assumed a life of adventure in the retinue of some lord, or set out for the Holy Land' (Evergates 1995: 17). Thus, external colonization was not merely the direct result of overpopulation and overcrowding, it was mediated and radicalized by exclusionary inheritance patterns due to changes in property titles. Henceforth, we can discern an accelerated 'international' circulation of knightly cadets.

Many cadets and younger children were of course sent to abbeys and monasteries for a life of celibacy. This was the fate of most daughters of noble birth who were not married off into other aristocratic families. However, it would be a profound mistake to detach the reproduction of ecclesiastical lordships from the general logic of the political economy of lordships. Placement in convents could not relieve population pressures indefinitely since the families of the prospective novices had to donate gifts, mostly in the form of land, upon the entry of their offspring. Ecclesiastical lordships could not admit an indefinite number of non-producing monks and prelates without sooner or later facing serious economic hardship themselves.[12] Indeed, the clergy was among the most ambitious in accumulating landed endowments in far-off places under the papal banner under the pretext of spreading the Roman liturgy. Indicatively, even those countries which were already Christianized before the millennium – Ireland and England – but escaped political integration into and economic exploitation and control by the post-Gregorian Church, found themselves subjected to the same ravages of conquest and colonization as their pagan co-victims.

We should further specify the structural preconditions for the great aristocratic expansion of the late eleventh century. Following Bartlett, aristocratic overpopulation was less a feature of the higher than the lower nobility, and in particular of the knightly class (Ganshof 1970: 69; Bartlett 1993: 48). What distinguished this class was its overwhelmingly non-landed character, which combined uneasily with its permanently militarized status. Eager to climb the feudal social ladder and to gain the highest goods in feudal society, land and labour, the knights were trapped between impoverishment and adventure. In response, they tied their fortunes to war-leaders – be it the pope, the emperor, kings, or greater territorial princes. For 'the way to make a fortune was not, of course, to launch out into the void. A young and ambitious knight would offer his services to a likely looking prince and hope that his lord would have success and be willing to share some of its profits' (Bartlett 1993: 36). The opportunities of conquest offered to knights extended to the summit of the feudal pyramid itself: royal title. Over the next two hundred years, new kingdoms sprang up in the Frankish periphery – Castile, Portugal, Bohemia, Jerusalem, Cyprus, Sicily, Thessalonica – to be manned by fresh dynasties, inspiring many an ordinary knight to risk his life beyond the borders of Latin Christendom. Strikingly, Bartlett reckons that of the fifteen monarchs to be found in 1350 Latin Christendom, 'only three families, the Folkunger of Sweden, the Danish royal house and the Piasts of Poland, were not of Frankish descent' (Bartlett 1993: 41).[13]

Here, then, we arrive at the point where the most active social group of the post-millennial century enters the 'international' historical stage with aplomb and panache: the knightly class, whose precarious economic position in conjunction with its over-militarized status made it the likeliest candidate for external aggression. Yet the differentiation of the ruling class into lower and higher nobility did not mean that it was the exclusive historical task of the knights to engage in large-scale conquest. It rather meant that the magnates of the old Frankish families, who had survived in the ex-marcher lordships of the Carolingian periphery (especially in Normandy, Catalonia, and Saxony), as well as the papacy found a willing and militarily able ally for such unlikely and unheard of ventures as the conquests of England, Spain, eastern Europe, and the Holy Land.

Before considering these conquests, let us pause and summarize the passage from the early to the high Middle Ages, which gave rise to a socio-political constellation propitious to geopolitical expansion and in whose train imperial hierarchy gave way to a multi-actor Europe.[14] Once Charlemagne's successors were no longer in a position to guarantee the incomes of their aristocratic followers, these magnates appropriated their political powers (the rights of the ban) and diverted the 'national' income into their own pockets. The collapse of the Carolingian war economy and the subsequent redistributional crisis removed the protective layer of public power from lord–free peasant relations. This translated into unmediated lordly access to peasant surplus and correspondingly higher exactions. The obverse side of the rise of the banal regime was generalized serfdom, intensified exploitation, and a thorough fragmentation of power. At the same time, the arrogation of banal rights required militarization by means of mounted armed forces (knights), ushering in a breakdown in ruling-class solidarity and inter-noble competition over land, labour, and privileges. The late Carolingian patrimonial state structures dissolved into 'feudal anarchy'.

In the aftermath of this restructuring of political power, the end of slavery, and the general conversion of free allodial peasants into serfs, demographic recovery swelled the ranks of both the ruling and producing classes. A process of internal colonization and land reclamation set in, vastly expanding the area under cultivation in the Frankish heartlands. However, the extension of arable land could not keep pace with demographic growth. It was particularly acute within the landholding class due to the introduction of primogeniture, a response to earlier changes in property relations that benefited territorially defined families. While primogeniture ensured the indivisibility of family property, it led to a surplus of non-landed, aristocratic cadets, especially among the lower nobility.

The extension and diversification of the ruling strata, now including a knightly class that also aspired to land, added a particularly restless, highly militarized, and aggressive element to the nobility. These knightly cadets were the bearers of late eleventh-century geopolitical expansion, for by around 1050 the redistribution of arable land within the post-Carolingian core areas came to a halt. Warlords had to look elsewhere to satisfy their thirst for land and booty. This marked the origins of expansion based on a radically feudalized, militarily individualized, and politically decentralized society. It is in this dynamic context of heightened inter-lordly competition over land and labour that the four great expansionary movements have to be situated. The insatiable feudal hunger for land exploded the fetters of territorial self-sufficiency. The transnational Frankish nobility set out to conquer Europe.

5. Post-Crisis Feudal Expansion as Geopolitical Accumulation (Eleventh to Fourteenth Centuries)

The ascent of banal lordship can thus be interpreted as a successful seigneurial reaction to a reduction in the redistributive capacities of the Frankish state: the lords inflicted a new mode of exploitation on the peasantry in the face of a crisis of income and status. The resolution of the crisis of the year 1000 imposed a new property settlement on large parts of Europe, extended the reach of feudalism into the European periphery, and established the basis for a system of feudal polities headed by dynasties.

Excursus – Demographic Growth and the Urban Revival

While we highlighted the geographical widening and social deepening of feudalism during the high Middle Ages, other accounts focus on the twelfth-century conjunction of demographic growth and urban revival as a key stage in the development of capitalism. However, this revival remained structurally tied to the feudal economy. Between the eleventh and four-teenth centuries, feudal Europe underwent a remarkable economic recov-ery, based on population growth, new arable land, and intensified exploitation of labour through the general imposition of serfdom. Growing lordly incomes translated into growing lordly demand, fanning the urban revival of the twelfth and thirteenth centuries. Noble demand for military equipment and conspicuous consumption established a system of Europe-wide long-distance trade, operated by non-capitalist burghers and mer-chants. However, these inter-urban trading networks remained entirely dependent upon noble demand and embedded in a labour-intensive agrarian economy. Wealth was not capital and mercantile exchange not capitalism (Wolf 1982: 83–8). Inter-urban trading networks and towns were to decline in the fourteenth century with the erosion of noble incomes. Thus, the expansion of trade was directly related to the first ascending phase in the eco-demographic cycle of the feudal agrarian economy. When this cycle peaked in the late thirteenth century, leading to overpopulation, soil exhaustion, bad harvests, the Black Death, and a marked decline in agricultural productivity, contracting noble demand directly impacted on the volume of urban trade. This is the secular context of the general crisis of the fourteenth century. The feudal economy, based on political relations of exploitation, could not generate a self-sustaining cycle of economic growth, since producers continued to produce primarily for subsistence, while non-producers continued to reproduce themselves by customary means, i.e., by trying to increase the rate of exploitation rather than trying to increase productivity by investing in the means of production. Investment in the means of violence and coercion, enabling successful (geo)political accumulation, remained the preferred strategy of reproduction of the noble class.

Michael Mann's claim that the twelfth century saw an 'embryonic transition to capitalism' is therefore questionable (Mann 1986: 373–415). Applying his pluralist IEMP model, which argues for the historical inter-dependence of four sources of social power (ideological, economic, mili-tary, and political), to the high Middle Ages, Mann argues that this 'embryonic transition to capitalism' was the result of a combination of factors, tied together in a cumulative long-term account of the rise of the West. On the one hand, the 'acephalous', i.e., politically fragmented, nature of feudal geopolitics allowed traders and other economic actors substantial economic and political autonomy. On the other hand, the revival of trade, assisted by technological progress, the intensification of agriculture, and the pacifying rational-normative order of Christianity, set

Europe on a dynamic developmental trajectory that led ultimately to the Industrial Revolution.[15] Similarly, Fernand Braudel suggested that the twelfth-century economic revival generated a first trial-run of the modern capitalist world-system, bringing different regions with different labour regimes into permanent trading relations, and thus setting off the modern cycle of successive capitalist world-systems (Braudel 1984: 92). But expanding commerce was not a breakthrough to capitalism, gradual or revolutionary. It was rather a continuation of the age-old practice of 'buying cheap and selling dear'. Thus, the high medieval urban revival remained structurally tied to its pre-capitalist context.

1. Patterns of Expansion: Socially Combined and Geographically Uneven Development

From the mid-eleventh century onwards, the post-Carolingian nobility pushed victoriously into the European periphery. Feudo-vassalic relations were introduced and adapted to prevailing eco-social conditions, creating for the first time a culturally and geographically homogeneous Europe. In the southwest, the Spanish *Reconquista* began to roll back Arab rule to its last continental stronghold, the Kingdom of Granada, replacing it with feudal structures. In the east, the Saxon aristocracy commenced its enormous Eastern Settlement, feudalizing and Germanicizing east-central Europe and the southern and eastern Baltic fringes. In the south and southeast, the Normans conquered southern Italy and Sicily as well as, for a good century, the feudal Crusader States in the Levant. In the north, the Franko-Normans overran Anglo-Saxon England and in the following centuries pushed the Celts into and over the fringes of the British Isles during the conquests of Wales, Scotland, and Ireland. Finally, France itself underwent a dramatic process of feudal state-building that saw the transformation of the banal regime into a consolidated feudal monarchy.

Hans Delbrück interprets the simultaneity of these four outward movements as the work of desperate central European knights:

> All of those who are constantly moving upward out of the lower warrior stratum approach, in doing so, the status of an aristocracy – one might even say of the ruling aristocracy. The Normans, who conquered England, lower Italy, and Sicily, were not by their lineage exclusively Nordics, but warriors of the most diverse origins who attached themselves to the nucleus formed by the Normans. The expansion of the hegemony of the German knights over Italy provided many a German knight the oppor-

tunity to attain higher position and property. The constant progress of the
German colonization toward the east created ever-increasing areas for new
ruling families. The French provided the largest contingent for the
crusades, which likewise included a colonizing movement. The Spaniards,
on their peninsula, drove forward against the Moors. (Delbrück 1982:
226; see also Wolf 1982: 104–8)

This surprising display of feudal vitality was thus the logical outcome of
geopolitical accumulation – or, more simply, land-grabbing, be it by
conquest, cultivation, or protracted colonization and settlement. What
distinguished these forms of conquest from the centrally organized Carolingian campaigns was their individualized and spontaneous or 'wild' manner.
Whereas the Carolingian warlords had systematically led the imperial
aristocracy in their annual springtime campaigns against neighbouring
polities so as to combine individual noble land hunger with the wider
security interests of the state, generating a geostrategic pattern of concentric
expansion, eleventh-century warfare was spasmodic, reflecting the essentially 'transnational' character of the mobile knightly class. The fighters on
horseback became (1) proverbial 'knights of fortune' and 'robber knights',
(2) mercenaries selling their labour to whoever needed it and could afford
it, (3) followers of greater warlords embarking upon more ambitious
ventures, promising not only plunder and booty but *a fortiori* opportunities
for landed lordships, or (4) crusaders combining these characteristics under
the religious veneer of God's will: *deus vult*! Consequently, aristocratic
power was spread by a 'transnational' military class – mobile and restless –
rather than a supreme warlord, a state bureaucracy, a nation-in-arms,
condottiere, or large-scale ethnic migration. Peasants came into play when
the conquerors could not draw on existing producers for agricultural
expansion, as in parts of the German Eastern Settlement. Under these
conditions, peasants had to be lured away from their homelands and could
often wring substantial concessions from their new lords in terms of legal
status and rents.

As the four expansionary movements encountered vastly different cultures with very different forms of economic organization – from sylvio-
pastoral, to primitive communal, to highly developed agrarian (as, for
example, in the Hispano-Arab irrigation cultures) and commercial – the
resultant forms of lordship did not simply replicate the knights' homelands.
Certainly, as a rule, the invaders tended to organize their newly acquired
lands according to their traditional estates system. Yet, depending on the
particular encounters between different aggressors and defenders, the outcomes of Frankish assertiveness were either (1) expropriation, expulsion, or

killing of the native ruling classes, as in England, Wales, eastern Ireland, Spain, Brandenburg, and other German marcher lordships; (2) assimilation and mutual accommodation through intermarriage, as in Scotland, Pomerania, or Silesia; or (3) 'clearance lordships' and new pioneer peasant villages, setting up new eco-political niches for the migratory nobility, as in east-central Europe. During this process of expansion, a range of political forms of lordships abounded – military, conquest, order, clearance – whose nature becomes intelligible within the framework of the social and geographical circumstances of clashing societies. This socially combined yet geographically uneven geopolitical accumulation laid the foundations for diverging long-term processes of state formation in different European regions on the basis of different constellations of lordly power. These divergences were particularly consequential with regard to England and France, the two archetypical and often falsely assimilated cases of modern state-building. The bifurcation in their long-term trajectories, beginning in the eleventh century and intensifying in the fourteenth-century crisis, has profound implications for reassessing the nature of the Westphalian states-system, revolving around absolutist France, and the modern states-system, revolving around capitalist Britain.

2. The Spanish *Reconquista*

In contrast to the sudden imposition of Franco-Norman rule on the British Isles, the conquest and settlement of Spain and trans-Elbian Germany were protracted and irregular. Here the bases of further expansion were the conquest lordships Charlemagne had established at the height of his power around 800: Catalonia and Saxony. Catalonia fragmented during its Feudal Revolution (1020–60) into a multiplicity of banal lordships inducing the familiar processes of general enserfment and *incastellamento* (Bonnassie 1991b, 1991c; Brenner 1996: 264–9). Inter-noble relations were radically feudalized, while the former count could no longer rely on imperial backing. However, due to the persisting opportunities for conquest and after a period of intense inter-Catalan feuding, Catalan lords accepted the overlordship of the comital dynasty of the Berenguers, while the count in return accepted 'private' lordly exploitation of a formerly free and tax-paying peasantry.

Catalonia thus emerged from the Feudal Revolution as the leading polity in the northwestern Mediterranean. Whereas pre-eleventh century Muslim–Frankish relations were marked by political expediency and mutual accommodation (the religious cleavage was secondary in trans-border relations), the counts of Barcelona began immediately to pay off their licence to rule (Fletcher 1987): from the mid-eleventh century on, they adopted an aggressive and systematic policy of conquest against those who only now came to be vilified as infidels (Bonnassie 1991c: 163–7). Catalonia's outward orientation was decisively reinforced by the influx of landless Frankish knights – Duby's 'youths' – from the old Carolingian core. In a shrewd diplomatic mobilization of dynastic marriage policies, Ramon Berenguer IV arranged his betrothal to the daughter of the king of Aragón, securing a union between formerly competing yet Christianized neighbours and combining forces against the Muslims to the south (Bisson 1986). The dynasty renewed pressures on the Taifa chieftains, attempted to capture Valencia, and engaged vigorously in the wider 'international' affairs of the Mediterranean, establishing ties with Norman Sicily and the incipient northern Italian trading cities. With the help of Frankish knights, it captured Majorca and renewed its suzerainty over Septimania and Provence. The driving ideological but also material forces behind this intensification of warfare were the reformed monasteries and a reinvigorated papacy. In a letter of April 1073, Gregory VII exhorted the French '"princes wishing to set out for the land of Spain"' that '"since the kingdom of Spain was from ancient times the property of St. Peter", all lands conquered by the French invaders must be held as fiefs from the saint' (Robinson 1990: 324). French Benedictine monks – themselves, of course, of noble origin by virtue of aristocratic monastic placement – were now appointed to recaptured Spanish bishoprics, busily administering Arab tribute payments to be transferred back to Cluny. 'By 1100 a large proportion of Spanish sees were ruled by French monks' (Lomax 1978: 56).

These mechanisms of geopolitical accumulation engendered a systematic manorialization of the conquered regions through the familiar cycle of count-led conquest and the granting of fiefs to lesser lords. These newly landed lords either enserfed their local peasantry or offered initially attractive conditions of settlements in the form of franchises to rural colonists in times of labour scarcity. Local Christian magnates and Frankish knights, clerics and the pope, had united in a long-term alliance, conducting a 'Holy War' to expand their dominion.

3. The German *Ostsiedlung*

The German *Ostsiedlung* was as variegated as and even less centrally organized than the Norman or even the Catalan undertakings, reflecting different starting conditions in the post-Carolingian Eastern Kingdom. Due to the Ottonian recovery of the tenth century, the feudalization of the state set in later and was never carried as far as in the French Western Kingdom. When the crisis came in the late eleventh century under the impact of external invasions, it took the unusual form of a power struggle between the Emperor Henry IV and the papacy, the Investiture Controversy (1060–1130). Whereas Henry IV tried to maintain his grip on the bishoprics, the reforming papacy allied with the German regional duchies (Mitteis 1975: 177–92). Ducal–papal victory meant the end of German imperial theocracy and its rights of lay investiture. It also led to the 'mediatization' of subvassals, institutionalized in the rigorous pyramidal stratification of the German *Heerschild*. In contrast to England, the German Hohenstauffen rulers failed to become territorial lords able to implement uniform trans-territorial policies beyond their royal desmesnes. 'German feudal law, as always, placed the interests of the vassals above those of the overlord' (Mitteis 1975: 251). The blocking of wider regalian public power by powerful territorial princes, who reserved the right to elect the emperor, cut the crucial protective link between the free peasantry and royal justice, leading to a new property structure of lordly estates worked by enserfed peasants (Anderson 1974a: 161–5; Arnold 1985: 1–22, 1991).

After the feudalization of inter-noble relations, the often-mythologized 'drive towards the East' revolved around two axes. On the one side, geopolitical accumulation unfolded across the countryside, orchestrated by the great trans-Elbian territorial marcher lordships. What Normandy was for England and Catalonia for Spain, Saxony became for eastern Europe. From the late twelfth century on, the familiar cycles of campaigning, land redistribution, and enfeoffment, followed by further campaigning and sub-infeudalization, projected German domination beyond the River Oder deep into Slav territory. In this process, landless knights of humble origin from the old areas of German settlement in Saxony, Lotharingia, or Frisia received immense landed wealth, which soon allowed them to supply their overlords with hundreds of retainers (Bartlett 1993: 33–9). The land-based political economy of feudal geopolitical relations seized on the oppor-tunities of noble upward social mobility offered by the Eastern Settlement and the 'moving' German frontier.

At the same time, German merchants set up a dense network of trading ports and towns along the southern and eastern shore of the Baltic, tapping the vast cereal, timber, and fur resources of eastern Europe. This form of commerce, co-ordinated by the Lübeck-based Hanseatic League, established a series of trading monopolies that were defended by military orders, of which the Teutonic Order came to dominate Prussia. Military orders pooled landless Frankish lords, securing naval trading routes and advancing the feudalization of the coastal Slav hinterlands. Originating in the Crusades, military orders recruited systematically from the Frankish knights and were characterized by extraordinary 'international' mobility and tight internal organization. Maintaining a dense network of strategic and logistic bases throughout the Mediterranean and along the Atlantic shore, they saw themselves as an emergency force for feudal Christendom (Christiansen 1980). In the Baltic, commercial and missionary interests combined with the martial capacities and land hunger of monastic lords in the colonization of the trans-Elbian regions.

4. The Papal Revolution and the Crusades

The novelty of military orders, which would have been regarded as a contradiction in terms in the eighth century, indicates a revolution in the constitution and ideology of the papacy. The very eleventh century that changed inter-noble relations so dramatically in the old Frankish heartlands also changed the relation between the secular and the ecclesiastical in the wake of the Gregorian reforms, establishing the papacy as a feudal power striving for European supremacy.

During the Carolingian era, the pre-Gregorian Church was subordinate to Frankish secular lords.[16] Bishops were nominated and invested by the emperor, enjoying special imperial protection and tax exemptions (indemnities); a system of noble proprietary churches prevailed at the local level. As a rule, the noble family that endowed the religious institution with land nominated parish priests and abbots, leading to the practices of monastic and conventual placement. Rome was merely a spiritual centre of pilgrimage. No separate legal framework separated the Latin clergy from the rest of feudal society. The pope was essentially a weak figurehead of the Roman nobility, appointed by the German emperor. Thus, pre-eleventh century Roman bishops were merely *primi inter pares*.

The structural position of the Church in medieval society began to change when imperial theocratic power was shattered by the banal lords' search for profit. Regional bishoprics, monasteries, and parish churches were the first to suffer from lordly pillage and confiscation. It was precisely at this time that the unarmed clergy, most affected by the feuding terror of the castellans, tried to find new ways of dissociating the realm of the sacred from the profane in order to escape the control of local lords (Mitteis 1975: 177ff).

First, the monastic reform movement, headed by the Benedictines, restructured relations among its scattered, loosely connected monasteries and lands into an extra-papal hierarchy under the jurisdiction of the abbot of Cluny. At the same time, monks formulated the doctrine of the Three Orders and invented a specific ethos of Christian chivalry that provided the ideological background for the Crusades. The formulation and dissemination of the lore of the trifunctional order, which stipulated that society was functionally divided into fighting knights, praying clerics, and a labouring peasantry, was the conscious policy of an economically threatened part of the ruling class that was defenceless against marauding lords.

Next, the episcopal peace movements tried to reimpose order by orchestrating first the 'truce of God' and later the 'peace of God' in the lands between Catalonia and Flanders (Flori 1992a). This bishop-led strategy of appeasement could not outlaw feuding, but it succeeded in specifying exemptions to war, first in terms of persons and objects, later in terms of time and space. However, precisely because the Church lacked powers of enforcement – the threat of excommunication went only so far – popes thoroughly redefined their war doctrines and tried to channel noble violence by directing it, as in their discourses on the Three Orders and the code of chivalry, outward against the 'infidels'. The intention of the Crusades was to pacify noble aggressiveness internally and to deflect it into external conquest. Promising not only land and booty but eternal salvation, the papacy co-opted Frankish lords, rebaptized them as *milites Sancti Petri*, and invented, in striking contrast to earlier notions of inter-Christian non-violence, notions of Just and Holy War. The idea of the Crusades was born (Flori 1986: 191–203, 215–19, 1992b: 133–46).

Finally, Church lore on war changed as rapidly as the institutions of the papacy tightened into a state-like, trans-territorially centralized administrative system based on canon law. Taking the Cluniac system as a model, the reform movement under Gregory VII struggled for papal supremacy over spiritual *and* secular matters by wrestling the Holy See from the German emperor (1075). This struggle for supremacy in the name of the *libertas ecclesiae* unleashed the famous Investiture Controversy. 'It was a struggle between two types of authority and legitimacy – each of which raised universalist demands with regard to the extent of their respective shares of influence. This conflict was brought to a head when Gregory VII in 1075, in his *Dictatus Papae*, declared the papacy to be politically and legally supreme over the entire Church, the clergy to be independent from secular control and the emperor to be subordinated to ultimate papal supremacy even in secular affairs.' (Axtmann 1990: 298) It soon gave rise to a series of Wars of Investiture between Gregory VII, mustering Norman mercenaries from Sicily and Frankish knights, and the German emperor, Henry V, who occupied Rome in 1111 (on Norman Sicily, see Tabacco 1989: 176–81, 237–45). After the Concordat of Worms (1122), the Ottonian imperial-theocratic system of government inherited from the Carolingians was a dead letter. The papal claim to supremacy over the whole of Christendom was established, though only the clergy was subjected to a systematized canon law whose court of last appeal was the papal *curia*.

It is in this context of revolutionary struggles that the Crusades (1096–99, 1147, and 1189), 'the foreign wars of the Papal Revolution' (Berman 1983: 101), must be understood. They were the result of the Vatican's policy of establishing a series of vassalic states in the Levant and the eastern Mediterranean, with military help from Frankish and Norman lords and financial support from the Italian city-states. Their constitutions perfectly reflected the feudal structure of the invading armies. Since each prince led his vassalic contingent of knights and mercenaries into battle, Syria was divided into a number of feudal principalities, owing nominal loyalty to the king of Jersualem and ultimately to the pope in his function as overlord. These developments *centralized*, *monarchized*, and *militarized* the Church. What used to be a centre of faith turned into a secularized church state (*Kirchenstaat*) with a power-conscious foreign policy. Henceforth, Christian universalism had several heads: monarchies defending their direct mandate from God and entertaining sacred notions of kingship on the one hand, a reinvigorated papacy insisting on its right to invest or depose temporal rulers on the other. While the pope's victory contributed to European political pluralism, the social conditions for the end of pan-European empire were laid in the crisis of the year 1000.

5. The Norman Conquest and Unitary English State Formation

Post-conquest England, in striking contrast to Capetian France, was a uniquely centralized, internally organized, and socially homogeneous feudal state. This unusual cohesion was the direct result of the rapid imposition of

Norman rule upon Anglo-Saxon England (Anderson 1974a: 158–61; Mitteis 1975: 199–212; Brenner 1985b: 255–8). Feudal social property relations were a direct consequence of the Norman Conquest and reflected the prevalent form of domination in the Dukedom of Normandy.[17] The Norman duchy around the lower Seine valley (840–911) was formed during the collapse of Carolingian power and the appropriation of banal powers by sub-imperial lords. The dukedom amalgamated a political structure inherited from the Scandinavian invaders, centring around a strong chieftain demanding retinue, with the initially granted and later usurped public authority of a Carolingian count (Le Patourel 1976: 13; Hallam 1980: 34–43). After a swirl of intense feuding (1030–47), William arrogated the comital authority of the ban in Normandy and succeeded in restoring order in his dukedom (Searle 1988: 179–89), but he needed to keep his magnates and followers at bay. His court became the natural locus of government, counsel, and conflict resolution. It was here that the plan to invade Anglo-Saxon England was hatched.

From the first, however, the Normans found themselves vying for land and labour with competing principalities (Flanders and Brittany). What allowed the duke of Normandy to expand across the Channel was the internal cohesiveness of his military elite, all of whom claimed personal kinship with the ducal family; his enormous wealth in land and treasure following the raid and settlement; and his power to collect taxes, receive judicial fines, levy tolls, and call out the *arrière-ban* – indeed, his *de facto* power of royal overlordship, the *bannum* (Le Patourel 1969, 1976: 281ff).

The Norman Conquest thus rested on the by now familiar predicament of feudal domination: internal cohesion among the lordly class was predicated on the overlord's capacity to reward his followers and disintegrated as land distribution made the newly landed lords rivals of the erstwhile leader.[18]

The Anglo-Saxon landholding class was dispossessed and killed within two decades of the Conquest, its lands redistributed among William's warriors, the barons. The sweeping nature of the Conquest resulted in the imposition of Norman dominion over England as a single territorial unit. A tenurial revolution steamrollered the country, bringing radical changes to the ownership, size, and constitutional status of lordships. Lords came to hold their estates 'of the king' – hereditarily, but not as private patrimonies. The king remained the supreme landowner of the entire territory. As Frankish Gaul disintegrated into countless independent banal lordships, England was unified en bloc. In contrast to France, the Norman and Plantagenet kings managed, in spite of regular baronial contestations, to retain the monopoly of the ban after 1066. All landholding Norman nobles had to swear direct fealty to the king (Oath of Salisbury, 1086), heading off the decentralizing consequences of vassalic 'mediatization' – so detrimental for Capetian France and Salian Germany. The 'king's peace', predicated on the power of the ban, minimized private feuding by providing recognized institutions for settling disputes over land, property, and privileges among the Anglo-Norman ruling class (Kaeuper 1988: 153ff).

The sudden imposition of the tightly organized manorial regime meant that *domestic lordship* went hand in hand with the large-scale enserfment of the Anglo-Saxon peasantry (Brenner 1985b: 246–53, 1996: 258–64). Due to better inter-noble self-organization, reflecting both the structure of ducal authority in Normandy and the military organization of the Conquest, the English peasantry was unable to shake off serfdom during the twelfth and thirteenth centuries. A centralized feudal state meant that royal law mitigated latent inter-lordly conflicts. Serfs fell under the exclusive jurisdiction of manorial lords (dampening lord–king tensions), free men under the royal jurisdiction of the common law. Revocable sheriffs staffed this supplementary layer of public legal power that operated alongside the traditional inter-noble bonds of vassalage. In a way, post-1066 authority relations were based on a dual property regime that resembled the Carolingian: Norman lords had a free hand to deal with their villeins (serfs) on their manors; free peasants (freeholders) were taxed by the king and enjoyed access to public courts. Not surprisingly, class conflict typically took the form of peasants contesting their social status (Hilton 1976a).

Furthermore, due to the vast lands of the British Isles and the overarching authority of William and his successors, the expansionary phase of geopolitical accumulation – and with it relative ruling-class cohesion – was sustained well into the fourteenth century. It was only broken by the onset of eco-demographic crisis and intensified inter-noble competition over declining revenues, setting off the Hundred Years' Wars and the subsequent 'civil' Wars of the Roses. By this time, of course, the French king had successfully centralized his lands to such a degree that he could match England. Between the eleventh and the fourteenth century, Anglo-Norman lords not only conquered Wales, Ireland, and Scotland, they also turned their attention to the fragmented duchies of western France, creating under the Plantagenets an empire that reached from the Hebrides to the Pyrenees (Le Patourel 1976; Davies 1990; Frame 1990). Martial superiority was both cause and effect of the extraordinary centralization of the English kingdom, expressed in the unchallenged monopoly of the royal ban. The continuity and relative stability of English pre-fourteenth-century state formation has to be seen against this background of a fixed, two-tiered property settlement that minimized noble competition over the peasantry. This inter-noble arrangement for mutual agrarian profit was buttressed by wider common strategies of geopolitical accumulation in northwestern Europe under the aegis of the king, 'Lord Paramount'.

6. France: from the Capetian 'Domain State' to Royal Consolidation

The pattern of feudal state formation in Capetian France was determined by the complete post-millennial fragmentation of political power (Brenner 1996: 251–5). From the late eleventh century, the princes and the king tried to reconsolidate their territories – internally against the castellans, externally among each other (Anderson 1974a: 156–8; Mitteis 1975: 267–79; Hallam 1980). The logic of French state-building thus unfolded under the constant pressure of geopolitical competition, i.e., intra-ruling class conflict, driving smaller lords into the hands of greater lords, and of inter-lordly political co-operation to retain the hold on the peasantry. The Capetian monarchy had to deploy the whole arsenal of feudal expansionary techniques to establish its suzerainty over Francia during the course of four centuries – from outright war and annexation, through dynastic marriage policies, alliance-building, and bribery, to simple confiscation and enfeoffment. The local aristocracy was suppressed, co-opted, intermarried, bought off, or tied to the king by unstable bonds of vassalage (Given 1990).

Because the concentric expansion of the Capetian monarchy was a gradual, piecemeal, protracted process, the French kingdom never achieved the unity of its English counterpart. Most importantly, French 'mediatization' ('The vassal of my vassal is not my vassal') meant that the authority of the king was far less recognized than in post-Conquest England. Due to this lack of intra-ruling-class organization, the French nobility competed with the king for powers to tax and control the peasantry. Precisely these competing claims to jurisdiction were decisive for the improving status of the French peasantry (Brenner 1985a: 21–3, 1985b: 220, 1996: 251–5). Despite unfavourable demographic pressures,[19] the peasantry succeeded in the course of the twelfth and thirteenth centuries in shaking off serfdom (commutation of labour rents into money rents) and establishing by the early fourteenth century *de facto* – though not *de iure* – property rights over customary tenures, including the right to inherit. Lords in need of cash sold charters of liberty regulating exactions to peasant communes. Rents (*cens*), but also other dues (fines, death dues, transfer dues) that still weighed on the plots, were fixed and thus eroded by inflation. Over time, lords were obliged to lease out desmesne land or sell land directly (Duby 1968: 242; Hallam 1980: 161ff, 225). Declining rents and lost property made their financial situation increasingly precarious. Many indebted castellans and knights were drawn into the service of greater noble households. Alternatively, they sold themselves as mercenaries or went 'abroad' to carve out lordships in the non-Frankish periphery. Crucially, the peasantry exploited the weakness and disorganization of its lords by appealing to royal courts to uphold the concessions it had wrought from banal lords. The king tended to side with the peasants, since their freedom gave him a new income base (no longer a rent but a tax base) and simultaneously weakened his noble rivals. Charters of liberty for rural communes and individual franchises dislodged much of the direct noble hold on the rural population. Wherever the local nobility tried to reimpose arbitrary taxation or customary levies to counteract their income crises, a combination of peasant revolts and the king's legal support led to the long-term decline of the decentralized banal regime.

The establishment of Capetian rule in the various French principalities was not so much an abrupt imposition as a regionally and chronologically uneven process of blending kingly patronage networks with those of pre-existing noble families through patrimonial and feudal techniques of domination. Here was not a state which grafted its bureaucratic administration upon a territory, but a feudal ruler who had to ensure the personal loyalty of political lords, who continued to reproduce themselves from their own lands, and patrimonial officers, who were always inclined to appropriate their farmed offices. Capetian rule meant, on the one hand, the integration of independent lords into the feudal hierarchy as vassals; and, on the other, the insertion of a network of royal jurisdiction, operated by royal agents, into the regional political landscape. This attempt to monopolize the right to arbitrate the chronic disputes between greater lords (lay or ecclesiastical), towns, petty *seigneurs*, and rural communities deeply enmeshed the royal agents into local politics. It was the changing alliances between the king, the regional nobility, the towns, and the peasants, and especially the royal interest in wresting control over towns and peasant communities away from the nobility, which gave French state formation its peculiarly uneven and piecemeal character.

By the beginning of the fourteenth century, the French 'state' came to rest on a new constellation of social classes. The king, in theory and in practice, had become a feudal suzerain trying to establish a rudimentary system of public offices in the provinces to supervise taxation and adjudication. The territorial princes were integrated into the feudal hierarchy. The independent class of banal lords and knights had vanished or turned into a petty nobility. Many towns had emancipated themselves from seigneurial control and enjoyed royal liberties. Finally, the peasantry had gained personal freedom and *de facto* property rights. Yet, for all the tendencies toward administrative centralization and territorial concentration, the realm remained thoroughly feudal – personalized and parcellized.

The Capetian rise to supremacy and the extension of the royal domain to four-fifths of contemporary France was not inevitable; nor was it the natural, unilinear, uninterrupted story of growth textbooks and national histories would have us believe. Indeed, the comparatively small royal domain of the *Île-de-France*, though it bore the important legitimation of ecclesiastical consecration and divine monarchy, was an unlikely contender against more powerful rivals, of whom the English Henry II and his successors were the most formidable. The very nature of feudo-patrimonial states – all the vicissitudes of a non-unified territory; the biological play of chance in dynastic reproduction and succession; *appanages* granted to royal cadets, alienated time and again – set absolute limits to French state formation. The territory contracted and fragmented; the uncertainty of the whole undertaking came clearly to the fore in the feudal crisis of the fourteenth century and the Hundred Years' War.

This is not an argument for the role of chance and contingency in history: rather, under a persistent interpersonal political property regime, the logic of state-building contains both a centralizing and a decentralizing drive, depending on the degree of self-organization of the ruling and producing classes. As in the ninth and tenth centuries, when the Carolingian Empire disintegrated under the combined impact of over-taxation and external threats, so the French monarchy struggled to keep its leading barons at bay in the crisis of the fourteenth. In other words, property relations established structural limits to state formation in high and late medieval France.

6. Conclusion: The Medieval Making of a Multi-Actor Europe

'Europe' expanded before the onset of capitalism. It expanded before the Italian, Flemish, and German ports established their far-flung commercial activities, and it expanded before the great absolutism-sponsored discoveries overseas. The agents of medieval expansion were the dissatisfied and economically threatened late Frankish nobility in search of new sources of income. The causes of feudal expansion were 'domestic': a prior internal restructuring of property relations in the late Carolingian European heartlands prompted the centrifugal dynamic of mass migration. Interpreting the tenth-century 'Feudal Revolution' as a dramatic seigneurial reaction to a crisis in income reveals the direct link between internal social relations and external conquest, 'domestic' and 'international' transformations.

Wherever the knights succeeded in holding on to their newly acquired lordships, feudal state formation followed. New kingdoms rose. The social transformation and geographic integration of the European periphery unified the continent in social, military, commercial, cultural, and religious terms under the spiritual umbrella of the political papacy. The Baltic Sea, the northern Atlantic, and the Mediterranean became Catholic lakes, increasingly dominated by commercial city-leagues and city-states, connecting Lübeck with Reval, Hamburg with Bruges and London, Genoa with Barcelona, and Venice with Constantinople and Alexandria. Yet while commercial and cultural unity spread, politico-territorial disunity became entrenched. Given the feudal character of colonization, post-millennial expansion did not engender dependent colonies but independent dynastic polities. This tendency was built into the interpersonal structure of the feudal mode of exploitation; it left room for power-political fissures, eagerly seized upon by parvenu dynasties, not for pan-European imperial domination. By the early fourteenth century, the political map of Europe shows that feudal statehood had shaken off the hierarchical ghosts of its imperial Roman and Carolingian pasts. While new empires (Spain and Germany), powerful monarchies (France and England), and a supremacy-claiming papal state emerged, the struggle for pre-eminence among the unequal polities of Europe remained undecided. Conversely, the rise of royal power within these polities prevented a repetition of the extreme fragmentation of the millennium. While the ascent of a multi-actor Europe was not irreversible, the emergence of multiple polities within the cultural unity of Christian Europe time and again frustrated universal imperial ambitions, fuelled by the persisting logic of (geo)political accumulation.

However, if a political pluriverse now came to be a constitutive feature of European geopolitics, it did not imply the fixed territorial identity of its units, nor did it inaugurate the rise of the modern state. Lordly colonialism was not a structural advance in social and political organization of the labour process, nor a leap in technological innovation. The persistence of coercive agrarian extraction during the Middle Ages meant that noble appropriation remained primarily territorially extensive and politically intensive. Precisely because direct producers remained in possession of the means of subsistence, the capitalist logic of systematic cost-cutting by replacing labour with technological innovations and resultant productivity increases predicated on systematic reinvestments, could not take hold. Thus, while extra-European expansion continued, inner-European competition over labour and territory and class conflict between lords and peasants over the rate of exploitation intensified on a par.

Trade was epiphenomenal to medieval colonialism, but the breakdown of the Carolingian Empire created political 'interstices' in which towns could wrest themselves from the political control of territorial princes (for Italy, see Tabacco 1989: 182–236). Yet, while urban political autonomy was gained in those regions where kings were too weak to reimpose their power after the Feudal Revolution (Germany, northern Italy, Flanders), these cities remained economically dependent on ruling-class demand. The rise and fall of medieval cities was directly pegged to the extractive powers of the landholding class and, in particular, to the solvency of borrowing kings. Unless towns succeeded in transforming themselves into land-based city-states with independent sources of non-commercial income (Venice), their fortunes followed noble demand governed by the rents extracted from the peasantry within the eco-demographic fluctuations of the agrarian economy. The resumption of long-distance commerce in the twelfth century was itself an upshot of heightened aristocratic demand based on intensified exploitation of a systematically enserfed peasantry. This, by the same token, intensified inter-noble military competition, which in turn powered the wheels of commerce. When the crisis of the fourteenth century set in, cities were the first to suffer.

This chapter has demonstrated the nexus between two important systemic transformations of medieval geopolitics and class conflict. Intra-ruling class struggle among late Frankish lords under outside pressure precipitated the implosion of the Carolingian Empire during the Feudal Revolution of the year 1000. Imperial hierarchy gave way to feudal anarchy. The restructuring of the mode of exploitation to a serf-based agrarian economy engendered the militarization of the Frankish countryside, while the territorialization and patrimonialization of lordships prompted the introduction of primogeniture, driving the lord's surplus sons beyond the borders of ancient Francia. Thereafter, migrating Frankish lords, legitimated by the political Church, attempted to replicate their traditional forms of political reproduction in the extra-Frankish periphery. New feudal kingdoms sprang up headed by knights turned dynasts. At the same time, the French monarchy consolidated its power. The new international order was characterized by a plurality of royal dynasties and other feudal actors. In sum, property relations explain the constitution, operation, and transformation of medieval geopolitical orders. Differences in medieval geopolitical organization reflect the differentiated power relations within different forms of lordship – banal, domestic, and land – that organized the social relations of exploitation and the inter-noble relations of authority.

We can now see why Neorealism and Realism are unable to explain the rise, reproduction, and decline of medieval geopolitical systems: the behaviour of actors in all three systems was not a function of system-structure (anarchy or hierarchy) in the Neorealist sense, but remained fundamentally governed by (geo)political accumulation, mediated by interpersonal feudal bonds and a common Roman Catholic culture. Feudal strategies of reproduction were compatible with different forms of international organization – imperial, individualized, and royal – as long as the essential unit of production and authority was the lordship. Political and geopolitical behaviour was rooted in the configuration of these lordship-based property regimes. The diverse experiences of extra-Frankish as well as inner-Frankish high medieval state-building found their institutional and 'modernizing' limits in the survival and export of structures of lordship. While the territorial extent of feudal Europe increased dramatically after the passage from the early to the high Middle Ages, and while its various rulers were no longer united under imperial authority, its socio-political organization did not change fundamentally. This meant that while the late medieval geopolitical order was not structured by the differentiation between the economic and the political, the reassertion of royal authority started to translate into an incipient differentiation between the domestic and the international. In one sense, feudalism created a world according to its own image. In a very different sense, however, feudalism created the lasting legacy of a European political geography divided along dynastic lines.

Notes

1 History, according to Hegel, is the resolution of contradictions that interpret themselves. Philosophy maintains the indeterminacy of these resolutions. Social science adopts the role of Minerva's owl and lays bare their retrospective intelligibility.

2 Tellingly, offensive wars were the preserve of the mounted imperial aristocracy, whereas the free peasant militia was mobilized only for defensive
purposes, i.e., in the face of enemy invasions in which there was nothing to
gain and everything to lose.

3 How Charlemagne dealt with recalcitrant nobles is exemplified by the
infamous bloodbath on the banks of the Aller, where the Franks massacred
4,000 free Saxons during Charlemagne's protracted conquest of Saxony.

4 The territorial and chronological unevenness of this process of fragmentation
must be stressed. In the Eastern Kingdom, fragmentation of public power
set in later and never went so far as in the Western Kingdom, due to
persistent opportunities of conquest in connection with the 'open' eastern
frontier. More generally, the powerful dukedoms and counties in the
marches were better able to resist the complete fragmentation of public
power due to their tighter internal organization in the face of invasion.

5 See also the debate on the Feudal Revolution in *Past and Present* (1996–97).

6 I follow Duby's interpretation of the end of slavery as resulting from class
struggle through the imposition of banal lordship on all peasants, whether
servile or non-servile, dating it around 1000 (Duby 1968: 188; Fourquin
1975). In an excellent survey article, Bonnassie, by refuting arguments which
peg the decline of slavery to the Christianization of the countryside,
difficulties in recruiting slave labour, the introduction of new productive
technologies, or economic growth in conjunction with demographic pressures, has forcefully reinstated Duby's explanation of feudalism as a serf-based
mode of production, associating its rise with the class struggles during the
Feudal Revolution (Bonnassie 1991a).

7 The nexus between pre-capitalist social property relations and lordly investment in the means of coercion is convincingly theorized in (Brenner 1986:
27–32) and exemplified for this period by Bartlett. The military elite's

> defensive armament consisted in a conical helmet, a coat of mail and a
> large shield; offensive arms included spear, sword and perhaps a mace or
> club; indispensable for offensive action was the heavy war-horse. These
> men were heavy cavalry because they were fully armed and, in particular,
> because they had the expensive mail coat. . . . They were heavy because
> they were clad in iron. A powerful force was one that was 'all of iron'.
> The mail coat must have been the most valuable single object that a
> knight owned and it is not surprising that they were sometimes pawned
> by knights in need. At a time when many agricultural implements were
> still made of wood, when the tool on which human survival turned, the
> plough, was often still made of wood or only tipped with iron, here were
> men who were dressed in iron. It represented a staggering investment.
> The full gear of an *armatus* or *loricatus* required approximately 50 lb of
> iron. When an army such as that raised by Otto II in the 980s included
> around 5,000 *loricati*, the iron carried by the heavy cavalry alone totalled
> 125 tons. The figure is all the more striking when we consider that, in
> this period, a German forge might produce only 10 lb of iron in a smelting

process taking two or three days. . . . The heavy horsemen of the Middle Ages lived in the wheat age but looked like men of the steel age. (Bartlett 1993: 61)

8 'Taking with one hand, receiving with the other, the knights were the real hub of the seignorial economy, the driving wheel of the system of exploitation' (Duby 1980: 155).

9 In a series of articles, Duby explored the 'correlation' between the rise of banal lordship and changing noble family forms. He could show that the introduction of clear-cut patrilineal genealogies was chronologically coeval with respective usurpations of the powers of command by single dynasties and the introduction of heredity and primogeniture. The further Duby descended in the noble hierarchy, the more recent the establishment of primogeniture turned out to be, reflecting the chronologically sequenced devolution of the ban from king, to princes, to counts, castellans, and finally to landed knights (Duby 1977b, 1977c, 1994). For the wider debate, see Bisson 1990.

10 'From 1030 there begin to be signs of primogeniture in castellan families. Finally, from 1025 the rights of sole legitimate descent become established. . . . At the moment of the crisis of feudalism, between 1020 and 1060, family relationships appeared to be seriously under strain and it is as if in response to these tensions that the closure of the lineage takes place' (Poly and Bournazel 1991: 108).

11 Duby first submitted a sociology of such eleventh- and twelfth-century 'youths', referring to that period in a noble man's life between his dubbing, usually in his early twenties, and that stage where 'he put down roots, became the head of a house and founded a family – which occurred often not before his forties' (Duby 1977a: 113).

12 Evergates comments that in the twelfth century,

> so many women entered convents, in fact, that many institutions by the end of the century had exhausted their meager endowments. In 1196, for example, Celestine III ordered Heloise's convent of the Paraclete to downsize through attrition to sixty nuns; shortly afterward the well-known convent of Avenay was restricted to forty nuns because it was 'burdened by debts owed to creditors', a complaint common in the thirteenth century. The Cistercian convent of Fervaques even sought Innocent III's protection from the 'nobles and powerful men' who reacted violently when their relatives were refused admission. (Evergates 1995: 18)

13 'By the late Middle Ages 80 per cent of Europe's kings and queens were Franks' (Bartlett 1993: 42).

14 Bartlett's fascinating account advances a threefold explanation for Frankish geopolitical expansion, granting pride of place to superior military technology, while remaining more hypothetical about the impact of changing aristocratic inheritance practices and the wider social rationale behind the pattern of aristocratic land-grabbing (Bartlett 1993: 18–23, 43–51, and 60ff).

Wickham takes him to task for not inquiring sufficiently into the internal socio-political transformations within the late Frankish kingdoms, antedating the actual outward movement (Wickham 1994). For an alternative 'multi-causal' account see Mann 1986: 373–415. Without mentioning the decline of the Carolingian Empire and the 'Feudal Revolution', the author's main conclusion is that the eleventh century saw 'an embryonic transition to capitalism' (Mann 1986: 409). Cf. the critical review by Wickham 1988. Ertmann, in turn, while choosing to neglect the serf-based dynamics of the contemporary agrarian economy, surmises that post-millennial economic expansion was due to the 'appearance of an agricultural surplus during the 900s', but warns that 'the exact origins of this surplus remains in some dispute'. He then argues that 'a favourable climatic shift may have played a role', and finally endorses Guy Bois's thesis (Bois 1992) that 'the collapse of central authority permitted the economy to establish, perhaps for the first time, a substantial measure of autonomy vis-à-vis the political order' (Ertman 1997: 50–51). Bois's account is critically examined in Teschke 1997.

15 Mann's multiple outbreaks of capitalism are derivative of the neo-utilitarian methodological-individualist assumptions that underlie his theory of subjectivity: 'Human beings are restless, purposive, and rational, striving to increase their enjoyment of the good things of life and capable of choosing and pursuing appropriate means for doing so' (Mann 1986:4). What Mann posits as a transhistorical theorem of human nature is for Weber, of course, only one ideal-type of social action (rational action). In Mann, Weber's heuristic device turns into an ontological axiom.

16 'There was a fusion of the religious and political spheres' (Berman 1983: 88).

17 Robert Brenner pointed to the socially uneven yet geopolitically combined dynamics of feudal political accumulation with regard to the Norman Conquest, systematically drawing out its long-term implications for English medieval class relations and state-building (Brenner 1985b: 254–5, 1996: 258–64). Cf. also Marx on the international relations of conquest:

> A similar relationship issues from conquest, when a form of intercourse which has evolved on another soil is brought over complete to the conquered country: whereas in its home it was still encumbered with interests and relations left over from earlier periods, here it can and must be established completely and without hindrance, if only to assure the conqueror's lasting power. (England and Naples after the Norman conquest, when they received the most perfect form of feudal organisation.) (Marx and Engels 1964: 92)

18 For a clear exposition of the constitutive contradictions of feudal political accumulation, see Le Patourel 1976: 279–318.

19 According to neo-Malthusian reasoning, a rising population would have meant an over-supply of labour, resulting in lower peasant incomes or a demotion of their legal status – none of which occurred in France.

4

Transitions and Non-Transitions
to Modernity:

A Critique of Rival Paradigms

1. Introduction: The Rise of the West?

With the end of the high Middle Ages, many scholars move to the beginning of the story of the 'Rise of the West'. After the crisis of the fourteenth century, the end of serfdom, and the progressive removal of feudal vestiges, a combination of the inexorable rise of the middle classes and rational bureaucracy in a competitive, state-centralizing context set Europe on a developmental trajectory radically different from the rest of the world. The IR literature has generally adopted this simplified version of the medieval-to-modern geopolitical shift, as both feudal geopolitics and projects of universal empire-building were replaced by the modern states-system, composed of sovereign, territorial states. In this perspective, these processes began after the fourteenth-century crisis and intensified in the sixteenth and seventeenth centuries, while France is singled out as the prototype of modern state formation.

In chapter 1, I criticized IR theories for their failure adequately to explain the formation of the modern states-system. We now need to examine three dominant models of long-term development and the transition to 'modernity' in historical sociology, and draw out their implications for explaining systemic change within IR: (1) the geopolitical competition model, (2) the demographic model, and (3) the commercialization model. The first emphasizes the competitive international relations of late medieval times; this military competition produced ever more consolidated and territorialized states eager to increase their war-making capacities, crystallizing in the modern states-system. The second model derives Europe's long-term economic dynamic from neo-Malthusian demographic fluctuations governing income distribution and phases of growth and decline. The third model views trade, the growth of towns, the increasing international division of labour, and the rise of the bourgeoisie as the long-term causes behind Europe's ascendancy in form of the modern world-system. All three theories have long theoretical pedigrees and enjoy periodic revivals in various guises. My argument, however, is that all three approaches are theoretically inadequate and substantively misleading accounts of early modern development and the passage to modernity.

Conventional IR paradigms, most notably those of Realist or Neorealist lineage, would of course challenge the very idea that the deep logic of international relations alters with the onset of modernity. Where there is no change, there is no need for explanation. This 'no-deep-change' model, which has dominated the discipline of IR, is, however, a disciplinary anomaly – the strange fruit of a branch of knowledge which mistook the expulsion of history for scientific rigour. My argument, by contrast, rests on explaining variations in the constitution, operation, and transformation of geopolitical orders. This argument is predicated on the assumption that we can discern both a deep 'generative structure' of international systems, which explains institutional and behavioural differences, and a 'transformative logic', which explains transitions from one system to another. The case for the theory of social property relations rests on its capacity to theorize the transition to modern international relations and to draw out implications for early modern and modern processes of state-building – and, by extension, the genesis of the modern European states-system.[1]

2. The Geopolitical Competition Model

The geopolitical competition literature developed outside the discipline of IR in the field of historical sociology. Its revival in the 1980s was largely a response to the perceived 'economic reductionism' inherent in Marxist historical sociology, notably Wallerstein's world-systems theory, which was held to have neglected the dimension of geopolitical competition in its reconstruction of the overall nature and dynamic of the modern world-system. While the more sophisticated approaches attempt to combine strategic interaction as a 'missing link' with domestic developments to argue for the relative autonomy of the strategic factor, the general thrust in this literature has moved towards asserting geopolitical competition as the primary level of determination to explain state formations and their variations.[2] Although IR's growing awareness of the problem of systemic transformation has led it to draw on this literature, it has failed to produce a systematic critique of its key assumptions and substantive conclusions

(Hobden 1998; Hobson 2000: 174–214; Hobson 2002b).[3] An excursion into the wider social sciences and historiography is therefore imperative if we want to demonstrate the superiority of the social-property view. I will therefore approach these models in the spirit of immanent critique, exposing how they are unable to provide coherent and convincing explanations with regard to their initial premises and the problems they set for themselves.

1. The Military Logic of State Formation

The sociological roots of the geopolitical competition model lie in the Weber–Hintze tradition of state theory, while its historiographical antecedents can be traced back to the Prussian Historical school and particularly to Leopold von Ranke's theorem of the 'primacy of foreign policy'. Otto Hintze classically expressed its core idea:

> If we want to find out about the relation between military organization and the organization of the state, we must direct our attention particularly to two phenomena, which conditioned the real organization of the state. These are, first, the structure of social classes, and second, the external ordering of the states – their position relative to each other, and their overall position in the world. It is one-sided, exaggerated, and therefore false to consider class conflict the only driving force in history. Conflict between nations has been far more important; and throughout the ages, pressure from without has been a determining influence on internal structure. It has even often suppressed internal strife or forced it into compromise. Both these forces have manifestly worked together in the design of the military order and the state organization. (Hintze 1975b: 183)

The essential causal sequence of the model may be schematically sketched as follows: international systemic competition ⇒ war ⇒ cost increases ⇒ increased resource extraction ⇒ new modes of taxation and fiscality ⇒ military-technological innovations ⇒ state monopolization of the means of violence ⇒ state centralization and rationalization (central representatives are Braun 1975; Finer 1975; Tilly 1975, 1985, 1992; Mann 1986, 1988a, 1988b; Downing 1992; Luard 1992: 30; Blockmans 1994; Reinhard 1996a, 1996b, 1999; Ertman 1997). In some versions, this dynamic chain of causation is also deemed to be crucial for the development of capitalism itself (Mann 1986: 454, 1988a, 1988b). The literature revolving around this core hypothesis constitutes the dominant paradigm of state-formation theory in contemporary scholarship and serves as one of the key intellectual legitimations for mainstream IR accounts of the rise of the modern states-system.[4]

The literature may be broken down into four closely related strands. A first strand emphasizes the role of military competition and its implications for the centralization and rationalization of military power in the hands of the state. A second strand focuses on changes in the techniques of revenue procurement and their consequences for state-building. A third concentrates on administrative and institutional innovations, and especially on the consequences of representative assemblies and 'bureaucracies' for state consolidation. And a fourth axis of inquiry revolves around the formation of a uniform legal system, a secular, codified body of civil and public law, and a centralized court system operated by professional jurists. But all four strands converge in regarding these partial developments as parallel and interrelated steps towards one core institution: modern sovereignty.

This literature is also in broad agreement on three fundamental propositions. First, the emergence of militarily, fiscally, administratively, and legally centralized states was essentially achieved in the main western countries by about the seventeenth, at the latest by the eighteenth, century. Second, these political phenomena can be equated with a broader notion of modernity. The sovereign state of the Age of Absolutism was a modern state. Third, the fundamental cause, the *primum mobile*, behind these processes was systemically induced pressure towards war, enforcing state rationalization. Again, Hintze pithily captures these assumptions:

> The constant rivalry between the Great Powers, which was still mixed up with confessional differences; the permanent political tension that invariably provoked further military exertions, in order that single states could preserve their independence and thus the basis of all prosperity and culture; in short, power politics and balance-of-power politics created the foundations of modern Europe: the international system as well as the absolutist system of government and the standing army of the Continent. (Hintze 1975b: 199)[5]

How does the Weber–Hintze tradition justify the arrival of modernity in the sphere of state formation? A first criterion for this equation is sought in the sphere of military organization, based on the Weberian distinction between a feudal oligopoly and a modern monopoly on the means of violence. The nexus between international rivalry, military rationalization, and state-building has been formulated in a simple and suggestive law-like generalization by Samuel E. Finer in an 'extraction–coercion-cycle', and by Charles Tilly in a 'war-making and state-making' model (Finer 1975: 96ff;

Tilly 1975: 23–4, 1985, 1992). The transition from the feudal host, based on interpersonal obligations and activated by the royal *arrière-ban*, to the modern standing army, financed and controlled by the monarchy, led to the state's monopolization of the means of violence. Driven by military technological innovations (the 'Military Revolution', 1550–1660), the 'irrationality', inefficiency, and unreliability of the feudal knights were replaced by a disciplined, trained, and publicly paid professional army (*miles perpetuus*), which was no longer organized along interpersonal lines predicated on the fief system, but into functional branches (artillery, cavalry, infantry, navy). The internal monopolization of the means of violence – outlawing feuds and crushing the noble right of resistance – went hand in hand with its external monopolization, evinced in states' closure to imperial and papal claims. Noble demilitarization and the concentration of war-making powers in the state were two sides of the same coin. While this allowed for rationalization and increased military efficiency, it also required extra-feudal financial resources.

Demand for additional resources affected taxation (second criterion), leading to the transition from the feudal 'domain state' to the modern 'tax state'.[6] In the modern tax state 'the "private" resources of the ruling power were exceeded in value by the "public" revenues derived from a system of general taxation' (Ormrod 1995: 123; Braun 1975). This passage from fiscal personalism, in which there was no real distinction between royal private income and public revenue (*le roi faut vivre du sien*), to fiscal institutionalism is held to have been consummated by the centralizing monarchy, which extended its fiscal supremacy over the entire realm. In this process, new modes of fiscality operated by new public institutions were invented and enforced against the autonomous powers of the nobility and the privileges and immunities of the clergy, leading to fiscal uniformity and institutional centralization (Ormrod 1995: 124–7).[7] The most important innovation was the shift from feudal military and financial assistance and inelastic, indirect taxation to generalized, elastic direct taxation. Feudal extraordinary aid gave way to regular and general taxation. Revenue extraction and expenditure became a public matter. Jean Bodin's maxim *pecunia nervus rerum* became state doctrine. This transition is held to have taken place in the leading West European monarchies between the fourteenth and seventeenth centuries under the pressure of 'state-constitutive wars', in which inter-state competition necessitated a state monopoly over taxation and the means of violence.

This in turn drove the transition from fragmented feudal to modern bureaucratic administration (third criterion). Both a standing army and a centralized tax regime require professional officials. Next to the standing army, a 'sitting army' of professional officers, employed and controlled by the state, came to challenge and finally supplant the independent local feudal administration. A nobility of service (*noblesse de robe*) grew at the expense of the old military nobility (*noblesse d'épée*).

The establishment of a legal system constitutes the fourth criterion. The welter of independent feudal courts gave way to a nationally unified legal system, regulated by a uniform tax code and operated by legal experts on the basis of an integrated court hierarchy, culminating in royal courts. Earlier feudal inter-lordly disputes were no longer resolved by archaic feuds, but by royal civil law. The long history of the royal suppression of aristocratic duelling records this process. The new modalities of fiscality required increasing powers of surveillance, enforcement, and discipline. Disputes between peasants and landowners were no longer decided by manorial courts, but were brought to royal courts. In short, military rivalry indirectly brought about the internal juridification of social relations.

Excursus – Michael Mann: Theoretical Pluralism, Historical Contingencies

Michael Mann's work presents arguably the most comprehensive and influential version of the geopolitical competition model, tied into a wider pluralist account of the ascendancy of Europe. Mann dates the origins of the European take-off to the twelfth century. He traces the interrelation between capitalism, the modern state, and the modern states-system through three successive phases, which are regarded as a cumulative process: 800–1155, 1155–1477, and 1477–1760, at which point the modern state and the modern states-system are held to have arrived.

Mann detects the origins of capitalism in the first phase. The 'acephalous' structure of feudal political authority created opportunities for profit-orientated economic behaviour.[8] The urban revival and the resumption of long-distance trade combined with technological developments, intensive agriculture, and the normatively pacifying framework of Christianity. The origins and interrelations of these power networks that drove the 'European miracle were a gigantic series of coincidences' (Mann 1986: 505). Only Christianity is deemed to have been a necessary condition, distinguishing Europe from rival civilizations (Mann 1986: 505).

In the second phase, two further accidents, one internal and one external, conditioned development. Internally, ecological (soil fertility) and geocommercial (Baltic–Atlantic navigational opportunities) factors contributed to agricultural intensification and commercial expansion. Simultaneously, the rise of 'co-ordinating states' (territorial federations that co-ordinated powerful domestic social groups) went hand in hand with growing intra-European geopolitical pressures and the Military Revolution, sparking the transition from feudal political fragmentation to a multi-state system. 'By 1477 these power networks were developing into their simpler, modern form: a multistate, capitalist civilization' (Mann 1986: 510). Externally, Islam blocked eastern expansion, with the conquest of Constantinople (1453) spelling the end of Orthodox Christianity. The closure of the East and the opportunities provided by the West ensured that power travelled towards the Atlantic. 'The two macro-patterns were political blockage to the East and agricultural-cum-trading opportunity to the West' (Mann 1986: 510).

The third phase was characterized by a rapid intensification of military rivalry, driving spiralling military expenditures, creating new modes of fiscality and administration, and generalizing the 'organic state'. Polities that failed to compete militarily were eliminated. While Mann recognizes the differences between French absolutism and the post-1688 British constitutional monarchy, he nevertheless subsumes them under the ideal-typical 'organic state'. Absolutist regimes, like France, were 'mobilized states' that enjoyed 'despotic power' over 'civil society' and 'a measure of financial and manpower autonomy' in a territory rich in manpower and poor in wealth (Mann 1986: 437). Constitutional regimes, like England and Holland, were 'fiscal states' with little despotic power but strong 'infrastructural powers' in territories poor in manpower but rich in wealth. But rather than developing these differences in regime type, Mann ultimately conflates them under a single category, subject to identical competitive pressures that produced identical state responses.[9] He concludes that 'the growth of the modern state, as measured by finance, is explained primarily not in domestic terms but in terms of geopolitical relations of violence' (Mann 1986: 490). The completion of this system-wide process is dated to the seventeenth and eighteenth centuries.

2. Modernity? Which Modernity? A Critique of the Geopolitical Competition Model

A closer re-examination of the geopolitical competition model reveals, however, a series of theoretical problems and historical misjudgements. Its inadequacies emerge when we (1) question the 'givenness' of a system of multiple states, and thus the lack of an account of the origins of the European political pluriverse; (2) reveal the lack of a social theory of war; (3) qualify the universal effects of geopolitical competition among the institutionally very different forms of political community of the late Middle Ages; (4) contest the explanation for the success or failure of these transformations in different regions; (5) challenge the definition of political modernity in these accounts; and (6) raise the issue of the role of capitalism.

We have seen that the model starts with the plurality of polities in late medieval and early modern Europe (see, e.g., Reinhard 1996b: 18). With the exception of Thomas Ertman,[10] this geopolitical pluriverse is taken as given; it lies outside the model's explanatory reach. While this pluriverse can, of course, not simply be 'read off' existing social property relations at any given point in time and space, I have shown how geopolitical fragmentation can be understood as the outcome of class conflicts which tore the last pan-European empire asunder. Geopolitical plurality was thus not a natural, geographical, ethnic, or cultural phenomenon, but an outcome of class conflict.

For all its insistence on the primacy of military rivalry, the geopolitical competition literature also lacks a social theory of war. Military, fiscal, and institutional centralization are held to derive from permanent geopolitical pressures. The focus then shifts to how power elites responded to these pressures by restructuring domestic techniques of revenue extraction, military mobilization, and institutional rationalization. But if every ruler had to respond to external pressures, who acted on what grounds in the first place? In other words, the geopolitical competition literature does not explain why the mere fact of territorial contiguity necessarily entails competition. This is not to dispute the historical record of geopolitical conflict, but to raise the question of causality. Radically put, the model fails to explain why early modern polities were expansionist.

This rather spectacular lack of a social theory of war results in two methodological dilemmas. In society-centred accounts, the initial stimulus is externalized to international forces; in system-centred approaches, it is attributed to a naturalized competitive inter-state system. But the mere geographical contiguity of polities cannot in itself explain why late medieval and early modern inter-state relations were bellicose, unless we assume an anthropologically questionable idea of man as a natural power-maximizer or a psychologizing rational-choice model, where risk minimization creates an inherent security dilemma. These dilemmas replicate the sociological impoverishment of Realist thinking and the dehistoricized abstractions of system-centred Neorealist thinking. The untenable hypostatization of systemic pressures thus calls for a framework of analysis wide enough to understand 'external' factors as *internal* to the system. It also needs to understand the system not as an abstracted 'third image' (Waltz 1959), operating above and beyond its constitutive actors according to its own logic, but as internally related to a 'generative structure' that explains the frequency of war. We must reconnect the social content of war to the social property relations that made it a necessary strategy of reproduction for the pre-capitalist ruling classes: geopolitical accumulation.[11] In other words, we need to denaturalize and deconstruct late medieval and early modern 'states' as geographically distributed members of a Europe-wide ruling class fighting over sources of income.

While war was universal, the responses to it were not. In other words, different states' responses to military pressure cannot be deduced from geopolitical factors, but have to be explained with reference to specific domestic social constellations and the timing of intensified military exposure. As a rule, the pure logic of international rivalry not only fails to cover the differential development of non-monarchical state forms (Spruyt 1994b; Körner 1995a: 394–5), it is equally unable to account for developmental variations in the dominant western monarchies, France, Spain, and England. Not only is it difficult from this perspective to explain why some feudal monarchies became territorial monarchies while others did not, it is even more difficult to explain why some European political communities – city-states, city-leagues, the Empire, the Church-state, merchant-republics, aristocratic-republics, and peasant-republics – maintained themselves in the emergent inter-state system, even though they often drew on much smaller territories and populations. 'This in turn prompts the comment that such alternative forms of state possessed a real dynamism and a capacity to modernize which also enabled structures that may appear archaic to survive' (Körner 1995: 394). In other words, we have to account not only for the success of territorial monarchies, but also for alternative state formations and state failures. In particular, we have to relate success, variation, and 'exit' to political and social diversity. The highly variegated political landscape of late medieval Europe did not constitute a 'natural field of selection', conceived in neo-evolutionary terms, in which bigger conflict units either subsumed smaller ones or forced them to adopt a similar socio-political regime, but a dynamic and mixed system in which the main causes for survival, transformation, or decline have to be sought in the nexus between internal revenue extraction and productivity, i.e., in class relations.[12] The universal logic of geopolitical competition has to be filtered through the social forces within polities. By failing to do so, sociologists and IR scholars tend to turn a historical outcome – the eventual victory of the modern territorial state – into a functionalist theoretical outcome.

To the extent that the geopolitical competition literature does try to theorize how regional power elites responded to military competition, the accounts are confined either to an abstract enumeration of new fiscal, military, and institutional innovations, or to the 'dialogue' within the power elite – usually between the king and some representative assembly composed of the clergy, the nobility, and burghers – leading to new modalities of inter-elite consultation and co-operation, explaining state-variations (see, for example, Hintze 1975c; Tilly 1975, 1985; Mann 1986; Ertman 1997).[13] Confining the processes of interaction to elites, while an important step beyond merely listing innovations, fails to extend this 'dialogue' to those most immediately affected by new modes of revenue extraction: the direct producers. In other words, we need to recognize the role of both horizontal, intra-ruling-class conflicts over the means of exploitation and distribution, and vertical class conflicts over the rate of taxation. When the analysis is extended to the peasantry, it usually appears not as a social agent with some influence over the level and forms of extraction, but as a neutral tax base or simply as 'the economy' – socially disembodied figures like population fluctuations or agrarian productivity, or formal terms like taxpayers, tax compliance, fiscal limit, or fiscal capacity.[14] The unwillingness to recognize the peasantry as the fourth party in the 'dialogue' between the king, the 'staff', and the estates is thus not merely an omission, but a decisive failure in assessing regionally specific solutions to the general problem of war-induced taxation.[15] Without considering the peasantry as a conscious class, defending its own interests, a fiscal sociology of 'the evolution of pre-modern fiscal systems in a comparative European framework' (Bonney 1995a: 2) is doomed to failure. In other words, class conflict in the form of struggles over the rate and distribution of taxation between and within the major classes of late medieval times, arising from varying degrees of self-organization and resulting in determinate balances of class forces, were decisive for regionally specific outcomes of state attempts to procure war finances. Regionally specific balances of class forces explain variations in the domestic responses to war understood as inter-ruling class competition over land and labour.

Yet this still does not tell us anything about the modernity of these state-building attempts. Crucially, we must reject the term modernity in connection with early modern state centralization. No early modern European state, with the exception of post-revolutionary England, achieved sovereignty in the modern sense of the term. Since the overwhelming majority of European states remained dynastic-absolutist up to the period between the mid-nineteenth century and the Treaty of Versailles, sovereignty was 'privately' held by the ruling dynasty; state territory was private patrimonial property. Nowhere was the crucial transition from patrimonial officialdom to modern bureaucracy achieved. The state apparatus remained highly personalized at all levels; no clear distinction was made between the public and the private. In dynastic-patrimonial states, venal officials reprivatized the rights of governance and taxation, so that state power was progressively alienated by a monarchy under financial duress. Administration remained an 'irrational' net of personal dependencies, characterized by venality, patronage, clientelism, nepotism, and favouritism. As a result, the means of violence were not monopolized by the state, but remained under personal-patrimonial control. The king's standing army was precisely the *king's* standing army, supplemented by mercenary forces. Military entrepreneurs remained outside the direct control of the state. Within the army, the practice of office venality meant that nobles bought colonelcies and entire regiments out of their private purses, recruiting, maintaining, and decommissioning soldiers at will.

The legal system, in turn, equally suffered the effects of venality, while the persistence of feudal courts and regional law-codes frustrated the principle of legal uniformity. Territory, finally, was determined by dynastic practices of military and marital political accumulation, so that dynastic states were in essence 'composite monarchies' (Elliott: 1992), never achieving the fixity and exclusivity of modern notions of state territory. In short, the early modern state evinced none of the traits typical of the modern state. While the transition from feudal monarchies to absolutist monarchies was an important development, it did not lead to the formation of the modern state and, by extension, the modern states-system. I shall show in the next chapter how the non-establishment of the modern state in early modern Europe can be understood on the basis of prevailing pre-capitalist social property relations.

Finally, the geopolitical literature is completely unclear about the definition and historical role of capitalism. The collective sigh of relief that the Weber–Hintze paradigm provided a powerful alternative to Marxist accounts has led on the one hand to completely omitting the question of the relation of capitalism to the modern state and of its effect on inter-state competition; at best, capitalism becomes derivative of the war-state, where externally induced state promotion requires 'commercial activity' or 'efficiency gains'. On the other hand, capitalism is regarded as ubiquitous, and irrelevant to the historically specific onset of geopolitical competition and the modern states-system. The one has little to do with the other, and when their historically independent trajectories happen to intersect, the state and the states-system merely subsume capitalism under their logic. In short, the geopolitical competition literature would do well to return to Hintze's admonition that the military logic should not replace class conflict, but be understood in relation to it. In other words, we shall have to bring the peasantry back in.

3. The Demographic Model

While the demographic model makes no claims about state formation, it does claim to have a general theory of pre-industrial long-term socio-economic development. Demographic fluctuations govern phases of econ-omic growth and decline, income distribution, and price movements. What distinguishes this model from those approaches that see the fourteenth-century and seventeenth-century crises as catalysts for economic moderni-zation is its altogether more 'conservative' interpretation of the chances for economic development, which it holds to be rooted in the age-old rhythms of the pre-industrial agrarian economy. Development is cyclical rather than linear, recursive not progressive. Let us see whether the demographic model can illuminate medieval and early modern economic and political developments.

During the fourteenth and fifteenth centuries, large parts of Europe, including France and England, entered into a deep and prolonged general crisis. Chapter 3 showed that this crisis was preceded by a sustained upswing between 1050 and 1250. Mark Bloch classically described this period as the 'second feudal age' (Bloch 1961). This eco-demographic upswing was not driven by any incipient form of capitalism, but by *horizontal expansion* – land reclamation, colonization, conquest – which in turn fostered demographic growth. This mutually reinforcing process came to a halt by about the middle of the thirteenth century, leading to a catastrophic population decline between 1315 and 1380, characterized by famines and the Black Death. The feudal economy stagnated from 1240 to 1320 and contracted from 1320 to 1440 (Duby 1968: 298ff.; Bois 1984), before 'the long sixteenth century' witnessed a period of economic expansion.

The standard explanation of this crisis draws on the neo-Malthusian account of the role of demographic fluctuations in general economic development (Ladurie 1966; Postan 1966; Abel 1978). According to neo-Malthusians, medieval economic history can be divided into two long-term cycles, the first between the eleventh and fourteenth and the second between the fifteenth and eighteenth centuries. Each cycle is divided into an ascending and a descending phase. The assumption is that demographic growth outruns productivity growth (given that resources, i.e., land and technology, remain constant), leading to periods of overpopulation, diminishing returns, and automatic 'homeostatic' adjustment through famines and plagues until population numbers and productivity rates are re-equilibrated. Then the cycle starts again. During the ascending phase, the population grows and more people have to survive on the same quantity of land. Consequently, the land is over-cultivated and over-exploited, leading to defertilization and soil exhaustion. At the same time, peasants bring less fertile soil (marginal lands) into cultivation. The overall result is a rising land/labour ratio and an aggregate fall in productivity. During the descending phase, over-exploitation and soil exhaustion induce bad harvests, malnutrition, and eventually famines and plagues, leading to 'natural' population reduction. Peasants withdraw to the more fertile lands, the land/labour ratio falls, and productivity rates grow again, ushering in a new ascending phase.

A model of income distribution is built into neo-Malthusian theory. During periods of demographic growth (ascending phase), the growing labour supply depresses wages and increases rents. Peasants lose and lords gain income. Grain, food, and land prices rise. Loss of peasant income and growing prices tend to intensify the effects of falling productivity on rates of reproduction, mortality, fertility, and life expectancy. The reduction of the number of direct producers during the descending phase leads to labour scarcity that causes rising wages, falling prices, and falling rents, reversing income distribution between producers and non-producers until the population starts to grow again. A new cycle takes off.

Robert Brenner identifies three fundamental flaws in this model (Brenner 1985a: 13–24, 1985b: 217–26). First, according to strict Malthusian reasoning, demographic recovery should have set in immediately after the mid-fourteenth-century plagues. However, recovery was delayed by about a century because lords tried to recuperate lost incomes by internecine and 'international' warfare (the Hundred Years' War), intensifying, radicalizing, and perpetuating the crisis in a downward spiral. Feudal property relations contained no self-correcting mechanism for resolving this crisis, since lords could not raise productivity through capital investments. Rather, they engaged in *distributional struggles* by relying on their extra-economic powers of coercion. Their compensatory tactics of squeezing the peasantry and feuding with rival lords unleashed sharp intra- and inter-ruling-class conflict. The crisis was not simply an eco-demographic but a *social crisis*.

Second, neo-Malthusians do not allow for variations in how collective actors translate resource pressure into social action. The basic demographic demand/supply mechanism operates in a socio-political vacuum and fails to account for regionally distinct relations between lords and peasants, largely determined by the balance of class forces. Since these balances diverged substantially in fourteenth-century France and England (and in Europe east of the Elbe), the different post-crisis outcomes must be read through the lens of different class constellations.

Third, the model fails to fit the evidence into a comparative perspective. As a result of these class conflicts, the Europe-wide fourteenth-century population drop-off resulted in the reimposition of serfdom in Eastern Europe, the consolidation of peasant freedom in France, and the eviction of peasants from their customary plots in England. Thus, similar population pressures generated very different responses. As we shall see, these regionally diverging outcomes shaped the general direction of long-term economic development *and* state formation in early modern France and England. Eco-demographic pressure was refracted through class conflict.

4. The Commercialization Model

1. *Le Monde Braudelien: Capitalisme Depuis Toujours*

The work of Fernand Braudel and the *Annales* school has deeply influenced postwar European historiography and, especially since the 1970s, the social sciences at large (Braudel 1972a, 1972b, 1977, 1984). Its appeal lies in a theoretical shift away from a discredited history of events and the short term to a history of conjunctures and structures, which predate and outlive individuals. The theoretical implication is a deep-rooted immobility at the heart of history, which is fundamentally determined by almost unalterable structures: geography, ecology, human infrastructures, and, later, mentalities. The cyclical lifetimes of economies, societies, states, and civilizations are treated as conjunctures, while high politics and war are merely events. Through Immanuel Wallerstein's reception of and collaboration with Braudel, the structural understanding of society-transcending socio-economic systems, first formulated by Braudel in his study *The Mediterranean and the Mediterranean World in the Age of Philip II*, gave rise to a distinct world-system paradigm (Wallerstein 1974, 1980, 1995). Since the late 1970s, it has made deep inroads into IR, where references to *la longue durée* and the conceptual triad *structure–conjuncture–événement* now abound (Ruggie 1989, 1993).

This section outlines the Braudelian background to Wallerstein's impos-ing, though, as I shall argue, defective theoretical edifice. The failure of the 'world-system' approach rests to a considerable extent on methodological assumptions of the *Annales* school that were themselves deeply problematic (good critiques are Hexter 1972; Vilar 1973; Gerstenberger 1987). I shall show how this methodological framework informs Braudel's historiograph-ical propositions, exemplified by such concepts as the world-economy, capitalism, and historical development.

Braudel's diminishing estimation of his three levels of historical time is captured in the preface to his seminal study on the Mediterranean. The history of structures 'is devoted to a history whose passage is almost imperceptible, that of man in his relationship to the environment, a history in which all change is slow, a history of constant repetition, ever-recurring cycles'. The history of conjunctures refers to a history 'with slow but perceptible rhythms . . . a *social history*, the history of groups and groupings'. Finally, the history of events captures

> surface disturbances, crests of foam that the tides of history carry on their strong backs. A history of brief, rapid, nervous fluctuations, by definition ultra-sensitive; the least tremor sets all its antennae quivering. But as such it is the most exciting of all, the richest in human interest, and also the most dangerous. We must learn to distrust this history with its still burning passions, as it was felt, described, and lived by contemporaries whose lives were as short and as short-sighted as ours.

To these analytically discrete histories correspond different temporalities: 'geographical time, social time, and individual time' (Braudel 1972a: 20–21). Space and time are correlated: the smaller the unit of analysis, the more time accelerates. Braudel's study is structured by these three levels of reality. Yet what was conceived as a heuristic device turns in the course of the book into three independent realities. Braudel thus works not with a conception of totality in which all phenomena are internally related, but with separate levels of history with their own temporalities, unfolding according to their own logics.[16] Braudel's conception of capitalism and its relation to the 'modern' state and the states-system can only be understood against this methodological background. We can then arrive at his under-standing of the dynamics that underlie and sustain this system.

There is one master-concept in Braudel's world, to which all other concepts stand in a dependent relation: world-economy. It is defined as 'an economically autonomous section of the planet able to provide for most of its own needs, a section to which its internal links and exchanges give a certain organic unity' (Braudel 1984: 22; see also Braudel 1977: 81–2).[17] In contrast to world-empires, it consists of a multiplicity of independent polities that are externally linked by trade, yet are at the same time tightly locked into a geopolitical system. It consists of a prosperous core with a dominant city, a subservient semi-periphery, and a dependent and backward periphery. A strict hierarchy relates these components, based on economic asymmetries arising from a mostly stable international division of labour and reproduced by unequal exchange and terms of trade politically manipulated by the privileged core countries.

Built into this hierarchical world-economy based on an international division of labour is a theory of the state. A state's form and strength stands in direct relation to its position in the world-economy:

> At the center of the world-economy, one always finds an exceptional state, strong, aggressive and privileged, dynamic, simultaneously feared and admired. In the fifteenth century it was Venice; in the seventeenth, Holland; in the eighteenth and still in the nineteenth, it was Britain; today it is the United States. (Braudel 1984: 51)

In the semi-periphery, as in absolutist France, the strength of the state is hampered by internal competition between the monarchy and the nobility. The colonial peripheries were governed from the metropolitan centres. However, not only does the form of the state follow from the exigencies of trade, the very relations of production and the status of the producer are a function of the structural location of each country in the exchange system:

> Every task, once allocated in the international division of labour, created its own form of control and that control articulated and governed the form taken by society. . . . In every case, society was responding to a different economic obligation and found itself caught by its very adaptation, incapable of escaping quickly from these structures once they had been created. (Braudel 1984: 62)

Wage-labour, share cropping, and serfdom and slavery correspond to the core, the semi-periphery, and the periphery.

Paradoxically, in spite of this rigid allocation of roles in the labour process and the forms of statehood, an enormous dynamic pervades the history of European-dominated world-economies. World-historical progress is conceived by Braudel in terms of a clear-cut succession of world-economies with ever more powerful world-cities at the centre commanding ever greater spheres of influence and rearranging the respective constellations between core, semi-periphery, and periphery. Braudel locates the beginnings of this sequence (in contrast to Wallerstein, who opts for the 'long sixteenth century') in the European thirteenth, if not eleventh century, which witnessed the growth of a town-centred trading network linking the Italian city-states and the northern European towns and city-leagues (Braudel 1984: 92).

Braudel explains the origins of and transitions between town-centred world-economies as follows: 'This break with the past appears as the result of an accumulation of accidents, breakdowns and distortions' (Braudel 1984: 85).[18] Hesitatingly, Braudel tries to understand the rise and fall of world-economies in the context of wider secular trends, such as the dominant neo-Malthusian one governing price movements and income distribution (Braudel 1984: 78–81). However, his discussion of the origins of world-economies and the mechanisms behind their shifts remains inconclusive. No general correlations are established and we are forced to turn to the contingent processes of causation Braudel provides in the narrative sections of his *opus magnum* devoted to each world-economy. However, even if we follow the crisis model of demographic fluctuations, Braudel is at a loss to specify why a particular country assumed the leading position in a restructured world-economy at a particular point in time. Transitions are conceived in evolutionary terms in which the same principles of an international division of labour, labour regimes, and corresponding state forms reappear on an ever-increasing scale. What changes – more or less accidentally – is the dominant actor at the centre of the world-economy which distributes political and economic attributes to all other actors in the system. We are left with a quantitative and evolutionary model of large-scale social change, based on a systemic, deterministic, economistic, and functionalist theory of economic and political development.

Why is Braudel led to advance such a sweeping conception? I contend that his theory is predicated upon an erroneous and fundamentally ahistorical conception of capitalism. His narrative fails to offer a consistent working definition of capitalism. Instead, we have a series of impressionistic insights resulting eventually in a conceptual distinction between capitalism and the market economy. Whereas the latter refers to the competitive sector of small-scale production, capitalism itself is equated with 'big business' and monopolies (Braudel 1984: 629; 1977: ch. 2 and 113–15). Market economies stand for local, transparent, equal exchanges in a marketplace based on competitive bargaining. The term capitalism is reserved for the privileged, hierarchical, secluded, long-distance sphere of merchant capitalism proper. This form of commercial 'monopoly-capital-ism' is the unifying and driving principle of Braudel's entire narrative. Here, the author conflates the distinction between contemporary private market monopolies, which are economic and not political monopolies, and pre-capitalist politically constituted trading monopolies. As long as the latter are discernible, capitalism, in Braudel's sense, exists. It is this political definition of capitalism that allows Braudel to bring the state back into the picture.

Whether we look at the medieval Flemish cities, the Hanseatic League, Venice, Holland, Great Britain, or the United States, his world-economies are invariably capitalist in so far as they exploit state-constituted monopolistic trade advantages vis-à-vis their semi-peripheries and peripheries. The only notable distinction within and among these centres is between city-based versus national market-based world-economies, a difference whose implications remain underexplored (Braudel 1977: 95ff). It is then not surprising to read that:

> I have argued that capitalism has been potentially visible since the dawn of history, and that it has developed and perpetuated itself down the ages. . . . Far in advance, there were signs announcing the coming of capitalism: the rise of the towns and of trade, the emergence of a labour market, the increasing density of society, the spread of the use of money, the rise in output, the expansion of long-distance trade or to put it another way the international market. (Braudel 1984: 620)

This statement squares with Braudel's conviction that there have always been world-economies, which, in turn, ties in with his conception of *'la longue durée'*, of which capitalism appears as one emanation. But because nothing ever really changes in the rise and fall of world-economies, Braudel remains a prisoner of his own system. 'Slavery, serfdom and wage-labour are historically and socially different solutions to a universal problem, which remains fundamentally the same' (Braudel 1984: 63).[19]

Excursus – Giovanni Arrighi: Westphalia under Dutch Hegemony

Let us now see how a more recent, modified version of the Braudel–Wallerstein model understands the Westphalian order. Giovanni Arrighi's account of the Peace of Westphalia is embedded in a wider Braudelian–Gramscian theory of the development of the modern capitalist world-economy. He starts from the assumption that the cycle of capital accumulation operative at the micro-level of the firm (MCM') can be transposed to the macro-level of the international system in order to explain the dynamic behind a series of hegemonic cycles of international capital accumulation (Arrighi 1994: 6–9).

The basic logic of these successive cycles can be summarized as follows. The rise of a hegemon is bound up with technological and organizational innovations, prompting a phase of material expansion. Inter-capitalist competition and declining returns, coupled with the catching-up of rivalling powers, lead to a displacement of the centre of accumulation to finance, prompting a phase of financial expansion. This constitutes a shift from fixed productive capital to flexible financial capital. The exhaustion of this second phase of capital accumulation and the rise of a rival leads to systemic crises, which are resolved by hegemonic war. The new hegemon successfully restructures its mode of production and administration. A new cycle of hegemonic expansion and capital accumulation sets in. Four systemic cycles of hegemonic accumulation span modern history, each defining a 'long century' and changing the structure of international relations:

> A Genoese cycle, from the fifteenth to the early seventeenth centuries; a Dutch cycle, from the late sixteenth century throughout most of the eighteenth century; a British cycle, from the latter half of the eighteenth century through the early twentieth century; and a US cycle, which began in the late nineteenth century and has continued into the current phase of financial expansion. (Arrighi 1994: 6)

This scheme rests on the distinct Braudelian definition of capitalism. Capitalism does not refer to a specific relation of production between capital and wage-labour, but to the 'top layer of the hierarchy of the world of trade' – a monopolistic 'anti-market' – from which a 'middle layer of the market economy' and the 'bottom layer of material life' are distinguished (Arrighi 1994: 24). Capitalism proper denotes exclusively the former. This notion of capitalism is understood to require state power (a fusion of state and capital), so that the concentration, accumulation, and expansion of capital are mediated by inter-state competition for mobile capital. The expansion of capital is thus a political and geopolitical process; it implies the restructuring of the states-system by a capitalist hegemon, a bloc of governmental and business organizations. From this perspective, 'the really important transition that needs to be elucidated is not that from feudalism to capitalism but from scattered to concentrated capitalist power' (Arrighi 1994: 11). While this account evokes a Weberian notion of the state as a 'power-container', the precondition for successful capitalist expansion, it also introduces the Gramscian idea of hegemonic power, echoing Neorealist Hegemonic Stability Theory.

Each international system is thus not simply structured by inter-state competition for mobile capital; each requires a 'world hegemon', which defines the rules of international conduct, order, and co-operation. Hegemonic systemic cycles of accumulation are not simply defined by the rise and decline of states within an invariant states-system; the very organizational structure, mode of operation, and geographical scope of the system are restructured under the aegis of each new hegemonic leader. Hegemony, in the Gramscian sense, implies not simply coercion, but leadership of 'the system of states in a desired direction', so as to pursue a perceived 'general interest', both among domestic subjects and among a group of states (Arrighi 1994: 29).

While Arrighi's account is open to many fundamental objections – his definition of capitalism; his prioritization of the logic of circulation in abstraction from the logic of production; his failure to theorize technological innovation in relation to production, to relate social change to class conflict, and to explore the domestic causes of hegemonic rise and decline; his bias towards the pre-British international system with respect to the alleged hegemonic role of oligarchic merchant republics rather than dynastic-absolutist states – his attempt to explain the Westphalian moment fails even on its own terms.

While the alleged hegemonic role of the Italian city-states, supervising a proto-capitalist world-system, is already qualified by Arrighi's admission that it remained 'enmeshed' in a medieval feudal world and 'never attempted individually or collectively a purposive transformation of the medieval system of rule', the United Provinces were able to 'transform the European system of rule to suit the requirements of the accumulation of capital on a world scale' (Arrighi 1994: 39–40).

> It was under these circumstances [the intensification of the European power struggle between France and the Habsburg Imperial House] that the United Provinces became hegemonic by leading a large and powerful coalition of dynastic states towards the liquidation of the medieval system of rule and the establishment of the modern inter-state system. . . . This reorganization of political space in the interest of capital accumulation marks the birth not just of the modern inter-state system, but also of capitalism as world system. (Arrighi 1994: 43–4)

This account is questionable. First of all, to what extent was the Thirty Years' War a hegemonic war? Its depiction as ushering in the decline of one hegemon – the Italian city-states – and the rise of another – the Dutch Provinces – obscures the much more obvious struggle between two blocs of territorial-absolutist states, among which France emerged victorious: the mixed-confessional alliance of France, Sweden, and the Protestant German Estates versus the Austrian-Spanish Habsburgs and the Catholic German Estates. The story of Dutch independence was minor next to the conflicts which restructured relations between the German Empire, France, the House of Habsburg, and Sweden.

To what extent did Holland succeed in consciously managing the transition from 'systemic chaos' to 'ordered anarchy', so as to become world-hegemonic? While the Dutch Provinces achieved independence, it does not follow that they achieved hegemony in Arrighi's sense, imposing a new mode of international organization and governance. By Arrighi's own admission, 'The Dutch never governed the system they had created. As soon as the Westphalia System was in place, the United Provinces began losing its recently acquired world-power status' (Arrighi 1994: 47). The series of post-Westphalian Anglo-Dutch commercial wars and Louis XIV's repeated attempts to conquer Holland undermine Arrighi's characterization of seventeenth-century Holland. If France and England failed to subjugate the Dutch, Holland certainly failed to impose its ascribed world-hegemony on them. The two dominant post-Westphalian powers were rather France and Sweden, who supervised the treaty provisions as quasi-hegemonic guaranteeing powers (*Garantiemächte*).

Finally, to what degree was Holland's rise bound up with innovations in the field of production and organization, Arrighi's first phase of material expansion? As Arrighi explains, Holland emerged as a European power not so much because of innovations in production as because of its ability to monopolize the carrying trade in the Atlantic and the Baltic, establishing itself as a major entrepôt (Arrighi 1994: 133ff). In this sense, Holland's rise was predicated less on internal productive innovations than on commercial profit-taking. The organizational advantages which Arrighi adduces – military reforms – testify not so much to Holland's rise as a capitalist power as to its ability to turn trading profits into military innovations, protecting and reproducing its control over the circuits of seaborne long-distance trade. This political response was prompted by the logic of geopolitical accumulation pursued by its territorializing dynastic-absolutist neighbours. Holland's post-Westphalian hegemony, in short, is an illusion. It neither restructured nor dominated international relations, nor did it alter the age-old commercial logic of unequal exchange sustained by military power.

2. A Critique of the Commercialization Model

The underlying inadequacies of the Braudel–Wallerstein model emerge most clearly when we try to understand the relation between capitalism, the modern state, the modern states-system, and social change. First, its account of the onset of capitalism and the modern state – its causes and timing – is inherently indeterminate. Wallerstein traces the origins of capitalism back to the 'long sixteenth century', which opened up intercontinental trade between Europe and the rest of the world – a necessary answer to the feudal crisis of the fourteenth century (Wallerstein 1974, 1979, 1980).[20] But precisely because Wallerstein refrains from specifying the nature and internal antagonisms of feudalism, his explanation rests on nothing more than a *post hoc ergo propter hoc* argument: the existence of commercial expansion does not explain its causal necessity for resolving the crisis (Brenner 1977). Furthermore, nothing in this perspective prevents us from identifying the origins of capitalism in the emergence of trading cities, usually with reference to the fourteenth-century Italian Renaissance city-states (Arrighi 1994); the commercial revival of medieval cities in the thirteenth and twelfth centuries (Braudel 1984: 92; Mann 1986, 1988b); the establishment of an intercontinental exchange system between India–Arabia and Europe during the same period (Abu-Lughod 1989); or, indeed, in trading relations between ancient Greece, Persia, and China (Wallerstein 1974: 16). *Capitalism in this sense becomes timeless* (Braudel 1984: 620), prompting speculations on its 5,000-year history (Frank and Gills 1993). If capitalism is understood as production for and exchange on the market with a view to accumulating profits in the process of exchange, then it is timeless not only with respect to the past, but potentially also with respect to the future. Neorealism's transhistorical assumption of anarchy is paralleled by a transhistorical assumption of capitalism. The crucial historical question is then not the transition from feudalism to capitalism, but, again in the words of Arrighi, the transition 'from scattered to concentrated capitalist power' (Arrighi 1994: 11). In other words, capitalism is not regarded as a qualitative, potentially reversible transformation of social relations, but simply a gradual quantitative expansion of the market since time immemorial.[21]

If capitalism is timeless, how, then, does it relate to the historically and chronologically specific onset of modern state formation? Since this disjuncture between an eternal capitalism and relatively late modern state formation creates theoretical problems, we could, of course, simply deny a causal nexus between the two phenomena – an option taken by scholars of various persuasions – or argue that capitalism acquires its dynamic, expansive character only once it is embedded in and managed by modern states – an option associated with Weber's idea of 'political capitalism', Braudel's idea of leading capitalist cities/states, and Arrighi's idea of a capitalist hegemon (Braudel 1984; Arrighi 1994). A third option, regularly adopted by world-systems theorists, consists in antedating the rise of the modern state to the 'proto-modern' Italian city-states. All three options are, however, problematic.

In fact, the Braudel–Wallerstein school has no theory of the specifically modern state at all; it only has a theory of differential power capacities of political communities within the world-system, in generic contrast to earlier world-empires in which bureaucracies absorbed surpluses so as to stifle world trade (Wallerstein 1974, 1980). In the Wallersteinian scheme, the form of the state is essentially a function of the timing of its incorporation into the international division of labour, which determines which regions specialize in what. This trade-dependent specialization in turn determines the 'regime of labour control' in the process of production, i.e., slavery, serfdom, or free wage-labour. A 'strong' state is associated with the capitalist core of the world-system, a 'weaker' state with the semi-periphery, and a 'weak' state with the periphery. Thus, a world-economy is politically structured by an international order divided into three zones of unequally powerful states. Without repeating the empirical objections that have been raised against this trade-dependent distribution of state power, we can note that neither Wallerstein nor Braudel recognize at any point the emergence of a *distinctly modern state*. Their concept of the state is as undifferentiated as their idea of capitalism (for critiques of Wallerstein's state theory, see Brenner 1977: 63–7; Gourevitch 1978b; Zolberg 1981; Imbusch 1990: 49–57; Skocpol 1994).

The Braudel–Wallerstein tradition further ignores the constitutive role of class conflict and revolution in historical development. While this may be advantageous from a non-Marxist point of view, it poses the problem of how to incorporate social conflict and socio-political crisis into the historical and theoretical equation. The standard response among world-systems theorists is either to omit the problem of class entirely (Arrighi 1994), or to give it a subsidiary and dependent role. In this case, the structure of class relations in the process of production becomes a function of a specific region's role in the international division of labour, determined by the timing of its integration into the world-economy (Wallerstein 1974, 1980, 1995).

Finally, the circulation paradigm cannot explain why it is that powerful indicators of the 'growth of the West' appeared first in northwestern Europe, and specifically in early modern England. While the great secular Malthusian fluctuations in the agrarian economy persisted in continental Europe well after the seventeenth-century crisis, England saw sustained economic, productivity, and population growth, as well as permanent technological innovation. The advocates of the circulation paradigm must eventually square their undifferentiated history of capitalism with the particular history of the emergence of economic, technological, and demographic growth. For these reasons, it is useful to see how capitalism understood as the 'logic of production' deals with these problems.

5. Capitalism, the Modern State, and the Modern States-System: Solutions and Problems

1. Capitalism as a Relation of Production

The puzzle that has now to be addressed is how an alternative conception of capitalism (a) explains the dynamic phenomena that we associate with capitalist economies (sustained economic growth, capital accumulation, technological innovation, and demographic growth); (b) accounts for the emergence and constitution of the modern state, based on the differentiation between a public state and a private market/civil society; (c) captures social crises, fundamental institutional ruptures, and large-scale transformations; (d) specifies the chronological and geographical origins of capitalism; and (e) illuminates the relation between capitalism and the modern states-system. The thesis I want to defend is that sustained economic growth, technological innovation, and demographic growth cannot be dissociated from the rise of capitalism. However, capitalism is not simply understood as an economic category but as a social property regime internally related to a specific form of political authority: the modern state. Again, everything depends on how we define not only modernity, but also capitalism.

Two dominant conceptions of capitalism can be distinguished in the literature. The first, derived from the Braudel–Wallerstein tradition, defines capitalism as an economic system of production for the market predicated on an advanced division of labour within and between centres of commercial production (towns), allowing for the accumulation of profits through inter-urban long-distance trade. Capitalism resides here in the 'logic of circulation' or in the *political relations of distribution* (Braudel 1977 and 1984;

Wallerstein 1979, 1995; Sweezy 1976; Abu-Lughod 1989; Arrighi 1994). The second defines capitalism as a social system based on a specific set of social property relations in which direct producers are separated from their means of subsistence, forced to reproduce themselves in the market by selling labour power as a commodity to the owners of the means of production to make a living. Profits are generated through the exploitation of labour power by siphoning off surplus value in the process of production itself. Capitalism resides here in the 'logic of production' or in the *social relations of exploitation* (Dobb 1976; Merrington 1976; Brenner 1977, 1985b, 1986; Wolf 1982; Comninel 1987; McNally 1988; Katz 1989, 1993; Gerstenberger 1990; Mooers 1991; Wood 1991, 1995c; Rosenberg 1994; Van der Pijl 1997; Harvey 2001).

The defenders of both conceptions claim to follow Marx's usage of the term. Yet while the production paradigm is held to be Marx's original contribution to the critique of classical political economy, the circulation paradigm has a longer pedigree that can be traced back to Adam Smith and is also compatible with Weberian understandings of capitalism. To put it in ideal-typical terms, while the production paradigm presupposes an objective set of social property relations as the necessary social and historical condition for capital accumulation and sustained economic growth, the circulation paradigm presupposes a (naturalized) subjective profit motive. Here, the profit motive entails rational economic action, specialization, and the division of labour once the 'artificial' impediments for its full flowering – be they cultural, religious, or military-political – are removed. The premise is that individuals will pursue market opportunities when left alone (Wood 2002). This conception of capitalism is clearly wedded to the utilitarianism that underlies the *homo oeconomicus* of neoclassical economics and projects specifically capitalist forms of subjectivity back on to the pre-capitalist past. The implications of these two meanings of capitalism are, however, not confined to Marxological disputes over the correct reading of his writings. They touch on the question of modern state formation, the significance of class conflict and revolutions in history, the origins, dynamics, and crisis character of capitalism, and the possibility of formulating strategies for its transcendence. In short, they have profound implications for understanding long-term historical development.

The definition of capitalism in terms of 'the logic of production' adopted here has been most powerfully and originally elaborated by Robert Brenner in a series of articles and a major historiographical monograph (Brenner 1977, 1985b, 1986, 1989, 1993). It can be summarized as follows. Capitalism denotes a social system predicated on determinate social property relations between direct producers, who have lost unmediated access to their means of subsistence and become subjected to market imperatives, and non-producers, who have come to own the means of production. This process of dispossession involves the qualitative transformation of essentially pre-capitalist social property relations into capitalist property relations. Once a capitalist property regime is established, specific and objective (meaning not subjectively motivated or intended) rules of reproduction and economic action follow on both sides of the labour process.[22]

On the side of producers, separation from the means of subsistence turns direct producers into 'free' labourers, compelled to reproduce themselves in and through the market. The commodification of labour-power, the establishment of a 'free' labour market, personal freedom (though not necessarily political rights and enfranchisement), and direct economic dependence on the imperatives of the market are four aspects of one and the same process.

On the side of capitalists, since direct producers are no longer coerced by extra-economic means to hand over a part of their surplus to, rent out from, or work for a lord – since workers are politically free – their reproduction also comes to depend on the market. The capital relation leads to a series of interconnected dynamics. The deployment of capital for production for the market implies inter-capitalist competition, regulated by the 'invisible hand' of the price mechanism, which tends to impose downward pressure on commodity prices. Capitalist survival (production 'at the socially necessary rate', i.e., maximizing the price–cost ratio) and expanded reproduction (the raising of additional income/capital accumulation) in the market require expanding the range of products (specialization), intensifying the division of labour, and underpricing competitors, which in turn requires reducing production costs. From this perspective, profit maximization is not a natural, subjective attribute of a timeless *homo oeconomicus*; it is an objective function of specific social relations mediated by private property. Cost-cutting takes the form either of lowering wages – a tendency assisted by competition among workers to sell themselves on the market – intensifying labour, or replacing wage-labour by technology. Technological rationalization in turn requires constant competitive reinvestment into production, driving a tendency towards technological innovation. A theory of technological progress is thus built into capitalist relations of production. This tendency towards productive reinvestment is also promoted by the fact that non-producers are no longer required to divert surpluses into the means of violence and conspicuous consumption, as under feudalism and absolutism. The transfer of surplus no longer involves direct physical coercion and the concomitant build-up of a privately owned and economically unproductive apparatus of violence. Simultaneously, productive reinvestment entails a systematic tendency to increase labour productivity by replacing 'absolute surplus labour' with 'relative surplus labour', and, everything else being equal, a decrease in commodity prices. As a rule, these processes drive economic development and growth, while pre-capitalist, neo-Malthusian limits on population growth are suspended. This definition does not, of course, imply that capitalism is a crisis-resistant economic system, or that political strategies cannot support or restrain its development. But it does imply that the capitalist market is qualitatively different from all other forms of production, distribution, circulation, and consumption.

These interconnected processes tend to generate economic and demographic growth, technological development, specialization, product diversification, and the territorial expansion of market relations (though not *eo ipso* capitalist property relations). Crucially, this interpretation of capitalism requires a historical account of the origins of capitalist relations of production. The development of capitalism is thus not to be sought in the geographic and quantitative expansion of more or less ubiquitous market exchange based upon fluctuations in the division of labour, but demands an account of the regionally specific transformation of social property relations in the transition from feudalism/absolutism to capitalism.[23] But since, as was shown in chapter 2, feudal social property relations determined rules for reproduction among lords and peasants that reproduced, rather than dissolved, the feudal system, the question of this transformation becomes the central problematique for theorizing long-term economic and political development. This also means that the whole complex of class conflict, socio-political crises, and revolutions remains decisively within its theoretical ambit. In sum, capitalism is based on and reproduces a series of constitutive contradictions (labour–capital, capital–capital) that lend the system a historically unprecedented and unique long-term dynamic. How this system emerged historically, rather than how it functions once it is in place, will be explored in chapter 8.

2. Capitalism and the Modern State

This conception of capitalism also entails a theory of the modern state (Sayer 1985; Wood 1991, 1995a; Brenner 1993; Rosenberg 1994, 123–58; Bromley 1995, 1999). For if the transition from a pre-capitalist to a capitalist property regime engenders a shift from a regime of political extraction (extra-economic coercion) to physically non-coercive exploitation, then we have identified the operative principle which underlies the differentiation between the political and the economic. Since ruling-class power in capitalist societies resides in ownership of and control over the means of production, 'the state' no longer needs to interfere directly in the processes of production and extraction. It can confine itself to maintaining the property regime and legally enforcing civil contracts among politically (though not economically) equal citizens. The modern state institutionalizes a private property regime in the form of a set of subjective private rights. While this basic function does not, of course, exhaust the historical role of the state, it establishes the link between capitalist property relations and the separation of a non-coercive 'economic economy' from a 'political state', which maintains the monopoly over the means of violence. State and market become two structurally differentiated, though internally related, spheres.[24]

Capitalist property relations are thus the condition of possibility for the appearance (in both senses) of a self-regulating market in which the anarchy of decentralized, individual decisions regarding production, consumption, and the allocation of resources is, in principle, governed by the price mechanism. Money (capital) replaces power as the dominant regulatory mechanism, the main form of intersubjectivity and co-ordination among individuals. This separation is, at the same time, the unacknowledged starting point for classical political economy as a separate discipline. Similarly, the abstract bourgeois individual now appears in utilitarian social philosophy and liberal political theory as the fictional individual in a pre-social state of nature who contracts to maximize utility and security.

This theoretical nexus also explains the necessary but absent social preconditions for Max Weber's typological definition of the modern state. Weber not only maintained, as Realists like to point out, that the modern state is 'a human community that (successfully) claims the *monopoly of the legitimate use of physical force* within a given territory' (Weber 1946: 78), but asserted that the separation of officials from the previously private means of administration is a social prerequisite for modern – impartial, independent, rational – bureaucracy (Weber 1968a). While Weber maintains that the conflicts over this separation were fought out under geopolitical pressure between centralizing kings and particularizing patrimonial officers (rulers and their staff) (Weber 1968a: 1086, 1103), the deeper preconditions for the state's withdrawal from direct economic exploitation (tax-farming etc.) cannot be understood on the basis of social domination and administration or geopolitical rivalry alone. Rather, the depoliticization and depersonalization of economic extraction and the pooling of political power in the sovereign state were bound up with the transformation of social property relations. The separation of the 'staff' from their private means of administration and exploitation was the obverse side of the commodification of labour. Politically enforced exploitation of the direct producer, which required either the fragmentation of politico-military powers under feudalism (the serf–lord relation mediated by rents) or centralized but still privatized rights of coercion under absolutism (the free peasant–venal patrimonial officer relation mediated by taxes), could be abandoned in favour of an impersonal tax-collecting bureaucracy – the backbone of the modern state. This left profit accumulation in the private economy intact. At the same time, public monopolization of the means of violence no longer served directly extractive purposes, but guaranteed the internal and external defence of law and order. Since the moment of exploitation travels under capitalism from the public to the private, the state appears now either as the Leviathan – the pure embodiment of power – or as the public locus of the general or universal will, that may even allow for liberal democracy. Henceforth, workers and capitalists appear as politically equal citizens, while remaining economically divided as bourgeois and proletarian.

This nexus also enables us to see why the ruling class does not rule directly in capitalist societies. While pre-capitalist societies exhibit an immediate identity between the personnel of the 'state' and the ruling classes – lords in feudal polities, the monarchy and a patrimonial nobility in absolutist states, a commercial oligarchy in merchant republics – this identity is no longer necessary in capitalist states. While the propertied classes did, of course, set up the first modern parliament in England during the English Revolution, maintaining legislation and the budget under direct ruling-class control, the enforcement of law and order could be left to an 'impartial' bureaucracy, separated from the means of administration and thus dependent on public salaries. Thus, a specific state form is internally related to capitalism as a social property relation: modern sovereignty.

3. Capitalism and the Modern States-System

While this analysis may explain the specific institutional form of the modern state, it can neither explain its territorially bounded nature, nor illuminate why capitalism exists in a system of states, a political pluriverse. If capitalism had developed within the framework of a universal empire, it is hard to see why it would have caused its break-up into multiple territorial units. In other words, there is no constitutive or genetic link between capitalism and a geopolitical pluriverse.

If capitalism and a system of states are not genetically co-constitutive and co-emergent, and if capitalism did not develop simultaneously in all early modern European states, what was the relation between capitalism and the states-system? This question points to a radically different reconstruction of the origins and development of modern international relations that is not premised on the assumption of a single structural break between feudal and modern geopolitics, while also rejecting the epochal importance of the Westphalian settlement of 1648. The argument that will be developed in chapter 8 is that capitalism developed first as the unintended consequence of class conflicts between the peasantry, the aristocracy, and the king in early modern England as each class tried to reproduce itself along customary lines. The seventeenth-century constitution of a specifically modern state/society complex 'in one country' in the context of an overwhelmingly absolutist states-system set in motion a long period of geopolitically combined but socially uneven European development, resulting in the gradual, crisis-ridden internationalization of the British state/society complex. While this process saw a series of changes in property regimes and political regimes, it did not transcend or negate the territorially divided nature of political authority in Europe. Its outcome was a universal system of territorially divided modern states, shadowed by a transnational world market. But it is precisely this constellation that may today be under attack.

Thus, the rise of capitalism was a phenomenon neither of the Italian Renaissance city-states nor of the trans-European 'long sixteenth century'; nor can the process of 'primitive accumulation' be broken down into a cumulative 'value-adding' sequence of nationally confined leading economies, as Perry Anderson argues (Anderson 1993). It was unique to early modern England (Brenner 1993; Wood 1991, 1996).[25] At the same time, the absence of capitalist social property regimes in early modern continental Europe implies *eo ipso* the absence of the modern state. Thus, the dynamics behind commercialization and war-driven state-centralization failed to produce the modern state and, by extension, the modern states-system. To this extent, the commercialization and geopolitical competition models present theories of *non*-transition to modernity. The formation of a territorially fragmented states-system preceded the onset of capitalism. This system was socio-economically and (geo)politically distinctly pre-modern, since its constitutive units were predominantly dynastic states and, to a lesser degree, oligarchic merchant republics. This pre-modern international order was precisely IR's Westphalian system.

However, maintaining that a states-system preceded the rise of capitalism does not imply that the formation of the European pre-capitalist states-system is not amenable to a Marxist interpretation. It rather means that the pressures towards the replacement of fragmented feudal polities by territorially more consolidated dynastic states were bound up with persisting non-capitalist social property relations, which necessitated strategies of (geo)political accumulation as well as peasant repression and exploitation. While the logic of political accumulation hardened European political space into a pre-modern states-system, the rise of capitalism in seventeenth-century England and its international repercussions occurred in an already established, dynastic-absolutist system whose 'generative grammar' and mode of operation were dramatically redefined by the geopolitically mediated spread of capitalist relations of production. *Ex hypothesis*, the arrival of modern international relations has to be theorized in terms of socially combined, geographically uneven development, which transformed European and world politics in the course of the nineteenth century.

Notes

1 For an alternative reading of such structural transformations see Colás 2002, especially ch. 2. Colás makes a case for the role of an internationalized civil society – and the class antagonisms inherent within it – in the transition towards a modern states-system.

2 The spectrum reaches from Aristide Zolberg 1980, 1981 to Charles Tilly 1992 and Michael Mann 1986.

3 While Hobson's (2002b) critique of first-wave Weberian historical sociology (Skocpol, Tilly, Mann) marks a first step in that direction, his model of structuration fails to transcend the limits of multi-causal factor analysis. A meta-theoretical critique can be found in Smith 2002.

4 While neo-Weberians rarely draw directly on Waltz, the intellectual affinity is clear. Waltz claims that all states are functionally alike because they are socialized by the pressures of geopolitical competition into the international system. This forces conflict-units over time to copy the successful practices of the leading states to reduce the power discrepancies between weak and strong states, converging in their domestic organization toward centralized governments with monopolies in the means of violence. States that fail to adapt and emulate are 'crowded out' of the system, leading to the homogenization of the units of the international system. Waltz 1979.

5 In Weber's multi-causal account of modern state formation, geopolitical competition is one factor among many. See Axtmann 1990.

6 The classical text is Schumpeter 1954. The couplet 'domain state–tax state' serves as the organizing concept for the volume on Theme B: Economic Systems and State Finance in the seven-volume edition on 'The Origins of the Modern State in Europe: 13th to 18th Centuries', edited by Wim Blockmans and Jean-Philippe Genet. 'The transition from the "domain state" to the "tax state" . . . is fiscal history's equivalent to the transition from feudalism to capitalism for economic history in general, and at times it has threatened to become the overarching theme of the book' (Bonney 1995a: 13). Compare Bonney's under-informed and dismissive remarks on Marxist understandings of state–economy relations (Bonney 1995a: 3–5). The transition from feudalism to capitalism and its implications for public finances and state formation are not mentioned again in the entire volume. I shall show in chapter 5 that the emergence of the tax state in seventeenth-century Europe has nothing to do with the emergence of capitalism or the modern state; indeed, it could be argued that the existence of a 'tax state' points precisely to the non-existence of capitalism.

7 In German parlance, this process is conceived as a transition from the feudal *Personenverbandsstaat* (state of associated persons) to the modern *institutioneller Flächenstaat* (institutionalized territorial state).

8 For a similar account, see Baechler 1995.

9 This non-differentiation flows from Mann's Weberian framework.

> Mann's classification is in need of refinement. As with Weber's typology in his sociology of domination in *Economy and Society*, it is constructed by focusing on the interaction of elite groups and neglecting the social relationships of the ruled among themselves and with these elite groups. . . . Mann's typology, which is built around different types of elite relations, would therefore have to be expanded to include differing types of class relations as well. (Axtmann 1993: 25–6)

10 In true Weberian–Hintzean style, the rise and fall of the Carolingian Empire is presented by Ertman purely in terms of the modalities of government and administration. Peasants and conflicts over sources of income do not appear (Ertman 1997: 39–48).

11 The social meaning of war is here and there acknowledged in fleeting comments in the Weber–Hintze literature, but it is not systematically theorized as arising out of distinct social property relations which made it an economic necessity, rather than the sport of princes. Cf., e.g.:

> As for the question of the acquisition of territorial rights, it was settled by combining the hereditary principle with an appropriate matrimonial policy. When succession disputes arose, armed force was usually the final means of action. Spending on external security by monarchical states should, therefore, be at least partly regarded as an investment for the acquisition of rights of domination, at least when war was followed by territorial aggrandizement. (Körner 1995a: 404)

12 For example, how can we explain that England, although it could nominally
   draw on a much smaller tax base during the Hundred Years' War, for
   centuries dominated France, with twice its size and three times its population? And how can we explain, short of having recourse to notions of
   military genius and historical contingency, that the Dutch Provinces freed
   themselves from the 'Spanish Yoke' and resisted repeated French bids for
   incorporation, despite their inferior natural resources and population?

13 Tilly distinguishes between three modes of state formation. In the *coercion-
   intensive mode*, the resource-seeking state had to build massive authoritarian
   structures to extract revenues from populations in non-commercialized
   agrarian economies. Russia, Prussia, and the Ottoman Empire serve as
   examples. In the *capital-intensive mode*, rulers formed alliances with commercial urban oligarchies, trading state protection against capital resources in
   market-orientated and monetized economies, leading to republican forms of
   government. Venice, the Netherlands, and northern Italy fit this category.
   In the *capitalized-coercion mode*, rulers struck a balance between capital and
   coercion, incorporating commercial classes into the state apparatus, while
   overall monarchical power remained unchallenged. England, France, Spain,
   and (later) Prussia are subsumed under this mode. This last type outper-
   formed competing states through a combination of a high concentration of
   military power and a high degree of mobilizing commercial interests. While
   this typology is flawed on empirical grounds, these variations in state modes
   are a result of inter-elite relations, excluding wider class relations. Whereas
   Tilly devoted in 1975 two and a half pages to the 'peasant base', the
   peasantry later drops out of the picture (Tilly 1992; see also Mann 1986,
   1988a; Ormrod 1995: 157–8; Bulst 1996; Reinhard 1996a, 1999). Ertman
   classifies eighteenth-century states according to how they combined regime
   types, determined by the locus of legislative power (absolutist or constitutional), with types of state infrastructure, determined by the nature of
   administration (patrimonial or bureaucratic). This results in a fourfold
   classification of state types: patrimonial-absolutist (France, Spain, Portugal,
   Tuscany, Naples, Savoy, the Papal States), bureaucratic-absolutist (the
   German principalities, Denmark), patrimonial-constitutional (Poland, Hungary), and bureaucratic-constitutional (Britain, Sweden). Three factors
   explain these differences. The first is the organization of local government
   after the collapse of the Carolingian Empire. The second is the timing of
   states' exposure to sustained geopolitical competition. The third is the
   independent influence of representative assemblies in constitutional regimes.
   The character of the representative assemblies that emerged in the twelfth
   and thirteenth centuries determined whether states developed in an absolutist
   or constitutional direction. Drawing on Otto Hintze, Ertman suggests that
   the uneven experience of Dark Age state-building generated feudal fragmentation and tricurial representative institutions in the Carolingian successor
   states (Latin Europe and Germany). Three-chamber houses were divided
   along the lines of functional status groups, creating disunity among them-

selves that weakened their structural bargaining position against absolutist rulers. On the fringes of the defunct Empire (England, Scotland, Scandinavia, Poland, Hungary), cohesive co-operative, and participatory self-government developed at county level, giving rise to bicurial representative assemblies. Two-chamber houses were not organized along functional but territorial lines, rooted in strong local self-government. The peripheral, bicurial regions were better placed to resist the development of absolutism, clearing the way for constitutionalism, whereas the tricurial regions failed to formulate and implement territory-wide anti-absolutist programmes. Next, whether constitutional and absolutist states developed patrimonial or bureaucratic administrative infrastructures depends, according to Ertmann, on the timing of their respective encounter with intensified military competition and the influence of national parliaments. In tricurial-absolutist states that experienced early geopolitical pressure (France), patrimonialism developed. In bicurial-constitutional states with early geopolitical pressures (England), proto-bureaucracies developed, because Parliament could resist patrimonialism. In tricurial-absolutist states with late geopolitical pressures (Germany, Prussia), proto-bureaucracies developed, because they learned from the early developers' mistakes and could borrow from their institutional successes. In bicurial-constitutional states with late geopolitical pressures (Hungary, Poland), patrimonialism developed, because ruling elites were entrenched in powerful national parliaments. The minimum that is required, but not provided, for an adequate explanation of these divergences is the decoding of geopolitical pressure as a social praxis among the pre-capitalist ruling classes and a sociological analysis of the social composition of different national parliaments that reflected specific and different proprietary interests among its members.

14 Bonney's assertion that 'it was the interaction of the state's demands with harvest fluctuations which determined the real fiscal burden carried by the majority of taxpayers' is symptomatic of the non-recognition of the peasantry as a social actor in the institutionalist literature (Bonney 1995a: 17–18). Whereas harvests are of course the 'natural', though eco-demographically mediated, condition for any dues, the social determination of the level of taxation was a result of the conflicts between those who imposed taxes and those who had to pay them. Although Bonney later tries to repoliticize taxation – 'If regional fiscal divisions were in large measure a question of privilege then we should not expect any clear relationship between economic wealth and fiscal burden' (Bonney 1995b: 501) – the conflict over the tax rate goes on between the ruler and the taxpayers.

15 A notable exception is Winfried Schulze. Although he also introduces the Schumpeterian couplet in passing, he then approvingly cites Marc Bloch on the social rationale behind royal *Bauernschutzpolitik* (policy of peasant protection). 'We may interpret this trend towards protection of the peasantry by the state as a "struggle between taxes and rents". This perspective has the advantage of linking the tensions between princes and their estates, between peasants and their landlords and between peasants and princes, various aspects

of which may be seen at work in the frequent rebellions against taxation' (Schulze 1995: 264).

16 While Pierre Vilar appreciates Braudel's emphasis on the 'deep structure of geography and nature', he makes the crucial objection: 'To think history geographically is not therefore contrary to Marxism. It would, however, be more Marxist to think geography historically' (Vilar 1973: 9).

17 The term was first introduced in Braudel 1972a: 387. '*Weltwirtschaft*, a world-economy, a self-contained universe. No strict and authoritarian order was established, but the outlines of a coherent pattern can be discerned. All world-economies for instance recognize a centre, some focal point that acts as a stimulus to other regions and is essential to the existence of the economic unit as a whole.'

18 'In the economic poker game, some people have always held better cards than others, not to say aces up their sleeves' (Braudel 1984: 48; see also Braudel 1977: 86).

19 For the argument that capitalism, beyond quantitative expansion, remained essentially unaltered, see Braudel 1977: 111–12.

20 'By a series of accidents – historical, ecological, geographic – northwest Europe was better situated in the sixteenth century to diversify its agricultural specialization and add to it certain industries', establishing itself as the core area of the modern, capitalist world-economy with tenancy and wage-labour as the modes of labour control (Braudel 1984: 18).

21 Robert Brenner criticized these accounts as 'neo-Smithean' since they assumed the very thing that had to be explained – namely, how the capitalist social property relations that drove a process of sustained economic growth actually emerged (Brenner 1977).

22 Brenner does not dispute that Adam Smith described correctly *how* modern economic growth functions but that he failed to specify *whether* and *under what conditions* sustained economic development actually occurs.

23 While Karl Polanyi also insists on the distinctiveness of capitalism as a social system, he attributes its origins to technological development *per se* – 'the machine' (Polanyi 1957).

24 This account of capitalist state-market relations does not preclude different degrees of intervention by the state into the economy, as the history of capitalist state-forms – liberal, imperialist, corporatist, welfare, neo-liberal – demonstrates. Furthermore, it implies no claims about the extent and form of the capitalist state's influence on economy and society, its relative autonomy, or the determination of policy-formation. It rather provides a specific understanding of the separation between, but internal unity of, politics and economics as a result of the commodification of labour and the creation of a private propery regime.

25 On the Dutch case, see Brenner 2001. While agrarian capitalist social property relations did emerge in some regions of Holland, their success remained dependent on the wider demand and supply patterns of pre-capitalist Europe.

5

L'État, c'est moi!:

The Logic of Absolutist State Formation

1. Introduction: Idealizing Absolutism

The analytical exposition of the relation between capitalism and the modern state is incomplete without a historical account of their combined emergence. Far from being simultaneous and system-wide, this was a regionally and temporally highly specific, though not contingent, process. But since the regional specificity of economic and political development is central for understanding the making of the modern states–system, we have to pursue the divergent trajectories of state formation in France and England to show that the assumption in IR and historical sociology of one medieval-to-modern shift is inadequate. The following chapters reconstruct this transition by further pursuing the diverging patterns of state formation in France and England. Contrary to conventional assumptions, I show how this divergence led to two very different international orders, the absolutist and the modern, which require two very different accounts of geopolitical systemic change – transition one from feudalism to absolutism in France and transition two from feudalism to capitalism in England. But since these transitions occurred simultaneously and not successively, I also show how the international coexistence of diverse political regimes combined to determine international relations in the Westphalian system and how it affected the transition to modern international relations. As a result, the standard IR account of Westphalia's modernity is radically rejected and revised.

What was the nature of the dominant early modern state form: absolutism? This chapter rectifies a fundamental error in the IR literature, which tends to equate absolutist sovereignty with modern sovereignty. Theoretically, IR's misconception and misperiodization of the Westphalian order rests on an idealization of early modern royal sovereignty and absolutist bureaucracy. Methodologically, this misinterpretation arises from four related tendencies. First, as a rule, in its preoccupation with the external marks of sovereignty, international relations are usually theorized in abstraction from the internal constitution of the units of geopolitical systems. In other words, the historically diverse nature of political communities is generally undertheorized and underdifferentiated. Second, if the concept of 'the state' is problematized in IR, its identity is generally understood in institutional, static, comparative terms. Third, to the degree that Max Weber's definition of the modern state is invoked to establish the identity of historically variable polities, it tends to be mistakenly projected on to differently structured pasts. Finally, theories of early modern international relations have generally drawn on the traditional interpretation of absolutism developed in the historiographical literature, and its ill-understood Weberian notions of state rationalization and bureaucratic centralization. This literature is today widely contested, if not simply outdated.

Section 2 provides a brief survey of the traditional historical-sociological state-centred interpretation of absolutism, which underwrites IR's standard account of the modernity of Westphalian international relations. This survey is followed by a short critique of the society-centred revisionist literature and a critical exposition of the Marxist debate on absolutism. Section 3 provides a reconstruction of the origins, nature, and long-term trajectory of the absolutist state. It explores the transition from feudalism to absolutism in early modern France and clarifies the meaning of proprietary kingship for the personalized nature of absolutist sovereignty. It then turns to the structure of absolutist rule, including office venality, the persistence of independent political centres of power, the logic of legislation, taxation, and fiscal crises, and the nature of the absolutist military and early modern warfare.

The conclusion summarizes the thesis that absolutist sovereignty was neither absolute nor modern, but defined by proprietary kingship. Given the nexus between a non-capitalist agrarian economy and a parasitic patrimonial state apparatus, the long-term trajectory of *Ancien Régime* France was politically crisis-ridden and economically self-exhausting. This explains both the bellicose nature of absolutism and the comparative military disadvantage it started to suffer during the eighteenth century, especially against Britain. The absolutist state was not only distinctively non-modern, it was not even transitional. The internal dynamic of absolutist class relations was a developmental dead end. Under these conditions, the origins of international modernity have to be sought in the rise of the first modern state, seventeenth-century England, which, driven by an

expanding capitalist economy, began to undermine the politically accumulative logic of the continental absolutist system in the eighteenth century,
and imposed its new capitalist logic in the course of the nineteenth and
early twentieth centuries. It was these processes that transformed the logic
of the absolutist system into the modern international order.

2. Debating Absolutism: Transition or Non-Transition?

Over the past three decades, the historiography of absolutism has seen an
important debate on the 'absoluteness' of royal government in relation to
political society. This debate opposed the defenders of an older, state-
centred orthodoxy against the followers – Marxist and non-Marxist alike –
of a revisionist strand determined to expose its limits.[1] Although the debate
covers all European political regimes, it came to focus on France, the
classical model of absolutist state formation. This is not simply because the
Bourbon state exemplified in ideal-typical form a general European
phenomenon. In some European polities, say, the Dutch General Estates,
England, Switzerland, or Poland – for reasons having to do with specific
resolutions of preceding class conflicts on the basis of different social
property relations – absolutism never took hold. Even those polities
conventionally taken to be absolutist – Spain, Austria, Russia, Prussia,
Sweden, or Denmark – had very different chronologies, dynamics, and
characteristics, although the differences between, for example, French
mercantilism and Prussian cameralism, are smaller than their commonalities
compared to what came before or after. However, if ever a state 'progressed
towards modernity' through a combination of state rationalization, a critical
discourse of Enlightenment, and a great revolution, it must have been
France. Or did it?

1. The Traditional State-Centred Interpretation:
the State as Rational Actor

The traditional interpretation starts from the assumption that from the
sixteenth century onwards the pressures of intensified geopolitical conflict
and the domestic turmoil associated with confessional disputes led to the
concentration of political, legislative, judicial, financial, economic, and
military decision-making powers in the monarch.[2] The state arrondized,
consolidated, and centralized its territory by systematically developing a

network of public institutions operated by loyal bureaucrats. Under the whip of external defence and demand for internal supra-confessional pacification, the king was progressively able to side-step the consultation and consent of intermediary powers and to arrogate 'legislative sovereignty', expressed in the formula *princeps legibus (ab)solutus*. His position beyond the law went hand in hand with a growing juridification and rationalization of what now came to be distinguished as the public and private spheres. The replacement of multiple and overlapping feudal rights and privileges by a centralized legal system emanating from the King's Council was mirrored by the monopolization of taxation, requiring the development of an officer class dependent upon the king. Powerful but revocable agents of the king, the *intendants*, carried his will into the provinces. The new service nobility, the *noblesse de robe*, staffed with literate burghers and clerics deriving their title from office, arose against the old sword-carrying nobility, the *noblesse d'épée*, which derived its titles from inheritance and landed property.

State economic development policies took shape in the form of mercantilism. State agencies improved national infrastructures, pressed for common weights and measures, supported manufacture and foreign trade, dismantled and replaced the mass of internal tariff barriers and the medieval toll system with a single customs unit, and introduced a common coinage to increase the wealth of the state. Economic planning created a unified internal market, while the pursuit of a positive national balance of trade geared external trade to the hoarding of bullion and treasure.

Informal mechanisms of domestic domination and conflict resolution (feuds) were replaced by institutionalized contracts and rules, based on positive legal principles. Older customary and contractual forms of state power among lords gave way to an impersonal state over and above its subjects, legitimized by Roman law. A distinct sphere of politics came to be distinguished from civil society. A new discourse of secular sovereignty, exemplified by Jean Bodin's *Six livres sur la république*, supplanted medieval lore of divine kingship, vassalage, the code of chivalry, and societal orders. The medieval conflation of public law and penal law gave way to the distinction between public international law and private criminal law: a police force started to discipline the non-noble population, while noble resistance became illegal. Feuds were criminalized as disobedience and rebellion, falling under the ultimate crime of treason, *lèse majesté*. Defiant nobles became enemies of the state.

At the same time, feudal forms of military organization based on the summons of the feudal host and the *arrière-ban* were supplanted during the 'Military Revolution' by the demilitarization of the nobility and the creation of standing armies (the *miles perpetuus*) under royal control, while state investments in military technology (artillery, warships, and fortifications) rendered feudal tactics obsolete. Foreign policy came to be an exclusive monarchical prerogative – the *arcana imperii* – in the name of *raison d'État*, while *ad hoc* diplomatic missions were replaced by permanent embassies, enjoying immunity under the new principle of extra-territoriality. The royal monopolization of the means of violence underwrote the transition from the late medieval *ius gentium* to the *ius inter gentes* and subsequently to the French-dominated *droit public de l'Europe*, transforming medieval hierarchy or heterogeneity into an 'anarchical' geopolitical order of legally equal states.

In theory, absolutist rule 'resided in the undivided and unlimited authority of an individual, who, as legislator, was not bound by the laws, who was independent of all control, and who exercised sovereignty without consulting any groups or institutions except those created by himself' (Vierhaus 1988: 113).[3] The Sun King, Louis XIV, came to embody the radiant omnipotence of absolute monarchy epitomized in his claim (ascribed or authentic) that '*L'État, c'est moi!*', while drawing an increasingly ornamental aristocracy into the artificial, baroque, purely ceremonial lifestyle of Versailles court society. In practice, it is maintained that the outcomes of the seventeenth-century struggles 'represented the conclusive establishment of the structure that is recognisable as the modern state, organized around an impersonal, centralized, and unifying system of government, resting on law, bureaucracy, and force' (Rabb 1975: 72). In sum, the 'state' is seen as the essential 'modernizer' of a society internally torn by conflicts among status groups and externally under threat of invasion.

It is this orthodox view of early modern politics, idealizing the rationality of absolutist public institutions while minimizing their differences from the modern state, which has informed the prevailing consensus within the discipline of IR: the mid-seventeenth-century Treaties of Westphalia perfected the architecture of European politics by laying down the rules of modern international relations for what were essentially modern states.

2. The Revisionist 'Society-Centred' Critique

Objections to the gradualist institutional account soon crystallized into a distinct revisionist literature, inspired by Roland Mousnier's concept of a society of orders (Mousnier 1979, 1984).[4] Empirically, it was pointed out that absolutist office venality, clientage, legal non-uniformity, tax-farming, mercenarism, and a host of cognate phenomena contradict the idea of a smooth progression towards the bureaucratic rationality of the modern state. This failure is held to be bound up with the lack of an inquiry into *Ancien Régime* France as a society of orders, comprising traditional interest groups competing over status and position. Institutional setbacks in the completion of the modern state were thus not temporary disturbances, but expressed the structural factional interests of political society opposed to the modernizing ambitions of the monarchy.

Yet while the non-Marxist revisionist literature – *Annalistes* and new institutionalists alike – persuasively unmasks the confirmationist bias towards the state perfection of the institutionalist literature, in many ways it only reverses its premises. While the old institutionalist account regards the state as the active, rational actor and society as a recalcitrant, irrational mass of particular interests, the revisionists maintain that the centre of *Ancien Régime* power is to be sought in 'society', which held the 'state' hostage to its particularistic interests. William Beik sums up this position:

> Thus historians have moved from viewing the state as a triumphant organizer of society to viewing it as a fragile organism struggling against a vast, turbulent society, and finally to the realization that forces in society were influencing, if not defining the very function of the state. The existence of these forces does not necessarily negate the state's progressive role, but it does call for a reassessment of the way distinctive early modern institutions interacted with a distinctive early modern society. (Beik 1985: 17)

While the burden of causality now rests on 'society', the basic premise that early modern state and society can be meaningfully theorized as two distinct and autonomous entities pursuing antagonistic interests was not abandoned. Whereas formerly, a modernizing state struggled victoriously against a recalcitrant society, now a backward-looking society frustrated the modernizing ambitions of the state. The idea that a common set of interests between privileged orders and the Crown may have created a field of compatibility of interests among the ruling classes, uniting them against the peasantry and thus reproducing a pre-modern state form, is excluded from the first. But while the ruling classes were united vis-à-vis the peasantry, they were divided over the distribution of peasant-produced tax proceeds. Thus, since political power remained personalized and shared between the monarchy and the privileged classes, the state–society dyad cannot be meaningfully employed for *Ancien Régime* France.

3. The Orthodox Marxist Interpretation: The 'Equilibrist–Transitional Paradigm'

Marxist authors most successfully attacked the view that the absolutist state could be conceptualized as something outside of and distinct from society, pursuing its own goals while disciplining society. Paradoxically, however, such interpretations of absolutism were long marred by the orthodox and formulaic stagist philosophy of history driven by a succession of ascending classes. On this view, codified in the *Communist Manifesto* (Marx and Engels 1998), the new progressive class, the bourgeoisie, developed gradually in the womb of the old order, overthrowing it in an abrupt revolutionary climax. The Age of Absolutism is taken as an object of research only in its preparatory role for the French Revolution, rather than treated as a social formation in its own right. The teleological theme becomes the 'transition to capitalism', and the genesis of its historical agent – the bourgeoisie – its fulcrum. While the state–society dyad is replaced by class analysis, it is determined by the rise of capitalism within the framework of the *Ancien Régime*. While neither Marx nor Engels ever put forward a systematic study of absolutism, the classical Marxist interpretation was canonized by Engels's famous statement that the absolutist monarchy 'held the balance between the nobility and the burghers', gaining autonomy from both classes until the bourgeoisie pushed through the integument of the old order (Engels 1876: 271).[5] In this 'equilibrist–transitional' perspective, the rise of capitalism was the outcome of the growth of a bourgeoisie whose interests were promoted and instrumentalized by the monarchy in order to counterbalance the reactionary particularistic interests of the landed nobility, until the monarchy was finally overthrown in a cataclysmic denouement by that class whose aspirations it helped to unleash.

This interpretation of absolutism is also supported by the fact that serfdom was dead in France after the fourteenth-century crisis. If feudalism is defined in terms of the lord-serf relations, post-fourteenth-century – not to speak of post-seventeenth-century – French society cannot qualify as feudal. More specifically, if feudalism is defined by serfdom and if capitalism is defined by wage-labour – both non-existent in early modern France – then the four centuries between the late fourteenth century and 1789 could only qualify as a long period of transition. The growth of urban mercantile activity, the monetarization of rural rents, and the general spread of commercialization and commodification support this interpretation.

These themes inform Boris Porchnev's and A.D. Lublinskaya's refinements of the equilibrist–transitional paradigm. Porchnev argues that the monarchy, under pressure from peasant rebellion, co-opted a capitalist bourgeoisie into the state by means of office venality, checking the reactionary aristocracy while preventing an alliance between the peasantry and the bourgeoisie (Porchnev 1963). Lublinskaya, in turn, argues for an equilibrium between an independent commercial and industrial capitalist bourgeoisie, supported by the monarchy, and a reactionary but unified sword and robe nobility (Lublinskaya 1968, 1980). Irrespective of the merits and problems of these two approaches, both authors fail to transcend the classical Marxist 'equilibrist–transitional paradigm'.

Excursus – Perry Anderson's Subterranean Transition to Capitalism

Rejecting the equilibrist interpretation, Perry Anderson's brilliant but not unproblematic synoptic account develops the transitional theme and its associated class relations. Anderson squarely identifies the absolutist state as feudal since it defended the interests of the old medieval aristocracy (Anderson 1974b: 428, 41–2). Starting from the observation that absolutist monarchies were 'exotic, hybrid compositions whose surface "modernity" again and again betrays a subterranean archaism' (Anderson 1974b: 29), he convincingly shows the non-modern nature of absolutist institutions – the army, bureaucracy, taxation, trade, diplomacy – by suggesting that the end of feudalism in its narrow sense, i.e., serfdom, was not tantamount to the disappearance of feudal relations of production (Anderson 1974b: 17). However, the dissolution of serfdom did end the unity of politics and economics – economic exploitation through politico-legal coercion – at the molecular level of the village, which defined parcellized feudal sovereignty as distributed in a hierarchical chain of inter-lordly relations. In its stead, on the instigation of an old noble class threatened with ruin, this cellular unity of extra-economic coercion was re-established on a national scale in the form of the absolutist state. 'The result was a displacement of politico-legal coercion upwards towards a centralized, militarized summit – the Absolutist State' (Anderson 1974b: 19). Localized, individualized feudal rents were replaced by centralized feudal rents in the guise of royal taxation:

> Absolutism was essentially just this: *a redeployed and recharged apparatus of feudal domination*, designed to clamp the peasant masses back into their traditional social position – despite and against the gains they had won by the widespread commutation of dues. In other words, the Absolutist State was never an arbiter between the aristocracy and the bourgeoisie, still less

an instrument of the nascent bourgeoisie against the aristocracy: it was the
new political carapace of a threatened nobility. (Anderson 1974b: 18)

While the mode of political organization had changed, the ruling class,
according to Anderson, remained the same – the feudal nobility supported
by the centralized power of the new state apparatus.

Yet, despite acknowledging the persistence of a pre-capitalist mode of
exploitation, Anderson nevertheless argues for a long transition to capitalism. His argument revolves around two axes. First, in the countryside, the
concentration of political power at the apex of the social system, mediated
by the commutation of labour rents into money rents, was complemented
by the *economic* consolidation of feudal property. Feudal conditional property gave way to exclusive private titles, aided by the reception of Roman
law. 'Landownership tended to become progressively less "conditional" as
sovereignty became correspondingly more "absolute"' (Anderson 1974b:
20). The creation of a land market fulfilled an essential condition for
establishing capitalist agriculture (Anderson 1974b: 424–6). Second, in the
towns, the same Roman civil law notion of quiritary ownership, rediscov-
ered by royal legists in order to defend the reconsolidation of feudal class
power on more centralized principles, was seized upon by the urban
bourgeoisie as the legal expression of free capital. Roman law, and
especially its differentiation between civil and public law, had the unintended effect of providing a legal idiom for the interests of the mercantile
bourgeoisie, a code of law and procedure, which guaranteed the security
of private property and contractual transactions (certainty, clarity, uniformity) (Anderson 1974b: 26):

> For the apparent paradox of Absolutism in Western Europe was that it
> fundamentally represented an apparatus for the protection of aristocratic
> property and privileges, yet at the same time the means whereby this
> protection was promoted could *simultaneously* ensure the basic interests of
> the nascent mercantile and manufacturing classes. (Anderson 1974b: 40)

Yet Anderson's analysis of absolutist France is not a self-enclosed case
study; it is embedded in a wider comparative history of uneven development. Again, the ultimate research-organizing question revolves around
the uniqueness of the 'West' and, in particular, the specificity of those
long-term conditions that were conducive to the rise of capitalism in
Europe. Here, the classical Marxist notion of world history as a simple
temporal sequence of modes of production (following the logic of replacement) is rejected in favour of, as Hegelians would put it, the dialectical
logic of 'sublation' (*Aufhebung* in its triple meaning[6]); the traces of the past

are abolished only to be preserved in a qualitatively transformed higher synthesis: 'The course towards capitalism reveals a *remanence* of the legacy of one mode of production within an epoch *dominated* by another, and a *reactivation* of its spell in the passage to a third' (Anderson 1974b: 421). More concretely, 'the *concatenation* of the ancient and feudal modes of production was necessary to yield the capitalist mode of production – a relationship that was not merely one of diachronic sequence, but also at a certain stage of synchronic articulation' (Anderson 1974b: 422). While the survival of a dense network of urban enclaves and the lingering memory of Roman law and rational forms of Roman modes of thought comprise the capitalism-assisting legacy of antiquity, the feudal fief – unknown outside Europe except in Japan – prefigured as a unit of economic exploitation the material matrix of capitalist private property in land. Absolutism was its period of incubation. Thus,

> in nature and structure, the Absolute monarchies of Europe were still feudal states: the machinery of rule of the same aristocratic class that had dominated the Middle Ages. But in Western Europe where they were born, the *social formations* which they governed were a complex combi-nation of *feudal and capitalist modes of production*, with a gradually rising urban bourgeoisie and a growing primitive accumulation of capital, on an international scale. It was the intertwining of these two antagonistic modes of production within single societies that gave rise to the transitional forms of Absolutism. (Anderson 1974b: 428–9)

In sum, for Anderson, absolutism resulted from a rallying of noble class power after the end of serfdom in the form of a centralized state. This state took over the formerly localized functions of extra-economic coercion on a national scale to the benefit of the nobility. The institutional innovations – unearthing the achievements of antiquity – which accompanied the new centralized mode of extraction, in conjunction with the spread of commo-dification and exchange, inadvertently created the conditions for private property and the rise of a capitalist bourgeoisie. In the transition from feudalism to capitalism, absolutism was a crucial step in a 'value-added' process (Anderson 1993: 17).[7] While the final clash between a rising bourgeoisie and a declining aristocracy was postponed until the bourgeois revolution proper, capitalism developed silently, even subterraneously.

There are, however, empirical and theoretical problems with Anderson's account of the rise, nature, and dynamics of French absolutism. It is doubtful that absolutism was ever actively pursued in the interest of, or was ultimately beneficial to, the old feudal class. Even if the old nobility survived within the absolutist state, its survival and functions cannot be derived from an original set of pre-fourteenth-century-crisis noble prefer- ences. The absolutist state and its 'centralized rent' was not the functional equivalent of local noble powers of exploitation. As we have seen, the crisis of the fourteenth century saw the monarchy side repeatedly with the peasantry against the old medieval nobility (Brenner 1985b: 288–9). Nobility and monarchy had clearly competing interests in the exploitation of the peasantry. The struggle between a feudal rent regime and an absolutist tax regime was ultimately decided against the interests and to the detriment of the old medieval nobility. Anderson's thesis that 'throughout the early modern epoch, the dominant class – economically and politically – was thus the *same* as in the medieval epoch itself: the feudal aristocracy' (Anderson 1974b: 18, see also 430) underestimates the changed class basis of the early modern nobility as well as the active role of the monarchy. Not only was there very little intergenerational continuity within the aristocracy between the fourteenth and seventeenth centuries, the very class basis of the medieval nobility was eroded and redefined in this process. The class that collected public taxes was not the same as the class that had reaped feudal rents.

Most importantly, while the aristocracy retained its land, it lost its political powers of representation. In other words, it was no longer the ruling class in the strict sense of the term. Nothing exemplifies the relative decline of the old nobility better than the non-convocation of the Estates General between the late sixteenth and the late eighteenth centuries.[8] This loss of political power translated into the sphere of international relations, where the arrogation of foreign policy by the king undermined the independent war-making capacities of the old nobility. While the majority of the *noblesse d'épée* had lost their arms-bearing status, the real beneficiary of the rise of absolutism was a new, state-sponsored, patrimonial officer class, the *noblesse de robe*. Its interests were directly bound up with the crown, imposing a qualitatively different dynamic of inter-ruling-class relations on French society as a whole.

Anderson's insistence on the persistence of the old feudal ruling class leads him to underestimate the transformations of inter-ruling-class rela- tions, i.e., the tensions between the monarchy, the sword-carrying nobility and the office-holding nobility, and thus the contradictions of absolutist sovereignty. On the one hand, centralized rents as the operative mechanism of surplus extraction clearly subordinated the nobility to the distributive favours of the monarchy. At the same time, public taxes and the royal monopolization of the means of violence elevated the dynastic principle to

the core of absolutist sovereignty and the cornerstone of early modern
international relations. Dynastic diplomacy was not the 'index of feudal
dominance' (Anderson 1974b: 39), but a sign of its relative decline. On the
other hand, while Anderson's discussion of office venality clearly shows the
limits of state rationalization, he fails to draw the more radical conclusion
that the privatization of offices implied a renewed tendency towards
decentralization. While Anderson is right to say that 'landownership tended
to become progressively less "conditional" as sovereignty became correspondingly more "absolute"' (Anderson 1974b: 20), the absolutization of
sovereignty was precisely reversed through the sale of offices. Domestically
it entailed a de-uniformization of legislation, taxation, and adjudication.
Venality, patronage, and corruption undermined legal clarity, certainty, and
uniformity.

Office venality not only blocked internal state sovereignty, it also tended
to divert urban and mercantile capital into state-constituted sources of
income – the purchase of sinecures, company charters, or loans to the
Crown. The monarchy thus became indebted to a growing parasitic officer
class, financiers, tax farmers, and mercantile adventurers, who tried to
recoup their public investments by exploiting their privately owned state-
granted titles to income. The net effect was a symbiotic and parasitic inter-
ruling-class relation between the monarchy, the *noblesse de robe*, financiers,
and town oligarchs that stalled any transition to capitalism. In this respect,
the 'lucrative if risky investments in public finance for usury capital'
connected with *rentier* sinecures in the royal bureaucracy, monopoly trading
charters, and colonial enterprises, did not 'accomplish certain partial functions in the *primitive accumulation* necessary for the eventual triumph of the
capitalist mode of production itself' (Anderson 1974b: 40). Rather, as will
be shown later, they represented speculative forays into state-backed forms
of political accumulation, which tied burghers to a Crown dispensing
official and commercial titles. While it is correct to say that 'economic
centralization, protectionism and overseas expansion aggrandized the late
feudal state while they profited the early bourgeoisie' (Anderson 1974b:
41), this bourgeoisie did not thereby become a *capitalist* bourgeoisie.

Anderson repeatedly insinuates that the consolidation of private property
as well as the commodification and commercialization of town and country
life acted as a condition for the rise of capitalism.

The maxim of *superficies solo cedit* – single and unconditional ownership of
land – now for the second time became an operative principle in agrarian
property (if by no means yet the dominant one), precisely because of the

spread of commodity relations in the countryside that was to define the long transition from feudalism to capitalism in the West. (Anderson 1974b: 26)[9]

Yet, although it is true that the commutation of labour rents into money rents turned the lordly domain into an economic estate which could be bought and sold, direct producers continued to possess their customary plots as *de facto* property. The implication for smallholders was that they were, as Anderson affirms at one point (Anderson 1974b: 17), not formally subsumed under capital, i.e., economically compelled to rent from or work for a landlord. Peasants reproduced themselves outside the market. Thus, while lordly estates became 'allodialized' (turned into absolute private property), neither landlords nor peasants had much incentive to consolidate their plots and estates, introduce novel farming techniques, or specialize. Investments were limited and did not follow the logic of economic production at a competitive rate because rural labour was not yet generally commodified, i.e., proletarianized. The introduction of Roman quiritary ownership, which allowed the contractual transfer of property, did not consolidate an agrarian capitalist regime of production. Antiquity was not a necessary condition for the rise of capitalism. In other words, Anderson does not show how his two conflicting claims – viz. that rural labour remained independent and that economic life was generally commodified – can be reconciled. In spite of the Althusserian idiom of 'articulation' and 'over-determination', Anderson fails to show how the 'feudal mode of production' and the 'capitalist mode of production' were actually, as he has it, 'intertwined'.

Relatedly, Anderson's treatment of the role of medieval towns is ambiguous. He starts off by noting that towns were internal to feudalism, since the parcellization of sovereignty allowed a decisive degree of political independence for urban communes (Anderson 1974b: 21). This is offered against those who argue in the Transition Debate, like Paul Sweezy, for the external dissolution of feudalism through the growth of towns and long-distance trade (Sweezy, Dobb et al. 1976). At the same time, according to Anderson, municipal political autonomy allowed towns to develop into centres of production – rather than remain parasitic centres of administration, distribution, and consumption, as in the Roman Empire and in non-Western agrarian empires – establishing 'a dynamic *opposition* between town and country' (Anderson 1974b: 422). In the long run, this led to the subordination of the country to the town, i.e., commercial production for urban markets. Thus the decentralized political structure of

feudalism was decisive for the town's eventual economic subordination of
the agrarian economy. This account not only assumes that medieval
burghers were either proto-capitalists from the beginning or evolved into
an urban bourgeoisie, it rests too on a misreading of John Merrington's
important work on medieval towns (Anderson 1974b: 21).[10] Although
Merrington stresses the political independence of medieval towns based on
feudal political decentralization, which were thus both internal and external
to feudalism, he also argues for their economic dependence on the demand
and supply generated by the countryside (Merrington 1976: 177–80).
Hence, although medieval towns evinced a political 'internal externality',
they were also economically internal to feudalism. The growth of exchange
and markets did not, according to Merrington, change this (Merrington
1976: 178).[11] Thus, even if one does not share Merrington's conclusion
that there was no dynamic opposition between pre-capitalist towns and
pre-capitalist agriculture, Anderson would have to demonstrate that the
dependency of towns upon the agrarian economy was reversed.

Finally, Anderson ends his introductory chapter with a short preview of
the 'bourgeois revolutions' and the establishment of capitalist economies
and states. Although the actual exposition of these themes belongs to the
projected third volume of his trilogy, he extends the logic of his earlier
argument to the revolutionary period: 'The rule of the absolutist state was
that of the feudal nobility in the epoch of transition to capitalism. Its end
would signal the crisis of the power of its class: the advent of the bourgeois
revolutions, and the emergence of the capitalist state' (Anderson 1974b:
42).[12] Without wanting to hold Anderson too closely to these preliminary
hypotheses, it should be remarked that powerful interpretations have
meanwhile appeared that cast considerable doubt on even an updated
reformulation of the classical Marxist social interpretation of the French
Revolution. George Comninel especially, supported by the recent wave of
revisionist literature on 1789, concludes (1) that the Revolution was not so
much a struggle between a rising bourgeoisie and a declining aristocracy as
the outcome of a dissatisfied patrimonial class, both nobles and bourgeois,
fighting for a greater share in the state's extractive capacities, and (2) that
the Revolution itself did not create a capitalist society, but rather further
entrenched petty peasant property while redistributing state offices to a
non-capitalist bourgeoisie (Comninel 1987: 179–207).

Thus, while Anderson clearly shows the non-capitalist character of the
early modern French state, and while he rejects the equilibrist interpretation, he still clings to the Marxist orthodoxy that the rise of capitalism was
the historical task of the bourgeoisie, which, assisted by the spread of

market opportunities and the revival of Roman law, developed in the interstices of the old feudal order. In this, Anderson and the old equilibrist–transitional interpretation parallel the modernizing bias of institutionalists, for whom the absolutist state acted as the unwitting midwife of the bourgeoisie.

To sum up, the 'equilibrist–transitional' interpretation of absolutism faces insuperable obstacles (Merrington 1976; Skocpol 1979: 51–67; Beik 1985; Comninel 1987; Parker 1996). First, the peasantry remained in direct possession of its means of subsistence throughout the early modern period. Second, mercantile activities did not create *eo ipso* a capitalist bourgeoisie, since the growth of trade did not act as a solvent of feudalism. Third, class relations between the bourgeoisie and the aristocracy were not fundamentally antagonistic, since both shared the same proprietary relation to the extra-economic means of exploitation. Fourth, the absolutist state remained patrimonial, absorbing a non-capitalist bourgeoisie and a defeudalized aristocracy through the sale of offices, trading charters, and other privileges. Fifth, the main axis of intra-ruling-class conflict – of which 1789 was a constitutive part – was not between a rising capitalist bourgeoisie and a declining aristocracy, but rather between a dissatisfied state-dependent class and the Crown. Finally, the Revolution itself neither created a capitalist economy nor a capitalist state, but rather further entrenched petty peasant property while redistributing state offices in favour of a non-capitalist bourgeoisie.

But if absolutism was neither a story of modern state-building, nor a society of orders which obstructed its modernizing ambitions, nor an arbiter between the aristocracy and the bourgeoisie, nor yet an instrument of the old aristocracy against the peasantry, 'overdetermined' by the rise of a capitalist bourgeoisie, what was it?

4. Political Marxists and the Critique of the 'Bourgeois Paradigm'

An answer to this question first requires a theoretical clarification. The orthodox Marxist theorem of the necessary co-development of a bourgeois class and capitalism has come under heavy attack from within the Marxist tradition on empirical as well as theoretical grounds. Marx and Engels failed to adequately theorize absolutism and the French Revolution because they uncritically accepted the liberal theory of bourgeois revolution in their early works (Beik 1985: 21; Comninel 1987: 53–76, 104–78; Brenner

1989; Parker 1996: 14).[13] Comninel and Brenner argue that much orthodox Marxist interpretation of the rise of capitalism remained under the
spell of the young Marx's adoption of a materialist, but distinctly liberal,
conception of general historical progress. This generates two opposing
narratives of the transition to capitalism in Marx's writings.

Scottish classical political economy and nineteenth-century French liberal restoration historiography significantly influenced the first interpretation, expounded in Marx's writings of the 1840s and early 1850s. Marx's
early writings attribute the rise of a capitalist bourgeoisie to the expansion
of market relations resulting from an increasing division of labour based on
the development of the forces of production in towns. The driving class
antagonism is identified between an urban class of burghers (which transformed itself into a capitalist bourgeoisie) and a reactionary, land-based
feudal aristocracy. While classical political economy revolved around the
idea of a 'natural' expansion of free-market relations, i.e., economic
liberalism, French liberal restoration historiography embraced the idea of
history as class struggle whose *terminus ad quem* was political liberalism.
Both traditions converged *au fond* in a liberal materialist conception of
historical progress, comprising a stagist theory of history.

The second interpretation, expounded in Marx's mature critique of
political economy in *Capital* and the *Grundrisse*, revolves around pre-
capitalist class relations between direct producers and lords. This conflict
gave rise to 'primitive accumulation', separating the direct producer from
his means of subsistence while subjecting him to the power of capital. In
this version, the *movens* of historical development lies not in the resolution
of class conflicts between the aristocracy and the bourgeoisie so much as
between the exploiters and the exploited, lords and peasants. It was the
historically unique resolution of these class conflicts that first established
capitalist relations of production in the English agrarian economy in the
course of the sixteenth and seventeenth centuries.

With the canonization of the first interpretation in the *German Ideology*
and the *Communist Manifesto*, much subsequent Marxist interpretation of
absolutism, the origins of capitalism, and the French and English Revolutions remained a prisoner of what Ellen Wood calls the 'bourgeois
paradigm', which posits that capitalism and the bourgeoisie are indissoluble
(Wood 1991: 2–11). In this perspective, the rise of capitalism can be found
in every early modern European country with cities and commerce. The
origins of this dilemma reach directly back to Marx and Engels's subsumption of France and England under one type of development: 'Generally
speaking, for the economic development of the bourgeoisie, England is

here taken as the typical country; for its political development, France'
(Marx and Engels 1998: 37). This abstract universal schema, culled from
the conflation of two very different national experiences and imposed on
other national developmental courses, leads to distorted and ahistorical
interpretations.

Brenner and Comninel argue that dissociating the bourgeoisie and
capitalism does not foreclose the possibility of a Marxist interpretation of
the crisis of the *Ancien Régime* and the transition to capitalism in both
England and France. With respect to early modern France, both base their
analysis on the rise of centralized extra-economic coercion on the basis of
a petty peasant property regime (Comninel 1987; Brenner 1985b: 288–91).
With respect to England, Brenner shows how capitalism resulted from class
conflicts in the countryside between direct producers and lords prior to the
English Civil War and the English Revolutions, which are consequently
reinterpreted as a struggle between a capitalist landed aristocracy and a
reactionary class alliance between the Crown and chartered merchants over
the form of the English state (Brenner 1993).[14] While they advance
powerful interpretations of the English and French Revolutions, they argue
that both were the result of regionally divergent trajectories of political and
economic development. On this basis, they reject the assimilation of France
and England as two variants of one path towards modernity, with the
former achieving political centralization a bit earlier while lagging behind
in economic development and the latter being economically precocious
while having to catch up politically.[15] Now, if early modern England and
France constitute structurally distinct state/society complexes and France
laid down the rules at the Westphalian settlement, what was the nature of
French absolutism?

3. The Development and Nature of French Absolutism

If the arguments of political Marxists hold, we have to show how the
French absolutist state was as structurally unable to transform itself into a
modern state as it was to unleash capitalism. Indeed, I shall argue that the
absolutist state–economy nexus not only failed to 'progress' towards political and economic modernity, but, on the contrary, imposed an economically self-undermining and politically highly divisive logic on early modern
France as a whole. The logic of French class relations resulted in the
hypertrophic growth of an ever-more parasitic and byzantine state apparatus
which weighed down the non-capitalist agrarian economy and eventually

led, under the impact of growing international competition especially from capitalist Britain, to the complete breakdown of absolutism.[16] But since this dynamic only impacted from the eighteenth century onwards and not from 1648, chapters 6 and 7 set out how long European international relations remained determined by distinctly non-modern, absolutist-dynastic forms of geopolitical interaction. Thus the beginnings of modern international relations should not be traced back to France, but are connected to a new set of pressures exerted by a qualitatively new state/society complex first achieved in England.

1. The Transition from Feudalism to Absolutism

How can we explain the fundamental bifurcation in French and English long-term patterns of social, economic, and political development? It is important here to realize that these two regions not only emerged differently from the fourteenth-century crisis, but that they already entered into it with diverging class constellations. We saw in chapter 3 that pre-crisis France experienced a gradual decline of the lords' capacity for surplus extraction, since they were caught between peasant resistance and royal support for petty peasant property. When eco-demographic crisis struck the French countryside in the fourteenth century, the seigneurial reaction failed due to the persistence of these two factors (Brenner 1985b; Root 1987). Peasants managed to consolidate their *de facto* property rights over their smallholdings, diminishing noble rights of direct extra-economic coercion. While French lords maintained *de iure* property rights, their political control over their lands was drastically reduced, especially since rents and entry fines were fixed at a low level.

As an alternative, lords turned against one another to recover income and increasingly took up 'state' offices during and after the Hundred Years' War. After the crisis, the state's extractive apparatus provided new income opportunities for a defeudalized nobility in the form of venal offices; the rational route to power, status, and wealth became ownership of a part of the state in the form of an office. Through the sale of offices the Crown 'could absorb into state offices many of those very same lords who were the casualties of the erosion of the seigneurial system' (Brenner 1985b: 289). This had the double effect of aligning noble interests with state interests and providing revenue for the Crown. And since royal office was attainable for non-noble burghers and other commoners, buying these offices was a major form of commercial investment, promising higher and more secure returns. Nobles and wealthy commoners were gradually and inextricably tied to the state apparatus. The result was the entrenchment of petty peasant property, now taxed by an increasingly centrally organized absolutist state revolving around the court, the centre of intrigue, faction, sinecure, and inter-noble rivalry. Despite recurrent waves of noble resistance, sixteenth- and seventeenth-century France saw the growing consolidation of the absolutist 'tax/office state' (Robert Brenner). This state form did not express the modern differentiation between the political and the economic, but continued the fusion of domination and exploitation characteristic of pre-capitalist societies. The general crisis accelerated the transformation of a feudal, lord–peasant rent regime into an absolutist, king–peasant tax regime. In other words, the parcellized sovereignty of medieval times, premised on private personal domination, gave way to the 'generalized personal domination' of *Ancien Régime* political authority (Gerstenberger 1990: 457–532).

After the fourteenth-century crisis, France (and much of Europe) experienced a period of economic and commercial recovery – the 'long sixteenth century'. However, this commercial upswing, the discovery of trading routes to the Americas and India, and the growth of long-distance trade was not a breakthrough to capitalism. It merely replicated, if on a larger scale, the nexus between growing noble incomes and urban revival during the twelfth century (Wolf 1982: 108–25, 130–261). As before, growing royal income was generally not reinvested in the means of production, but spent primarily on military equipment and conspicuous courtly consumption. This drove the build-up of the permanent war-state while sapping the agrarian economy. The sixteenth-century spurt of mercantile expansion was predicated on growing royal and noble demand, mediated by rising tax proceeds drawn from a demographically expanding but still pre-capitalist agrarian economy, rooted in petty peasant property. The towns were not mini-laboratories of proto-capitalism led by an entrepreneurial bourgeoisie in opposition to the king. Rather, the burghers were forced to co-operate with the king, who sold royal charters to monopoly companies, tying merchants to the king and absorbing urban elites into the state apparatus.[17] Commercial profits were reaped only in the sphere of circulation, based on unequal exchange. The exploitation of price differentials between sellers' and buyers' markets generated windfall profits. The king provided protection for overseas commerce (convoys, ports, armed merchant fleets, etc.). Buying cheap and selling dear, not free economic competition based on price competition, was the maxim of the day. As I shall show later in greater detail, out-gunning, not under-pricing, characterized the logic of the great maritime-mercantile empires. What European merchants did not do, according to Eric Wolf, was 'use their wealth as capital to acquire and transform means of production and put them in motion through the purchase of labour power offered for sale by a class of labourers' (Wolf 1982: 120). Braudel's second reincarnation and Wallerstein's first manifestation of the modern capitalist world-system remained derivative of pre-capitalist, agrarian economies.

The absolutist tax/office state failed to establish the conditions for economic take-off, instead perpetuating the logic of (geo)political accumulation. Punitive peasant taxation combined with peasant production for subsistence rather than competitive production for the market. Plots were subdivided (*morcellement*) rather than consolidated, products were diversified rather than specialized, and technology stagnated (Brenner 1985b; Parker 1996: 28–74, 212–13). Royal protection of peasant ownership prevented seigneurial attempts to enclose, consolidate, and improve farms.[18] While the customary sector was never destroyed in absolutist France, *de facto* peasant proprietorship over smallholdings and access to common lands left peasant reproduction outside the market. The attraction of local and municipal markets that provided incentives for commercial farming was time and again negated by the 'safety-first' considerations of subsistence. While peasants had to sell *on* local markets to pay taxes and levies, they were under no compulsion to systematically reproduce themselves *in* the market. The proceeds of taxation, in turn, were pumped back into the apparatus of coercion and conspicuous consumption. The general result of this social property regime was a comparatively stagnant agrarian economy, especially in terms of productivity rates, still subjected to the rhythms of eco-demographic fluctuations (Goubert 1986; Crouzet 1990; Parker 1996).

When crisis struck again in the early seventeenth century, intensified class conflict over the distribution of income led to a cycle of peasant revolt, noble unrest, and royal repression. This crisis of reproduction also explains the system-wide attempts at geopolitical accumulation in the form of the Wars of Religion and the Thirty Years' War, in which France played a leading role. Pre-capitalist France, caught between excessive taxation and spiralling military expenditures, underwent a series of fiscal crises during the course of the eighteenth century before it collapsed in the French Revolution.

2. Absolutist Sovereignty as Proprietary Kingship

What are the implications of this social property regime for absolutist sovereignty? The modern notion of sovereignty is predicated on an abstract, impersonal state, existing apart from the subjective will of its executive. The modern state endures independently of the life-spans of its representatives; it is based on the separation of public office from private property. It is through this separation that modern state territory retains its clearly demarcated boundaries irrespective of the private accumulation of bureaucrats or the political class, as was the case in pre-modern times.

This non-separation of public authority and private property not only characterized European feudalism, it persisted in most European states well into the eighteenth and nineteenth centuries, if in altered form. In absolutist states, this fusion of the public and the private can best be understood in relation to dynasticism and proprietary kingship (Rowen 1961, 1969, 1980). Proprietary kingship meant personal property of the state by the king.[19] But in what sense did the king own the state? Ownership could not refer to territory, since noble and non-noble absolute landed property was widespread and the king's private lands – the royal domain – were distinguished from non-royal lands. Furthermore, the notion of royal territory contradicted the Salic Law, which prohibited the permanent alienation of state territory (Mousnier 1979: 649–53). Territory was to be used by the king as a usufructuary and had to be passed on undiminished as dynastic patrimony. Ownership of the state, therefore, meant the legitimate and exclusive right of command within the realm and, in particular, personal ownership of the rights of taxation, trade, and legislation. '*L'État, c'est moi!*' implied royal ownership of public power – the basis of absolutist sovereignty.

How did proprietary kingship relate to developments in property relations within society? The feudal notion of kingship as overlordship rested on decentralized rights of appropriation held by lords, predicated on direct producer's possession of the means of subsistence. Lords held land on the condition of fulfilling specified military and political obligations, establishing a relation of mutuality between king and vassal (*auxilium et consilium*). Politically constituted rights of appropriation in turn entailed various degrees of personal unfreedom for the direct producer – from slavery to serfdom to other forms of bonded labour. As we have seen, even before the fourteenth-century crisis, the French peasantry had succeeded in shaking off serfdom and gaining *de facto* property rights to their plots. The

lords, in turn, while losing many political powers of seigneurial exploitation, retained property rights in their desmesnes and turned them into
landed estates, leased out to or worked by peasants paying rents, engaging
in sharecropping, or receiving wages. Yet while many peasants took
advantage of these opportunities (mainly to pay for taxes), they were not
compelled to do so, since they were not driven off their customary lands.
The conversion of lordships from political units into economic estates
undermined the conditionality of feudal property as laid down in the
vassalic contract. Noble '*dominium utile*', aided by Roman law, became
absolute private property (Rowen 1980: 29).[20] Political property as rights
of command over subjects turned into economic property over objects
(land). The king's overlordship (*dominium directum*), in which the rights of
command were dispersed among lords, became proprietary kingship, con-
centrating the powers of command and taxation in the king while exempting the nobility from taxation. The transition from a rent regime to a tax
regime allowed the king to monopolize public power in his personal
capacity. 'Feudalism involved specifically the merger of economic and
political powers; the rise of the sovereign territorial state did not destroy
this merger in the case of the dynastic monarchies but confined it
increasingly to the monarch' (Rowen 1961: 88). Absolutist sovereignty
expressed the fusion of the economic and the political in the person of the
king. Yet, while the king monopolized the rights of sovereignty, he never
actually controlled the means for its exercise.

This disjunction between rights and means pervaded the structure of
power in absolutist France. The personalized character of absolutist sovereignty left its imprint on all absolutist institutions. The following sections
show how their hybrid character, pointing towards modernity while
betraying time and again backwardness, was determined by the organizing
principle of early modern French society: the nexus between petty peasant
property, politically constituted rights of exploitation, and proprietary
kingship. The following investigation of absolutist core phenomena –
'bureaucracy', political institutions, legislation, taxation, the army – revolves
around the following questions. How 'absolute', 'modern', and 'efficient'
was absolutist rule? And to what extent did absolutist practices of rule and
economic organization stimulate a transition to modern forms of political
and geopolitical organization?

3. Office Venality as Alienation of State Property

The persisting unity of the political and the economic had direct implications for the patrimonial, non-bureaucratic character of office-holding in absolutist states. As a rule, state officers accumulated private wealth in pre-revolutionary France through privately owned public offices. Officers were never separated from their means of administration and coercion. But offices were not only privatized, they were venal. Office venality 'marked an acceptance of property in public offices below the level of kingship at the very time that jurists were striving to persuade their readers that the kingship itself was not only the highest office in the state, but also that it was not patrimonial property' (Rowen 1980: 55). In fact, Francis I institutionalized office venality by setting up the *bureau des parties casuelles* as an administrative branch officially selling royal posts. Offices could only be sold on the assumption that public power was indeed the full property of the dynasty, held not by divine grace but by right of inheritance. Not only did provinces, cities, and other corporate institutions retain powerful rights, even those royal agents operating within royal institutions usually owned their offices.

'Appropriation by virtue of leasing or sale of offices or the pledge of income from office are phenomena foreign to the pure type of bureaucracy' (Weber 1968a: 222; see also Weber 1968: 1038–9a). Against the evidence of Weber's writings, much of the literature on absolutism exaggerates the continuity between the absolutist and the modern, rationalized state by projecting Weberian notions of a modern salaried bureaucracy, separated from its means of administration, back on to the *Ancien Régime*. The anachronistic application of Weber's ideal type of rational bureaucracy to pre-revolutionary France – even, in Spruyt's case, fourteenth-century France – transforms it into a modern state.[21] However, the qualitative step towards a modern bureaucracy was never taken, precisely because the sale of offices implied a repatrimonialization – in some cases even a refeudalization – of state power. Venality included not only the sale of offices, but also the sale of honours and special privileges – the right to collect taxes, monopolize an industry, control trade, and exercise a specific profession. Private shares in public power pervaded all spheres of political society. Even the highest posts in government were exploited to accumulate private riches. Both Richelieu and Mazarin, the acclaimed masterminds behind absolutist state-making, did not pursue policies of *raison d'État*, but systematically built up their private empires within the state:

Although the idea of reason of state had begun to circulate in political pamphlets, leading political figures still acted primarily on the basis of a careful calculation of their personal interests. Both Richelieu and Mazarin exploited their own positions shamelessly. In the nine years after the Fronde Mazarin amassed one of the greatest fortunes in the history of the old regime, comprising abbeys, properties, duchies, lands in Alsace granted by the king, diamonds, claims on the throne, and cash – including large deposits near the borders of France in case he should ever have to flee again. He had also safeguarded his position among the magnates by marrying his nieces into important families. (Kaiser 1990: 82)[22]

Selling offices was one strategy of income provision pursued by a monarchy under financial duress:

> Between 1600 and 1654 some 648 million *livres* were received by the *bureau des parties casuelles*, the special treasury set up to administer revenues from office-holding. This constituted over 28 per cent of ordinary revenue of the crown for the same period. At the peak of the fiscal exploitation of office-holders (which seems to have occurred in the 1620s and 1630s), revenues from this source represented over half the ordinary revenue of the crown. (Bonney 1991: 342)

The history of French offices reflects the nexus between the ever-increasing royal demand for income and the increasing liberty and security granted to incumbents. Roughly speaking, we find the acceptance of perpetuity under Louis XI, of venality in the period between Louis XII and Francis I, and of heredity under Henry IV. 'Henry IV not only accepted – and emphasized – his own proprietorship in the state; he also gave venal office, which institutionalized government offices as private property, full legality in the French state' (Rowen 1980: 54–5). The proliferation of offices and increasing security of tenure went hand in hand with foreign wars, especially during the period of the Italian Wars and the Thirty Years' War. According to Le Roy Ladurie, the overall number of office holders in the kingdom rose from 4,041 to 46,047 between 1515 and 1665 (Ladurie 1994: 17). There was a direct correlation between the intensification of warfare and office proliferation, the pursuit of inter-national geopolitical accumulation and the domestic hollowing out of state power.[23] 'It was precisely in 1635, the year of France's entry into the war against Spain, that the sale of offices reached its highest point with a massive flooding of the market with every sort of financial and judicial office from presidents of *parlements* to sergeants and clerks in the lesser jurisdictions' (Parker 1996: 158). Decisively, these sales did not merely alienate parts of state property; they engendered a whole series of practices beyond royal control – practices incompatible with any notion of a modern bureaucracy, modern public finance, or modern sovereignty.

The price of an office was based on its value, which was determined by the personal profits accruing to the incumbent. If an office was deemed to be particularly lucrative and prestigious, competing bidders drove up its value. In other words, the office became a commodity. Moreover, offices did not only confer title, prestige, and political influence, they were treated by bearers as interest-bearing capital investments. To the king, they represented a form of interest-free credit, since interest was covered by the income derived from the office (Hoffman 1994: 230–35). Although some office holders did receive salaries, these *gages* were regarded as returns on investment and were of minor importance compared to the fees flowing from office (Schwarz 1983: 178). However, since this form of investment was not ploughed back into the economy but invested in the means of political and geopolitical accumulation, these credit structures had nothing to do with capitalism.[24] They simply thrived on the existence of political privilege. 'Frenchmen preferred to buy offices rather than to invest in commercial or industrial activities' (Bonney 1991: 344). These investments valourized *rentier* capital but did not turn it into entrepreneurial capital. Rather, these *rentier* credit structures provided a new financial link between the internal exploitation of the peasantry qua office-backed political power and external appropriation qua military-backed political power.

Given the commodified nature of offices, sales were usually a matter for seller and purchaser alone – a transaction that precluded a conscious royal policy of recruitment, though it formally required the king's dispensation. Offices were traded among 'private' bidders – the *resignatio in favorem tertii* (Reinhard 1975; Schwarz 1983: 177). Thus a veritable market in offices sprang up. If the king wanted to remove an incumbent, he had to be reimbursed. A range of dysfunctional practices followed. Once most offices had become hereditary by 1604 through the introduction of the *paulette* (an annual tax on venal offices) and tended to be auctioned to the highest bidder, how was professional competence to be secured? Once offices were purchased as a means of personal enrichment, how could misadministration, fraud, and corruption be controlled? Once the office was its holder's private property, who could stop him from creating and selling new sub-offices on his own initiative? Since the office was a commodity, it was handled like an economic asset. It could be pawned, sublet, or divided upon inheritance. Finance ministers even required finance officers to make loans to the state to cover budgetary deficits – loans guaranteed by office revenues. Over time, a credit structure developed which was guaranteed by largely fictitious future incomes and turned the Crown into a debtor to its own creation – the (private-patrimonial) officer class.

The only layer of officers often (but incorrectly) taken to satisfy the Weberian criteria of non-patrimonial bureaucrats, the *intendants*, did not alter the fundamental logic of the pre-modern French bureaucracy. These revocable royal commissioners, equipped with extraordinary powers to supervise the collection of taxes and the administration of justice in the provinces, were created by Richelieu and Mazarin in response to the fiscal pressures of the Thirty Years' War and its aftermath, testifying to the financial logic of office proliferation in seventeenth-century France. They were immediately seen by most patrimonial officers as a direct attack on their prerogatives and thus provoked open resistance during the *Fronde*. The *intendants* were themselves drawn from the higher magistracy and did not lose their venal offices while sent on commission. Thus, through the cumulation of offices and the sharing of the same social background, their interests did not set them fundamentally apart from venal officers so as to form a separate officer class in the hands of the king (Salmon 1987: 202; see also Beik 1985: 14–15; Mettam 1988: 23; Parker 1996: 176). And, as royal commissioners, they did not turn into independent state bureaucrats (with lifelong tenure), but simply formed a new officer class which, precisely because it did not own its offices, could be freely dismissed by the king (Hinrichs 1989: 91).

In other words, office venality and office-trading were not mere epiphenomenal forms of corruption or anachronistic legacies of the feudal past. Rather, they were recognized, institutionalized, and legalized forms of early modern government in a regime of exploitation that gave the French administrative system its peculiarly inert, 'irrational', crisis-ridden character. The king was forced to share control over the state with private 'dilettante' office holders – not through bureaucratic delegation, but through real alienation of state power to private persons: 'This was a development of the greatest importance, because it put brakes on the creation of royal absolutism. . . . The powers that the crown had gained in thinning out the feudal system beneath it, retaining for itself the sole status of possessor of full power, was now given away again, not to vassals but to office-holders' (Rowen 1980: 56–7). Thus,

> a full realization of the implications of venality has had the effect of 'demodernizing' seventeenth-century government. Venality tied absolut-ism to its feudal past by consecrating a new form of private ownership of public authority which enabled rich and influential subjects – noble or bourgeois – to share in the profits and prestige of the state. It was a new

expression of the king's inability to control his society without conciliating his most powerful subjects. (Beik 1985: 13)

The structural nexus – a relation of mutual dependence – between the absolutist ruler and the officer corps did not evolve in the direction of a truly modern state, but reproduced and entrenched the existing arrangements until it led the state to systemic breakdown.

4. Political Institutions in Early Modern France

The demystification of absolutist 'bureaucracy' involves a broader clarification of the institutions of the French polity. For only if all political institutions derived their legitimacy from royal fiat and carried the king's will into the regions would it make sense to speak of internal sovereignty. Early modern French political institutions expressed a rather different spirit. They functioned not so much as faithful relays of royal policies as bodies mediating between the interests of the Crown and diverse yet powerful regional elites. Political power was wielded by a welter of independent corporate bodies, coexisting side by side and often fusing with monarchical institutions. By 1532, after the incorporation of Brittany, the last great principality, into the realm, the idea of the principality as a feudal fief, whose membership in the polity was based on the classical feudal contract, was dead. Thereafter all former principalities were not fiefs but provinces headed by royal governors, who nevertheless usually happened to be the largest provincial landowner. As such, the governor did not simply represent the king in the province (without compensation), but mediated between the interests of the king and those of regional elites, including himself.

Royal and independent corporate political institutions competed for the rights of political domination. On the one hand, the highest court – the *Parlement de Paris* – and the Royal Council were truly royal institutions, owing their very existence to the Crown. Yet even the higher magistrates staffing these institutions – the higher *noblesse de robe* – came to own their offices. On the other hand, independent provincial corporate institutions – provincial estates (in the *pays d'état*), town councils, noble and clerical assemblies, village assemblies, and regional *parlements* – did not owe their existence to royal fiat. However, such a clear-cut distinction is only feasible if we take their original independence as the defining criterion. In practice, corporate institutions were the target of royal penetration through the placement of royal agents. But since royal agents were often drawn from the local nobility, the clergy, and the town patriciates, and since their offices were proprietary, the corporate bodies became hybrid institutions. Instead of imposing a hierarchical relation of bureaucratic subordination, they mediated the dialogue between Crown and province. Furthermore, although the offices run by the service nobility offered lucrative channels of upward mobility for 'new men', they cannot be regarded solely as a manipulative device in the hands of the king against the aristocracy, since intermarriage between robe and sword was common and sword status was still more prestigious.

Most importantly, although these 'new men' were often drawn from prosperous families which had made their fortunes in commerce, industry, or finance – enabling them to purchase an office in the first place – this was not a bourgeoisie which slowly but surely undermined the class position of the sword nobility, but a privileged group of parvenues which remained financially dependent on the favours of the king:

> The venal office-holder, whether of the *noblesse de robe* or of humbler rank, would have felt that he had little in common with the merchant or the master craftsman, even though the money with which his family had purchased its first office, perhaps at a date long in the past, might well have come from the profits of trade or industry. Now, as an *officier*, he carefully cultivated all the habits of the old landed nobility, in whose circles he wished to be accepted. (Mettam 1988: 22)

In sum, the king could not rule without the privileged orders since he needed their support to rule the country, rooting the king in a net of patrimonial alliances. The privileged orders, in turn, realized that their survival and privilege, in terms of both their hold over the peasantry and their collective defence against rival kingdoms, depended on the profits of royal office as well as royal military protection. The class dynamics of the absolutist state did not follow the logic of a Crown pushing through its 'historical task' of modern state-making assisted by the legal expertise and financial resources of a conniving bourgeoisie to the detriment of a retrograde feudal nobility; rather, the Crown attempted to create a new state class that fused the town patriciate and the old nobility into a nobility of service. Thus, in spite of an objective contradiction between Crown and regional ruling classes over the rights of domination and exploitation, their relations amounted neither to a zero-sum game[25] nor to an amicable sharing of political power based on consent and partnership (Henshall 1992, 1996). Rather, the scope and intensity of intra-ruling-class conflict were circumscribed by the double threats of peasant rebellion and geostrategic pressure. These forces kept French state-building, that is, inter-ruling-class co-operation, on track.

5. *Legibus solutus?*

By the end of the Thirty Years' War, sovereignty as supreme power over a certain territory was a political fact, signifying the victory of the territorial princes over the universal authority of emperor and pope, on the one hand, and over the particularistic aspirations of the feudal barons, on the other. The inhabitant of France found that nobody but the royal power could give him orders and enforce them. This experience of the individual French citizen was duplicated by the experience of the king of England or the king of Spain; that is to say, the supreme authority of the French king within French territory precluded them from exerting any authority of their own within that territory save by leave of the French king himself or by defeating him in war. But if the king of England and the king of Spain had no power in France, they had exclusive power in their own territories. These political facts, present in the experience of contemporaries, could not be explained by the medieval theory of the state. The doctrine of sovereignty elevated these political facts into a legal theory and thus gave them both moral approbation and the appearance of legal necessity. The monarch was now supreme within his territory not only as a matter of political fact but also as a matter of law. He was the sole source of man-made law – that is, of all positive law – but he was not himself subject to it. He was above the law, *legibus solutus* (Morgenthau 1985: 328–9).[26]

How does Morgenthau's conventional benchmark of absolutism – legislative sovereignty – fare when confronted with widespread venal officialdom and regionally autonomous political institutions? Despite real steps towards 'legislative sovereignty' through the expansion and refinement of royal law, the alleged transition of the king from personal dispenser of justice, based on feudo-theological conceptions of divine kingship, to sovereign lawmaker was arrested by strong countervailing forces (for a contrary view, see Spruyt 1994a: 106–7). The desire for legal uniformity, promoted by recourse to Roman law and the Justinian conception of undivided sovereignty flowing from one supreme source, did not so much supplant the principle that autonomous rights of justice emanated from possession of land and office as supplement it (Parker 1989). Not only did autonomous seigneurial courts persist (even as they tended to become integrated into an appellate system) – and with them the principle that litigants ought to appear before their 'natural' judges – the higher courts did not draw their legitimacy from royal delegation but from a real devolution of authority. Higher magistrates had authority not by virtue of their function, but by virtue of their status.[27]

The patrimonial character of legal office – proprietary, hereditary, and irrevocable – turned the legal system into an incongruous network of patronage. Clientelism ran beyond royal control, developing its own self-reproductive logic. The idea that legal uniformity imposed by the king implied the formal equality of 'equal citizens before the law' ran time and again into traditional social hierarchy, based on the possession of land, title, and privilege. Precisely because the kingdom was yoked together over several centuries by force as well as concessions, elites in the provinces enjoyed various liberties, tax exemptions, and powers of self-government. The king, in spite of all his propaganda for *legibus solutus*, was not *iure solute* – provided we understand by *ius* the ensemble of customary rights and privileges enjoyed by the members of the ruling class, which forced the king to make legislative concessions. For example, many local lords retained independent rights of justice over their peasants; lawcourts (the *parlements*) could obstruct royal 'legislative sovereignty' by refusing to register royal edicts; the provincial estates in the *pays d'états* (the provinces which used to be powerful principalities) retained the right to vote on taxes; important cities held up their charters of liberty against royal legislative incursions (Hoffman 1994: 226–9). 'Rights and privileges embodied a discourse of ancient customs, contracts and charters: their sanction was the past' (Henshall 1996: 30). The king's pretension to absoluteness did not absolve him from acting within the inherited boundaries of 'right'.

Even the political discourse on absolutism, classically expressed in Jean Bodin's *Six livres sur la république*, evinced a de-absolutization of sovereignty by retrieving the 'framework of natural and divine law within which a just monarch is morally obliged to operate' (Parker 1981: 253). This is not simply a question of dismissing the discourse of *raison d'État* as an ideological weapon, forged and wielded by a host of thankful pro-royal publicists and pamphleteers, for even the most ultra-royal political literature did not dare to challenge the fundamentals of absolutist society: property rights. 'Invasion of property rights without consent was condemned even by allegedly "absolutist" thinkers like Bodin: force was unlawful' (Henshall 1996: 30).[28] There was a clear conceptual line in contemporary political consciousness between absolutism and despotism, between *monarchie absolue* and *monarchie arbitraire* (Mettam 1988: 36). Given the inherited structure of vested interests, royal positive law coexisted with customary, feudal, and divine law. Legal sovereignty remained divided.

6. The Costs and Consequences of War

The relation of mutual dependence between the king and 'his' patrimonial and parasitic corps of officers not only stalled the formation of a modern state, it repeatedly threw state finances into crisis. The tendency towards financial breakdown had its roots in the tension between the limited productivity of the pre-capitalist agrarian economy and the ever-increasing costs of warfare imposed by the logic of geopolitical accumulation.

The move to 'privatize' the rights of appropriation and domination through tax-farming and patrimonial adjudication was one strategy to fill the coffers for war. War, in turn, was a common dynastic strategy for amassing territories and riches as well as the customary means of settling inter-dynastic property disputes. Yet these revenues did not come close to covering escalating war expenditures:

> It was under Francis I and his successors that the expenditure of the French monarchy began to increase significantly. But the hegemonic policies of the seventeenth and eighteenth centuries produced an expend-iture explosion, the first peak beginning with the Thirty Years' War and direct French intervention during the 1630s and 1640s. After a brief cessation of war with the advent of Colbert, expenditure rose again with the Dutch War and that of the League of Augsburg, reaching a second peak with the War of the Spanish Succession, and a third with the Seven Years' War. (Körner 1995a: 417–19)

The arrival of the permanent war-state intensified the super-exploitation of the peasantry. 'In 1610, the fiscal agents of the State collected 17 million *livres* from the *taille*. By 1644, the exactions of this tax had trebled to 44 million *livres*. Total taxation actually quadrupled in the decade after 1630' (Anderson 1974b: 98).[29] Next to selling offices and raising taxes, borrowing came to be the preferred royal instrument of raising revenue. However, since the king was an unreliable debtor, interest rates spiralled, leading the Crown to ever more desperate and grotesque measures of income provision. Overall,

> French revenues grew consistently, gross revenue amounting to 20.5 million in 1600 and reaching nearly 32.8 million *livres* in 1608 and 42.8 million in 1621. Moreover, with the declaration of war against Spain in

1635, French revenues continued to expand, averaging some 115 million *livres* a year, although much of this came from borrowing at very high rates of interest. (Bonney 1991: 352–3)

What we see is thus a self-perpetuating upward spiral of raising revenues to finance ever more costly wars – in part, of course, to pay back creditors through plunder, the acquisition of territories, or the payment of indemnities or satisfactions – and an ever-growing diversion of peasant-produced wealth into non-productive military consumption.

The net effect was that the public credit structure turned the king into the prisoner of 'his' state officers and financiers, making the tax and the credit system virtually immune to non-violent reform. This credit structure did not develop towards a modern system of central banking, for credits were not administered and guaranteed by a national bank but by a welter of private agents, the *financiers* (Mettam 1988: 106–17). Confidence in this credit system rested on the Crown's capacity to service his debts. Finance remained tied to the person of the king; the entire credit structure stood and fell with him. In striking contrast to France, the English revolution in public finance had led by the end of the seventeenth century to the establishment of the Bank of England. It was essential for raising loans, sustaining governmental credits, and providing long-term credit security beyond the life-spans of individual monarchs. Government loans were based on parliamentary guarantees, and Parliament could raise money more effectively by taxing the propertied classes, i.e., themselves and those they represented (Anderson 1988: 154). In France, by contrast, state debts were the king's debts (Bonney 1981). As such, they were not transferred from king to king, but risked forfeiture on the death of the original debtor.

The fiscal crises and bankruptcies of 1598, 1648, and 1661 – roughly marking the ends of the Wars of Religion, the Thirty Years' War, and the war with Spain – and again of 1748 and 1763 – marking the ends of the Austrian War of Succession and the Seven Years' War – were thus not those of the French state, but of the French monarch. What is more, the king's debts were political in the sense that loans were often demanded and payments simply defaulted, so that lending to the king was very risky (Hoffman 1994: 232–3; Parker 1996: 197). The king systematically turned his new sovereign prerogatives into instruments of fund-raising by selling not only offices, but also other privileges like noble titles, professional qualifications, and monopoly charters on trade and commerce. Thus were extra-economic powers of accumulation distributed and decentralized (Bien 1978).[30] Unlike in the medieval world, it was now one ruler decentralizing his powers, not a plurality of autonomous lords vying to centralize their fragmented powers through the system of vassalage.

The state's reform efforts to establish greater geographical uniformity and centralization, replace proprietary office holders with revocable royal commissioners, and diversify the instruments of taxation while increasing tax rates, ran time and again into the vested interests of patrimonial officers. A few examples elucidate this nexus between war, kingly debts, internal revolts, and institutional reforms. After each war, war debts triggered insolvencies and fiscal crises, translating into inter-ruling class conflicts with important institutional consequences (Mettam 1988: 102–5; Hoffman 1994: 242–8). Royal initiatives to cut through the system of privilege and corruption met stiff opposition. The end of the Wars of Religion brought the *paulette*, which granted office holders heredity in return for an annual payment. The financial crisis of 1638, after France's entry into the Thirty Years' War, brought the *intendants*, created to supervise more effective tax collection. The end of the Thirty Years' War brought the *Fronde* (1648–53), pitting defrauded owners of government offices and holders of government *rentes* against the king, while magnates and princes of the blood led foreign armies into the land, and peasant tax rebellions sprang up around the country (Kaiser 1990: 75–81). On return from exile, Mazarin restored the *intendants* system, reimposed heavy taxation, and renewed relations with the financiers. Overall, these piecemeal institutional innovations could not dislodge the fundamental contradiction of king–patrimonial officer relations:

> There were . . . numerous financial office-holders established in the local *bureaux des finances* and *élections*. Their offices could not be abolished, and the owners reimbursed, because this would be too heavy a burden on the king's already badly strained finances. The offices could not be abolished without compensation, because this would be tantamount to an attack on private property. On the other hand, the existence of a large number of semi-autonomous accountants and financial office-holders ruled out an efficient system of direct administration (*régie*) since the crown had no direct control over their activities. If the king wanted a new and unpopular tax to be levied, it was by no means certain that his accountants or financial office-holders, men with property interests in the locality, would be co-operative. (Bonney 1981: 16–17)

The counterproductive dynamic of the tax/office state fixed a structure of ruling-class power that was inherently unable to reform itself. Arguably, royal attempts to generate resources for war did not broaden the scope of central government (although institutions multiplied); it reduced royal autonomy by signing away more and more government powers to private agents. Given this structural blockage, the Crown could only generate additional income by punitive taxation of the peasantry or geopolitical accumulation abroad – be it in the form of war, marriage, or mercantilist foreign trade – intensifying its political dependency on a network of privileged men and undermining the productivity of the agrarian economy. If the (il)logic of the absolutist war-state nexus was madness, it still had method: Unreason of state.

7. The Military Constitution of the Old Regime

In the modern state, the monopolization of military might is institutional-ized in public armed forces. Soldiers are permanently garrisoned, disci-plined, uniformed, trained, hierarchized, and under public pay. The specialists of violence do not privately own the means of violence. Soldiers are not decommissioned and disarmed after conflicts, but return to their garrisons. Soldiery is a profession. In principle, the military apparatus functions according to the Weberian precepts of modern bureaucracy. What were the major traits of the military constitution in absolutist states? Spruyt assures us that 'the standing army, since the late fifteenth century, thus became an instrument of the state rather than an instrument for the defence of the king's private property' (Spruyt 1994a: 165). *Contra* Spruyt, this section argues that in spite of the transition from a feudal to an absolutist military regime, none of the traits of modern military organization are visible in the absolutist states.

The social relations of warfare in the European Middle Ages were based on the conditionality of property in land. Noble land tenure entailed military obligations to the land-granting overlord for a stipulated period, since peasant possession of the means of subsistence necessitated forms of extra-economic labour control. Lords bore arms. Military decentralization determined the form of the medieval state (the state of associated persons) as well as its military constitution, the knightly army. The commutation of peasant dues from rents in labour and kind to money rents from the twelfth century onwards was reflected in a shift to military payments to the king. Wealthy nobles could 'buy off' their military duties, allowing the latter in turn to pay mercenaries. However, mercenary knights supplementing the old feudal levy did not undermine the basic social logic of feudal military organization (Wohlfeil 1988: 119). They merely increased the king's dependence on noble military contributions based on feudal law.

The military emancipation of the king from inter-noble arrangements through the rise of the 'tax/office' state restructured the social relations of exploitation and the social relations of military organization. As the old *noblesse d'épée* blended with the new *noblesse de robe*, many nobles took up office in the king's standing army. Thus, in France, at the latest after the Ludovician military reforms of 1661, the king disposed of a permanent army, a special military budget, an institutionalized system of recruitment, a military hierarchy of regiments and ranks, an officer corps with defined competencies and regulated promotions, royal academies for training cadets, a civil administration for the provision of the army, and specially commissioned civil inspectors (*intendants d'armée, comissaires des guerres*, and *contrôlleurs des guerres*) for its control. The king was the chief of the army.

But does the transition from a knightly feudal host to a royal standing army strengthen the view that at least one criterion of modern sovereignty – the state monopoly in the means of violence – is applicable to absolutist France? To start with, it was not the state that sought to monopolize the means of violence, but the king. Officers did not swear allegiance to an abstract state, but to the person of the king. The proprietary conception of kingship did not in fact allow the crucial separation of the means of violence from the 'office' of kingship; it merely continued the essential fusion of the means of violence and personal domination, if now in the more centralized form of the royal army. 'The army was, as it were, a foreign body in the state. It was an instrument of the monarch, not an institution of the country. It was created as a tool of power politics in the foreign sphere, but at the same time it served to maintain and extend the sovereign's power at home' (Hintze 1975b: 200–201). The army was, strictly speaking, the personal property of the king, at his disposal, under his command, and financed by him (Burkhardt 1997: 545).[31]

As 'states' were personalized ('*L'État, c'est moi!*'), so were wars ('*La guerre, c'est moi!*') (Krippendorff 1985: 284). Yet royal unlimited control and absolute discretion over the army remained a fiction. Max Weber commented that, 'there is a decisive economic condition for the degree to which the royal army is "patrimonial", that means, a purely personal army of the prince and hence at his disposal also *against* his own political subjects: the army is equipped and maintained out of supplies and revenues belonging to the ruler' (Weber 1968a: 1019). Since the French army was constantly growing, from a few thousand men in 1661 to 72,000 in 1667, to 120,000 in 1672, and to more than 150,000 in the early 1680s, adding considerably to the non-productive army of civil officers, its maintenance strained royal finances (Kaiser 1990: 145). Yet, since its financing out of royal coffers was restricted by chronic deficits, the king had to resort to other strategies of maintaining 'his' army.

Thus, in striking parallel to the general phenomenon of office venality, the sale and trade of army offices was widespread (Mettam 1988: 42–4, 217–24; Muhlack 1988: 260, 273; Gerstenberger 1990: 330, 333ff). As in civil administration, officer posts could be sold because the king owned the army. This meant the systematic alienation of kingly property, here the alienation of control over the means of violence, to private agents. From the highest echelons in the ministries of foreign affairs and war, through posts in civil army administration (*intendants d'armée*), down to regimental, company, and recruiting officers, office holders used their quasi-irremovable position to build up independent networks of clientelism by creating and subletting new posts:

> In one respect . . . the French army remained highly conservative and backward-looking. In it more completely than in many other regiments and companies were still the property of their colonels and captains and could be bought and sold like other sorts of property. Colonelcies were not cheap. By the 1730s and 1740s prices of 20–50,000 *livres* for infantry regiments were normal, though one at least fetched as much as 100,000. Not until 1762 did the government lay down maximum prices which could be charged for them. They could also, however, be extremely profitable: in 1741 a French guards regiment . . . yielded its owner an income of 120,000 *livres*. (Anderson 1988: 101, 46)

Veritable military dynasties grew inside the army, appropriating entire regiments whose commands were handed down from generation to generation (Parker 1988: 48). Precisely because powerful office holders staffed the institutions over which they presided with relatives and dependants, Muhlack observes that 'towards the end of Mazarin's time in government, the king's army was in fact replaced by the cardinal's army' (Muhlack 1988: 269). In addition, recruiting officers, almost exclusively of noble origin, simply mustered soldiers from their own lordships, so that surviving feudal relations of dependence on lordly estates were carried over into the army. The desperate royal attempts to control these practices – most strikingly in the *Code Michau* of 1629 – by outlawing office venality and insisting on the royal right of nomination ran time and again into financial requirements (Kaiser 1990: 68). The proprietary character of the means of violence pervaded all levels of the army hierarchy. The relation of mutual dependency between the Crown and the officer class reproduced the precarious symbiosis between the members of the ruling class. Neither could do without the other. The net result was a new form of military devolution to private agents.

Furthermore, until the reforms of 1661 – i.e., until well after the Westphalian peace treaties – the royal standing army was not the only military institution in France. This was even less the case in other parts of Europe. Since monarchs could hardly ever afford to maintain armies that matched their ambitions, they turned to military entrepreneurs to carry out their foreign policy objectives.[32] These *condottiere* came to characterize European warfare in the period up to and including the Thirty Years' War. These military entrepreneurs were wealthy private agents employed (*condotta* = contract) by rulers, raising, equipping, commanding, and paying their own armies, and in turn receiving titles and land from their employers (Krippendorff 1985: 257–67):[33] 'It has been estimated that during the Thirty Years War there were in the different German armies in all close to 1,500 'military enterpriser' commanders, colonels and generals who owned regiments, and in the great majority of seventeenth-century armies . . . regiments were known, quite logically, by the names of their colonels' (Anderson 1988: 47).

Wallenstein was the most outstanding example of these men who made war their private business. Operating from his estates in Bohemia – the newly created Duchy of Friedland – bought cheaply from the emperor who had confiscated it from rebellious Bohemian nobles, he received the Duchy of Mecklenburg in compensation for his services and credits granted to the emperor and was promised the Electorate of Brandenburg, provided he could conquer it – an act which would have made him the mightiest lord in the Holy Roman Empire.[34] Military entrepreneurs enjoyed considerable independence from central control (Hintze 1975b: 198–9; Kaiser 1990: 21ff). They were sometimes in complete control of armies that outsized regular royal troops, posing a serious threat to and entailing incalculable risks for their nominal masters. Wallenstein's murder by Viennese agents illustrates this lack of public control. Yet precisely because these entrepreneurs entered into private contracts, they formed essentially transnational armed forces, freely employable by whoever could afford them and always on the brink of pursuing their own interests. The composition of their soldiery was polyglot and trans-confessional. Demand for mercenaries created an international market for military labour. As a rule, mercenaries came from humble backgrounds. They were often criminals who had fled their homelands, impoverished peasants, or simply prisoners enlisted in their former enemy's army. Mercenary armies commanded by unscrupulous businessmen and employed for private profit constituted not only powerful challenges to monarchical claims to absolute power by privatizing war, they posed a serious threat to European international stability.

If we turn from the military constitution of early modern states to the social relations of warfare, we find other decidedly non-modern character-istics. Armies, like their feudal predecessors, still 'lived off' the countryside during campaigns. They simply sequestrated what they could lay their hands on, confiscated goods, cattle, and food, looted homesteads, villages, and towns, demanded 'protection money' from surrounding settlements in return for letters of protection, and imposed *ad hoc* military taxes (in fact, ransom) in the form of regular peasant contributions to the fighting forces. It was these confiscations that largely financed the Thirty Years' War, with catastrophic economic and demographic effects. Yet armies lived not only off the countryside, they also lived off the enemy. Defeat meant plunder and appropriation. In striking contrast to modern conventions, victory implied booty for each combatant:

> A battle might produce thousands of prisoners, whose personal effects immediately became the property of the captor, and whose ransoms would be divided between him and his commanders in a fixed proportion. Even greater opportunities for gain were provided by the capture of an enemy town. Although there were some dissenting voices, most military experts agreed that towns could be legitimately sacked if they refused to surrender before the besiegers brought up their artillery. After that happened, if the town were captured, its inhabitants forfeited liberty, property and even life, thereby turning every soldier in the victorious army into a prince. (Parker 1988: 59)

Ideally, war should pay for itself (*Bellum se ipse alet*). Beyond the gains from victory and plunder, soldiers received privately negotiated wages, not publicly stipulated pay. Mutiny was common when territorial princes were in arrears and military entrepreneurs readily sold their services to the enemy. Since mercenaries owned their weapons and were not garrisoned during or after campaigns, they created a serious problem for order, continuing their marauding after wars were formally terminated.[35] This lack of public discipline thus contributed to the prolongation of wars and their recurrent transformation into civil strife. The *Sacco di Roma* of 1527 at the hands of unpaid German mercenaries exemplified these anarchical tendencies. War was still a means of private and personal enrichment.

In sum, the absolutist military apparatus could not qualify as a modern army. Though the king sought to arrogate and centralize the means of violence, he merely personalized and privatized them under his own command and for his own interests, which he tended to equate with those of the state. He was further forced to reprivatize and decentralize them through the systematic sale of officer posts and the employment of military enterprisers. He thus had to share military power with other independent actors. In the early modern period, military might remained divided and personalized, if on a new basis.

4. Conclusion: The Modernizing Limits of Absolutism

The regionally specific resolution of class conflicts in high and late medieval France resulted in the end of serfdom and an early modern property regime characterized by petty peasant ownership. Generalized peasant smallholding implied that the peasant sector reproduced itself essentially outside the market, resisting the incentives towards commercialized agriculture and the creation of consolidated farms. The relations of exploitation shifted from a feudal rent regime to a dynastic tax regime. The feudal unity of the political and the economic in the lordship was reconstituted in the tax/office structure of the absolutist state. The monarchy became an 'independent, class-like surplus extractor' (Brenner 1985a: 55), trying to increase central control of taxation.

While the rise of absolutism destroyed the feudal system of vassalic relations between politically independent lords, absolutism was not a zero-sum game in which the growth of royal centralized power meant the inevitable decline of regional aristocratic or patrimonial authority. On the contrary, it gave rise to a variegated political landscape of symbiotic authority relations between a strengthened monarchy, the *noblesse d'épée*, the *noblesse de robe*, and urban and ecclesiastical oligarchies. Absolutism's *differentia specifica* vis-à-vis feudalism lay in the direct dependency of these privileged classes upon the monarchy. Thus the elevation of the king from a feudal overlord to a dynastic sovereign meant that private political interests had to be defined in direct relation to the king in order to maintain or have access to extra-economic means of income, as the king was forced to govern through semi-public channels: 'The very system of political rule, which was in essence a royal system, required close collaboration with the larger monarchy and precluded any real autonomy on the part of the provincial ruling class. Only the king could maintain hegemony' (Beik 1985: 332). Conversely, sovereignty as proprietary kingship had to be signed away in various ways. The penetration of royal institutions into the countryside did not so much dislodge existing hierarchical structures as create additional layers of patronage and clientelism which tied royal agents to prevailing political arrangements, while local nobles and town oligarchs aspired to insert themselves into these channels.

The driving force behind these developments was class conflict between direct producers and non-producers over the rate of exploitation and intra-ruling-class conflict over the relative share in the politically constituted means of appropriation.[36] Thus the main axis of intra-ruling-class conflict was not a clash between a rising capitalist bourgeoisie and a retrograde nobility, balanced and manipulated by the Crown. Rather, it was differential access to extra-economic income opportunities – be it in form of venal offices, royal monopolies, or land. In this, absolutism did not promote – intentionally or unintentionally – a capitalist bourgeoisie, but rather enlisted the services of a non-capitalist class of merchants, financiers, and manufacturers for its own ends, co-opting these actors into the state apparatus through the sale of offices and royal monopoly titles to production and commerce. Whenever the king upset the proprietary status quo with administrative innovations and office proliferation, the redistribution of royal favours stirred significant conflict between the defenders of the *status quo ante* and newly privileged men. Each crisis translated into an *ad hoc* reconfiguration of the established *modus vivendi* between the ruling classes without fundamentally redefining its essential rationale.[37] 'The most unwieldy state apparatus in the world was turning over only in order to stay in place' (Zolberg 1980: 706). These conflicts did not neatly follow the lines between an old nobility, a new office nobility, and a non-capitalist bourgeoisie. But the privileged classes were both united and set against each other, as factional interests bound the king. Intra-ruling-class strife found its limits in internal peasant resistance as well as international rivalry.

The debate over the nature of absolutism has greatly qualified the older conception of the absoluteness of absolutist rule. It has certainly shattered the idea that the *Ancien Régime* state was modern, rationalized, and efficient. Legal sovereignty remained divided, military power personalized and privatized, taxation and finance hedged by privileged regional interests, and political discourse abided by custom. Steps towards administrative centralization were undermined by decentralized networks of patronage, clientelism, and corruption, which blurred the lines between public power and private advantage. The persistence of political property precluded the establishment of a modern bureaucracy. Venality constituted a structural brake to the modernization of absolutist rule.

Absolutist France not only failed to become a modern state, it was not even a precursor or transitional stage towards a modern state, as the classical 'equilibrist–transitional' Marxist interpretation and many Weberian accounts suggest. Although the institutional structure of the absolutist state, whose centralizing advances were radicalized by Napoleon, was the historical condition in which French capitalism would develop in the nineteenth century, it was not logically necessary for its development. This does not imply that the *Ancien Régime* should be subsumed under the general type of feudalism, for the transition from a regime of lordly rent extraction to a system of royal tax extraction represented an important development. Direct lordly exploitation was superseded by 'generalized personal domination' by the king, transforming feudal inter-noble relations mediated through military vassalage into absolutist inter-ruling-class relations mediated through patronage (Gerstenberger 1990: 510–22). The absolutist state was thus a dynastic-patrimonial state. Kingship was no longer a 'contractual' affair between the mightiest lords in the country, but an institution which appropriated the rights of command in a sovereign fashion. The legitimacy of kingship no longer derived from the ensemble of pre-constituted feudal lordships; it was 'divine'. Yet divine kingship did not confer state autonomy. Its form and dynamic were never external to prevailing relations of exploitation, but co-constituted and maintained them.

On a higher level of abstraction, however, both feudal and absolutist polities operated on and were limited by the parameters set by non-capitalist property relations and the corresponding internal as well as external logic of (geo)political accumulation. Therefore, the structural similarities between absolutist and feudal France are indeed greater than those between absolutist France and late-nineteenth-century France. 'Extra-economic coercion is a motif which can be applied both to the fundamental class relationships under feudalism and to the social and legal trappings of absolutist society' (Beik 1985: 30; see also Henshall 1996: 36). However, absolutism cannot be subsumed under feudalism or the 'feudal mode of production'; it was neither a peculiarly transitional combination of feudalism and capitalism, as suggested by Perry Anderson, nor a transitional society preparing the ground for the modern state (Giddens 1985: 98 passim). It was a *sui generis* social formation, displaying a specific mode of government and determinate pre-modern and pre-capitalist domestic and international 'laws of motion'. Absolutism's 'relations of exploitation' provide the surest guide to their explanation.

In developmental terms, the reproductive imperatives of the ruling elite, depending entirely upon the well-being of the king, occasioned a recurring pattern of predatory foreign policy, punitive taxation, public borrowing, and the sale of offices. The rationale of foreign policy was not power politics but geopolitical accumulation – social power politics – in which territory and the exclusive control over trade routes were the highest prizes. Over-militarization and nearly permanent warfare induced a series of fiscal crises and state bankruptcies. Additionally, the long-term logic of these strategies of political accumulation implied an ever-greater alienation of state property to an ever-growing parasitic officer class, which, being exempted from taxation, shifted its burden almost exclusively on to the peasantry, while indebting the king to his own officer corps. It was this structural contradiction that exhausted French financial capacity and inten-sified class antagonisms between the peasantry, the officer class, and the Crown. Super-exploitation of peasant surplus through over-taxation stalled productive reinvestment and induced soil exhaustion, entailing the persist-ence of pre-capitalist eco-demographic crises well into the eighteenth century. Ruling-class investment in the means of violence diverted funds from productive investment, explaining the torpor of French agriculture compared to England and its 'Agricultural Revolution'. Precisely because economic development remained stifled by a pre-capitalist property regime, the logic of (geo)political accumulation was in the long term economically counterproductive, socially conflictual, and ultimately self-undermining (Gerstenberger 1990: 406–8). These underlying contradictions arrested consensual reforms and set the limits on the 'modernization' of the French state. In developmental terms, absolutism was a dead end. In a way, *war did not make the state; it rather unmade it.*

That the French state was finally transformed into a modern state cannot be deduced from developments internal to the *Ancien Régime*. It required the complete breakdown of the social property relations which made up absolutist society. This process set in with 1789 and was, arguably, not completed until the late nineteenth century. 'The separation of the public political sphere of the state from the economic sphere of civil society never really occurred in France before the establishment of the Third Republic, by which time capitalism can at last also be said to have existed' (Comninel 1987: 204). Since France could not generate a modern government out of pre-modern socio-political relations – since each class tried to reproduce itself as it was – the impetus for change was 'externally' imposed. The violent terminus absolutism suffered at the end of the eighteenth century must be explained by relating its inner dynamic – especially the mismatch between its low productivity and its war-making ambitions – to the external dynamic of the European states-system. This mismatch placed

France at a comparative coercive-financial disadvantage against capitalist Britain. Change derived, *ex hypothesis*, from the geopolitically mediated pressures of an inter-state system in which one state, England, successfully transformed itself into a capitalist society by the late seventeenth century and made its ascendancy internationally felt in the eighteenth. However, until the overthrow of the Bourbon monarchy, the privileged classes tried to defend their position at the top of society by conventional means. While ruling-class reproduction was domestically based on strategies of political accumulation, external strategies of geopolitical accumulation held sway. It is to these strategies of international relations, systematized in the Westphalian order, that I now turn.

Notes

1 The revisionist literature is now vast. Non-Marxist accounts include Elias 1983 and 1994; Root 1987; Mettam 1988; Hinrichs 1989; Kaiser 1990, 7–202; Henshall 1992 and 1996; Hoffman 1994; Asch and Duchhardt 1996; Oresko, Gibbs, and Scott 1997. Marxist accounts include Anderson 1974b; Beik 1985; Parker 1989, 1996; Gerstenberger 1990.

2 Two widely read studies, which are often adduced in the IR community as evidence of the modernity of the Westphalian state, are Poggi 1978 and Strayer 1970. For Poggi, 'the new, absolutist system of rule . . . is widely considered the first mature embodiment of the modern state' (Poggi 1978: 62). Strayer is invoked by Gilpin 1981: 116–23 and Spruyt 1994a: 78–108. See also the influential study edited by Tilly 1975; Tilly 1985; Giddens 1985: 83–121.

3 Vierhaus himself advanced as early as 1966 a much more nuanced picture of absolutist rule than implied by the classical definition and asserted that 'since WWI, at the latest since WWII, such a view of absolutism can be regarded as outdated in academic circles (even if it survives in popular historical perceptions)' (Vierhaus 1985: 36).

4 Summaries of the more recent debates can be found in Beik 1985: 3–33 and Parker 1996: 6–27.

5 Further variations of this position can be found in Marx 1976a: 326, 333; 1976c: 328.

6 *Aufhebung* in German can simultaneously mean raising, preservation, and cancellation.

7 'For Marx the different moments of the modern biography of capital were distributed in cumulative sequence, from the Italian cities to the towns of Flanders and Holland, to the empires of Portugal or Spain and the ports of France, before being "systematically combined in England at the end of the 17th century". Historically, it makes more sense to view the emergence of

capitalism as a value-added process gaining in complexity as it moved along a chain of inter-related sites.' (Anderson 1993: 17).

8 Although Anderson discusses aristocratic discontent, he nevertheless insists that absolutism was ultimately – and even in spite of its own original intentions – beneficial to the old aristocracy, which survived not only economically but politically. 'No class in history immediately comprehends the logic of its own historical situation, in epochs of transition: a long period of disorientation and confusion may be necessary for it to learn the necessary rules of its own sovereignty' (Anderson 1974b: 55).

9 Cf. also: 'The new form of noble power was in its turn determined by the spread of commodity production and exchange, in the transitional social formation of the early modern epoch' (Anderson 1974b: 18).

10 Merrington's study was first published in 1975, but Anderson refers to an unpublished draft.

11 Merrington therefore argues against the dissolving effect of towns on feudalism. 'This absence of revolutionary vocation on the part of towns, the constant "betrayals" of the bourgeoisie to the old order (as the *creditor* of the old order) . . . must be seen in terms of their objectively *convergent* interests vis-à-vis the exploitation of the countryside so long as rent remained, in its various forms, the principal mode of appropriation of the surplus and capital remained external to the productive process' (Merrington 1976: 180).

12 'In the West, the Spanish, English, and French monarchies were defeated or overthrown by bourgeois revolutions from below' (Anderson 1974b: 431).

13 In spite of the evidence amassed in his study, Beik still subscribes to the transition paradigm: 'Absolutism must be seen accordingly, not as a modern state grafted on to a pre-modern society, but as the political aspect of the final, highest phase of a venerable, though modified, feudal society – a society in transition, if you like, from feudalism to capitalism' (Beik 1985: 339).

14 See also Wood's clarification of the theoretical link between Brenner's earlier work on the origins of English agrarian capitalism and his later work on the role of merchants in the English Civil War (Wood 1996).

15 Parker 1996, Gerstenberger 1990, and Beik 1985: 4, also stress the incommensurability between France and England. According to Anderson, 'England experienced a peculiarly contracted variant of Absolutist rule' (Anderson 1974b: 113). More systematic treatments of French absolutism can be found in Gerstenberger 1990: 261–463 and Mooers 1991: 45–102.

16 Skocpol makes a similar argument about pre-revolutionary France. However, by basing her account on the rise of agrarian capitalism in sixteenth-century England on the work of Robert Brenner, she fails to acknowledge that international military pressure had no influence on the English social revolution and relatively little influence on the English political revolution. The endogenous development of capitalism in England presents thus a straightforward vindication of Marxist class analysis. (Skocpol 1979: 140–44). It is noteworthy that although Skocpol sketches the contours of the notion

of combined and uneven development for a world-historical explanation of social revolutions, the *fons et origo* of this whole process, the English case, receives only cursory attention. The methodological problems deriving from Skocpol's adoption of a comparative historical sociology are drawn out in Burawoy 1989.

17 The central theme in early modern France was thus not, as argued by Spruyt, a town-king alliance, driving the construction of a modern and efficient state (Spruyt 1994a, 1994b), but the conflict between a noble rent regime and a royal tax regime that drew urban oligarchs, merchants, financiers, and a service nobility into the royal orbit, driving the construction of a patrimonial, pre-modern, and ultimately 'inefficient' state.

18 The move to commercial farming was even largely unsuccessful in the Paris basin (Comninel 1987: 182–96).

19 The state was the private property of the king – not only '*L'État, c'est moi*', but, as Herbert Rowen put it, '*L'État, c'est à moi!*' (Rowen 1961).

20 Whether land was henceforth allodial, or Roman quiritarian, is a matter of debate.

21 Spruyt asserts that by the late Middle Ages, 'the king benefited by having a professional and remunerated bureaucracy' (Spruyt 1994a: 102). For contrary views cf. Hinrichs 1989: 82; Henshall 1992: 15; Parker 1996: 176.

22 See also Bergin's study on the connection between Richelieu's tenure of political office and his accumulation of private and family wealth (Bergin 1985).

23 This does not mean, as John Brewer claims, that 'the spread of venality was a direct response to the financial pressures created by war' (Brewer 1989: 19). Rather, the ability by rulers to resort to office venality under fiscal pressure deriving from war reflects the internal social property regime and class relations. In sixteenth- and seventeenth-century England, office venality was far less pervasive, not because of diminished geopolitical pressure, but because Parliament resisted it.

24 Reinhard's account is therefore unconvincing. He first argues that 'it is today generally acknowledged that office venality was inimical to economic growth since it implied the withdrawal of capital from the economy', but then asserts – citing Marx – that venality and state debts were one of the most decisive levers behind 'primitive accumulation' (in Marx's sense), 'since the existence of public debts strengthens a very uneven distribution of wealth, because only rich people can gain from these investments and profit opportunities' (Reinhard 1975: 316). Finance capital and commercial capital neither presuppose nor engender capitalism. Rather, they thrive on the persistence of political privilege. Parker writes that 'there are those who argue that the French state, simply by virtue of the scale of the financial transactions which it stimulated, was *ipso facto* capitalist. This view is unconvincing not only because of the way state fiscalism drained the economy of resources and imposed a punitive level of taxation on the labouring population but also because the money raised was rarely trans-

formed into productive capital' (Parker 1996: 203). The 'insufficiency of theories which seek to explain the rise of Capitalism by the effects of monetary exchanges or the influence of government finance (debts, armament orders, etc.) consists in the fact that they emphasize only sources of enrichment and provide no explanation of how from a society of small owner-producers a vast proletarian army was born' (Dobb 1946: 186).

25 This is the older view: estate-building and state-building were mutually exclusive.

26 Note Morgenthau's use of the term citizen – anachronistic before 1789. Note also his collapsing of French and English early modern sovereignty into one concept.

27 'The struggle of the jurists to reconcile the idea that all justice derived from the king with a situation in which it still seemed firmly attached to the possession of office and land produced rather conflicting views and a considerable lack of clarity' (Parker 1989: 50).

28 See also Anderson 1974b: 50; Vierhaus 1985: 56–7; Wood 1991: 24–7 and ch. 3.

29 Figures vary, but the trend is unequivocal. See Kaiser 1990: 74; Bonney 1999.

30 Finely shown by Bien in his case study of the proliferation of the *secrétaires du roi*.

31 'Most British visitors to Frederick the Great's Prussia were struck by the remarkable degree of *personal* control that the king exercised over his army and administration' (Brewer 1989: 43). However, this surprise was limited to British visitors. For eighteenth-century continental visitors to Britain, it was surprising to see that the army was under *national* and not dynastic control.

32 Kaiser argues that upon entry in the Thirty Years' War, 'France had virtually no standing army. The only battleworthy troops available belonged to the Protestant military entrepreneur Bernhard of Saxe-Weimar, whom Richelieu enlisted into French service in exchange for a large annual subsidy and a promise of the territory of Alsace' (Kaiser 1990: 73).

33 Contrary to Krippendorff's interpretation, privately paid military labour-power has nothing to do with modern armies or capitalism (Krippendorff 1985: 249, 262).

34 Mercenarism was, of course, not a capitalist enterprise as Michael Mann avers (Mann 1986: 456).

35 'In Brandenburg during the Thirty Years' War, the soldier was still the predominant owner of the martial implements of his business' (Weber 1968a: 982).

36 'There was a basically unified dominant class – one that appropriated surplus directly or indirectly primarily from peasant agriculture' (Skocpol 1979: 56).

37 Mettam concludes that 'there was scarcely anything which could meaningfully be called "modern" in the France of Louis XIV' (Mettam 1988: 12; see also Kaiser 1990: 135).

6

The Early-Modern International
Political Economy:

Mercantilism and Maritime Empire-Building

1. Introduction: The 'Long Sixteenth Century' and Mercantilism

The long sixteenth century (1450–1640) marks for Wallerstein the break-through towards the modern, capitalist world-system (Wallerstein 1980: 8). From this perspective, mercantilism 'has historically been a defensive mechanism of *capitalists* located in states which are one level below the high point of strength in the system' (Wallerstein 1979: 19). This situation applied to absolutist France. Irrespective of regionally diverse regimes of labour control, the early modern international economy is a *capitalist* world-economy, the ruling classes in France are *capitalist*, 'success in mercantilist competition was primarily a function of productive efficiency', and 'the *middle*-run objective of all mercantilist state policies was the overall effi-ciency in the sphere of production' (Wallerstein 1980: 38).

This chapter rejects this assessment by setting out how early modern property and authority relations shaped the pre-capitalist, pre-modern structure and dynamic of the early modern international economy. It begins by clarifying the nature of mercantilist trade policies, understood as politically constituted unequal exchange prolonging medieval practices into the early modern world. This interpretation rests on the fundamental distinction between commercial capitalism, with profits generated exclu-sively in the sphere of circulation, and modern capitalism, involving a qualitative transformation of relations of production. Section 2 explores the class character of early modern trade, draws out the 'territorial' conse-quences of this type of militarily protected maritime geocommerce, and shows its competitive and bellicose consequences. It then turns to the question of whether mercantilist geocommerce and industrial economic policies promoted a transformation of labour relations in the direction of full-blown capitalism. Section 3 seeks to determine whether mercantilism's development of closed trading states entailed their economic unification. Finally, I try to substantiate the basic difference between mercantilist trading practices and modern capitalism by drawing out some counterproductive long-term developmental tendencies of early modern commerce in relation to its constitutive class alliances in order to arrive at an adequate periodization of international economic modernity.

2. Theoretical Premises: Mercantilism as Commercial Capitalism

According to the conventional interpretation of mercantilism, central rulers gained control over national economic policies and foreign trade with the arrogation of territorial sovereignty and the concomitant integration of towns into the realm. Medieval scholastic economic teaching, still guided by moral and religious considerations, gave way to secular, 'scientific' ways of fathoming the sources of wealth, while mercantilism promoted for the first time a public economic policy on a 'national' scale. Grand state designs – especially from Colbert on – pursued a conscious policy of unifying a fragmented economic space into a national economic territory. Trade policy, protectionism, export subsidies, the abolition of internal tariffs, the construction of transport networks, and the encouragement of import-substituting manufacture and demographic growth present enormous developments over spontaneous, uncoordinated medieval practices. The theorem of a positive balance of trade premised on bullion as the mainstay of national riches came to inform public economic policy. The very existence of state economic policy, channelling economic life to public ends, was a step in the direction of a bounded economic territory.

But do these developments qualify as modern? Did mercantilism promote capitalism? Did it inaugurate the era of the modern international economy, as world-systems theorists argue? What was the relationship between mercantilism and absolutism? And how far did the creation of a uniform home market go? In other words, do these changes override the differences between mercantilism and economic liberalism?

In an article published in 1948, Jacob Viner challenged the standard view that mercantilism clearly subordinated the pursuit of plenty to the pursuit of national power. The prevailing conception that plenty was only a means to a superordinate political end arose, according to Viner, from a lack of 'economic understanding' (Viner 1969: 71) by merchants who, so the implication, were otherwise motivated. Mercantilist writings suggest that plenty and power were 'joint objectives', 'both sought for their own sakes' (Viner 1969: 74). Viner's conflation of power and plenty fails to make sense of what was a circular mode of reasoning: just as state power depended on the accumulation of wealth, so the accumulation of wealth depended on state power. This leads to the hasty conclusion that the two objectives enjoyed equal status. What Viner misses are the specific social conditions for the accumulation of wealth in the early modern period.[1]

Due to the persistence of the unity of economics and politics in early modern Europe, accumulation remained politically constituted. If we turn to mercantilist trade policy, this meant that the early modern world market established circuits of exchange that remained fundamentally tied to the 'archaic' logic of commercial capitalism, based on asymmetrical terms of trade. Such a commercial capitalism, however, had characterized virtually all preceding trade systems, like those of the Hanseatic League, the Italian Renaissance cities, or the medieval trading circuits of the Indian Ocean. According to Maurice Dobb, mercantilism

> was a similar policy of monopoly to that which at an earlier stage the towns had pursued in their relations with the surrounding countryside, and which the merchants and merchant-manufacturers of the privileged companies had pursued in relation to the working craftsmen. It was a continuance of what had always been the essential aim of the policy of the Staple; and had its parallel in the policy of towns like Florence or Venice or Bruges or Lübeck in the thirteenth and fourteenth centuries, to which in an earlier chapter the name of 'urban colonialism' was given. (Dobb 1946: 206)

Gustav Schmoller observes of the policies of medieval towns that 'the soul of that policy is the putting of fellow-citizens at an advantage, and of competitors from outside at a disadvantage. . . . All the resources of municipal diplomacy, of constitutional struggle between the Estates (*Stände*), and, in the last resort, of violence, were employed to gain control over trade-routes (*Straßenzwang*) and obtain staple rights' (Schmoller 1897: 8, 10). In Marx's words, 'not only trade, but also trading capital, is older than the capitalist mode of production, and it is in fact the oldest historical mode in which capital has an independent existence' (Marx 1981: 442). These trading circuits flourished precisely because merchants relied on politically constituted trade privileges granted by rulers, which established monopolies for specific trades linking territorially separated centres of production and exchange and creating profits through the exploitation of existing price differentials (Wolf 1982: 83–8). Trade monopolies were granted either for a particular region or a particular commodity. Wealth was obtained only in the sphere of circulation. 'Buying cheap in order to sell dear' was the maxim of commercial capitalism – a principle that worked only because price differentials were artificially, i.e., politically and militarily, maintained through monopolies, preventing economic competition (Marx 1981: 447).[2] 'Without regulation to limit numbers and protect the price-margin between what the merchant bought and what he sold, merchant capital might enjoy spasmodic windfalls but could have no enduring source of income' (Dobb 1946: 200).

It was precisely the circumvention of world prices that allowed privileged traders to reap the profits of unequal exchange, sparing them from investing systematically in production to undercut competitors. Traders, of course, profited twice: first by selling domestic goods overseas (exports), where monopoly supply met competitive demand, driving up prices; and second by selling foreign goods at home (imports), again profiting from being the monopoly supplier in the face of competitive demand:

> In the cruel rapacity of its exploitation colonial policy in the seventeenth and eighteenth centuries differed little from the methods by which in earlier centuries Crusaders and the armed merchants of Italian cities had robbed the Byzantine territories of the Levant. . . . 'The large dividends of the East India companies over long periods indicate plainly that they converted their power into profits. The Hudson's Bay Company bought beaver pelts for goods costing seven to eight shillings. In the Altai the Russians sold iron pots to the natives for as many beaver skins as would fill them. The Dutch East India Company paid the native producers of pepper about one-tenth the price it received in Holland. The French East India Company in 1691 bought Eastern goods for 487,000 *livres* which sold in France for 1,700,000 *livres*. . . . Slavery in the colonies was another source of great fortune'; sugar, cotton and tobacco cultivation all resting on slave-labour. (Dobb 1946: 208, quoting F.L. Nussbaum)

Under a regime of politically maintained price differentials, there was no long-term tendency towards the equalization of profit rates. Politically hedged commercial bilateralism was the opposite of modern 'free' commercial multilateralism. The only options for expanding commercial accumulation were quantitative growth in the volume of trade, political expulsion of competitors from markets (at home as well as abroad), or conquest of new markets and trading routes. Everything therefore depended on fostering the national and international political conditions for maintaining or expanding this dominant strategy of ruling-class reproduction.

3. The Class Character of Sea-Borne Trade and its Geopolitical Implications

The geopolitical upshot was that maritime trading routes in the medieval Mediterranean and along the northern Atlantic and Baltic seaboard, as well as in the early modern trans-Atlantic zone, became 'territorialized'. This meant that they had to be protected by military means, which explains the lamentations over protection costs and the build-up of naval forces. Merchants were forced to travel in convoys, accompanied by naval vessels (Mettam 1988: 299).[3] Alternatively, merchantmen were militarized in order to combine the twin tasks of shipping and warfare.

The logic of political trade meant that, beyond the coastlines, states sought exclusive control over the seas. The notion of the 'sovereignty of the sea' gave rise in the sixteenth and seventeenth centuries to the *mare clausum* versus *mare liberum* debate, in which England, France, and Holland sought to challenge the Spanish claim to exclusive property over the oceans (Grewe 1984: 300–322). While England first argued for the liberty of the sea against Spain, John Seldon later adopted the Spanish position in order to defend the Stuarts' *de facto dominium maris* against the Dutch, whose cost advantages in the carrying trade led them to develop the *mare liberum* argument (Hugo Grotius). The liberty of the sea did not mean its depoliticization and internationalization, however, but its division among the leading commercial maritime powers. While the mid-nineteenth-century 'open door' doctrine, which enshrined the principle of equal opportunity in trade, was predicated on capitalist free trade, *mare liberum* practices remained tied to the system of competitive national mercantilism (Grewe 1984: 559–66). The partition of the oceans did not establish geographically contiguous maritime spaces, but followed the criss-crossing lines of seaborne commerce. In practice, sovereignty travelled with the merchant convoys; convoys did not traverse sovereign grounds. As the sovereignty of coasts came to be set by the range of mainland artillery, so the sovereignty of the seas was realized through the military protection of trading routes: *terrae dominium finitur, ubi finitur armorum vis* – 'the control over land ends where the force of arms ends' (Grewe 1984: 386). The efficacy of armed might delineated the boundaries of maritime sovereignty. To put it graphically: the sea was 'territorialized' along the lines of trading routes, dotted with trading posts, bastions, and walled entrepôts. And as the sea was 'territorialized', trading ports and their hinterlands were connected through these lines of militarily protected commerce to respective metropolitan countries. The early modern intercontinental empires were thus essentially seaborne empires.

Under these conditions of geocommercial exchange, economic competition took the form of politico-military competition between rival polities over market monopolies, colonies, and circuits of exchange.[4] Competition was 'primarily "extra-economic", involving piracy and retaliation, diplomacy and alliances, trade embargoes, and outright armed struggle against rival merchants and towns' (Katz 1989: 99). It translated directly into almost permanent maritime trade wars between political rivals – the dominant logic of interaction between seafaring international actors in this period. 'Commercial competition, even in times nominally of peace, degenerated into a state of undeclared hostility: it plunged nations into one war after another, and gave all wars a turn in the direction of trade, industry, and colonial gain, such as they never had before or after' (Schmoller 1897: 64).

However, wherever cities had failed to become oligarchic merchant republics, like the United Provinces, the fundamental difference between the trading cities of the European high and late Middle Ages and the trading states of the early modern period was that powerful territorial monarchs had arrogated the rights to dispense trading monopolies and charters to towns and merchant companies within their territories.[5] Thus, merchants could not organize themselves politically in city-republics or city-leagues, but had to turn to the Crown to negotiate these crucial political titles to wealth in return for royal military protection at sea. This monopoly policy 'was the former "policy of the town writ large in the affairs of the state"' (Dobb 1946: 206; see also Münkler 1992: 208).

The outcome of this class alliance was the organization of foreign trade under royal trading companies – gigantic military-commercial machines whose vessels, though sailing under the royal flag and on a royal commission, were owned and commanded by private entrepreneurs who shared costs and profits with the Crown (De Vries 1976: 128–46). As joint-stock companies, trading companies were private enterprises; as chartered companies, depending upon royal trading concessions and privileges, they were public agencies, carrying rights of sovereignty. For example, 'in England, of the twenty-five ships which had made up Drake's expedition to the West Indies in 1585 only two were supplied by the Queen; and though he sailed as Elizabeth's admiral and had official instructions, only about a third of the cost of fitting out the expedition was met by the government' (Anderson 1988: 27). It was these semi-independent naval companies that stood on a permanent footing of undeclared war overseas.

The near-permanent state of war between the leading trading nations was graphically illustrated by Louis XIV's foreign policy. His gambit for the West Indies, promoted by the creation of the French West India Company, led to the failed attempt to take over Dutch commerce by the direct conquest of the United Provinces in 1672. This was in turn followed by the Anglo-French trade war of 1674 and the struggle with Spain over the *asiento* (the right to supply slaves) during the War of the Spanish Succession (Kaiser 1990: 151–2). The English and Dutch East India Companies, for their part, were bitter rivals in southeast Asia. Cromwell's protectionist Navigation Act (1651) struck directly at Dutch dominance in the lucrative carrying trade and led to the escalation of Anglo-Dutch geocommercial rivalries. The English Navigation Acts (1651, 1660, 1662) occasioned the Anglo-Dutch naval conflicts of 1652–54, 1665–67, and 1672–74 – here in connection with Louis XIV's invasion of the Dutch Republic. The English objective in all three wars was to destroy Dutch shipping and trade, notably Dutch control over the West African slave trade. Early modern trade was predicated upon ever-vigilant naval policy and commercial legislation. It was buttressed by the power of states. Commerce, strategy, and security formed one undifferentiated whole.

At the same time, these hybrid public–private corporations were hard to keep under effective government control. Consequently, the line between privateering and outright piracy was hard to establish, and rulers were none too keen to draw it. On the contrary, privateering was part and parcel of aggressive geocommerce. Juridically, corsairs were private captains with royal orders to capture foreign vessels, whereas pirates attacked ships indiscriminately. Pirates were lawless criminals; corsairs were political enemies (Grewe 1984: 354ff). France, for example,

> came to rely more heavily than any other state on privateers as a weapon in maritime war, and developed the strongest privateering tradition in Europe. To many Frenchmen this seemed an ideal form of war at sea. It would be cheap, since most of the cost would be borne by speculators in search of profits from captured English and Dutch ships. (Anderson 1988: 96–7)

Since by the beginning of the early modern period the Crown enjoyed a monopoly over the rights of circulation, we find everywhere in territorial monarchies a long-term inter–ruling-class alliance between the Crown and 'its' privileged merchant-manufacturers. While monarchs vied for the returns from customs and profited from selling charters and patents, assisting the expansion of overseas trade, merchants sought royal monopolies and military protection. This alliance controlled entry to commerce (Brenner 1993: 48). Such a structural nexus between the economic and the political constitutes, of course, the opposite of modern capitalism, which was expressed in the sphere of maritime trade in the shift to 'open door' principles, allowing the free flow of goods in open markets. Here, competition is regulated only by the price mechanism and not through domestic monopolies and war. Under-pricing rather than out-gunning characterizes capitalist trade. As a result of the Glorious Revolution, backed by the class alliance between capitalist aristocrats and new merchants, Parliament diluted the monopolies of the old trading companies to allow for freer and greater mobilization of capital in overseas enterprises (Brenner 1993: 715). Eventually, the English Levant Company was dissolved in 1823, the East India Company by the mid-nineteenth century, and the Hudson's Bay Company in 1859. Privateering was officially outlawed in 1856 (Grewe 1984: 368; see also Thomson 1994). This shift, which did not come about on an international scale until the nineteenth century, indeed marked a sea-change in maritime international relations. It meant nothing less than the 'de-bordering' of the sea. In terms of political economy, this was the shift from Antoyne de Montchrétien, John Seldon, and Thomas Mun to Adam Smith.[6]

Mercantilist trade thus remained subordinate to and dependent on the political power of the Crown. It did not usher in a modern world-system, based on a new mode of territorial organization and international relations, but essentially extended the pre-modern logic of absolutist territorial organization into the non-European world. As Rosenberg argues, the 'international economy of the absolutist empires is not structurally commensurate with the modern world economy' (Rosenberg 1994: 92).[7] Commercial capitalism under dynastic conditions was a geographical strategy of extending the accumulating reach of pre-modern states, not a qualitative change in the logic of world order. The 'logic of commercial capitalism . . . ultimately found intercontinental expression in the imperial organisation of early modern world trade' (Boyle 1994: 355). Precisely because world-systems theorists equate long-distance trade with capitalism, which thus becomes a phenomenon of virtually all international economic systems, they are forced to push the existence of a modern world-system back into ever more distant pasts, leading to meaningless speculation about 5,000 years of the world-system (Abu-Lughod 1989; Frank and Gills 1993).

4. Did Mercantilism Promote Capitalism?

Early modern mercantilism not only failed to establish a new logic of international economic relations (although it extended their geographical reach), it did not even generate any unintended consequences which would have pushed this system in the direction of modern capitalism and thus modern international relations.

Linking insulated centres of production does not necessarily imply control over direct producers, although this was sometimes done by organizing the labour process both at home and in overseas markets.[8] For the most part, it sufficed to secure a monopoly foothold in these trading ports, where quasi-extra-territorial merchant communities sprang up, in order to affirm and exploit favourable terms of trade, i.e., to maintain a profit margin between the price in the market of purchase and the price in the market of sale:

> With a few exceptions, such as West Indian sugar plantations worked by negro slaves, such investment was an accessory to trading ventures rather than an independent enterprise, valued for its own sake; and the preoccupation of practical men and of economic theorists alike was essentially with the terms of trade rather than with the conditions for investment abroad. Herein lay the crucial difference between the Old Colonial System of the Mercantile period and the colonial system of modern Imperialism. (Dobb 1946: 217)

As a rule, privileged chartered companies had little interest in reorganizing the labour process since this necessitated risky, long-term capital investments that were difficult to supervise. True, the stimulus of market exchange could orientate production towards exchange. But under conditions of unfree labour, this stimulus tended merely to intensify the use of extra-economic coercion by those in control of labour, be they lords, slave owners, or merchant manufacturers operating putting-out systems. The entrenchment or even introduction of pre-capitalist property relations in the wake of trade was most spectacularly evidenced in American slave plantations, the introduction of the 'second serfdom' in fifteenth-century eastern Europe, and other versions of tributary relationships (Wolf 1982: 101–25).[9] This reduction of peripheries to dependency and underdevelopment through unequal terms of trade is, of course, the mainstay of dependency and world-systems theory. But this was not capitalist trade.

The logic of the putting-out system, for example, was based on the political exclusion of craftsmen from the trading guilds, which monopolized the raw materials necessary for the craftsmen's trade and fixed prices. Craftsmen were thus not only forced to work exclusively for the guilds, they had to sell the finished goods to them as well. Merchants were thus in a position to force down the prices of production for export goods.

> Merchants also used political power more directly to regulate wages, hours and working conditions; 'anticombination' laws sought to destroy or prohibit the formation of craftsmen or journeymen fraternities designed to raise prices or wages. The leading burgess groups in the towns would thus augment profits by depressing the economic conditions of existence of the direct producers. (Katz 1989: 100)[10]

The fates of the once-prosperous Venetian cloth and Genoese silk industries are a case in point. As soon as the English 'new draperies' under-priced Italian products during the seventeenth century and the Italian city-republics were unable to defend their maritime trading monopolies, the Italian industries were unable to react competitively because home producers were not completely subject to capital. Italian putting-out systems remained regulated by rigid guilds (Brenner 1993: 33–9). Since competition was not between capitalist entrepreneurs but between appropriating agents in politically protected markets, profits were maximized by intensifying labour (forcing down wages, extending labour-time) rather than by creating cost advantages through investment. Reducing production costs remained secondary to protecting monopoly markets and reducing labour costs, precisely because the latter remained politically controlled. This comparative disregard for productive efficiency came to the fore in the disputes over the general welfare effects of mercantilism. Critics argued that monopoly prices drove up prices and that chartered trading companies restricted free enterprise (Buck 1974: 155–9).

Since commercial capitalism did not set in motion a self-sustaining logic of economic growth based on 'free labour', factor mobility, and reinvestment in the means of production, Marx postulated an inverse relationship between the development of trade and the development of capitalist production:

> The law that the independent development of commodity capital stands in inverse proportion to the level of development of capitalist production appears particularly clearly in the history of the carrying trade, as conducted by the Venetians, Genoans, Dutch, etc., where the major profit was made not by supplying a specific national product, but rather by mediating the exchange of products between commercially – and generally

economically undeveloped communities and by exploiting both the producing countries. (Marx 1981: 446)

However, in his important chapter 'Historical Material on Merchant Capital' Marx remarks that commercial capitalism acted as a 'solvent' of pre-capitalist relations of production by subjecting production more and more to the demands of capital. Yet he hastens to add that 'how far it leads to the dissolution of the old mode of production depends first and foremost on the solidity and inner articulations of this mode of production itself' (Marx 1981: 449). In other words, it is the political grip of the ruling classes on existing social property relations that defines the extent of this dissolving effect: it depends on the class constellations defining the political constitution of the respective polity.[11] Market stimuli, Marx explains, are 'insufficient to explain the transition from one mode of production to the other' (Marx 1981: 444). Since commercial capitalism only mediates the exchange of surplus already extracted by political means, it does not fundamentally change the social relations of production.[12] Trade does not in itself generate surplus-value, or even value; it merely realizes profits. Trade in no way generates aggregate economic growth; it merely redistributes existing surpluses. Merchant wealth is therefore not capital.

Internationally, this redistribution through unequal exchange was a zero-sum game (Anderson 1974b: 37); total wealth was thereby not increased. This zero-sum conception, which conceived of total wealth as finite, was elevated into an economic law in mercantilist doctrine, precisely because the sphere of production remained outside its theoretical scope. Nationally, economic growth was thought of in terms of absolute population growth, absolute gains from trade, the surplus inflow of bullion, or absolute territorial gains. The mercantilist theory and praxis of wealth creation thus remained typically limited to policies of labour immigration, land reclamation, and peasant protection by absolutist rulers who were subsequently hailed as 'enlightened'. Frederick the Great's economic policies are often seen in this light, failing to observe that his *Bauernschutzpolitik* (policy of peasant protection) was less to benefit Prussian peasants than to disadvantage the landed nobility and fill royal coffers. Since the peasantry constituted the tax base, there was nothing altruistic or 'enlightened' in these policies. Kunisch notes that 'absolutism had no conception of the citizenry (*Staatsvolk*) other than in the form of the mercantilist category of population, the mass of subjects whose nationality and language constituted no part of *raison d'État*' (Kunisch 1979: 15). Strictly speaking, mercantilism had no conception of economic growth, only an idea of the asymmetric accumulation of existing wealth. Domestically, of course – at least for the western metropolitan countries – mercantilist teaching led to the hoarding of treasure, bullionism, and the mistaken belief that a positive balance of trade was the source of national wealth. Consequently, profits from trade were not systematically reinvested in the means of production but in the means of violence, so as to guarantee the reproduction of political exchange. Trade-driven military demand promoted the development of new industries – armaments, shipbuilding, metallurgy, textiles, etc. – but always in the 'antediluvian' form of state-granted monopolies (Katz 1989: 91ff). When state demand and state protection disappeared, the industries collapsed.

This ancient logic of commercial capitalism was not even challenged by the new Dutch trading system, which, by specializing primarily in bulk goods, gained trade advantages by lowering transaction costs. The competitive edge was not maintained so much by lowering production costs as by maximizing 'carrying capacity subject to the constraint of low construction costs [of vessels] and low operating costs' (De Vries 1976: 117). Dutch trade thrived by offering lower freight charges, based on new shipbuilding techniques. This strategy in turn lost out to English exports during the seventeenth century. The English began to under-price competitors not only by means of low transaction costs, but by real cost advantages in commodity production itself. This, however, presupposed the prior transformation of labour relations in the English countryside – not as a response to market opportunities, but as an unintended result of struggles between feudal lords and peasants over rents. After the establishment of capitalist agrarian labour relations, economic competition among farmers induced reinvestment, product diversification, specialization, and rising levels of agrarian productivity. This social property constellation created the conditions for new manufacturing industries. The main contemporary trade, the 'new draperies' produced in English textile industries running on capitalist principles, began to dominate international cloth markets through comparative advantages in the context of contracting European demand during the seventeenth-century crisis (De Vries 1976: 125; Brenner 1993: 38–9). These English developments were the starting point for the new logic of international trade relations which came to supplant politically regulated geocommerce. However, these processes belong to the late eighteenth and particularly the nineteenth century.

Thus the early modern geographical subdivision of the non-European world into territorialized colonies, extending the reach of European metropolitan countries into previously uncharted lands, not only expanded the theatre of inherently bellicose inter-European relations; it also created a configuration of political space in which the essentially a-territorial logic of modern capitalism later had to operate. When capitalism burst on the international scene in the nineteenth century, most parts of the world had already been territorially demarcated by mercantilism. Bounded, though not fixed or static, territoriality preceded the rise of capitalism.

5. Closed Trading States: Uniform Economic Territories?

Mercantilism meant essentially the private ownership and accumulation of state-sponsored titles to wealth for the mutual benefit of king and privileged traders and manufacturers. Metaphorically, this was no struggle between Mercury and Mars; Mercury could only succeed by standing on Mars's shoulder. Yet mercantilist policies had the side-effect of building up economically unified territories, closed trading states. Or did they? Yes and no (Mettam 1988: 288–308). What is required is a distinction between external closure and internal uniformity. The idea that closed trading states, i.e., states with high tariffs or quotas on imports and state-sponsored subsidies on exports, were tantamount to unified home markets evaporates if we consider not only the effects of politically maintained monopolies on foreign trade, but also their effect on the structure of production and consumption in domestic markets. For monopolies granted to certain home industries and the systematic build-up of state-subsidized manufactures did not establish an open and competitive home market. Rather, royal political power was expressed through a series of bilateral agreements with different towns, companies, and corporate actors. 'Thus, the question at issue was not, at the outset, whether the various town privileges should be blended in one body of rights enjoyed equally by every citizen of the territory, but simply whether the princely government should secure a moderate increase of its power as against each particular town' (Schmoller 1897: 22). Mercantilism promoted a unified, though imperfect, domestic market in the sphere of circulation – Colbert reformed the national customs system in 1646 – but it did not free the sphere of production (Mettam 1988: 303). It merely regulated production for the mutual benefit of a privileged burgher class and the Crown.

Since the property relations governing agrarian production remained untouched, mercantilism entrenched a dual economy consisting of a low productivity agrarian sector and an artificially promoted, high productivity sector of manufactures, catering to export and domestic luxury consumption. Prices remained inelastic, especially in the luxury goods (leather, armaments, metal, tapestries, glass, silk, carpets, porcelain, spices) primarily promoted by the Crown, whose 'natural' buyers were, of course, precisely the court and the higher classes (Dobb 1946: 196–7). In short, protection of the guild system, export-orientated manufacture, and non-competitive prices were ultimately to the detriment of private buyers. The corollary was that mercantilism entrenched a politically differentiated internal sphere of production while removing obstacles to circulation. Since, according to mercantilist doctrine, one man's gain was another man's loss, internal trade meant redistribution within the national economy. Surplus, affecting the balance of trade, was only to be reaped from foreign trade. The construction of an open, homogeneous home market, an economically unified space based on the complete mobility, i.e., commodification, of all factors of production, was impossible to achieve under mercantilism. This was not, of course, simply the effect of economic doctrine, but the expression of the persistence of pre-capitalist social property relations. Nevertheless, a bounded though internally differentiated economic territory, emerged in the leading West European monarchies by the late seventeenth century: the closed trading state.

6. Conclusion: The 'Wealth of the State' versus the 'Wealth of the Nation'

In sum, mercantilism was not designed to increase the 'wealth of the nation' but the wealth of the state. The state, however, was first and foremost the king. But since he could not realize the profits of unequal exchange without the assistance of privileged merchant strata, mercantilism involved the systematic deployment of political titles for private wealth. This class structure drove the logic of politically constituted and militarily protected trade. Mercantilism's social rationale was based on the persistence of non-capitalist social property relations, which necessitated the internal and external accumulation of surplus by political means, either through the direct political coercion of direct producers or through politically maintained unequal exchange.

This had five important long-term consequences. First, the military struggle over monopoly markets and trade routes constituted the dominant *logic of interaction* among European seafaring countries throughout the sixteenth, seventeenth, and eighteenth centuries. Near-permanent warfare was not derivative of systemic anarchy, but expressed the reproduction strategies of rulers within the given structure of property relations. Second, the geopolitical struggle over access to monopoly markets and the progressive removal of internal barriers to trade hardened economic space into bounded, though internally differentiated, territorial shells. The closing of home markets in conjunction with the logic of commercial capitalism strengthened a new *territorial order* – multiple bounded territories. Third, to the extent that the Crown tended to promote foreign trade as well as domestic industry, it instrumentalized these economic means for its own power-political aspirations. Mercantilism was a rationalization strategy of absolutist rulers to maximize politically constituted income and not a defensive mechanism of the capitalist classes. While it failed to promote, either intentionally or unintentionally, capitalist industry, it attempted to rationalize income opportunities within the given confines of pre-capitalist relations of exploitation. Power and wealth were not simply joint objectives, two separate goals; the accumulation of wealth was predicated on the exercise of power. Security and reproduction were inseparable. Fourth, the Crown's demand for ever-greater resources to secure the framework of political extraction led mercantilism to degenerate into pure fiscalism (Hinrichs 1986: 355–6). Punitive taxes on the peasantry, the high protection costs of trade routes, a growing apparatus of parasitic officers, artificially maintained and uncompetitive prices, monopoly enterprises, protectionism and import substitution, capped by unproductive investment in the means of violence, posed clear limits to economic growth under mercantilism. In fact, these strategies were counter-productive and self-exhausting in the long run. Fifth, the symbiosis between privileged merchants and the title-dispensing Crown became a long-term, self-perpetuating class alliance. This class alliance had a vested interest in the maintenance of the status quo. When it was later vigorously contested by the 'new merchants' during the English Revolution, it became 'reactionary' and backward-looking. It had everything to lose and little to gain by free-trade.[13] This new free trade regime brought with it the forces that undermined the ancient logic of commercial capitalism during the nineteenth century, inaugurating the era of the modern world-market.

Theoretically, it was precisely mercantilism's abstraction from the sphere of production and its focus on the sphere of circulation that gave it a distorted, 'antediluvian' character:

> The first theoretical treatment of the modern mode of production – mercantilism – necessarily proceeded from the superficial phenomena of the circulation process, as these acquire autonomy in the movement of

capital. Hence it only grasped the semblance of things. . . . The genuine science of modern economics begins only when theoretical discussion moves from the circulation process to the production process. (Marx 1981: 455; see also Dobb 1946: 199)

However, since by the seventeenth century political control over the rights to circulation was mostly in the hands of territorial monarchs, mercantilism, according to Schmoller, was 'in its innermost kernel . . . nothing but state making' (Schmoller 1897: 50).[14] The state distributed these titles to private agents who, in turn, remained dependent on state power for their realization. The state, however, was the king.

Notes

1 The failure to theorize the politically constituted nature of mercantilism is a recurrent theme in the historiographical literature. Burkhardt, for example, asserts that 'all examples of early modern economic policy, whether we look at single countries or at the epoch as a whole, show much politics and little economics', and takes this to be a non-Marxist argument for the primacy of power politics (Burkhardt 1997: 557; see also Buck 1974).

2 Douglass North, in contrast, suggests theorizing the rise of merchant empires on the basis of a neoclassical supply/demand model, built on comparative advantage, plus a model of declining transaction costs (North 1991; see also Tracy 1990; Chaudhuri 1991).

3 This commercial insecurity and the associated credit risks are semantically reflected in the term 'merchant adventurers', and formed part of the Florentine discourse of *fortuna* (Münkler 1982: 209–12).

4 For early modern Portugal and Spain, see Rosenberg 1994: 91–122.

5 For pre-revolutionary England, cf. Brenner 1993: 51–94 and 199–239. For France, see, e.g., De Vries's account of the fate of the Calvinist city of La Rochelle, its reincorporation into the royal state, and the resulting arrangements between its merchant traders and the king (De Vries 1976: 238).

6 Burkhardt conceives the fusion of the political and the economic under mercantilism as a 'deficit of state-autonomy in economic and fiscal matters' and points out with reference to Karl Polanyi that 'a new form of international economic thinking' – classical political economy – was necessary to autonomize the state from the economy. Since Burkhardt fails to relate these changes in economic theory to secular social property relations, his remarks on the nature of mercantilism stand theoretically on their head (Burkhardt 1997: 560–61).

7 If this is true, however, then it is difficult to say that early modern Spanish, Portuguese, Dutch, French, and English empire-building were 'different moments of primitive accumulation', as Marx wrote in one passage (Marx

1976b: 915.) They may represent different stages of capital accumulation, but not necessarily steps in the transformation of relations of production, i.e., they did not generalize the capital relation.

8 Chartered merchants often had no interest in setting up entirely new systems of production in the colonies, preferring to concentrate on trade itself (Brenner 1993: 92–112).

9 It should be pointed out that the seventeenth-century American plantations were not developed by old-style company merchants, but by what Brenner calls colonial-interloping merchants, a new non-privileged class of traders who acted as capitalist entrepreneurs in colonial production (Brenner 1993: 684ff).

10 On the rigid guild structure of the fifteenth-century Florentine cloth industry and the double dependency on export and import markets, see Münkler 1992: 146–8, 162–3.

11 On Marx's two paths to the transition to capitalism, see Brenner 1989.

12 Hinrichs comments that 'the majority of the members of the French trading companies regarded their participation in trade merely as an object of monetary investment, similar to a royal office or a clerical prebend, not as a mercantile adventure which required initiative and risk' (Hinrichs 1986: 351). It is, therefore, doubtful whether mercantilists ever really 'spelled out the inner nature of capitalist production' (Zech 1985: 568).

13 'And it is to this fact that we must evidently look for a part of the reason why older and established sections of the bourgeoisie have always become so quickly reactionary and showed such readiness to ally themselves with feudal remnants or with an autocratic régime to preserve the *status quo* against more revolutionary change' (Dobb 1946: 219). Robert Brenner has explored the consequences of this class alliance between king and privileged traders and its contestation by new colonial merchants and capitalist landlords during the English Revolution (Brenner 1993).

14 Schmoller's tract deserves attention in so far as it – as a member of the 'Younger Historical School of German Economists' – spells out, fired by national sentiment, the hostile nature of commercial international relations in the age of mercantilism, which was often prettified by apologetic writers of the dominant Western trading powers. 'Does it not sound to us to-day like the irony of fate, that the same England, which in 1750–1800 reached the summit of its commercial supremacy by means of its tariffs and naval wars, frequently with extraordinary violence, and always with the most tenacious national selfishness, that that England at the very same time announced to the world the doctrine that only the egoism of the individual is justified, and never that of states and nations; the doctrine which dreamt of a stateless competition of all the individuals of every land, and of the harmony of the economic interests of all nations?' (Schmoller 1897: 80). Theoretically, Schmoller's writings are set in the German historicist tradition, which harshly criticized methodologically individualist theories of economic action by placing economic agents into the context of historically grown

communities which determined their economic behaviour. Although Schmoller's account of macro-historical development is couched in evolutionary-functionalist terms as successions of ever larger and 'more adequate' economic territories (here: from towns to territories), his insistence on the historical specificity of 'economic laws' unmasks the universalizing and naturalizing doctrines of classical political economy as the ideology of the nineteenth-century hegemonic power. The writings of the nineteenth-century German historical economists provided the 'scientific' and ideological legitimation for Prussia's rise to the status of a European great power just as British writers could confidently proclaim the principle of free trade as soon as a capitalist home market had raised productivity to such an extent that British goods under-priced competitors in their own markets. Dobb remarked that 'whereas England at the time, as an importer of corn and cotton and as a pioneer of the new machinery, who had everything to gain and nothing to lose by opening markets abroad to her manufactures, could afford to elevate freedom of foreign trade to the level of a general principle, other countries could seldom so afford' (Dobb 1946: 194).

7

Demystifying the Westphalian States-System

1. Introduction: Theorizing the Constitution, Operation, and Transformation of Geopolitical Systems

I argued in chapter 4 that conventional accounts of Europe's pre-industrial long-term economic and political development – the geopolitical competition, demographic, and commercialization models – are flawed on empirical and theoretical grounds. I then suggested that accounts of the transition to modernity need to register two transformations – from the medieval to the early modern, and from the early modern to the modern world. I further argued that these two transformations are bound up with the radically divergent trajectories of state/society formation in early modern France and England, based on variations in the balances of class forces that led to a transition from feudalism to absolutism in France and from feudalism to capitalism in England. These different passages provide the key to unlock the incommensurable patterns of geopolitical conflict and co-operation in the early modern and modern international systems. In chapter 6, I demonstrated these pre-modern patterns in the early modern international political economy, based on mercantilism, politically consti-tuted unequal exchange, and maritime empire-building. We can now draw out the wider implications of this understanding for reconstructing the general nature of early modern international relations and the meaning of the Westphalian peace treaties. Thereafter, we will turn more fully to the English experience to reconstruct the transition to modern international relations.

To recapitulate: this research agenda attracted the attention of IR scholars in response to John Ruggie's charge that Neorealism cannot account for systemic change, and especially the medieval-to-modern shift (Ruggie 1986, 1993). While important new interpretations of this instance of systemic change, largely of Constructivist persuasion, are now available (Spruyt 1994a; Burch 1998; Hall 1999; Philpot 2001), the conventional Realist account of Westphalia's significance as the epochal turning point in the history of international relations remains intact. 'The Peace of West-phalia, for better or worse, marks the end of an epoch and the opening of another. It represents the majestic portal which leads from the old into the new world' (Gross 1948: 28–9; cf. also Morgenthau 1985: 293–4, 328–9; Butterfield 1966; Wight 1977b, 1978; Bull 1977).[1] Independent of theoret-ical premises, there is a broad consensus in the IR community that specifically modern principles or constitutive rules of international relations – state sovereignty, exclusive territoriality, legal equality, secular politics, non-intervention, standing diplomacy, international law, multilateral con-gresses – were codified at the Westphalian Congress against the background of the demise of feudal heterogeneity and universal empire (Ruggie 1986: 141–9; Kratochwil 1986, 1995; Holsti 1991: 20–21, 25–6; Armstrong 1993: 30–40; Spruyt 1994a: 3ff; Arrighi 1994: 36–47; Burch 1998: 89; Hall 1999: 99; Buzan and Little 2000: 4–5, 241–55).[2] Henceforth, inter-state anarchy, power politics, and the balance of power as the systemic regulator of international relations prevailed.

But does this shift in system structure matter for determining geopolitical behaviour? Paradoxically, for Neorealists this shift is irrelevant, since the transition from feudal anarchy to inter-state anarchy involves no change in the basic structuring principle of international relations. Fischer's Neorealist analysis of feudal geopolitics concludes that 'conflict and power politics are a structural condition of the international realm – present even among individuals in a stateless society' (Fischer 1992: 425). The Neorealist thesis of a basic invariance in the conduct of conflict units, regardless of their identity and social composition – provided that the international system is multipolar and thus anarchical – precludes recognizing 1648 as a fundamen-tal break in the logic of international relations. Westphalia merely reaf-firmed the timeless logic of anarchy. The players may have changed, but their conduct did not. Constructivists, by contrast, stress that modern anarchy is grounded in exclusive territoriality, resulting from the early modern redefinition of fundamental constitutive rules of social life (modern subjectivity, private property rights, etc.) that transformed the international 'rules of the game'. While this account does not contest the competitive mode of operation of modern international relations, it claims to have identified its 'generative grammar' and allows for variations in international behaviour, exemplified by medieval Europe. But since the mode of territoriality constitutes for Constructivists like Ruggie the decisive criterion, current processes of de-bordering and deterritorialization of political rule may support the claim for the move toward a postmodern international system.

My interpretation of the Westphalian order leads to radically different conclusions. My argument is that distinctly non-modern geopolitical relations between dynastic and other pre-modern political communities characterized the Westphalian system. While these relations were competitive, they were determined neither by structural anarchy, nor by a new set of constitutive rules agreed upon at Westphalia, nor by exclusive territoriality. Rather, they were rooted in pre-capitalist social property relations. The logic of inter-dynastic relations structured the early modern geopolitical order until the regionally highly uneven and protracted nineteenth-century transition to international modernity.[3] The social constitution of the absolutist geopolitical system, its mode of operation, and the logic of its transformation are, however, insufficiently understood in standard IR theories, be they of (Neo-)Realist or Constructivist provenance. It follows that, if European geopolitics was characterized by dynasticism well beyond 1648, we need to reconsider the significance of the 'Westphalian theme' as a geopolitical turning point for the IR community.

Three basic theoretical arguments, relating to the constitution, operation, and transformation of geopolitical orders, inform the following exposition. First, although the medieval, early modern, and modern geopolitical systems are all characterized by anarchy, they reflect fundamentally different principles of international relations. Given the indeterminacy of anarchy, variations in the character of international systems, the political regimes of their constitutive actors, and their forms of conflict and co-operation can be theorized on the basis of different social property relations. They form the *constitutive core* of different geopolitical orders. Schematically, personalized, decentralized, feudal political authority was replaced by personalized but more centralized absolutist rule, which was in turn replaced by depersonalized, centralized capitalist political order: modern sovereignty. Absolutist sovereignty, in striking contrast to modern sovereignty, was proprietary in character, personalized by the ruling dynasty, and rooted in absolutist pre-capitalist property relations.

Second, property relations not only explain the constitution of different political regimes and geopolitical systems, they also generate the historically bounded and antagonistic strategies of action that govern international relations. The persistence of pre-capitalist property relations in *Ancien*

Régime states implies that the reproduction of the dynastic–absolutist ruling classes continued to be driven by the logic of (geo)political accumulation. Dynastic sovereignty and geopolitical accumulation determined the conduct of early modern international relations. Proprietary kingship entailed empire-building, political marriages, wars of succession, dynastic 'international' law, bandwagoning, and an inter-dynastic compensating equilibrium that eliminated smaller polities. These core institutions structured early modern modes of aggression, conflict resolution, and territoriality. Dynastic strategies of reproduction explain the *mode of operation* of the absolutist geopolitical system.

Third, while differences between international systems can conceptually be clearly established, a historical reconstruction faces the problem of coming to terms with the temporal coexistence of heterogeneous international actors in a 'mixed-case' scenario. During the seventeenth-century crisis, regionally uneven solutions to domestic class conflicts and geopolitical struggles over the politically constituted powers of extraction spawned important regime variations among European polities. The result was a heterogeneous geopolitical system. France, Austria, Spain, Sweden, Russia, Denmark–Norway, Brandenburg–Prussia, and the Papal States were absolutist. The Holy Roman Empire remained a confederal elective monarchy until 1806. The Dutch General Estates established an independent oligarchic merchant republic. Poland was a 'crowned aristocratic republic' and Switzerland a free confederation of cantons. Whereas Italian merchant-republics struggled against being transformed into monarchies, England became a parliamentary constitutional monarchy presiding over the world's first capitalist economy. Yet, despite this diversity, the early modern international system was dominated by the numerically and power-politically preponderant dynastic states. This account of geopolitics is thus not predicated upon the homogeneity of its constitutive units, but comprehends the Westphalian order as an open system dominated by dynastic states, in which *system maintenance and system transformation* were actively contested.[4]

2. Structure and Agency in the Westphalian Order

This section briefly recapitulates the nexus between the structure of absolutist property relations and early modern sovereignty, and shows how these property relations define the ruling-class strategies that explain international conduct.

1. Structure: The Absolutist State, Property Relations, and Economic Non-Development

What was the elementary structure of social property relations in seventeenth-century continental western Europe? I demonstrated in chapter 5 that between the fourteenth- and seventeenth-century crises, the passage from a feudal rent regime to an absolutist tax regime transformed fragmented medieval domination into centralized royal sovereignty. The 'parcellized sovereignty' of the medieval polity was superseded by the still personalized but more centralized domination of the absolutist tax/office state. The (imperfect) royal monopolization of the means of violence and the rights of appropriation – in the form of the standing army and centralized surplus extraction by taxation – deprived the lords of direct extra-economic powers of extraction. However, absolutist sovereignty did not entail a separation of public and private, of politics and economics, since sovereignty was personalized by the king as patrimonial property. *Ancien Régime* sovereignty meant proprietary kingship.

But, despite its pre-capitalist basis, can the absolutist tax/office state be considered a modern state, as much of the IR literature assumes (Ruggie 1993; Spruyt 1994a: 79; Hall 1999: 78)? Politically, the transformation of France from a feudal to an absolutist monarchy did not entail the establishment of modern sovereignty as defined by Max Weber (Weber 1946: 78–83). As demonstrated in chapter 5, the revisionist literature on absolutism has shown that office venality, patronage, and clientelism blocked the establishment of a modern bureaucracy and modern political institutions. Taxation remained non-uniform. Noble exemption from taxation implied the absence of permanent representative assemblies. The court became the centre of patronage, intrigue, sinecures, and faction. Different laws operated in different regions and for different status groups. There was no modern system of public finance. The means of violence were not monopolized by the state but personalized by the king, who sold army posts to patrimonial officers. Mercenarism further undermined royal aspirations to a monopoly of violence. Mercantilism was precisely the public economic policy of a pre-capitalist state. In short, all the institutional trappings of the modern state were absent in early modern France.

Economically, the loss of lordly feudal powers entailed the end of serfdom and *de facto* peasant possession. Direct producers were under no direct market pressures, but continued to produce primarily for subsistence. Precisely because the peasantry was not yet separated from its means of subsistence and subjected to market imperatives, surplus appropriation still occurred in the sphere of redistribution by extra-economic means and not in the sphere of production itself. The corollary was that the competitive logic of capitalism could not gain hold in the countryside, explaining economic non-development.

2. Agency: Political and Geopolitical Strategies of Accumulation

How does this property structure translate into international conduct? Under non-capitalist agrarian property relations, ruling-class strategies remained tied to the logic of 'political accumulation', predicated on investment in the means of appropriation. These strategies can be analyti-cally divided into (1) arbitrary, coercive, and punitive taxation of the peasantry and (2) the sale of offices, professional monopolies, and public borrowing. Externally, these strategies were matched by (3) geopolitical accumulation through war and dynastic marriage policies and (4) politically maintained and enforced unequal exchange by royal sales of trading charters to privileged merchants. Strategies (3) and (4) are the necessary external counterparts of internal strategies (1) and (2). Consequently, the two main sources of war were dynastic territorial claims and commercial monopolies and trading routes.

(Geo)political strategies of accumulation were dictated by political society's dependency on the economic well-being of the king, who had to maintain himself at the top of the ruling classes. To the degree that monarchs ceaselessly struggled to maintain and enhance their power bases at home against the threat of revolt, they were driven to pursue aggressive foreign policies. This allowed them to meet the territorial aspirations of their families, repay debts, satisfy the desire for social mobility of the 'sitting' army of officials and the 'standing' army of officers, and share the spoils of war with their growing networks of clients, financiers, and courtly favourites (Malettke 1991). These elites, in turn, pegged their fortunes to the royal warlord, provided he respected the absolutist historical compro-mise of aristocratic non-taxation, repaid his debts, and offered prospects for social promotion and geopolitical gain. In other words, geopolitical accu-mulation was necessary for the expanded reproduction of the ruling elites, revolving around the monarch at the apex of the social hierarchy. The *Fronde* (1648–53) illustrates what happened when absolutist rulers failed.

The logic of (geo)political accumulation gave rise to a series of state-constituting, state-selecting, and state-consolidating wars, accounting for the frequency and intensity of combat during the Age of Absolutism. However, these processes drove absolutist, not modern state formation. Between the end of the fifteenth century and the Napoleonic Wars, few years passed without war in Europe (Krippendorff 1985: 277; Burkhardt 1992: 9–15). Quincy Wright suggests that there were 48 important battles in 1480–1550, 48 in 1550–1600, 116 in 1600–50, 119 in 1650–1700, 276 in 1700–50, and 509 in 1750–1800, before we see a significant reduction in the nineteenth century (Wright 1965: 641–4).[5] These wars were often preceded and followed by domestic conflicts and civil wars. Although the feudal age, which lasted roughly until the rise of the 'new monarchies' in the fifteenth century, was equally a culture of war based on political accumulation, the absolutist age drastically increased the frequency, intensity, duration, and magnitude of military conflict. Furthermore, the medieval feuds and campaigns of lords, knights, and vassalic hosts were dwarfed by the martial activities of vastly better-organized permanent war-states, raising the size of armies, the cost of warfare, and the rate of surplus extraction through taxation.[6]

The success of all four strategies of income provision depended on the balance of forces between the producing and non-producing classes. This determined the tax rate and thus the resources available for war. All strategies prioritized investment in the means of violence – the build-up of standing armies, navies and militarized merchant fleets, and a police force – rather than in the means of production. It was the pressure of (geo)political accumulation, rather than systemic geopolitical competition *per se*, that explains the violence of early modern international relations. It was these inter-ruling class conflicts, and not some autonomous military technodeterminism, that drove the military-technological innovations associated with the 'Military Revolution'. Finally, it was class conflict and not the Hintzean logic of international rivalry systematized by Charles Tilly's 'states make war and war makes states' model that explains absolutist state formation (Hintze 1975a, 1975b; Tilly 1985). Yet these factors do not explain the rise of capitalism or the modern state. The diversion of economic surplus into the non-productive apparatus of violence and conspicuous consumption reproduced the politically punitive and economically self-defeating logic of the absolutist war-tax state (Bonney 1981).

Given existing social property relations and a non-self-sustaining national income, which reduced the options for expanded reproduction to (geo)political accumulation, absolutism was not only domestically rapacious, it also produced a structurally aggressive, predatory, expansive foreign policy. Consequently, the arrival of the permanent war-state and the intensification and increased frequency of war cannot be reduced to the mere contiguity of power-maximizing and security-driven unitary states or the conventions of intersubjective norms. They were bound up with the domestic structure of pre-capitalist polities.

Proprietary kingship meant that public and, *a fortiori*, foreign policy was conducted in the name not of *raison d'État* or the national interest, but of dynastic interests. It was precisely in diplomatic and foreign affairs that monarchs were most concerned to impose their 'personal rules' in order to negotiate their private titles to sovereignty with fellow monarchs:

> Reason of state thus closely linked the state with its monarch and dynasty, but not with its people or nationality; that link was only beginning to emerge in some countries. Louis XIV's idea of the state as dynastic patrimony (*L'État, c'est moi*) still prevailed in much of Europe, and if the Enlightenment notion of the monarch as the first servant of the state was beginning to make headway, the distinction made little difference in practice, especially in foreign policy. (Schroeder, 1994a: 8; see also Symcox, 1974: 3)

Thus, instead of unearthing the earliest stirrings of the first modern state ascendant in the ever more distant past – usually in absolutist France or the 'proto-modern' merchant republics of Renaissance Italy or seventeenth-century Holland – and antedating the origins of the modern states-system correspondingly, this chapter seeks to show how long European international politics was governed by practices and principles which remained thoroughly embedded in pre-capitalist social relations. Despite the 'surface modernity' of early modern international relations, their substance betrays a greater continuity with the Middle Ages.

3. Westphalian Geopolitical Relations: Foreign Policy as Dynastic Family Business

Proprietary kingship meant that the social relations of international intercourse were largely identical with the 'private' family affairs of monarchs. The biologically determined play of chance of dynastic genealogy and family reproduction – like problems of succession, marriage, divorce, inheritance, childlessness – did not simply 'contaminate' the otherwise purely political mechanisms of the balance of power or undermine the rationality of intersubjective conventions; it determined the very nature of early modern geopolitics. Since sovereignty was transmitted by birth, royal sex, as Marx argued in his critique of Hegel's *Philosophy of Right*, was directly political: 'The highest constitutional act of the king is therefore his sexual activity, for through this he *makes* a king and perpetuates his body' (Marx 1975: 40). This is the meaning of sovereignty by birth, or, as Marx quipped: 'His Majesty: sovereignty!' Since public political power was still personalized, European politics was not the affairs of states but the affairs of its ruling families. 'Proprietary dynasticism was displayed at its strongest in ordinary times in the conduct of foreign affairs, with the concern for family interests all too obvious' (Rowen 1980: 34–5).[7] But since all dynastic ruling classes engaged in predatory foreign policies, non-monarchical states were forced to comply with the competitive patterns of inter-dynastic European relations on pain of extinction. The bounded rationality of individual actors came to define the irrationality of the system as a zero-sum game over territorial rights.

1. *Monarchia Universalis*: Parity or Ranking?

Given the political economy of territoriality as a natural monopoly under pre-capitalist agrarian property relations, prevailing conceptions of geopolitical order revolved around notions of universalism and hierarchy in monarchical states well after 1648 (Burkhardt 1992: 30–63, 1997; Bosbach 1986; Rosenberg 1994: 91–122). The concept that captured the self-understanding of contemporary rulers was *monarchia universalis*, which dominated public discourse – although with important shifts over time – from the fifteenth to the end of the eighteenth century (Bosbach 1986: 12; Hinsley 1963: 167ff). Etymologically, monarchy means rule by one, so that the fragmentation of the *res publica christiana* into a plurality of monarchies was understood as a contradiction in terms. While the discourse of power-balancing started to challenge the idea of universal monarchy in the late seventeenth century and the two principles stood in stark tension throughout the period, it is the longevity of universalizing ideas that has to be explained. At the same time, as I shall show later, inter-dynastic relations and their universalizing interests did not bring about automatic power-balancing, but generated a distinct dynastic practice of equilibrium through elimination.[8]

Lingering imperial foreign policy practices and discourses vitiate any conventional argument that Westphalian political actors treated each other as equals, or recognized the legitimacy of the given territorial order. France claimed to be the *arbitre de l'Europe*, Austria the *caput mundi*, Sweden the *dominium maris baltici*. In 1771, Peter the Great adopted the Latin title *imperator*, a title which the Habsburgs claimed exclusively for themselves. The contraction of a plurality of feudal pyramidal polities into coexisting sovereign monarchies did not *eo ipso* imply the general acceptance of formal parity of conflict units after the Westphalian settlement. Quite the reverse was the case: 'The ranking of individual monarchs and the relative standing of their states were crucial dimensions of early modern international relations' (Oresko, Gibbs, and Scott 1997: 37).[9] Clashes over precedence in diplomatic negotiations were symptomatic of the persistence of hierarchical conceptions of inter-state organization. This was not IR's notion of hierarchy, implying complete subordination, but a dynastic convention that endorsed the formal inequality of the members of the inter-dynastic society. If many polities were 'sovereign', some were less sovereign than others. This inequality was not the effect of disparities in *de facto* power capabilities – leading to the non-juridical distinctions of great, middle, and small powers – but a generally recognized international norm, flowing from princely status (Luard 1992: 129–48).

A scale of ranks placed sovereigns on a descending ladder. The Holy Roman Emperor was given pride of place, followed by the 'Most Christian King', the king of France. Hereditary monarchs were, as a rule, placed above elective ones and republics below monarchies, followed by non-royal aristocrats and free cities. The standing of England was seriously weakened as a result of the various Commonwealth governments, and serious conflicts over precedence occurred wherever there was a mismatch between *de facto* importance and title of state, as in the Dutch and Venetian cases. Peter the Great's adoption of the imperial title in 1721 aroused considerable resentment not only in Vienna, but also in Britain, which recognized the title only in 1742, and France, which followed suit in 1745. Towards the end of the seventeenth century, many German rulers sought royal titles, since ducal or *Kurfürsten* (Elector) status tended to exclude them from international politics. While the Hohenzollern, the Wettins, the Wittelsbachs, and the Welfes succeeded, the remainder had to resign themselves to their lesser status. Anxiety over reputation and dignity should not be dismissed as ceremonial quibbles. It was an outgrowth of competition over status and rank within a dynastic international society in which hierarchy loomed large. Accepting a demoted place at diplomatic meetings was tantamount to accepting one's own inferiority and could have material implications in inheritance struggles. It thus should not surprise us that dynastic discourses were couched in the semantics of reputation, honour, and dignity. 'In an age where rulers looked on their states as their personal family property, it was inevitable that they should stress their personal honor, reputation, and prestige. This also explains why most international disputes tended to be over dynastic claims' (McKay and Scott 1983: 16).

2. 'States' Marrying 'States': Dynastic Unions and Wars of Succession

Two conflicting practices dominated early modern patterns of co-operation and conflict. On the one hand, proprietary kingship induced dynastic marriage policies as a political instrument for acquiring territory and enhancing wealth. 'For the ultimate instance of legitimacy was the *dynasty*, not the territory. The state was conceived as the patrimony of the monarch, and therefore the title-deeds to it could be gained by a union of persons: *felix Austria*. The supreme device of diplomacy was therefore marriage – peaceful mirror of war, which so often provoked it' (Anderson 1974b: 39). Inter-dynastic marriages not only characterized 'international' relations, they constituted a ruler's single fastest and most cost-effective expansion strategy. This was a geopolitical order in which 'states' could marry 'states'. As late as 1795, Immanuel Kant found himself pressed to demand in his philosophical sketch *Zum Ewigen Frieden* (On Perpetual Peace) that 'no independent nation [*Staat*], be it large or small, may be acquired by another nation by inheritance, exchange, purchase, or gift'. Here, Kant indicts the most quotidian practices of *Ancien Régime* territorial acquisition. He expands:

> everyone is aware of the danger that this purported right of acquisition by the marriage of nations [*Staaten*] to one another – a custom unknown in other parts of the world – has brought to Europe, even in the most recent times. It is a new form of industry, in which influence is increased without expending energy, and territorial possessions are extended merely by establishing family alliances. (Kant 1983: 108)

The proverbial adage '*Tu, felix Austria, nube!*' was not only the political maxim of the *casa d'Austria*. The marital accumulation of royal and noble titles led to personal unions that 'bundled' the most socially heteroclite and diverse territories into one political space. European politics was the affair of its ruling houses – the Habsburgs, the Bourbons, the Stuarts, the Hohenzollern, the Romanovs, the Wasas, the Orange-Nassaus, the Wittelsbachs, the Wettins, the Farnese, etc. (Weber 1981). Political marriages were not confined to the ruling dynasties but were also pursued at the higher levels of the aristocracy, leading to a welter of criss-crossing, transnational inter-noble alliances (Parrott: 1997). Finally, leading ministers engaged in diplomatic marriages aiming to balance personal family interests with those of the kingly state (Bergin 1985 on Richelieu; Oresko 1995 on Mazarin).

On the other hand, the resulting European-wide web of transregional dynastic family alliances simultaneously contained the seeds of disorder, partition, and destabilization. 'Private' inter-family and intra-family disputes, physical accidents, and pathological calamities were immediately translated into 'public' international conflicts (Kunisch: 1979): 'Since the ruler alone guaranteed under absolutism the dynastic bracket of his territory, his death led automatically to a systemic crisis' (Czempiel 1980: 448). Systemic crisis was not confined to the ruler's death. A whole range of dynastic family matters – structurally produced accidents – recurrently shook the inter-state system to its bones. The end of a dynasty and the accession of a new family to the throne almost automatically entailed a general realignment of alliance patterns. Minorities led to foreign claims to the throne and the takeover of foreign policy by strong ministers. Regencies presented dangerous power vacuums, eagerly seized upon by powerful courtiers and queen mothers who, if of foreign origin, staffed offices and positions with favourites from their home countries. In cases of divorce, rival claims to the throne and territories abounded. Multiple marriages with multiple heirs created problems of precedence. Illegitimate offspring claimed rights of inheritance. In cases of childless marriages, the lack of a direct male heir, as well as insanity and physical weakness due to generations of inbreeding, domestic as well as inter-dynastic disputes arose over the legitimacy of claims to succession.

Claims to hereditary precedence were usually resolved by war. Next to mercantilist trade wars, wars of succession and, more broadly, wars over hereditary claims, became the dominant form of international conflict. But since dynastic family disputes, mediated by the web of inter-dynastic family relations, automatically affected almost all European states, any succession crisis could turn easily into a multilateral, Europe-wide conflagration. The War of the Polish Succession (1733–38) in the wake of the Saxon–Polish king's death was largely fought over non-Polish issues, driven by a France eager to recover its pre-Utrecht possessions. Sonless Emperor Charles IV's death occasioned the War of the Austrian Succession (1740–48), despite the Pragmatic Sanction. The death of heirless Bavarian Elector Max Joseph in 1777 produced the War of the Bavarian Succession (1778–89), with Prussia and Austria fighting over the kingless territory. In 1700, the death of childless Spanish king Charles II and Louis XIV's acceptance of the

Spanish Empire for his grandson Philip of Anjou triggered the War of the Spanish Succession (1702–13/14), which involved all the major western and central European powers. From a contemporary perspective, it must seem a world-historical irony that the pathological history of a child, Charles II of Spain, and his eventual recovery and survival postponed the division of the world for thirty years. Yet these 'follies' were inscribed into the proprietary nature of the dynastic states-system. As long as proprietary kingship was the dominant political regime in Europe, international relations were decisively structured by inter-dynastic family relations.

3. Dynastic Rules of Succession as Public International Law

Given the vagaries of dynastic family relations, the fixation of rules of succession and inheritance became a matter of international concern; their internationally recognized codification was a form of preventive action. *Contra* Constructivism, however, an exhaustive understanding of these constitutive rules requires a prior recognition of the social conditions of dynastic sovereignty. In this context, 'private' family law became part and parcel of not only constitutional but also international 'public' law – indeed, a matter of extreme urgency for European rulers. Constitutional lawyers studied dynastic genealogies more than positive principles of constitutional and international law. Indeed, the latter could be read as a catalogue of the former.[10] Consequently, the ruling houses' ever-present concern with regulating questions of succession was a conscious strategy of managing structurally produced property conflicts. Inheritance law became the linchpin of absolutist reason of state and, by extension, of the absolutist states-system (Kunisch 1979, 1982; see also Czempiel 1980: 447; Grewe 1984: 48–339).

Order in these delicate matters, however, meant wresting testamentary control from single monarchs and investing it in codified laws of succession that thus entered into the body of '*loix fondamentaux*'. In Denmark after the state-threatening Nordic Wars (1655–60), the *Lex Regia* of 1665 laid down the principle of male primogeniture and the indivisibility of territorial possessions. Dynastic continuity, not the contingent will of the ruler, was to guarantee territorial integrity as well as political stability. In this perspective, sovereignty lay with the dynasty, not with the individual monarch. What we see is thus an attempt to subject the whims of private family law to the more enduring principles of *raison d'État* – *lex fundamentalis et immutabilis*. This was the intention; the reality was entirely different, precisely because the proprietary character of kingship was not overcome and no institution was powerful enough to penalize contraventions once the estates had ceded absolute sovereignty to the king. The constitutional semantics of stability, defining sovereignty as inalienable, unlimited, irrevocable, indivisible, and imprescriptible, ran time and again into inherently fickle dynastic practice.

Let me illustrate the failure of dynastic succession rules with reference to the famous Austrian Pragmatic Sanction of 1713 (Kunisch 1979: 41–74; McKay and Scott 1983: 118–77; Duchhardt 1997: 79). The Habsburg monarchy, unlike France, was a monarchical union that united three different territorial complexes with three different succession laws. After the experience of the Spanish War of Succession, the partition of the Spanish Empire, and Charles IV's lack of a male heir, the Pragmatic Sanction unified and fixed new female succession rules. Female succession was to safeguard Charles IV's huge territorial gains. Acceptance of the Pragmatic Sanction was not only sought from the Austrian Estates and the German Imperial Diet (*Reichstag*), but also from the great European dynasties in order to diplomatically guarantee the property of the House of Habsburg. International recognition was achieved through a series of bilateral treaties that effectively incorporated the Pragmatic Sanction into the *Ius Publicum Europaeum*. In keeping with the proprietary character of public power, these bilateral treaties involved Austrian compensation for foreign acceptance – a sequence of 'swaps' of territories, rights of domination, and declarations of guarantee.

Prussia recognized the Pragmatic Sanction in 1728 in return for Austrian acceptance of Prussian succession rules and its support for Prussia's claims in the disputed territories of Jülich-Berg against the pretensions of the Bavarian House of Wittelsbach. Denmark–Norway (1732), Spain (1731), and Russia (1732) followed suit in return for Austrian acquiescence in their respective succession regulations. In 1731–32, the maritime powers, Britain and the Dutch General Estates, agreed to guarantee the inviolability of the Pragmatic Sanction in the Second Treaty of Vienna on condition that (1) the Austrian emperor's daughter, Maria Theresia, did not marry a Bourbon prince, (2) no Austrian subject traded with East Asia, and (3) the Austrian Ostende Company was dissolved. In 1732, the German Imperial Diet recognized Austrian succession laws against the votes of Bavaria and Saxony. France, predictably, battled more persistently against the Pragmatic Sanction until recognition was given in 1738 in exchange for the formerly Austrian kingdom of Naples and Sicily, which went to Spain.

However, on the death of Charles VI in 1740, the delicate diplomatic and territorial architecture largely masterminded by Walpole imploded in the wake of the succession crisis between the two lines of the House of Habsburg. The resulting power vacuum was seized by Frederick II of Prussia, who, describing the situation as a *'conjoncture favorable'*, invaded Austrian Silesia in the winter of 1740–41 with no dynastic claim to the Austrian monarchy whatsoever, but out of dismay at Charles VI's decision to exclude Prussia from the Jülich-Berg succession. Spain demanded Tuscany and Parma. Bavaria renewed its claim to the imperial title and made attempts to seize Bohemia, while France made a play for the Austrian Low Countries. In fact, all the Austrian lands were regarded as estates by European dynasts. Far-fetched legal titles were mobilized, and the break-up of Austria appeared imminent. In the absence of an international court of family law, the inheritance struggle turned into a Europe-wide military conflict. In spite of its misleading name, the War of the Austrian Succession was largely a Franco–British war over European hegemony. Yet while France pursued traditional territorial imperialism, Britain pursued no direct continental territorial goals but heavily subsidized the anti-French coalition (McKay and Scott 1983: 172). It took eight years to settle the disputes in the Peace of Aachen (1748), which codified the territorial *revirement*, while Maria Theresia emerged battered but not beaten.

In sum, the ensemble of succession rules formed the 'hidden' European 'public' international law. The fact that succession rules and partition schemes were often secretly agreed upon as part of the *arcana imperii* did nothing to stabilize European politics. Conflicts of inheritance did not always provide the immediate *casus belli*, but they created the discourse of legitimacy in which many declarations of war and peace settlements were couched. While the language used to legitimize interventions and conquests was framed in terms of legality, military conflict constituted the ultimate regulator of the absolutist system of 'states'. Since territory was first and foremost a source of income, 'political Europe was like an estate map, and war was a socially acceptable form of property acquisition' (Hale cited in Bonney 1991: 345). Dynastic succession crises based on proprietary kingship and recurring crises of the European states-system continued to be the norm until states were depersonalized, that is, until a new property regime deprivatized political power.

4. Circulating Territories, Circulating Princes

According to the standard account in IR theory, the modern system of territorial states rests on a configuration of territoriality structured by mutually exclusive, geographically fixed, clearly demarcated, and functionally similar political spaces (Gilpin 1981: 121–2; Giddens 1985: 89–91; Ruggie 1993, 1998: 875–6; Spruyt 1994a: 153–5). The construction of modern territoriality results from the confluence of private property rights, the separation of public and private realms, and the sovereign's monopolization of the legitimate use of force, generating the spatial demarcations of internal and external realms, legitimized by reciprocal international recognitions From this perspective, the genesis of the modern states-system is located in the period between the Renaissance and the Baroque Age (Kratochwil 1986: 51; Ruggie 1993; Luard 1992: 174–84).[11]

However, proprietary kingship imposed a rather different territorial logic upon the spatial configuration of early modern geopolitics. Territoriality remained a function of private dynastic practices of territorial accumulation and circulation, frustrating a generic identity or fixity between state and territory. Since absolutist sovereignty was imperfect and feudal and patrimonial practices survived, territory remained non-exclusive and administratively non-uniform. The diversity of early modern sovereign actors – hereditary and elective monarchies, merchant republics, confederations, aristocratic republics, constitutional monarchy, cities, states of estates – precluded their functional similarity, let alone equality. Consequently, the formation of the modern states-system, based on exclusive territoriality operated by a depersonalized state, must be pushed up to the nineteenth century.

The dynastic structure of inter-state relations had direct implications for the changing geographies of territoriality. The politics of inter-dynastic family relations led to supra-regional territorial constructions – especially dynastic unions – which defined the logic of territorial (dis-)order and defied the logic of territorial contiguity and stability. Marital policies and inheritance practices, mediated by war, led to frequent territorial redistribution among European princes. Territorial fixity was thus prevented. Territorial unity meant nothing but the unity of the ruling house, personified by its dynastic head. Territorial continuity was identical with the smooth transmission of sovereign title from dynastic head to dynastic head. Any dynastic vacancy directly threatened the territorial integrity of the monarchy and opened it up to foreign claims. Territory was not constitutive of sovereignty, but a proprietary appendage of the dynasty. It was thus handled like an economic asset in international relations – a disposable mass for inheritances, compensations, exchanges, securities, cessions, donations, partitions, indemnities, satisfactions, sales, and purchases (Arentin 1981; Grewe 1984: 462–3; Klingenstein 1997: 442). Dynastic interest, not national interest or reason of state, defined the logic of early modern territoriality (Mattingly 1988: 108–9, 117–18; Schroeder 1994a: 8).

But the unity of the house was not co-terminous with the geographical contiguity of its lands. Although these territories were nominally 'bounded' in the sense that they belonged to one sovereign, they were geographical conglomerates, governed by diverse legal codes and tax regimes, criss-crossing the dynastic map of Europe. Early modern Europe was a system of 'composite monarchies' (Elliott 1992; see also Holsti 1991: 51). At the same time, the ever-changing size of early modern 'states' intensified the problem of internal administrative cohesion. Austria, Spain, Sweden, Russia, and Prussia exemplified the scattered and disjointed mosaic of early modern territoriality, combining multi-ethnic provinces with little in common except their rulers. For example, in 1792 it was calculated that 'the territories over which the House of Austria ruled included seven kingdoms, one archduchy, twelve duchies, one grand duchy, two margravates, seventeen counties [*Grafschaften*], and four lordships. The order in which these were listed was significant, since the geographer and statistician adhered to the strict ranking dictated by the feudal hierarchy' (Klingenstein 1997: 449). These territories did not form a geographical continuum and were governed according to the tenets of *aeque principaliter*, each region keeping its customary legal system (Elliott 1992: 52, 61). The geographical consolidation into compact territories and administrative unification of these lands was time and again negated by the vagaries of dynastic relations and resulting wars. Consequently, early modern territoriality was not primarily a state-centralizing, national, ethnic, denominational, geostrategic, topographical, cultural, or linguistic construction, but the protean outcome of dynastic nuptial policies of war-supported territorial redistribution.

Dynasticism implied no organic identity between a state and its territory. A state did not possess its own territorial identity independently of dynastic property titles; state territory followed the actions of the monarch. It was the ensemble of accumulated rights to specific domains, bundled together through proprietary kingship (Sahlins 1990: 1427). This generic non-identity replicated the mobility of feudal lords, who readily took up rights of lordship in the most diverse places, transferring their family seats from one end of Europe to another. Although the frequency of dynastic changes

receded with the growing juridical and institutional embeddedness of
dynasts in 'their' states, sovereignty was still not pegged to an abstract state
apparatus, but travelled with the Crown. The Habsburg ancestral lands lay
in northwestern Switzerland, yet the dynasty rose to power in Vienna and
Madrid. The Hohenzollern began in Württemberg, yet the accumulation
of dynastic territories occurred around Königsberg and Berlin after the
family acceded to the Prussian throne. While the Bourbons came from
Navarre, they built up their court at Versailles, and, after the Treaty of
Utrecht, a branch of the family took its seat in Madrid to rule what
remained of the Spanish Empire. When the Scottish Stuarts were sent into
exile, the Dutch Orangians took over in London, while the Hanoverians
hailed from northern Germany. The House of Savoy came from Cham-
béry, but 'found' a throne and established a court in Turin. In principle,
dynasties had little problem 'finding' new thrones. Succession, marriage,
election, and conquest were the conventional means of gaining a new
kingdom. Territories frequently and legitimately changed their masters.

The personalized and imperfect nature of dynastic sovereignty as well as
the additive logic of territorial acquisition implied administrative non-
uniformity. Even in the alleged model of successful political centralization,
France, different law-codes, tax regimes, and privileges, eagerly defended
by independent domestic centres of power, rendered administrative fragmentation unavoidable (Oresko, Gibbs, and Scott 1997: 8–9). Especially
the distinction between *pays d'État* and *pays d'élection* barred any progress
towards uniformity. Bounded enclaves like cities, ports, abbeys, bishoprics,
fortresses, and lordships reproduced the logic of geographical non-conti-
guity and administrative non-uniformity. In France, the *princes étrangers*,
members of foreign dynasties at the Bourbon court, enjoyed sovereign
status and entered into contractual feudal relations with the king, while
having landed possessions, offices, and inheritance claims in France and
elsewhere in Europe (Parrott: 1997).

At the same time, it is misleading to portray the history of dynastic state
formation as remorselessly linear, teleological territorial accumulation. Not
only were there setbacks and reversals, the logic of dynastic territoriality
qua political accumulation witnessed both building-up and building-down.
The succession provisos of indivisibility and inalienability were honoured
more in the breach. In the merry-go-round of territorial exchanges,
accumulation and disintegration, marriage and succession disputes, war and
peace, were two sides of the same coin.

Any attempt to define the modernity of international relations in terms
of seventeenth-century bounded territoriality must therefore be revised.

Territoriality remained non-exclusive, administratively non-integrated, and geographically fluid – the proprietary asset of composite states. Post-feudal bounded territoriality was not modern territoriality, since it remained first and foremost a function of dynastic strategies of geopolitical accumulation.

5. Dynastic Predatory Equilibrium and the Balance of Power

Were there any systemic limits to absolutist geopolitical expansion? Can we identify any generally acknowledged principles of geopolitical order in the early modern period? These questions may be answered by setting them within the context of the two rival conceptions of geopolitical order: empire and the balance of power.

1. Dynastic Equilibrium qua Territorial Compensations

Dynastic actors, despite the existence of a collectivity of independent polities, clung to universal schemes of geopolitical order which legitimized aggressive foreign policies driven by (geo)political accumulation. Yet the terminology of power-balancing emerged for the first time as a distinct discourse in the seventeenth century and became a recognized norm, enshrined in the Peace of Utrecht during the eighteenth century (Butterfield 1966; Fenske 1975). Does this disprove the thesis of Europe's multiple universalisms? Much depends here on the time-bound meanings of the balance of power and historically contextualizing the identity of its respective protagonists. Realist analyses, in spite of the many historical examples adduced, are thoroughly ahistorical, since they first establish an ideal type of the balance of power as a 'universal concept' and then subsume diverse historical cases under it, modifying, subdividing, and diluting the ideal type in an *ad hoc* fashion (Butterfield 1966; Wight 1966a, 1978: 168–90; Bull 1977: 101–26; Morgenthau 1985: 187–240; Mearsheimer 2001).[12] The ahistorical and socially disembodied character of Realist theories of the balance of power thus presupposes what has to be explained. For example, Morgenthau's assumption that actors seek 'territorial aggrandizement' prevents him from theorizing the fundamental difference between dynastic equilibrium and modern power-balancing (Morgenthau 1985: 222). Constructivist accounts of early modern equilibrium, while disconfirming Neorealism, fail to spell out the social sources of dynastic interests that drive its construction as a time-bound convention (Kratochwil 1982: 12–20).

In fact, two opposed yet interacting practices of the balance of power – respectively operated by the continental dynastic powers and the British parliamentary-constitutional monarchy – can be discerned: eliminatory equilibrium and active balancing. Although the two conceptions operated on the basis of incommensurable premises rooted in different state/society complexes, in practice they fused as the British conception manipulated and came to govern the continental one.

On the side of absolutist powers, power-balancing during the eighteenth century did not rest on the idea that each political actor possessed its own legitimacy and independence based on natural law, to be preserved against any aggressor by an alliance; nor was it the automatic, law-like, depersonalized function of anarchy, which mechanically stabilized or re-equilibrated the distribution of power and territory (Waltz 1979; Morgenthau 1985: 189). Rather, absolutist power-balancing was an inter-dynastic technique of territorial expansion through proportional aggrandizement that routinely eliminated weaker states.

Individually, each dynastic actor sought to maximize wealth and territory. Since the goal was universal monarchy, none of the leading absolutist-dynastic powers consciously wanted a balance in Europe; dynastic equilibrium resulted from antagonistic interests, while its realization was a chimera. Equilibrium, however, implied practices incommensurable with the conventional understanding of the balance of power. Systemically, since no single actor was strong enough to impose its universal scheme on Europe, aggression provoked responses that went far beyond simple balancing and the re-establishment of the *status quo ante*. The objective of early modern coalition-building was, as Mattingly suggests, not balancing but outweighing (Mattingly 1988: 141, 150). Outweighing implied the possibility of the complete destruction of the adversary, followed by its territorial apportionment among the victors. If these practices appeared in the guise of ruthless power politics, they were usually rationalized by far-fetched legal claims ingeniously constructed or invented through the Europe-wide network of often-recondite dynastic genealogical connections.

Schemes for the partition or complete break-up of even the mightiest polities were common. In 1668, France and Austria signed a secret partition treaty against the Spanish Empire. After the War of the Spanish Succession, the Utrecht settlement effectively dismembered the Spanish monarchy. During the War of the Austrian Succession, the very existence of the Habsburg state was at stake. In the First Treaty of Vienna (1725), Austria and Spain agreed to partition France in case of war. During the Seven Years' War, Russia considered the complete division of Prussia. The three partitions of 1772, 1793, and 1795 eclipsed Poland. Since the war objective of coalitions was outweighing to the point of complete partition, the attacking power often aimed at unconditional victory (McKay and Scott 1983: 83). As a rule, wars were brought to an end not by self-restraint or the recognition of the international legitimacy of any one power, but by mutual economic, financial, and military depletion. Peaces were peaces of exhaustion (Duchhardt 1997: 56). The diplomatic semantics of saturation expressed tactical arguments by ascending powers, like Prussia, eager to gain international recognition for the *faits accomplis* of already annexed lands, and by no means indicated a strategy of self-restraint. Moderation was a temporary respite for economic, financial, and military recovery.

If the Carthaginian objectives of outweighing or total victory could not be achieved, dynastic power-balancing was directly linked to the idea of *convenance*, which demanded a consensus among the major powers over territorial alterations (Duchhardt 1976: 51, 1997: 17). The desired objective was 'just equilibrium', consciously negotiated by the leading powers. The operative principle was that each territorial gain by any one power justified claims to territorial or other equivalents by others (McKay and Scott 1983: 212, 214, 228; Schroeder 1994a: 6–7). To be left out of any round of territorial aggrandizement was to fall behind. Few dynasts could afford to stay neutral. *Convenance* became the regulative principle of the dynastic balance of power or, as Martin Wight suggested, 'the diplomatic counterpart of hereditary absolute monarchy' (Wight 1966a: 171, see also 1978: 186; Butterfield 1966; Gulick 1967: 70–1; Fenske 1975: 972). The dynastic balance of power thus had a clear affinity to the mercantilist balance of trade. As wealth was conceived of as absolute and finite, so that any trade deficit had to be made up by an inflow of bullion or was regarded as an absolute loss, territory was finite and any acquisition required compensation to re-establish a 'just equilibrium'. The territorial equivalent of mercantilism thus came to be cameralism, which gauged state power in terms of taxable population and territory in terms of soil fertility.

Convenance intensified war and territorial changes, for each territorial gain immediately induced claims to equivalents in order to offset the perceived disadvantage. Equilibrium was thus restored, if on a new level. This made non-intervention next to impossible. Intervention did not violate international law, it was regarded as legitimate behaviour (Grewe 1984: 392–3). The implication was that bilateral wars immediately occasioned a multilateral *renversement* of positions, driven by the search for territorial equivalents. Legitimate claims for compensation entailed a series of practices incommensurable with the preservation of or return to the *status quo ante*. Territorial exchanges, cessions, indemnities, pensions, and subsidies negotiated through outright haggling were the mark of the age. Usually, the arithmetic of *convenance* meant that weaker powers were carved up by stronger ones. Successive peace treaties codified the disappearance of smaller states as pawns in the international game of territorial compensation. Compensation often meant liquidation.

2. The Case of the Polish Partitions: Balancing or Compensatory Equilibrium?

The three Polish Partitions of 1772, 1793, and 1795, pursued by Prussia, Austria, and Russia, exemplify the state-eliminating and compensatory dynamic of inter-dynastic equilibrium. According to (Neo-)Realist predictions, power-balancing should have prevented Poland's break-up. Yet no counterbalance emerged. The first partition was justified and carried out by Prussia and Austria as compensation for Russian acquisitions in the Balkans against the Ottoman Empire. The second and third partitions were justified as indemnities for Prusso-Austrian war efforts against France in the Wars of Revolution after the defeat at Valmy (1792), while Russia claimed to put down 'Jacobinism' in Warsaw in the interest of the European dynastic fraternity (McKay and Scott 1983: 248). Britain remained neutral, having no direct interests in the region. Nor was it only geographical circumstances that permitted the break-up of Poland. Poland's social property regime generated a constitution in which power lay with the aristocrats, who individually enjoyed the famous *liberum veto*, enabling any member of the Polish Diet to exercise a personal veto over legislation. This prevented Poland's elective monarchy – the 'crowned aristocratic republic' – from developing the absolutist administration and military centralization of its neighbours. The inherent weakness of the aristocratic constitution opened Poland up to foreign dismemberment, since it was regarded as a power vacuum in eastern Europe.

The tripartite seizure of Polish territory did not restore the status quo before the Russian acquisitions in the Balkans or the French Wars of Revolution; it adjusted the balance on the basis of a new territorial settlement. Power-balancing failed, but liquidatory equilibrium worked. Dynastic equilibrium promoted war, not peace. Yet war did not re-equilibrate the distribution of power among a constant number of actors, it led to the systematic eclipse of smaller states. And it was this practice of dynastic equilibrium, not the modern balance of power, which incurred as late as 1793 the censure of Enlightenment philosophers like Immanuel Kant: 'The maintenance of universal peace by means of the so-called Balance of Power in Europe is – like Swift's house, which a masterbuilder constructed in such perfect accord with all the laws of equilibrium, that when a sparrow alighted upon it, it immediately collapsed – a mere figment of the imagination' (Kant cited in Wight 1966a: 170–71). In other words, the Polish episode did not undermine the spirit of dynastic power-balancing, it was its clearest expression (von Arentin 1981; Grewe 1984: 395–7).[13]

As an explanatory device, the balance of power is indeterminate since it accounts for any outcome, depending upon whether a systemic or a unit-level perspective is adopted. If a state survives, it is due to the stabilizing and protective function of the balance of power; if it perishes, it is due to the necessity of a new systemic balance. Neither Realist, Neorealist, nor Constructivist theory is able to understand the historical character of the Polish Partitions, the forces that caused them, or their outcome. As long as the time-bound practices of power-balancing and alliance formation are not taken seriously, universalizing IR theories will be unable to grasp historical specificity.

In sum, not the preservation of the status quo or the re-establishment of the *status quo ante*, but territorial gain was the goal of early modern power-balancing. It was a conscious technique of expansion, driven by dynastic political accumulation, which destabilized and restabilized the territorial distribution in ever-changing configurations, not an automatic mechanism operating behind the backs of political actors. If the aggressor did not succeed, *convenance* ensured proportional aggrandizement to his detriment. But dynastic equilibrium did not need aggressors, it needed victims. It thus invited *bandwagoning* rather than balancing (Luard 1992: 335–7; Schroeder 1994b).[14] The dramatic decline in the number of European sovereign actors between 1648 and the nineteenth century did not come about despite the balance of power, but because of the policy of predatory equilibrium and bandwagoning. Dynastic power-balancing did not mean preserving an even distribution of power. It did not become 'a means of maintaining state independence' (Holsti 1991: 69), or put 'a break on territorial changes' (Butterfield 1966: 144). It meant equality in aggrandizement (Wight 1966a: 156, 1978: 187; Gulick 1967: 71). The logic of dynastic anarchy generated a dynamic system of collective wealth maximization among predatory monarchs. The balance of power is not the natural and universal function of anarchy, it is the outgrowth of the specific interests of the members which constitute diverse geopolitical systems. Given the persisting logic of geopolitical expansion, it is doubtful that the system of dynastic states could ever have generated a general interest in the preservation of the status quo. The dynastic practice of equilibrium qua *convenance* was an instrument of geopolitical accumulation. But, as we shall see in the next chapter, this was to change significantly with Britain's new post-1688 foreign policy.

6. Demystifying the Peace of Westphalia

1. Proprietary Dynasticism versus Sovereignty

How do the Westphalian peace treaties themselves square with the interpretation of early modern geopolitics set out above? Rather than formulating principles designed to transcend these dynastic practices, the following textual reinterpretation of the peace treaties demonstrates the extent to which Westphalia expressed precisely the nexus between premodern forms of rule and geopolitical accumulation. The most obvious indicator of Westphalia's non-modernity lies in the nature of the contracting political regimes. The treaties were not concluded between states but between rulers, or, to be more precise, between private persons and corporate bodies. The preambles carefully establish the character of the major signatories: the kings of France and Sweden, the German emperor and the German Estates of the Empire – the *Reichsstände*, consisting of the nine electors, the remainder of the German princes, and the fifty-one imperial free cities (Symcox 1974: 40–1; Steiger 1998; generally Dickmann 1972). They proceed to list each of the major party's long collections of titles of dominion, indicating 'functionally different' rights in the different territories of their internally differentiated realms. These lists are not simply symptomatic of a time-bound conception of honour and representation; they show that these rulers held bundles of rights in personal union over variegated dominions. The treaties thus reflect the fact that the basic units of international politics were not states, but persons and associations of persons, who literally owned their respective realms and dominions. In other words, none of the signatories to the treaties headed a modern state, nor did any contracting polity become one as a result of 1648.

The bulk of the treaty stipulations refer to questions of territorial changes, dynastic succession, proprietary restitutions, and indemnities (e.g., articles 4, 10–14 IPO, and clauses 70–89 IPM).[15] The treaties did not abandon the dynastic principle so as to remove the root cause of recurring destabilizations, but only laid down strict rules of succession, namely primogeniture, to ensure the stable transmission of returned proprietary titles (e.g., article 4 IPO). The necessary failure of this project was demonstrated by the fact that few wars in seventeenth- and eighteenth-century Europe were not wars of succession. As we have seen, in a system in which 'states' could marry 'states', it should not surprise us that honeymoons turned quickly into nightmares.

This leads to the issue of territorial changes. Since the treaties were concluded between rulers rather than states, territory did not refer to administratively uniform geographical space but to bundles of rights of domination over differentiated dominions. These are carefully listed as rights, privileges, properties – in short, *regales* – over cities, bishoprics, abbacies, lordships, ports and roads, garrisons and jurisdictions. France received the Bishoprics of Metz, Toul, and Verdun as well as the right-Rhenanian fortress of Breisach and, most importantly, Alsace.[16] Sweden gained the Archbishopric of Bremen, the Bishopric of Verden, the Baltic port of Wismar and, most importantly, the western part of the Duchy of Pomerania. These territories were ceded as imperial fiefs, so that the Swedish Crown became a vassal of the emperor. This implied the internationalization of the confederal Empire, since the Swedish king became an imperial estate with voting rights in the Imperial Diet as duke of Bremen (art. 10, 9 IPO). Thus, these territorial rights were not adjudged to France and Sweden qua states; rather, they were incorporated into their dominions by their respective rulers.

2. Restoration versus Modernity

The treaties' terminology reveals the ubiquity of such concepts as 'restoration', 're-establishment', and 'restitution' (e.g., art. 3, 1 IPO) – a reaffirmation of 'ancient rights and liberties' which the signatories and especially the German Estates had enjoyed long before the outbreak of the Thirty Years' War. The semantics of restoration reflected the prevailing consensus that the treaties should not enact new principles of international public law, but rather codify the reversal to the *status quo ante bellum*. The Thirty Years' War was not regarded as a great modernizing geopolitical convulsion that forced decision makers to adopt new rules of international relations, but rather as a deplorable diversion from pre-war international customs that had to be restored (Osiander 1994: 44). Let me exemplify these restorative tendencies in relation to three phenomena: (1) territorial redistributions, (2) confessional regulations, and (3) the 'sovereignty' of the German Estates.

First, the aforementioned territorial redistributions raise a difficult question. If the aim of the peacemakers was to restore international order to the *status quo ante*, how were these territorial changes to be dealt with? The apparent contradiction is resolved if we understand how the victorious powers legitimized their territorial gains. France and Sweden did not receive these lands as 'rights of conquest', but rather as indemnities or 'satisfactions' for the services they had rendered to their German allies. This might seem to be hair-splitting, but the language of indemnities and satisfactions is not an auxiliary legal construction; it points to the fact that the rights to these lands were indeed purchased. The French agreed at Münster to pay three million *livres* in accordance with convention – the purchase of territory was an acknowledged form of pre-modern international relations between personal rulers. Furthermore, the insertion of what amounts to a contract of purchase into the peace treaties shows the enormous importance attributed to the principle of legality in accord with ancient customs (Osiander 1994: 49). Admitting right of conquest as a principle of international public law would have undermined the dominant principle of international stability.

Stability and restoration were also the leitmotivs in the treatment of confessional issues. In the IR literature, there is general agreement that the Peace of Augsburg of 1555 was a precursor of modern statehood in so far as the maxim *cuius regio eius religio* allowed each ruler to impose and change the religion in his lands at will (*ius reformandi*). Religious autonomy in the German territories broke the 'Spanish Servitude'. In so far as this principle broke the empire's monopoly on determining the official faith in the wake of the Reformation, it did, of course, represent a major change in sixteenth-century European politics. The question is, a change in which direction? To the extent that rulers gained the right of religious self-determination, that of their subjects was lost. Subjects were forced to adopt the faith of their rulers. The maxim *cuius regio eius religio* was thus decidedly absolutist in character. If anything, 1555 points to the non-separation of politics and religion in the sixteenth century: the state was not secular, even if denominational pluralism was allowed within the empire. Spanish religious universalism was selectively replaced by plural religious absolutisms.

To what degree did Westphalia dissolve this nexus? The principle that each ruler could decide and impose his faith on his lands was abandoned and replaced by the rule (art. 5, 2 IPO) that every territory was to retain 'in perpetuity' the religion it had on 1 January 1624 – the famous *Normaljahr* (reference year), which served as a standard for determining the restoration of pre-war territorial-religious allegiances. What we see is therefore nothing less than an international prescription of the territorial distribution of different confessions – a reversal of Augsburg. While rulers could change their creeds, the official faith of the land was there to stay (Asch 1988: 124). The Estates became the guardians of the religious status quo. This meant that the *ius reformandi* of the territorial princes was severely restricted. In specific cases, as in the Bishopric of Osnabrück, the treaties fixed an alternation between Catholic and Protestant rulers. Again, we see an attempt to 'freeze' the distribution of confessions so as to minimize conflict. An international treaty that imposes religion on territories can hardly be deemed a step towards internal sovereignty. Although the followers of the respective minority faiths were allowed to exercise their religion in private, most of them emigrated to lands of their faith (Burkhardt 1992: 176). In sum, 1648 constituted the internationalization of territorial confessional status – a turning back of the religious clock to 1624, and in constitutional terms to before 1555 – not in order to achieve self-determination, be it either princely or popular, but to ensure peace. In this sense, international politics was not secularized, but the *res publica christiana* was renewed by a *pax christiana*.

Restoration was also reflected in the international order laid down in the peace provisions. The partisans of the modernity thesis usually refer to the key provision of article 8, 2 (IPO) and clauses 62–6 (IPM), laying down the right of the German Estates to conclude treaties, enter into alliances, and declare war (*ius foederis et ius belli ac pacem*). The rights to make treaties, declare war, legislate, levy armies, and impose taxation are held to fulfil the criteria of modern sovereignty. However, there are a series of important qualifications to be made.

First, even this icon of international modernity did not constitute an innovation. As Andreas Osiander pointed out, 'contrary to what is sometimes implied or asserted, this was really a clarification of the existing legal custom. The faculty for the estates to conclude alliances had been legally established since the Middle Ages' (Osiander 1994: 47; see also Dickmann 1972: 325–32). The Estates' *ius foederis* was recognized as early as 1356 in the Golden Bull. While this right had a long pedigree, it was never absolute but subject to classically feudal reciprocal limitations vis-à-vis the emperor, the feudal overlord. The treaties of 1648 reaffirmed and further qualified

it. This should not be taken to imply the proto-modernity of the pre-1648
German medieval Estates. It rather points to the *sui generis* dual character of
the German imperial constitution, in which the 'liberty' of the estates and
the territorial princes – their *ius armorum* – antedated and survived 1648
(Burkhardt 1992: 101, 105). The codified right to conclude alliances
conformed to prevailing constitutional practice in the German Empire. In
this sense, the *ius foederis* was part and parcel of medieval conceptions of
reciprocal fealty among semi-independent lordly actors (Böckenförde 1969:
458–63; classically Brunner 1992). Its roots lay in the medieval lordly right
of resistance, based on the arms-bearing status of lords within the wider
context of feudal relations of exploitation. The medieval right of resistance
and the right to negotiate treaties were inseparable.

   Second, these rights were significantly hedged by further stipulations.
Most centrally, the Estates' *ius belli ac pacem* and the *ius foederis* were
restricted to defensive alliances and operations. Further provisions prohibited alliances against the *Reichslandfrieden* (Imperial Peace) and the Westphalian settlement itself (art. 8, 2 IPO). These limits were perfectly in line
with the *ius territoriale* (*Landeshoheit*/territorial lordship) enjoyed by the
Estates, but not with the modern notion of sovereignty. The repeated
transgression of these provisions points to social and political processes that
lie outside the reach of legal interpretations. There were further express
conditions. The treaties forbade, for example, intervention in the Burgun-
dian Circle of the Empire, i.e., the Spanish Netherlands (clause 3 IPM). In
other words, neither the emperor nor the German polities were allowed to
join the Spanish in their continuing war against the French in this theatre.
This reflected an essential French war aim, namely the isolation of Spain
from its imperial ally. Thus, from the French perspective, the Westphalian
treaties represented a separate peace (*Separatfrieden/Sonderfrieden*), prohibiting interference in Franco-Spanish relations and freeing France to deal with
Spain on a one-to-one basis. France and Spain signed the bilateral Treaty
of the Pyrenees eleven years later.

   Third, at the same time that the German Estates and princes reaffirmed
their alliance-concluding powers, they continued to enjoy the '*ius suffragii*',
i.e., the right to co-decide imperial foreign policy through the pan-German
Imperial Diet (*Reichstag*) (art. 8, 4 IPO; clause 65 IPM).[17] It met first in
1653 and then from 1663 to 1806 in Regensburg as a permanent assembly
of representatives of the Estates, guarding their liberties and helping
determine imperial policy. While the German Estates remained embedded
in imperial institutions, their alleged sovereignty was further compromised
by provisions prohibiting alliances against the emperor – reasserting the

custom of imperial loyalty (*Reichstreue*)[18] – as well as war among themselves (clause 116 IPM). They were obliged to submit their disputes to the Empire's two supreme courts, the *Reichskammergericht* (Imperial Cameral Court) and the *Reichshofrat* (Imperial Aulic Council), in a process known as *Reichsexekution*. It is worth noting that these courts not only settled disputes between Estates, they also heard complaints and suits brought by subjects against their direct territorial lords. The referral of inter-Estates disputes to a higher authority clearly showed the Empire's supremacy. While the *Reichstag* stalled Germany's transformation into an absolutist empire, it equally stalled Germany's complete fragmentation into small, independent mini-absolutisms. The Empire was and remained a multi-layered, semi-feudal, semi-monarchical federation and the constitutional status of the German princes and Estates remained embedded within it. The German Estates did not enjoy full sovereignty (Steiger 1998: 68).

3. Dynastic Collective Security System versus the Balance of Power

The implication of the German Estates' limited 'sovereignty' (territorial lordship) was that Westphalia was not exclusively an international settlement, but also an intervention into the 'internal' structure of the imperial sub-system (art. 17, 2 IPO). The treaties thus had a dual character, being at once instruments of international *and* German constitutional basic laws (*leges fundamentales*) (Böckenförde 1969; Oestreich 1982; Steiger 1998: 51). Since the Thirty Years' War was also a constitutional struggle within Germany between centralizing-absolutist and particularistic-representational principles of state organization, 1648 was in part a settlement of the peculiar mixed German constitution – a halfway house between corporative-representational privileges supported by the estates and absolutist prerogatives claimed by the emperor. In IR terms, the German sub-system retained a *sui generis* structure, combining particularistic, 'anarchical' principles and universal, 'hierarchical' principles, though these terms have very little purchase on explaining imperial inter-actor behaviour.

Crucially, however, this settlement was not only a German affair. The elevation of the German constitution to an element of public international law meant the internationalization of German politics. The constitutional independence of the German Estates against the emperor was to be guaranteed by France and Sweden. Conversely, the peace treaties were incorporated into the corpus of German imperial law. Both powers assumed the task of guaranteeing the post-Westphalian order. In this

respect, 1648 represented in essence France's victory over the House of
Habsburg's repeated attempts to turn the German Empire into a hereditary
absolutist state. In order to maintain German disunity, France reserved the
right to intervene in German affairs if Westphalian clauses were violated.
When the Empire dissolved under Napoleon in 1806, Sweden protested
that it was not consulted as a guarantor of the Peace of Westphalia
(Oestreich 1982: 243).

It follows that the core of the treaty was neither the establishment of full
legal sovereignty for all involved nor the 'liberty' or autonomy of the
German Estates, but rather the establishment of peace in the interest of and
supervised by France (Duchhardt 1989b). While political self-determination
in the form of the right to conclude alliances was affirmed, it was severely
limited. Although the signatories were formally elevated to agents of peace
and war, their recourse to war was strictly circumscribed. In other words,
1648 did not put forward principles of international public law by recognizing the internal and external sovereignty of the signatories; it established
a system of collective security which tried to 'freeze' a legal, confessional,
and territorial status quo favourable to the two victorious powers, France
and Sweden (clauses 115–17 IPM and art.18, 5–7 IPO) (Duchhardt 1989b:
533; Osiander 1994: 40–42). Power politics was not acknowledged as the
legitimate basis of foreign policy conduct in a rulerless society; the
regulative idea behind international politics was not yet conceived in terms
of the balance of power, through which the independence of any one actor
would be 'naturally' guaranteed by the free play of shifting alliances
(Repgen 1988; Duchhardt 1989b: 536; Burkhardt 1992: 202; Osiander
1994: 80–82; Steiger 1998: 78).[19] On the contrary, 1648 was an attempt
to fix 'for perpetuity' the territorial status quo of an international system
imagined as highly static (Osiander 1994: 43). Thus 1648 represented the
(ultimately failed) attempt to juridify European politics, guaranteed by
France and Sweden, which gained superordinate rights of arbitration and
intervention. In fact, the treaty did not remove universal/hierarchical claims
to international authority, but relegalized European politics with specific
reference to the German states. Whereas the core idea of 1648 was peace,
not self-determination, the core idea of the balance of power is self-
determination, not peace.

In sum, the political regimes of the treaties' parties, the restorative and
backward-looking substance of its provisions, and the collective security
intentions of the peacemakers provide considerable evidence of the pre-
modern nature of the settlement. Far from establishing the classical model
of international relations based on anarchy between modern sovereign

states, as the IR literature asserts, it enshrined constitutional relations among the actors of the German Empire and decidedly non-modern dynastic states. To this extent, 1648 was more of an end than a beginning.

7. Conclusion: The End of 1648

The specificity of the Westphalian order cannot be adequately understood on the basis of naturalized great power rivalries driven by *Realpolitik* and regulated by a universalized balance of power. Nor can it be explained by the pressure exerted by an anarchical and competitive states-system in abstraction from the internal character of its constitutive conflict units, as demanded by Neorealism (Waltz 1979; Gilpin 1981; Mearsheimer 1995). My argument also challenges the plausibility of Constructivist approaches. Constructivism explains variations in and transformations of international relations either in terms of the intersubjectively negotiated quality of institutions qua conventions that may alter policy outcomes, or changes in the identities of political actors based on changing sources of legitimacy (Kratochwil 1989; Onuf 1989; Adler 1997; Ruggie 1998; Burch 1998; Reus-Smit 1999; Hall 1999; Wendt 1999). Without systematic inquiry into the property-related social sources of identity formation, which define particular interests and generate specific institutions, Constructivist claims remain ungrounded. While all social phenomena are mediated by language and norms, the extra-normative conditions sustaining the rise, reproduction, and fall of specific constitutive rules fall outside the scope of Constructivism. After all, norms are only valid during normal times and require coercion and sanctions for their maintenance.

In sum, the overwhelmingly dynastic nature of the Westphalian order set it apart from its modern successor. Its distinguishing properties were bound up with the persistence of non-capitalist property relations that blocked the development of modern sovereignty. IR's failure to correctly theorize and periodize 1648 thus rests on its conflation of absolutist and modern sovereignty. Consequently, demystifying Westphalia requires retheorizing absolutist sovereignty. I suggested that changes in the class structure subsequent to widespread French peasant liberation of the thirteenth and fourteenth centuries led to the absolutist tax/office state. 'Parcellized sovereignty' was transformed into royal proprietary sovereignty. Pre-capitalist property relations led to political strategies of domestic income extraction by royal houses and their courtly clienteles, and by the same token to external strategies of geopolitical accumulation. This explains the frequency of war and the persistence of empire-building. Proprietary and personalized sovereignty promoted political marriages, wars of succession, and the elevation of dynastic 'private' family law to the status of 'public' international law. The proprietary nature of state territory made it an exchangeable appendage of dynastic fortunes. Inter-dynastic compensatory equilibrium promoted bandwagoning, eliminating smaller states. In sum, proprietary statehood implied the regulation of contemporary inter-actor relations on the basis of predatory dynasticism and inter-personalism. The peace treaties of Westphalia – in intention, wording, and outcome – remained embedded in this geopolitical configuration. European early modern international relations, codified in the Westphalian settlement, had their own 'generative grammar', a distinct territorial logic, and historically specific patterns of conflict and co-operation.

Notes

1

The modern system of international law is the result of the great political transformation that marked the transition from the Middle Ages to the modern period of history. It can be summed up as the transformation of the feudal system into the territorial state. The main characteristic of the latter, distinguishing it from its predecessor, was the assumption by the government of the supreme authority within the territory of the state. The monarch no longer shared authority with the feudal lords within the territory of which he had been in a large measure the nominal rather than the actual head. Nor did he share it with the Church, which throughout the Middle Ages had claimed in certain respects supreme authority within Christendom. When this transformation had been consummated in the sixteenth century, the political world consisted of a number of states that within their respective territories were, legally speaking, completely independent of each other, recognizing no secular authority above themselves. In one word, they were sovereign. (Morgenthau 1985: 293–4)

[I]mperial orders constituted merely a system of states, not what Hedley Bull characterized as an international 'society'. International conflict was at once economic, social, political, and civilizational. This was true until the Treaty of Westphalia. (Gilpin 1981: 111)

If we say that the states-system becomes apparent in the later seventeenth century or early eighteenth century, we are left with the task of providing a description for the European system between the Council of Constance and the Congress of Westphalia. And however we describe it, this system has a greater resemblance to the states-system that succeeds it than it has to the medieval system that precedes it. The real break, prepared through the fourteenth century, becomes manifest in the fifteenth . . . [Thus] at Westphalia the states-system does not come into existence: it comes of age. (Wight 1977b: 151)

By the mid-seventeenth century both the states' *de facto* monopoly of military force and their exclusive right to exercise that force were widely established and accepted. Even the sovereign principalities of the historically anachronistic Holy Roman Empire had their right to wage war explicitly recognized in the *Peace of Westphalia*. (Holzgrefe 1989: 22)

2 These contemporary authors, while more cautious about the epochal significance of 1648, do not challenge the classical account. Cf., e.g., 'My discussion ends at about the time of the Peace of Westphalia (1648), which formally acknowledged a system of sovereign states' (Spruyt 1994a: 27). 'Elements of sovereign statehood had been accumulating for three centuries, making Westphalia the consolidation, not the creation *ex nihilo*, of the modern system' (Philpot 2001: 77). Two exceptions are Reus-Smit 1999 and Osiander 2001. While both accounts identify the nineteenth century as the century of transition, their explanations remain marred by one-sided, 'ideational' Constructivist approaches.

3 For Marx and Engels's own accounts of nineteenth-century international relations, see Soell 1972 and Teschke 2001.

4 While it is plausible to suggest that these 'unlike' actors were, in the long run, 'socialized' into the system (Waltz 1979), we still need to know (1) why they were heterogenous in the first place, (2) why the completion of this process took several centuries, (3) the exact mechanisms of this 'adaptation', (4) on which specific type of state/society complex they converged, and (5) why states repeatedly try to break away from this system and even attempt to transcend and transform it (European Union etc.). It is equally clear that it is one-sided to assume a permanent process of 'passive-adaptive' state-emulation. It is necessay to demonstrate how revolutionary states – be it seventeenth-century England or eighteenth-century France – either transformed the very nature of the system or altered its rules in significant ways. For a richer conception of 'competitive homogenization' see Halliday 1994: 94–123.

5 While Quincy Wright's statistics are methodologically not unproblematic, they indicate a clear tendency.

6 For figures on public revenues and expenditures in various European regions and the percentages dedicated to war, see Bonney 1996, 1999.

7 'Once we understand that the state was a piece of property heritable within a particular family, it is easier to appreciate the dynastic basis of war and diplomacy in the seventeenth and eighteenth centuries' (Symcox 1974: 5; see also Marx 1986).

8 Morgenthau defines the goal of power-balancing as 'stability plus the preservation of all the elements of the system' (Morgenthau 1985: 189). On the automatic conception of the balance of power, see Waltz 1979.

9 'The hierarchical organization of states was one that all Europe took for
   granted as the outward expression of power and prestige, and changes were
   not easily made' (Hatton 1969: 157; see also Wight 1977b: 135; Osiander
   1994: 82–9).

10 The transition from the medieval *ius gentium* to the Spanish-dominated *ius
   inter gentes* and the French-dominated *droit public de l'Europe* failed to establish
   a body of general abstract norms of international law (Grewe 1984: 420–22).
   This failure was bound up with the personalized nature of dynastic sovereignty. Through an additive and issue-related series of peace conventions,
   trade agreements, and coalition treaties, early modern international law
   mostly enshrined the interpersonal relations of the European princely class.

11 It is puzzling to see how Luard's rich historical exposition disproves his main
   argument, namely that 1648 'ushered in a wholly new age', where 'competition now took place among sovereign states, competing for territory, status
   and power' (Luard 1992: xii).

12 On the multiple meanings of the balance of power, see Claude 1962: 25–39;
   Gulick 1967; Luard 1992.

13 Morgenthau (1985: 199, 222) submits that the Polish Partitions 'reaffirmed
   the essence' of the balance of power, since Poland was divided into equal
   parts; later, he claims that it failed, since it could not protect Poland from
   destruction. Wight (1966a: 157, 1978: 189) argues that the partitions
   discredited the balance of power. Gulick (1967: 37–42) argues that it
   depends. For Bull (1977: 108), 'the partition of Poland was not a departure
   from the principle of balance of power but an application'. Luard (1992: 24)
   refers to them as the result of a 'balance of advantage'. Schroeder (1994a:
   18) calls them a 'system conforming behaviour'. Sheehan (1996: 61) indicts
   them as an 'aberration'.

14 While Schroeder's survey of the historical record confirms the prevalence of
   bandwagoning, he offers no explanation.

15 IPO stands for *Instrumentum Pacis Osnabrugense*, the peace treaty of Osnabrück.
   IPM stands for *Instrumentum Pacis Monasteriense*, the peace treaty of Münster.

16 Although it is often pointed out with reference to clauses 71–82 (IPM) that
   the Habsburg dominions of Alsace were given in 'full sovereignty' to France
   (Osiander 1994: 68–70; for the opposite view see Symcox 1974: 39), clause
   112 (IPM) qualifies this transfer in that the Bishoprics of Strassbourg and
   Basel, various abbacies, the ten Alsacian imperial cities and the nobility of
   lower Alsace remained in immediate dependence upon the Empire.

17 See Burkhardt on the Empire as a 'third way' of early modern state
   organization (Burkhardt 1992: 108–25).

18 Burkhardt even judges the explicit acknowledgement of *Reichstreue* in
   relation to the right to conclude alliances as a success for the emperor
   (Burkhardt 1992: 106).

19 The plenipotentiaries to the Peace Congress did entertain ideas of international equilibrium, but power politics and the balance of power were not
   acknowledged as principles of the treaty.

8

Towards the Modern States-System:

International Relations from Absolutism to Capitalism

1. Introduction: From 'Structural Discontinuity' to a 'Mixed-Case' Scenario

How should we understand the transformation of absolutist into modern international relations? My argument is that this shift was directly linked to the formation of capitalism, the emergence of a modern state in England, and Britain's eighteenth-century rise as the world's major international power. In the period between the end of the Glorious Revolution and the accession of the first Hanoverian king, George I, in 1714, British foreign policy shifted on the basis of a capitalist social property regime that revolutionized the British state. Henceforth, this new state/society complex would play a pivotal role in the long-term restructuring of the European states-system.

The property relations approach thus entails a theory of *systemic transformation* that insists on the centrality of class conflict for changes in property regimes, forms of political authority, and international orders. Routinely, clashing strategies of reproduction are about income distribution within the confines of given property relations. However, in times of general crisis, the very structure of the property regime may be at stake, bringing a period of violent transformation. Rethinking the transition from pre-modern to modern geopolitical relations in terms of class conflict generates a new set of propositions for IR. The decisive shift towards modern international relations is not marked by the Peace of Westphalia, but comes with the rise of the first modern state: post-revolutionary England. After the establishment of an agrarian capitalist property regime and the transformation of the militarized, landholding feudal nobility into a demilitarized, landed capitalist class with full and exclusive property rights in late seventeenth-century England, political authority was redefined in terms of parliamentary sovereignty. The shift from dynastic to parliamentary sovereignty signals the consolidation of modern sovereignty. After 1688, England started to employ new foreign policy techniques while remaining surrounded by territorially accumulating dynastic states.

Although late seventeenth-century England constitutes the point of departure for retheorizing and reperiodizing the development of the modern international system, no single event or date can be unequivocally singled out as the decisive system-wide caesura of inter-state modernity. There was no 'structural rupture' that divided pre-modern from modern international relations. Rather, international relations from 1688 to the First World War and beyond were about the geopolitically mediated and contested negotiation of the modernization pressures that emanated from capitalist Britain. International relations in this long period of transformation were thus not modern, but *modernizing*. Structural analysis has to cede to a processual historical reconstruction. The expository problem of theorizing geopolitics among coexisting heterogeneous actors in a 'mixed-case' scenario thus also applies to the British-led development of the modern states-system. Reassessing the transition to generalized modern international relations requires a systematic reinterpretation of the geographically combined and socially uneven generalization of the English state/society complex.[1] *Ex hypothesis*, in a series of geopolitically mediated international crises, Britain undermined the continental *Ancien Régimes* – starting with the French Revolution and ending with the First World War – forcing them through a series of revolutions and reforms (revolutions from above) to adapt their economic and political systems to its superior economic performance *and* military power. During this protracted transition, specifically modern inter-state relations gradually replaced the old Westphalian logic of inter-dynastic relations.

2. The Transition from Feudalism to Capitalism in England

In early modern England, state formation and economic development started on a radically different long-term trajectory. When the eco-demographic crisis struck England, expressed in the Black Death, lords tried to recuperate falling income by increasing rents in spite of population decline. The seigneurial reaction failed in the face of protracted peasant resistance, culminating in the rebellion of 1381 (Hilton 1973). The English peasantry removed many feudal controls, gained full personal freedom, and came to hold its land on a copyhold basis (long-term leases), which increased security of tenure. The fifteenth century saw a marked improvement in peasant status and income, while lords progressively lost their capacity to take coerced rents. However, in contrast to French developments, the English peasantry failed to gain legally protected property rights to their plots (freeholds), since landlords succeeded in turning copyhold agreements into leaseholds, renewable only at the lord's will. This enabled lords to drive up rents and charge variable and large entry fines. As a result, the peasantry was gradually evicted from its customary lands during the sixteenth and seventeenth centuries. Landlords drove peasants off their land, consolidated and enclosed their holdings, and leased them out to large capitalist tenants, who farmed commercially by employing wage-labour (Wolf 1982: 120–21; Brenner 1985a: 46–54, 1985b: 291–9).[2] The enclosure movement that started in the sixteenth century and continued, backed by a series of post-1688 Acts of Parliament, well into the eighteenth century, destroyed the commons and subsistence farming. English peasants were not protected by the monarchy due to tight co-operation between the king and his landholding aristocracy, blocking a French-style peasant/king alliance and the growth of an absolutist tax/office state. The result was the destruction of the old feudal powers of political surplus extraction and the beginning of a new class constellation revolving around the triad of large landlords, capitalist tenant farmers, and wage-labour. What explains the Franco-English variation is differences in class constellations. The relatively centralized self-organization of nobility and king fostered a higher degree of inter-ruling-class co-operation in England than in France, where the competitive relations between nobility and king inadvertently secured both peasant freedom *and* peasant possession.

In England, then, the market no longer represented an opportunity for selling surplus produce, but an economic compulsion in which landlords, tenant farmers, and wage-labourers had to reproduce themselves (Wood 2002). Lords no longer received rents in kind, labour, or cash. Landlords received a capitalist ground rent, while tenant farmers received capitalist profit. Labour and capital were subjected to the competitive laws of the market, so that ruling-class reproduction was no longer a function of military but of economic competitiveness. Cost-cutting through innovation and specialization became the means of increasing productivity and competitiveness in commercial farming. Systematic reinvestment in the means of production brought agricultural improvements, large-scale commercial farming, the break-up of the Malthusian cycles in the countryside, and the beginning of a self-sustaining 'Agricultural Revolution' (Kerridge 1967;

Wrigley 1985; Crouzet 1990; Overton 1996). Rapidly growing agrarian productivity rates and shrinking agricultural employment supported both a continuously growing population and a growing home market for industrial goods and proletarianized labour, leading eventually to the Industrial Revolution, while urbanization increased apace. The seventeenth-century crisis in England was therefore not a conflict over the distribution of shrinking total output in a contracting agrarian economy, as in France, but a conflict over the nature of property relations and, ultimately, the form of the state.

3. The Glorious Revolution and Modern Sovereignty

Politically, the transformation of a militarized feudal class into a demilita-rized class of capitalist landlords provided the social basis for the new constitutional monarchy. The new capitalist aristocracy sought to secure its private property rights, commercial rents, and political liberties against the Stuart reaction of 1603–40, which tried to foster absolutism. This conflict was not between an old feudal aristocracy and a rising bourgeoisie, composed of merchants and the gentry/yeomen, but between a landed and unified capitalist aristocracy, supported by the new colonial-interloping traders, and a patrimonial monarchy, supported by courtiers, the ecclesias-tical elite, and the privileged overseas company merchants (Brenner 1993: 638–716; Wood 1996). The growing divergence of interests between the landed capitalist classes and the pro-Catholic, pro-Bourbon, and pro-absolutist monarchy led Charles II to strike up an alliance with France, while Parliament remained suspended between 1674 and 1679, forcing the capitalist aristocracy to lean on radical movements in London.[3] The Stuarts' attempt to internationalize the conflict by mobilizing French support provoked Parliament to invite William of Orange, the arch-Protestant head of the House of Orange and Stadtholder of the United Provinces, to restore internal order and fend off absolutist restoration. However, in the face of popular radicalism, the parliamentary anti-absolutist reform pro-gramme had to be toned down to allow the restoration of the monarchy after the republican Commonwealth governments. Caught between the 'revolution from below' and Stuart absolutism, the landlords settled in the Glorious Revolution for a compromise that maintained overall stability while promoting their essential interests: sovereignty became 'the King-in-Parliament'. In a series of royal concessions – the 1689 Bill of Rights, the 1694 Triennial Act, and the 1701 Act of Settlement – the capitalist aristocracy secured essential control over taxation, the army, jurisdiction, foreign policy, and the right of self-convocation. In other words, Parliament became the locus of centralized state power.

Parliamentary control of military power de-patrimonialized the army and created a *public monopoly in the means of violence*. Parliament exercised exclusive control over the military's funding, size, internal regulations, and deployment, leaving the king the notional title 'supreme commander' (Brewer 1989: 43–4). Parliament's control over taxes ended the royal prerogative of extra-parliamentary taxation and the king's reliance on customs and excise, which had previously allowed him to circumvent Parliament. The eighteenth-century 'financial revolution' combined a new, modern system of public credit with a new system of taxation. Tax-farming gave way to direct collection carried out by centrally appointed government officials, establishing an effective tax system that provided regular income supervised by the Treasury Board. 'This enabled Britain to become the first major European state to keep full accounts of total government revenue and expenditure' (Brewer 1989: 129). The land tax, i.e., direct taxation, became the third pillar of public revenue, next to customs and excise. It did not rely on force but on consensus, since it was the key mechanism through which the landed classes taxed themselves (Parker 1996: 218ff). 'The Land Tax was a tax on *capitalist ground rents* paid to the owners of large estates by their capitalist tenants as a portion of the proceeds realized from the exploitation of rural labor' (Mooers 1991: 162). The landed classes resorted to self-taxation precisely because customs and excise (indirect taxation) were the key sources of income for the monarchy and thus associated with absolutism. While the importance of the land tax declined as a percentage of overall state income after 1713, it represented the main source of state revenue between 1688 and 1713, accounting for between 37 and 52 per cent of all receipts (Brewer 1989: 95). Thus, during the crucial period of Parliament's consolidation of its fiscal rights in the face of sporadic royal attempts to reassert fiscal prerogatives, self-taxation meant control. Once the new regime was entrenched, the reliance on customs and excise was, of course, more convenient to the propertied classes. In contrast to France, the British tax system did not degenerate into a heterogeneous welter of locally and socially differentiated and particularistic tax deals, but was *national, uniform*, and *effective*. The side-effect of systematized public tax collection and fiscal control was the creation of a superior public credit system. Precisely because tax returns were predictable and secure, creditors had greater incentives to provide loans to the government. Public debt was no longer the king's debt – liable to fraud –

but became the National Debt (1693), managed by the newly established Bank of England (1694). Lower interest rates on government bonds were accepted by investors in return for greater security, especially in the servicing of long-term debts, while they also kept government debt-servicing under control. At the same time, eighteenth-century Britain experienced an enormous expansion and transformation of the administrative apparatus, which gradually took on the Weberian traits of modern bureaucracy – professionalism, salaries and pensions, examinations, appointments, merit-based promotion, a hierarchical career path, records and bookkeeping, procedure, seniority, accountability, and a sense of public duty. While pockets of venality, corruption, and patrimony persisted in the state edifice, state offices were not, as in France, the private property of a venal and uncontrollable officer class (Brewer 1989: 64–87). The old spoils system gave way to an increasingly depoliticized and deprivatized civil service, while corruption was no longer a privilege but delegitimized and criminalized as 'corruption'.[4]

Parliament not only revolutionized the military, fiscal, financial, and administrative systems, it immediately broke the monopolies of the great chartered overseas companies, allowing for freer and greater capital investments in overseas enterprises. 'It chartered the New East India Company in 1694, thus undermining the old company; deprived the Hudson's Bay Company of its exclusive privileges in 1697; destroyed the Royal Africa Company's monopoly in 1698; and broke the Russia Company's control over the Muscovy tobacco reexport trade in 1699' (Brenner 1993: 715). Having gained state control, the 'committee of landlords' passed a series of enclosure acts during the eighteenth century that completed the transformation of peasant-held customary land into consolidated capitalist farms. In this context, it was equally important to find a religious settlement that safeguarded the Protestant succession, since absolutist restoration was invariably associated with opposing Catholic forces – the papacy, which fought to reverse the independence of the national Church controlled by Parliament; the arch-Catholic rival powers, Spain and France, which actively supported Stuart restoration; the patrimonial monarchy itself; and some surviving old feudal English magnates. Protestantism became the common medium of identity for the capitalist aristocracy. While the international context was an important factor in the resolution of England's century of crisis, it only modified a socio-political configuration that was essentially endogenously created (for a different view, see Zolberg 1980: 704–13).[5]

The self-organization of capitalist landlords in Parliament meant that sovereignty was centralized and pooled in a state that was no longer directly involved in political accumulation. The feudal unity of the political and the economic dissolved and gave way to their separation – the *disiecta membra* of one social totality. Political surplus appropriation was replaced by the nexus between private, purely economic capital accumulation and public, impersonal political authority: modern sovereignty. A capitalist aristocracy, rather than a mercantile bourgeoisie, came to dominate Parliament and determine affairs of state.

> The political corollary of these distinctive economic relations was a formally autonomous state which represented the private, 'economic' class of appropriators in its public, 'political' aspect. This meant that the 'economic' functions of appropriation were differentiated from the 'political' and military functions of rule – or, to put it another way, 'civil society' was differentiated from the state – while at the same time the state was responsive, even subordinate, to civil society. (Wood 1991: 28)

The rise of capitalism was not the necessary result of contradictions in the feudal mode of production, of interstitial emergence, or the preordained middle-range telos of world history. Most importantly, it was not the project of a rising urban bourgeoisie in mortal conflict with a retrograde landed aristocracy. It was the result of specific class conflicts between exploiters and exploited in a specific region of Europe. In other words, as Robert Brenner argues, the establishment of agrarian capitalism was the *unintended outcome* of class conflicts over property rights as each class tried to reproduce itself as it was. Capitalism need not have come into existence at all. Capitalism, however, rose in conjunction with the first modern state – but this was capitalism in one country (Wood 1991; on the controversial Dutch case, see the essays in Hoppenbrouwers and Zanden 2001). Thus, France and England were not two variations on the same theme. Whereas in France, the tax/office state was a competitor of the pre-capitalist landed class, promoting its absorption into the patrimonial state through the sale of offices, in Britain, the state became the instrument of the capitalist landed classes for the joint management of their common affairs. France and England were two incommensurable social totalities.[6] But the effect of capitalism was not confined to the island nation. Rather, capitalism came to be the general ether that gave all subsequent developments, domestic and international, a specific colouring.

4. British Uniqueness: Capitalism, Modern Sovereignty, and Active Balancing

Analytically, I argued that while feudalism implied the decentralized, personalized rule of the lords, creating the parcellized sovereignty of the medieval 'state', and absolutism implied the more centralized but still personalized rule of the dynasties, capitalism implies the centralized, depersonalized rule of the modern state. Since ruling-class power in capitalist societies is based on private property and control over the means of production, 'the state' is no longer required to interfere directly into processes of production and extraction. Its central function is confined to the internal maintenance and external defence of a private property regime. This entails legally enforcing what are now civil contracts among politically (though not economically) free and equal citizens subject to civil law. This, in turn, requires a public monopoly over the means of violence, enabling the development of an 'impartial' public bureaucracy. Political power and especially the monopoly over the means of violence now come to be pooled in a deprivatized state above society and the economy. While this does not, of course, exhaust the historical role of the modern state, capitalist property relations allow the separation of a non-coercive 'economic economy' from a purely 'political state'. But since capitalism is not predicated on the logic of domestic political accumulation, we should expect it to bring about the decline of the external geopolitical accumulation that defined the war-driven international conduct of the feudal and absolutist ages.

Does this argument hold empirically for post-revolutionary British foreign policy? *Prima facie*, the historical record seems to contradict this thesis. Britain was centrally involved in all major eighteenth-century conflicts – the Nine Years' War (1688–97), the War of the Spanish Succession (1702–13), the War of Jenkins's Ear and Austrian Succession (1739–48), the Seven Years' War (1756–63), the American War of Independence (1775–83), and the conflicts surrounding revolutionary France and Napoleon. However, Britain's role, strategy, and objectives in European politics changed decisively as a result of its new domestic arrangements. 'For almost three centuries (from about 1650 to 1920) Great Britain had available to it a highly distinctive system of national security' – blue-water policy (Baugh 1988: 33; see also Baugh 1998). How did it come about and what were its effects on European politics? At the end of the seventeenth century, British sovereignty lay no longer with the king but with Parliament. Britain's new attitude towards Europe was based on the decoupling of foreign policy from dynastic interests, brought about by Parliament's right – gained in the 1701 Act of Settlement – to limit, co-articulate, and even determine British foreign policy (Zolberg 1980: 74; Black 1991: 13–20, 43–58).[7] After these constitutional changes, British foreign policy was no longer conducted exclusively on the basis of dynastic interests as formulated in *Kabinettpolitik*, but increasingly on the basis of the 'national interest' as formulated by the propertied classes in Parliament. This was a world-historical *novum*. The decisive new regulator of Britain's readiness to go to war was taxation, and especially the land tax, through which the landed and commercial classes taxed themselves.

The personal union of the United Kingdom with Hanover, which wedded the German ancestral lands to the British Isles, was regarded by both the Tories and Whigs as a disturbing continental legacy and caused much resentment in Parliament (McKay and Scott 1983: 104; Black 1991: 31–42). Hanoverian monarchical interests as German Electors ran time and again into those of changing parliamentary majorities.

> Much of the debate about war and diplomacy in eighteenth-century Britain was about reconciling the dynastic and personal interests of the monarch – William III's concern with the balance of power in Europe, the first two Hanoverians' desire to protect their beloved Electorate – with a broadly defined public interest. Such a debate only occurred because the national representative, as well as the crown, exercised some control over Britain's armed forces. (Brewer 1989: 43)

Whereas the Hanoverian dynasty remained enmeshed in the absolutist territorial game of inter-dynastic relations, Parliament sought to deterritorialize British policy on the Continent (Sheehan 1988: 28; Schroeder 1994b: 136; Duchhardt 1995: 182–3).[8] In addition, post-revolutionary foreign policy had to avoid alliances with the Catholic powers, notably Spain and France, since this would have threatened domestic socio-political arrangements, especially the power of Parliament. The revival of dynasticism had to be avoided at all costs. Given these conditions, foreign policy had to be insulated as far as possible from continental affairs.

The first manifestation of the new British attitude came with the Nine Years' War (1688–97), in which the post-revolutionary constitutional settlement and the Protestant Succession were tested in the struggle against the Bourbons, who supported the restoration of the Stuarts (Sheehan 1988: 30; Duchhardt 1989a: 33). Britain's ability to sustain the war against absolutist France was predicated on the Parliament-backed creation of the first modern financial system, relying on the National Debt and the Bank of England. Wars were no longer to be financed out of the 'private' war chest of the dynastic ruler, but by a reliable credit system. It was superior in raising funds, since public debts were guaranteed by Parliament (Parker 1996: 217–21). Investment in these loans had the effect of uniting the propertied class behind the British war effort, creating a commonality of purpose. Credit security was guaranteed by the self-taxation of the capitalist classes in Parliament. 'During the Nine Years' War the commercial and landed classes represented there managed to double the country's revenues by effectively taxing their own wealth for the first time' (McKay and Scott 1983: 46).

The uneven development of different state/society complexes in early modern Europe meant that while continental states continued to operate absolutist regimes of domestic tax extraction and dynastic foreign strategies of geopolitical accumulation, England developed a dual foreign policy strategy (Black 1991: 85–6; Duchhardt 1997: 302). While it continued its aggressive mercantilist 'blue water' policies overseas, fanned by an expanding capitalist economy that financed naval superiority, Britain assumed the new role of balancer of the European pentarchy (Van der Pijl 1998: 86) and disengaged from direct territorial claims on the Continent after the Treaty of Utrecht.

> Blue water warfare was a form of technically advanced warfare emphasizing economic pressure. The military weight of the Continental powers was to be opposed by naval skills, superiority of equipment, and abundance of money and resources, as well as access to resources. All of these were chiefly derived from domestic industry and seaborne commerce. (Daniel Baugh, cited in Brewer 1989: 257)

As long as the dominant European powers were dynastic states based on pre-capitalist social property relations, Britain remained engulfed in a hostile world of politically accumulating states. This explains why Britain's struggles overseas with Spain and France retained a military-mercantilist character. Utrecht, in turn, exemplified not simply Britain's rise as a great power, but also its willingness and ability to regulate European affairs on a new principle of active balancing, though on the old territorial basis (continental predatory equilibrium). The British peace plans were a major departure from earlier schemes (for a contrary view, see Holsti 1991: 80). Her strategy was to contain France by keeping her militarily occupied on the Continent while defeating her overseas by means of Britain's superior naval forces. While France was Britain's 'natural enemy' due to its military power, geopolitical situation, and oceanic access, the negotiation of a bilateral Anglo-French separate peace treaty in 1713, which, much to the dismay of Austria, preserved France as a viable power, was inscribed in the logic of balancing. French elimination would have buttressed Austrian hegemony on the Continent. Significantly, Britain's only territorial gains on the Continent at Utrecht were the strategic posts of Gibraltar and Minorca, while the acquisition of trading posts and commercial rights overseas, like the *asiento*, dominated her peace agenda (Rosenberg 1994: 38–43; Schroeder 1994b: 142). Territorial gains on the Continent – apart from strategic posts that allowed the policing of the main European trading routes – were of little interest for a commercial nation (Baugh 1988: 46). If Britain's direct military interventions on the Continent were already significantly reduced after 1713, they veered towards zero after the Seven Years' War, which established Britain overseas as the hegemonic naval power. At the same time, Frederick the Great was heavily subsidized by Britain, guaranteeing Prussia's survival. America was indeed conquered in Germany. It is indicative that of the seven Anglo-French wars between 1689 and 1815, Britain lost only one, the American War of Independence, which was precisely the only conflict in which she had failed to forge a continental anti-French alliance. While Britain's security interests lay in Europe, her economic interests lay overseas.

After 1713, British foreign policy no longer operated on the principle of 'natural allies' – the 'Old System', which allied England, the Dutch Republic, and Austria against France – but on the fluid principle of rapidly changing coalitions, earning her on the Continent the epithet 'Perfidious Albion'.[9] This nickname owed as much to the dynasts' failure to grasp the nature of changing parliamentary majorities as to their failure to understand the logic of post-dynastic foreign policy and active balancing in the context of an overwhelmingly dynastic system of states. The new idea was to stop fighting once the weaker ally had recovered (e.g. Prussia) rather than to eliminate the common enemy. This was, as Sheehan explains, a policy of achieving minimal aims rather than the maximal aims of the dynastic coalitions (Sheehan 1996: 64). The logical choice of Britain's continental partners against France were those land-based powers – like Austria, Prussia, and Russia – which had no overseas ambitions. Walpole squashed Austria's only foray in this direction, the Austrian Ostende Company, in exchange for recognizing the Austrian Pragmatic Sanction. Prussia's promotion of the tiny port of Emden set off alarm bells in London's merchant community. Russia's predominance as a trading power in the Baltic was of more concern to Parliament than her vast territorial gains in Siberia. Even a *rapprochement* with France was possible in the 1730s when it was realized that Austria could again dominate European politics. 'To paraphrase a statement of Palmerston: While the holder of the balance has no permanent friends, it has no permanent enemies either; it has only the permanent interest of maintaining the balance of power itself' (Morgenthau 1985: 214). But what was to be balanced here were not modern but dynastic states. This explains why the balance of power did not assume the form of the automatic 'invisible hand' reminiscent of Adam Smith's idea of market self-regulation (as argued by Rosenberg 1994: 139). It was manipulated by a structurally privileged and self-conscious balancer: Britain's hand held the scales.[10]

This meant that during the eighteenth century, two regimes of power-balancing were operating in Europe. While absolutist states continued the policy of territorial equilibrium, partitions, and compensations, parliamentary Britain sought to manage the balance of the European system by indirect interventions, in the form of subsidies and pensions to smaller powers, while countering any imperial-hegemonic ambition (McKay and Scott 1983: 96).[11] Britain's neutrality in the War of the Polish Succession (1733–38) was a clear indicator of her disengagement from the fruits of the *convenance* system of territorial compensations. Power-balancing operated primarily through diplomacy and the payment of huge subsidies, while war became the *ultima ratio*.

> In all the major wars of the eighteenth century the government spent substantial sums subsidizing other troops to fight on its behalf. During the War of Spanish Succession over £7 million or nearly 25 per cent of all money voted for expenditure on the army was assigned to foreign subsidies. Similarly, between the outbreak of the War of Jenkins's Ear (1739) and the end of the Seven Years' War (1763) some £17.5 million or 21 per cent of the sums voted for the army went on foreign soldiers. Between 1702 and 1763 the British government spent over £24.5 million in this fashion. Sometimes these monies were paid to small corps of foreign troops who fought in allied armies alongside the British; occasionally, as during the Seven Years' War, they subsidized an entire army like the 40,000 enlisted with the Duke of Brunswick. (Brewer 1989: 32)

While this was, of course, expensive and a major source of concern, it was manageable and sustainable. The War of the Austrian Succession 'cost Britain £43 million, of which £30 million was added to the National Debt. With the land tax at 4s in the pound, alarmists in the government raised the cry of national bankruptcy' (McKay and Scott 1983: 172–3). Yet, while Britain sustained the huge financial burden, the French financial system, despite its greater taxable population, collapsed. This pattern was repeated throughout the history of Anglo-French conflict in the eighteenth century.

Taking account of the Franco-British divergence in financial responsiveness to war is central to avoiding the fallacy of subsuming both states under one model of war-driven polity. Clearly, Britain became in the eighteenth century not simply Europe's major power, it became a 'fiscal-military state' (Brewer 1989) – bellicose, militarized, and on a near-permanent war footing, like any other comparable European power. This has led many commentators in the Weber–Hintze tradition to overlook the structural differences between Britain and the rest of the continent. For Michael Mann, for example, the arrival of the permanent war state in early modern Britain is primarily a function of geopolitical rivalry. While Britain was a constitutional regime, this was the result of its privileged geostrategic position, which rendered a standing army superfluous.[12] In the absence of a standing army as an instrument for internal repression, the path towards absolutism was blocked. However, his emphasis on a 'standing navy' and the general drive towards a fiscal state primarily organized for war minimize, according to Mann, the significance of regime-type differences – constitutional and absolutist – both being subject to the pressure of geopolitical competition. He concludes that 'the growth of the state's size is occasioned throughout the whole period [1130–1815] by warfare between states and only marginally by internal developments' (Mann 1988c: 110; cf. also Mann 1986: 478).[13]

The best way to demonstrate the significance of domestic arrangements is to observe different state responses to military pressure. In Britain as in France, public finances were dominated by war expenditures. Englishmen were more heavily taxed than their European neighbours, with 17.6 *livres* per capita in annual taxes by the first quarter of the eighteenth century (compared to 8.1. *livres* in France), rising to 46 *livres* (compared with 17) by the 1780s. What is indicative, however, is that although Britain spent between 61 and 74 per cent (excluding debt-servicing) of total government expenditure on military costs between 1689 and 1783 – in effect, *more* than France – this constituted only between 9 and 12.5 per cent of national income (Brewer 1989: 40, 89). Why, then, was the percentage of national income dedicated to war smaller than France's, while total war expenditure was higher? Why and how did British subjects sustain the higher tax burden? Why did it not lead to domestic strife, as in France? Given that Britain faced neither bankruptcy nor major tax riots during the entire eighteenth century, it seems plausible to suggest that Britain's financial resilience and health was underwritten by a *dynamic and expanding capitalist economy* and a post-revolutionary political settlement that made the raising of taxes and tax-collecting a *national* and relatively *conflict-free* affair.

Britain's position as balancer was based on a productive capitalist economy that financed naval supremacy. She was no longer placed in either of the two scales but held the balance itself in her hands.[14] 'Continental Powers have always noted that while Britain traditionally claimed to hold the balance of Europe with her right hand, with her left hand she was establishing oceanic hegemony which refused for two centuries to admit any principle of equilibrium' (Wight 1966a: 164). Britain was not the accidental insular *tertius gaudens* of dynastic power-balancing (Wight 1978: 171), but the conscious regulator of a system of European politics from which she was socio-economically, rather than geographically, set apart. The apparent unity of eighteenth-century European politics conceals two different conceptions of geopolitical order, held by capitalist Britain on the one side, and the continental dynastic powers on the other.

5. Geopolitically Combined and Socially Uneven Development

We can thus see how a more differentiated and historical account of international relations, one based on the social property relations within states, leads to a radically revisionist picture of the Westphalian system. Chronologically, the fundamental break with the old territorially accumulative logic of international relations came with the rise of capitalism in England. The onset of agrarian capitalism in sixteenth-century England, the change from dynastic to parliamentary sovereignty in the late seventeenth century, and the post-Utrecht adoption of a new foreign policy resulted in the gradual deterritorialization of British interests on the Continent. At the same time, Britain began to manipulate the old inter-dynastic predatory equilibrium through a new conception of active balancing.

Yet, developmentally, the eighteenth-century world was not yet capitalist. This explains why Britain's post-1688 trajectory remained heavily influenced by the geopolitically accumulating logic of dynastic states. As we have seen, geopolitical pressure massively inflected post-1688 British state formation (without however unsettling its core structure) such that a smooth transition to a minimalist liberal state was not possible. The key difference compared to its continental neighbours was that the eighteenth-century British 'military-fiscal' state was sustained by a productive capitalist economy, an increasingly rationalized state apparatus, and the ultimately consensual national policies of a unified ruling class, while the same pressures led to recurrent crises, intra-ruling class strife, and finally state collapse on the Continent. During the formation of the absolutist world-system, Britain was the 'third hand' that consciously balanced the imperial pretensions of pre-capitalist states. This technique was initially a defensive mechanism, designed to safeguard domestic arrangements. But by the late eighteenth century, British balancing no longer served the exclusive function of security and order, but had the side-effect of forcing continental states to respond to and finally adjust to the superior socio-political British model, especially under the impact of the Industrial Revolution. In this process, active balancing became the major conduit for distributing pressure on continental states that had, in the long run, a transformative effect on politico-economic organization in 'backward' state/society complexes. *Ex hypothesis*, this suggests that it was under pressure of geopolitical competition, especially between France and Britain after the French defeat in the Seven Years' War and the victorious but financially ruinous campaigns in the Americas, that a militarily weakened and financially bankrupt France was eventually forced, in a period of dramatic class conflicts, to violently alter its internal social property relations. Relying on its expanding capitalist economy, Britain continued to play non-capitalist actors off against each other until they were financially and economically exhausted (Van der Pijl 1996: 62–3; 1998: 89ff). The method of change was not direct military conquest or imposition (certainly not in mainland Europe) but 'financial attrition' (Baugh 1989: 56). This forced them to undergo a series of geopolitically mediated crises – the French Revolution, the Napoleonic Wars, the Wars of Liberation, and a sequence of further 'Revolutions from above'. These entailed agrarian reforms, peasant liberations, and state transformations. While France's transformation was most directly affected by Britain, Prussia's revolution from above was initiated by Napoleon's victories, who was ultimately defeated by Britain. Only after the Europe-wide spread of capitalism, the European revolutions of the late eighteenth and nineteenth centuries, and the 'freeing' of markets, did the new logic of free trade impose a non-territorial logic of international surplus appropriation, based on non-political contracts between private citizens.

Substantiating this thesis would of course require a far-reaching synthesis of an enormous amount of historiographical material into a new theoretically controlled account. While this is beyond the scope of this book, the basic contours of this project can be sketched out. Karl Marx and Friedrich Engels famously suggested that the spread of capitalism was to create a world after its own image:

> The need of a constantly expanding market for its products chases the bourgeoisie over the whole surface of the globe. It must nestle everywhere, settle everywhere, establish connections everywhere. The bourgeoisie has through its exploitation of the world market given a cosmopolitan character to production and consumption in every country. . . . In place of the old local and national seclusion and self-sufficiency, we have intercourse in every direction, universal interdependence of nations. . . . The cheap prices of its commodities are the heavy artillery with which it batters down all Chinese walls, with which it forces the barbarians' intensely obstinate hatred of foreigners to capitulate. It compels all nations, on pain of extinction, to adopt the bourgeois mode of production. (Marx and Engels 1998)

This sketch was still heavily influenced by liberal cosmopolitanism and conceived of the expansion of capitalism in *transnational* rather than *international* terms.[15] Any reconstruction of capitalist expansion must not only register its chronological unevenness, but also start from the premise that this course was geopolitically mediated, i.e., refracted through the existence of societies territorially organized in states. This means that capitalism cannot have caused the states-system, but had to 'work itself through' multiple, pre-established sovereignties. As we have seen, while absolutist territoriality was still a function of dynastic geopolitical accumulation, the (imperfect) centralization of early modern sovereignty gave territory a more bounded character. Although it remained fluid – contracting and expanding as the result of war, marriage policies, and inheritances – it had overcome the parcellized sovereignty of the Middle Ages. External and internal were increasingly demarcated by boundaries. Thus the political organization of the modern world into a territorially divided states-system was not a function of capitalism. Rather, capitalism was 'born into' a system of dynastic polities that had consolidated their territories during the absolutist period. Capitalism emerged in a territorially prefigured states-system.[16]

Neo-Weberian historical sociology has stressed this chronological and causal dissociation of capitalism and the states-system: 'Nothing in the capitalist mode of production (or the feudal mode if that is defined economically) leads of itself to the emergence of many capitalist *systems* of production, divided and at war, and of an overall class structure which is *nationally* segmental' (Mann 1988c: 120). Theda Skocpol, in turn, argues that

> The international states system as a transnational structure of military competition was not originally created by capitalism. Throughout modern world history, it represents an analytically autonomous level of transnational reality – *interdependent* in its structure and dynamics with world capitalism, but not reducible to it. (Skocpol 1979: 22)

But the *historical* observation that a states-system preceded capitalism does not warrant the *theoretical* conclusion that it represents a transhistorically independent or autonomous structure (level of analysis) that affirms the call for theoretical pluralism. Quite the contrary: I have demonstrated that a territorially preconfigured pre-capitalist multi-state system was the result of a long history of class conflicts over sources of income that began in the tenth and intensified in the fourteenth and the seventeenth centuries. It was not states that competed against each other for power and security, but ruling classes organized in territorially centralizing communities struggling over their relative international share of territory and other sources of income. The fragmentation of the European ruling class into multiple, separately organized states was neither theoretically necessary nor historically contingent, but it is retrospectively intelligible. Capitalism and a political pluriverse are chronologically and causally not coeval, but pre-capitalist geopolitical accumulation and a pluriverse are. Capitalism and the states-system are the diachronical *disiecta membra*, synchronized in one contradictory totality.

Contra Marx and Engels in *The Communist Manifesto*, the expansion of capitalism was not an *economic* process in which the transnationalizing forces of the market or civil society surreptitiously penetrated pre-capitalist states, driven by the logic of cheap commodities that eventually perfected a universal world market. It was a *political* and, *a fortiori*, *geopolitical* process in which pre-capitalist state classes had to design counterstrategies of reproduction to defend their position in an international environment which put them at an economic *and* coercive disadvantage. More often than not, it was heavy artillery that battered down pre-capitalist walls, and the construction and reconstruction of these walls required new state strategies of modernization. These strategies were not uniform; they ranged from the intensification of domestic relations of exploitation and the build-up of an increasingly repressive state apparatus for military and fiscal mobilization, via 'enlightened' policies of neo-mercantilism and imperialism, to the adoption of liberal economic policies. But in one way or another, on pain of extinction, pre-capitalist states had to accommodate, assimilate, or adjust – or invent radical counterstrategies, most notably socialism. These variations in state responses express the explosive confluence of the different

timing of competitive exposure to Britain and other advanced capitalist
states and pre-existing domestic class constellations that ruled out certain
state strategies while ruling in others. While the initial impetus towards
state modernization and capitalist transformation was geopolitical, state
responses to this pressure were refracted through respective class relations
in national contexts, including class resistance. In this sense, the 'alignment
of the provinces' generated nothing but national *Sonderwege* (special paths).
If Britain showed its neighbours the image of their future, it did so in a
highly distorted way. Conversely, Britain never developed a pristine culture
of capitalism, since she was from the first dragged into an international
environment that inflected her domestic politics and long-term development. The distortions were mutual.

The transposition of capitalism to the Continent and the rest of the
world was riddled with social conflicts, civil and international wars,
revolutions and counter-revolutions, but its essential mechanism was geopolitically combined and socially uneven development.[17] This concept
allows us to avoid repeating the geopolitical competition literature's mistake
of externalizing military rivalry to a separate and reified level of determination, while at the same time avoiding economic reductionism. Post-1688
international relations were not a continuation of the succession of dominant great powers in an otherwise unchanging structure of anarchy, but
expressed the unfolding of this gigantic human drama. It was a long and
bloody transformation – a transitional period – in which the twin processes
of capitalist expansion and regime transformation were generalized –
schematically speaking – from 1688 to the First World War in Europe,
from the First to the Second World War in the rest of the non-socialist
world, and from 1917/45 to 1989 for the socialist world.[18] Thereafter, a
fully integrated world-economy may be said to have come into existence.
The international relations during this long period of transformation may
be termed *modernizing*, rather than modern. This history is yet to be
written.

However, while the expansion of capitalism entailed a series of class and
regime transformations, it did not challenge the principle of multiple
politically constituted territories that was a legacy of pre-capitalist state
formation. It universalized the differentiation between the economic and
the political, but it did not reverse the differentiation between the domestic
and the international. The creation of the transnational 'empire of civil
society' did not entail the destruction of the states-system and the construction of a territorially coextensive and congruous political empire. Capitalism neither caused the territorially divided states-system nor required a

states-system for its reproduction – though, as Justin Rosenberg argues (Rosenberg 1994), it is eminently compatible with it. Capitalism's *differentia specifica* as a system of surplus appropriation consists in the historically unprecedented fact that the capital circuits of the world market can in principle function without infringing on political sovereignty. As a rule, capitalism can leave political territories intact. Contracts are concluded, in principle, between private actors in the pre-political sphere of global civil society. Capitalism, then, is the condition of possibility for the universalization of the principle of national self-determination. Within the wider framework of the long transformation, international relations in the capitalist heartland assumed a pacified form, replacing military with economic competition.

However, while the horizontal separation between the world market and the states-system creates a field of compatibility, the vertical separation of the world into territorially confined centres of political power creates a field of tension. International relations among capitalist states consist in the effort of living with and negotiating this fundamental contradiction at the heart of twentieth-century international order. While political power is organized in competing sovereign states, transnational economic accumulation requires a stable international order that adheres to a minimum of common rules. The functioning of the world market is predicated on the existence of states that maintain the rule of law, guaranteeing contract-based private property and the legal security of transnational transactions so as to maintain the principle of open national economies. Multilateralism and collective security, rather than power politics and the balance of power, correspond to this matrix. The evolution of international organizations – the League of Nations after the First World War for the capitalist heartland, the United Nations and GATT after the Second World War on an expanded international scale, the World Trade Organization after the collapse of the Soviet empire on a global scale – punctuate this process. While international organizations express and reproduce the power of the capitalist heartland, they provide an arena of peaceful inter-capitalist conflict resolution and are instrumental for the accommodation and control of contender states. It follows that the key idea of modern international relations is no longer the war-assisted accumulation of territories, but the multilateral political management of global capital's crisis-potential and the regulation of the world-economy by the leading capitalist states. International economic accumulation and direct political domination are disjoined. A universalized capitalist world market must and can coexist with a territorially fragmented states-system. While the logic of political accumulation qua war that was built into pre-capitalist dynastic states has been eliminated, the major lines of military conflict run between states that are locked out of the world market and those that reproduce the political conditions of the open world market, backed up by the principle of collective security.

But is this international configuration now in the process of being transcended by globalization and global governance, ringing in a post-Westphalian, postmodern geopolitical order that is no longer international but rather global? Are we moving towards a global state? I have argued that the Westphalian system as a historical phenomenon – and not as IR's conceptual shorthand for modern international relations – was rooted in pre-capitalist property relations and dynastic sovereignty. If those IR theorists that identify a shift towards post-Westphalian international relations want to get their chronology right, they will have to argue for a post-post-Westphalian order. However, if we understand the period from 1688 to 1989 as a long transformation characterized by modernizing international relations and the legacy of Westphalia and absolutism as a rudimentary system of territorially bounded states, then we may well understand the current processes of debordering and (asymmetrical) loss of state power not as a move towards a postmodern world, but rather as the erosion of pre-modern territoriality: modern international relations may just have arrived on a global scale.

Notes

1 Van der Pijl conceives of this process as a three-century cycle in which the Anglo-American liberal-capitalist 'Lockean heartland' is repeatedly challenged by a series of 'Hobbesian contender states' (Van der Pijl 1998: 64–97).

2 McNally and Mooers argue that agrarian capitalism in England was the result of an internal differentiation within the peasantry. The rise of richer peasants (yeomen) during the fifteenth and sixteenth centuries undermined village solidarity to allow the gentry to enclose the lands of impoverished peasants (McNally 1988: 1–21; Mooers 1991: 155–61).

3
    If the English aristocracy provided no social base for absolutism, it also, and for the same reasons, lacked the means to withstand any absolutist project by the Crown without forging alliances with other forces and accepting a dangerous degree of popular mobilization – as occurred in the 1640s and again during the exclusion crisis of 1679–81. The particular nature of the English state and social property relations created, to put it

simply, a structural disposition to political alliances which acquired a momentum of their own. (Wood 1996: 218–19)

4 Brewer's assessment contrasts with Mooers', who argues that the post-revolutionary British state was 'an *unrationalized* capitalist state which distinguished it from the 'rationalized' bureaucratic, but non-capitalist states of the Continent' (Mooers 1991: 165). For Anderson, the seventeenth-century revolutions 'transformed the structures but not the superstructures of English society' (Anderson 1992: 29).

5 This is not to argue that the emergence and survival of Britain's new state/society complex was inevitable, since absolutist intervention may have crushed the new regime.

6 Arno Mayer, in contrast, argues that 'neither England nor France had become industrial-capitalist and bourgeois civil and political societies by 1914. . . . All alike were *anciens régimes* grounded in the continued predominance of landed elites, agriculture, or both' (Mayer 1981: 11). Sandra Halperin revisits the Mayer-thesis and argues for the survival of the *ancien régime* in Europe as a whole, dislodged only after the two World Wars. 'In Europe, a landowning elite survived from the days of feudalism through the ages of absolutism and nationalism and into the twentieth century. . . . The nation-state system which succeeded absolutist states and empires in Europe was set up to serve the interests of what at that time was still the dominant group within European society: the land-owning aristocracy' (Halperin 1997: 23–4).

7 While the monarchy remained, of course, an important actor in post-revolutionary diplomacy, the *differentia specifica* of the British system was the constitutionally enshrined parliamentary right to co-determine foreign policy.

8 'The policy of European involvement was regularly castigated as costly; it was also condemned as a "Hanoverian" measure, giving higher priority to the protection of the monarch's "country seat" in Hanover than to England's overall strategic interest' (Brewer 1989: 174).

> The Continental orientation, however, was steadily favoured by the Hanoverians, at least the first two Georges, and they were able to find leading politicians who shared or were willing to support their view. However, these politicians were usually unable to gain sufficient support in Parliament for a strongly Continentalist policy. . . . On balance, the decisions tended against military commitment on the Continent. . . . Hanover was a millstone, its only strategic value its capacity to provide loyal mercenaries. (Baugh 1989: 34, 47)

9 'The British participation in the War of the Spanish Succession, the War of the Austrian Succession, and the Seven Years War, all ended with Britain abandoning her major ally' (Sheehan, 1996: 63). For Britain's fluctuating alliance-patterns see Gulick 1967: 68.

10 Although the balance of power was already discussed in England prior to

1688, it only became a foreign policy maxim after 1688; see Sheehan, 1988: 33.

11 Towards the end of the War of the Austrian Succession, 'the Austrians increasingly felt they were becoming British mercenaries in an Anglo-French war' (McKay and Scott 1983: 172).

12 Mann's general lack of attention to variations in state formation is captured thus: 'Political canniness, windfalls in foreign policy, and financial expediency would steer one state toward absolutism, another toward constitutionalism' (Mann 1986: 478). His basic explanatory variable is land-based versus sea-based states. The former veers towards absolutism, the latter towards constitutionalism, but both state forms are sub-types of a single form of state: the 'organic state'.

13 While Mann insists on trying to avoid a 'military reductionism', the primary level of determination for state formation remains the international. 'Thus the English Civil War does not figure in my narrative as a revolution, nor do the events of 1688. These were not massive social changes but failed royalist coups' (Mann 1986: 469).

14 While this is sometimes acknowledged, its causes are either attributed to Britain's insularity (Gulick 1967: 65–6) or her political skill, when they are explained at all (Claude 1962: 47–8, 59–60). Luard (1992), for example, draws no distinction between early modern Britain and her continental neighbours and has no concept of a balancer.

15 Marx and Engels revised this perspective in their later works, see Soell 1972; Kondylis 1988; Kandal 1989; Teschke 2001: 327–31.

16 This idea is elaborated in its implications for globalization by Lacher (forthcoming).

17 The concept of combined and uneven development is explored in Rosenberg 1996.

18 To be sure, many of the state socialist countries were highly integrated into international capitalism well before 1989, while one would have to date the integration of many 'Third World' countries well after 1945. I owe this clarification to James Ingram.

Conclusion:

The Dialectic of International Relations

The historical turn in IR has helped us break out of the state-centric straitjacket of orthodox IR. It has shifted the focus of attention to geopolitical relations in a stateless society and provided explanations of the formation of the modern states-system, explanations of the constitution of modern anarchy. But in this process historicizing Neorealists have merely transposed the rational-choice model that, according to Neorealism, underlies the operation of the international system to the very process of its constitution – the logic of neo-evolutionary selection as a *theory of development* fuses with the logic of rational choice as a *theory of operation*. Not only does this approach misdate the timing of the origins of the modern states-system – reproducing the myth of 1648 – it fails to explain the variable conduct of political actors across different geopolitical orders, as it obscures the uneven nature of state formations and geopolitical transformations that are rooted in class relations.

Constructivist IR theory has provided a series of innovative approaches, social and historical, that challenge the positivist certainties of mainstream IR. But whether the stress is on different modes of territoriality, modes of legitimacy, or the intersubjective construction of norms that fix the 'rules of the game', based on the Weberian idea of value-communities, it has largely depoliticized and desocialized the construction and reconstruction of international relations. Empirically, its obsession with early modern France as the proto-type of modern state formation and its neglect of England has led it into a historical cul-de-sac, whose familiar terminus is 1648.

Historical sociology has further enriched the field. But it remains hampered by a neo-Weberian pluralism that can only conceive of historical development in terms of the external interaction of independently constituted spheres of reality. The failure of neo-Weberianism resides not so much in privileging geopolitical competition as the overriding level of determination, but in its inability to decode the geopolitical as a social relation and to overcome its orthodox pluralism. Ever since Theda Skocpol's important comparative analysis of social revolutions, it has become a standard criticism of Marxism that it fails to incorporate the 'relative autonomy of the state' and its position in the states-system as independent factors into comprehensive explanations of the origins, course, and outcomes of social revolutions and the general nature of long-term historical development. This study has avoided the dual fallacy of conceiving of historical development either in terms of a single world-historical pattern, or by narrowing our focus to a single-society perspective that abstracts from international contexts. But rather than subscribing to a Weberian model of plural causations, it has demonstrated how international relations are internally related to politically instituted class relations (social property regimes) and how geopolitical pressure affects the course of socio-political development. But these geopolitical pressures – be they war or diplomacy – have not been reified and externalized to the 'international', but internalized and deciphered as social praxes linked to prevailing social property regimes. Conversely, this study has not only shown how international relations restrained, accelerated, or deflected the development of revolutionary state/society complexes, but how social revolutions influenced and transformed the nature of international relations. This included an explanation of the very constitution and development of the European multi-actor system as an outcome of class conflict. However, these propositions are incompatible with a Weberian perspective that insists on the interaction of independent spheres of reality, but derive from a dialectical understanding of Marxism, revolving around the core concepts of praxis, contradiction, and totality. While the Marxist tradition may have under-theorized the relevance of international relations for world-historical development, Karl Marx's conceptual apparatus, pace Skocpol, Mann et al., provides a surer guide to its explanation.

In contrast, I have demonstrated that the economic and the political, the domestic and the international, are never constituted independently of each other. I have argued that the core of their interrelations resides in social property relations. These relations – be they feudal, absolutist, or capitalist – are not simply an economic phenomenon, but are internally related to political and military power and to differentiated sets of subjectivity. In turn, the political and the military are intrinsically linked to their reproduction and expansion, both in their domestic and international aspects. Politically constituted social property relations form a contradictory and manifold dynamic totality.

The constitution, operation, and transformation of international relations are fundamentally governed by social property relations. The theory of social property relations demonstrates how geopolitical orders express authority structures that are rooted in relations between producers and non-producers. Variations in geopolitical conduct and systemic transformations can be understood on this basis. International relations cannot be adequately theorized by deriving foreign policy from pre-constituted political communities, generically reduced to conflict units in an anarchical environment. Structuring principles – anarchy or hierarchy – tell us very little about how political actors behave. Anarchy is indeterminate. Aggressive geopolitical conduct can be compatible with anarchy and hierarchy, as we saw for the Middle Ages; co-operative conduct can be compatible with anarchy. But international relations have to be historicized and socialized to see these differences.

The theory of social property relations not only explains geopolitical conduct, it can theorize the constitution and transformation of geopolitical orders – shifts in system structure, in contemporary IR terms. But it shows that these systemic transformations are always bound up with profound social conflicts that reorganize both the relations of domination and exploitation *and* the relations between the internal and the external – the domestic and the international. The relation between structure and agency is not a repetitive and recursive cycle in which structure determines agency and agency re-enacts structure. Nor can this relation be comprehended by a simple polarizing opposition between rationalism, seeking causal explanation, and reflectivism, seeking interpretive understanding. It is a contradictory and dynamic process that also interprets itself, leading to qualitative transformations. It is clear too that these transformations do not follow a schematic succession, but are highly uneven, socially, geographically, and chronologically. They do not follow a transcendent telos, but they are retrospectively understandable. History is not only dynamic, it is also cumulative. Traces of the past have to be accommodated in a reorganized present. The old and the new fuse in unforeseen ways. Structure and agency, necessity and freedom, combine in different ways, both domestically and internationally. This is a world of our making, but this making is neither the aggregate of voluntary and intentional actions, nor the outcome of desubjectified mechanisms of structural emergence. This is not a process of structuration, but of dialectical development.

International Relations is a *social* science. As a social science, it does not stand outside the daily reproduction of structures of domination and exploitation. But the dominant IR paradigm, Neorealism and its rationalist sibling Neoliberalism, remains wedded to a positivist conception of science to explain international politics. The subsumption of international behaviour under one general covering law claiming objectivity is as theoretically impoverished as it is intellectually debilitating. Politically, it is dangerous and all too often complicit with the aggressive policies of the hegemonic state. In some versions, it is scandalous. Neorealism is a science of domination. It is a technology of state power prevaded by instrumental rationality. Its grotesque craggy melody parades as the siren song for all undergraduates. In terms of explanatory power, it obscures more than it reveals and compresses the rich history of human development into a repetitive calculus of power. The elevation of anarchy and the balance of power to transhistorical principles that determine geopolitical behaviour in a mechanistic way rests on a series of unfounded assumptions and generates behavioural propositions that are easily falsified. The projection of a rational choice model on political actors in a 'system of survival' reduces political will to a response to 'iron laws' and hides massive historical transformations in the constitution of the social and the political world. Epistemologically, Neorealism's survival is predicated on its move to cut off the political from the social and the structural from the processual in order to maintain an autonomous and universal science of IR. Its technique of testing amounts to perpetual self-validation, whereby history is mined for confirming cases, while contradictory evidence is castigated as non-system-conforming behaviour – irrational anomalies.

The reasons for Neorealism's continuing dominance are manifold. Academic socialization into an Americanized discipline that never quite cut its umbilical cord with the German tradition of *Geopolitik* reinforces a vocabulary and a collective disciplinary mind-set that narrows the options for free thought. The lure of consultancies and the prospects of involvement in the political establishment – advice for the prince – short-circuit critical thought. The intensifying commodification of thinking corrupts emancipatory impulses. Contemporary education and science policy encourage 'practical' social science research while penalizing reflection on the direction and purpose of social science as a democratic exercise. The establishment of universities as autonomous, self-governing bodies was a great victory of the Enlightenment. They had the purpose of creating a secular social space, a public sphere governed by reason, debate, and critique, against the dogmatism of the Church, the power of the state, and the profitability of the market. This space is in danger of being subsumed under the logic of capital. Not only is research today evaluated by bureaucrats in largely quantitative terms; it has to conform to the categorical imperative of producing value, of being valorizable. This book has been written largely against these tendencies. It is a critical intervention against an ongoing worldwide process of exploitation and domination. The pulse of dialectic is quickening.

Bibliography

Abel, Wilhelm, *Agrarkrisen und Agrarkonjunktur*, 3rd edn, Hamburg [1935] 1978.

Abu-Lughod, Janet L., *Before European Hegemony: The World System A.D. 1250–1350*, New York 1989.

Adler, Emanuel, 'Seizing the Middle Ground: Constructivism in World Politics', *European Journal of International Relations*, vol. 3, no. 3, 1997, pp. 319–63.

Adorno, Theodor W., *Einleitung in die Soziologie*, Frankfurt/M [1968] 1993.

Agnew, John and Stuart Corbridge, *Mastering Space: Hegemony, Territory and International Political Economy*, London 1995.

Anderson, Matthew S., *War and Society in Europe of the Old Regime, 1618–1789*, Leicester 1988.

——, *The Rise of Modern Diplomacy, 1450–1919*, London 1993.

Anderson, Perry, *Passages from Antiquity to Feudalism*, London 1974a.

——, *Lineages of the Absolutist State*, London 1974b.

——, 'Origins of the Present Crisis', in P. Anderson, *English Questions*, London [1967] 1992, pp. 15–47.

——, 'Maurice Thomson's War', *London Review of Books*, no. 4, November 1993, pp. 13–17.

Arentin, Karl Otmar von, 'Tausch, Teilung und Länderschacher als Folgen des Gleichgewichtssystems der europäischen Großmächte: Die polnischen Teilungen als europäisches Schicksal', *Jahrbuch für die Geschichte Mittel- und Ostdeutschlands*, vol. 30, 1981, pp. 53–68.

Armstrong, David, *Revolution and World Order. The Revolutionary State in International Society*, Oxford 1993.

Arnold, Benjamin, *German Knighthood, 1050–1300*, Oxford 1985.

——, *Princes and Territory in Medieval Germany*, Cambridge 1991.

Arrighi, Giovanni, *The Long Twentieth Century. Money, Power, and the Origins of Our Times*, London 1994.

Asch, Ronald G., 'Estates and Princes after 1648: The Consequences of the Thirty Years War', *German History*, vol. 6, no. 2, 1988, pp. 113–32.

——, and Heinz Duchhardt, eds, *Der Absolutismus – ein Mythos? Strukturwandel monarchischer Herrschaft in West- und Mitteleuropa (ca. 1550–1700)*, Cologne 1996.

Ashley, Richard, 'The Poverty of Neorealism', *International Organization*, vol. 38, no. 2, 1984, pp. 225–86.

Aston, Trevor, ed., *Crisis in Europe, 1550–1660: Essays from Past and Present*, London 1965.

——, and C.H.E. Philpin, eds, *The Brenner Debate: Agrarian Class Structure and Economic Development in Pre-Industrial Europe*, Cambridge 1985.

Axtmann, Roland, 'The Formation of the Modern State: A Reconstruction of Max Weber's Arguments', *History of Political Thought*, vol. 11, no. 2, 1990, pp. 295–311.

——, 'The Formation of the Modern State: The Debate in the Social Sciences', in Mary Fulbrook, ed., *National Histories and European History*, London 1993, pp. 21–45.

Ayton, Andrew and J.L. Price, 'Introduction: The Military Revolution from a Medieval Perspective', in Ayton and Price, eds, *The Medieval Military Revolution: State, Society, and Military Change in Medieval and Early Modern Europe*, London 1995, pp. 1–22.

Baechler, Jean, *Le Capitalisme: Tome 1. Les Origines*, Paris 1995.

Bartlett, Robert, *The Making of Europe: Conquest, Colonization and Cultural Change, 950–1350*, London 1993.

Baugh, Daniel A., 'Great Britain's Blue-Water Policy, 1689–1815', *International History Review*, vol. 10, no. 1, 1989, pp. 33–58.

——, 'Withdrawing from Europe: Anglo-French Maritime Geopolitics, 1750–1800', *International History Review*, vol. 20, no. 1, 1998, pp. 13–32.

Beik, William, *Absolutism and Society in Seventeenth-Century France: State Power and Provincial Aristocracy in Languedoc*, Cambridge 1985.

Bergin, Joseph, *Cardinal Richelieu: Power and the Pursuit of Wealth*, London 1985.

Berman, Harold, *Law and Revolution: The Formation of the Western Legal Tradition*, Cambridge, MA, 1983.

Bernstein, Richard J., *Praxis and Action*, London 1972.

Bien, David D., 'The *Secrétaires du Roi*: Absolutism, Corps, and Privilege under the *Ancien Régime*', in Ernst Hinrichs, Eberhard Schmitt, and Rudolf Vierhaus, eds, *Vom Ancien Régime zur Französischen Revolution: Forschungen und Perspektiven*, Göttingen 1978, pp. 153–68.

Bisson, Thomas N., *The Medieval Crown of Aragon: A Short History*, Oxford 1986.

——, 'Nobility and Family in Medieval France: A Review Essay', *French Historical Studies*, vol. 16, no. 3, 1990, pp. 597–613.

——, 'The "Feudal Revolution"', *Past and Present*, no. 142, 1994, pp. 6–42.

Black, Jeremy, *A System of Ambition? British Foreign Policy 1660–1793*, London 1991.

Bloch, Marc, *Feudal Society*, transl. L.A. Manyon, London [1940] 1961.

——, *French Rural History: An Essay on its Basic Characteristics*, transl. Janet Sondheimer, Berkeley [1931] 1966a.

——, 'The Rise of Dependent Cultivation and Seignorial Institutions', in M.M.

Postan, ed., *The Cambridge Economic History of Europe: The Agrarian Life of the Middle Ages*, vol.1, 2nd edn, Cambridge [1941] 1966b, pp. 235–90.

——, *The Royal Touch: Sacred Monarchy and Scrofula in England and France*, transl. J.E. Anderson, London [1924] 1973.

Blockmans, Wim P., 'Voracious States and Obstructing Cities: An Aspect of State Formation in Preindustrial Europe', in: Ch. Tilly and W.P. Blockmans (eds.), *Cities and the Rise of the States in Europe, A.D. 1000 to 1800*, Boulder, Co., 1994, pp. 218–50.

Böckenförde, Ernst-Wolfgang, 'Der Westfälische Frieden und das Bündnisrecht der Reichsstände', *Der Staat*, vol. 8, no. 4, 1969, pp. 449–78.

Bois, Guy, *The Crisis of Feudalism: Economy and Society in Normandy, c.1300–1550*, reprint, Cambridge [1976] 1984.

——, *The Transformation of the Year One Thousand: The Village of Lournand from Antiquity to Feudalism*, transl. Jean Birrell, Manchester [1989] 1992.

Bonnassie, Pierre, 'The Survival and Extinction of the Slave System in the Early Medieval West (Fourth to Eleventh Centuries)', in Bonnassie, *From Slavery to Feudalism in South-Western Europe*, transl. Jean Birrell, Cambridge/Paris [1985] 1991a, pp. 1–59.

——, 'From the Rhône to Galicia: Origins and Modalities of the Feudal Order', in Bonnassie, *From Slavery to Feudalism in South-Western Europe*, transl. Jean Birrell, Cambridge/Paris [1980] 1991b, pp. 104–31.

——, 'The Formation of Catalan Feudalism and its Early Expansion (to c. 1150)', in Bonnassie, *From Slavery to Feudalism in South-Western Europe*, transl. Jean Birrell, Cambridge/Paris [1985] 1991c, pp. 149–69.

Bonney, Richard, *The King's Debts: Finance and Politics in France 1589–1661*, Oxford 1981.

——, *The European Dynastic States, 1494–1660*, Oxford 1991.

——, 'Introduction: Economic Systems and State Finance', in Bonney, ed., *Economic Systems and State Finance*, Oxford 1995a, pp. 1–18.

——, 'Revenues', in Bonney, ed., *Economic Systems and State Finance*, Oxford 1995b, pp. 423–505.

——, ed., *The Rise of the Fiscal State in Europe, c.1200–1815*, Oxford 1999.

Bosbach, Franz, *Monarchia Universalis: Ein politischer Begriff der frühen Neuzeit*, Göttingen 1986.

Boyle, Chris, 'Imagining the World Market: IPE and the Task of Social Theory', *Millennium*, vol. 23, no. 2, 1994, pp. 351–63.

Braudel, Fernand, *The Mediterranean and the Mediterranean World in the Age of Phillip II*, 2 vols., transl. from the 2nd rev. edn 1966 by Siân Reynolds, London [1949] 1972a.

——, 'History and the Social Sciences', in Peter Burke, ed., *Economy and Society in Early Modern Europe: Essays from Annales*, London 1972b, pp. 11–42.

——, *Afterthoughts on Material Civilization and Capitalism*, transl. Patricia Ranum, Baltimore 1977.

——, *The Perspective of the World*, vol. 3, transl. Siân Reynolds, Berkeley [1979] 1984.

Braun, Rudolf, 'Taxation, Sociopolitical Structure, and State-Building: Great Britain and Brandenburg-Prussia', in Charles Tilly, ed., *The Formation of National States in Western Europe*, Princeton, NJ, 1975, pp. 243–327.

Brenner, Robert, 'The Origins of Capitalist Development: A Critique of Neo-Smithian Marxism', *New Left Review*, no. 104, 1977, pp. 25–92.

——, 'Agrarian Class Structure and Economic Development in Pre-Industrial Europe', in T.H. Aston and C.H.E. Philpin, eds, *The Brenner Debate: Agrarian Class Structure and Economic Development in Pre-Industrial Europe*, Cambridge 1985a, pp. 10–63.

——, 'The Agrarian Roots of European Capitalism', in T.H. Aston and C.H.E. Philpin, eds, *The Brenner Debate: Agrarian Class Structure and Economic Development in Pre-Industrial Europe*, Cambridge 1985b, pp. 213–327.

——, 'The Social Basis of Economic Development', in John Roemer, ed., *Analytical Marxism*, Cambridge 1986, pp. 23–53.

——, 'Feudalism', in J. Eatwell, M. Milgate, and P. Newman, eds, *The New Palgrave: A Dictionary of Economics: Marxian Economics*, London 1987, pp. 170–85.

——, 'Bourgeois Revolution and Transition to Capitalism', in A.L. Beier, David Cannadine, and James M. Rosenheim, eds, *The First Modern Society: Essays in English History in Honour of Lawrence Stone*, Cambridge 1989, pp. 271–304.

——, *Merchants and Revolution: Commercial Change, Political Conflict, and London's Overseas Traders, 1550–1653*, Cambridge 1993.

——, 'The Rises and Declines of Serfdom in Medieval and Early Modern Europe', in Michael L. Bush, ed., *Serfdom and Slavery: Studies in Legal Bondage*, London 1996, pp. 247–76.

——, 'The Low Countries in the Transition to Capitalism', in Peter Hoppenbrouwers and Jan Luiten van Zanden, eds, *Peasants into Farmers? The Transformation of Rural Economy and Society in the Low Countries (Middle Ages–19th Century) in Light of the Brenner Debate*, Turnhout 2001, pp. 275–338.

Breuer, Stefan, *Max Weber's Herrschaftssoziologie*, Frankfurt/M 1991.

Brewer, John, *The Sinews of Power: War, Money and the English State, 1688–1783*, New York 1989.

Bromley, Simon, *American Hegemony and World Oil: The Industry, the State System, and the World Economy*, University Park 1991.

——, 'Rethinking International Political Economy', in John Macmillan and Andrew Linklater, eds, *Boundaries in Question: New Directions in International Relations*, London 1995, pp. 228–43.

——, 'Marxism and Globalisation', in Andrew Gamble, David Marsh, and Tony Tant, eds, *Marxism and Social Science*, London 1999, pp. 280–301.

Brunner, Otto, *Land and Lordship: Structures of Governance in Medieval Austria*, transl. from the 4th rev. edn by H. Kaminsky and J. Van Horn Melton, Philadelphia [1939] 1992.

Buck, Philip W., *The Politics of Mercantilism*, New York [1942] 1974.

Bull, Hedley, *The Anarchical Society: A Study of Order in World Politics*, London 1977.

Bulst, Neithard, 'Rulers, Representative Institutions and their Members as Power Elites: Rival or Partners?', in W. Reinhard, ed., *Power Elites and State Building*, Oxford 1996, pp. 41–58.

Burawoy, Michael, 'Two Methods in Search of Science: Skocpol versus Trotsky', *Theory and Society*, vol. 18, no. 6, 1989, pp. 759–805.

Burch, Kurt, *'Property' and the Making of the International System*, Boulder, CO, 1998.

Burkhardt, Johannes, *Der Dreißigjährige Krieg*, Frankfurt/M. 1992.

——, 'Die Friedlosigkeit der frühen Neuzeit. Grundlegung einer Theorie der Bellizität Europas', *Zeitschrift für Historische Forschung*, vol. 24, no. 4, 1997, pp. 509–74.

Butterfield, Herbert, 'The Balance of Power', in H. Butterfield and Martin Wight, eds, *Diplomatic Investigations: Essays in the Theory of International Politics*, London 1966, pp. 132–48.

Buzan, Barry and Richard Little, eds, *International Systems in World History: Remaking the Study of International Relations*, Oxford 2000.

Chaudhuri, K.N., 'Reflections on the Organizing Principle of Premodern Trade', in James D. Tracy, ed., *The Political Economy of Merchant Empires: State Power and World Trade 1350–1750*, Cambridge 1991, pp. 421–42.

Christiansen, Eric, *The Northern Crusades: The Baltic and the Catholic Frontier, 1100–1525*, London 1980.

Claude, Inis, *Power and International Relations*, New York 1962.

Colás, Alejandro, *International Civil Society: Social Movements in World Politics*, Cambridge 2002.

Collins, Randall, *Weberian Sociological Theory*, Cambridge 1986.

Comninel, George C., *Rethinking the French Revolution: Marxism and the Revisionist Challenge*, London 1987.

Cox, Robert W., 'Social Forces, States, and World Order: Beyond International Relations Theory', *Millennium*, vol. 10, no. 2, 1981, pp. 126–55.

Crouzet, François, *Britain Ascendant: Comparative Studies in Franco-British Economic History*, transl. Martin Thom, Cambridge [1985] 1990.

Czempiel, Ernst-Otto, 'Strukturen absolutistischer Außenpolitik', *Zeitschrift für Historische Forschung*, vol. 7, nos 1/4, 1980, pp. 445–51.

Davies, Rees, 'Frontier Arrangements in Fragmented Societies: Ireland and Wales', in R. Bartlett and A. MacKay, eds, *Medieval Frontier Societies*, Oxford 1989, pp. 77–100.

——, *Domination and Conquest: The Experience of Ireland, Scotland, and Wales, 1100–1300*, Cambridge 1990.

Delbrück, Hans, *History of the Art of War within the Framework of Political History. Vol.III: The Middle Ages*, transl. Walter Renfroe, Jr, Westport, CT [1923] 1982.

De Vries, Jan, *The Economy of Europe in an Age of Crisis, 1600–1750*, Cambridge 1976.

Dickmann, Fritz, *Der Westfälische Frieden*, 3rd edn, Münster [1959] 1972.

Dobb, Maurice, 'Capital Accumulation and Mercantilism', in M. Dobb, *Studies in the Development of Capitalism*, London 1946, pp. 177–220.

Downing, Brian, *The Military Revolution and Political Change: Origins of Democracy and Autocracy in Early Modern Europe*, Princeton, NJ, 1992.

Duby, Georges, *La Société aux XIe et XIIe siècles dans la région maconnaise*, Paris 1953.

——, *Rural Economy and Country Life in the Medieval West*, transl. Cynthia Postan, Columbia, SC [1962] 1968.

——, *The Early Growth of the European Economy: Warriors and Peasants from the Seventh to the Twelfth Century*, transl. Howard B. Clarke, London [1973] 1974.

——, 'Youth in Aristocratic Society', in Duby, *The Chivalrous Society*, transl. Cynthia Postan, Berkeley [1964] 1977a, pp. 112–22.

——, 'The Structure of Kinship and Nobility', in Duby, *The Chivalrous Society*, transl. Cynthia Postan, Berkeley [1967] 1977b, pp. 134–48.

——, 'The Origins of Knighthood', in Duby, *The Chivalrous Society*, transl. Cynthia Postan, Berkeley [1968] 1977c, pp. 158–70.

——, *The Three Orders: Feudal Society Imagined*, transl. Arthur Goldhammer, Chicago [1978] 1980.

——, 'The Relationship between Aristocratic Family and State Structures in Eleventh-Century France', in Duby, *Love and Marriage in the Middle Ages*, transl. Jane Dunnett, Cambridge [1988] 1994, pp. 113–19.

Duchhardt, Heinz, *Gleichgewicht der Kräfte, Convenance, europäisches Konzert: Friedenskonresse und Friedensschlüsse vom Zeitalter Ludwigs XIV. bis zum Wiener Kongreß*, Darmstadt 1976.

——, 'Die Glorious Revolution und das internationale System', *Francia*, vol. 16, no. 2, 1989a, pp. 29–37.

——, 'Westfälischer Friede und internationales System im Ancien Régime', *Historische Zeitschrift*, vol. 249, no. 3, 1989b, pp. 529–44.

——, ed., *Rahmenbedingungen und Handlungsspielräume europäischer Außenpolitik im Zeitalter Ludwigs XIV*, Berlin 1991.

——, 'Droit et droit des gens – structures et métarmophoses des relations internationales au temps de Louis XIV', in Reiner Babel, ed., *Frankreich im europäischen Staatensystem der frühen Neuzeit*, Sigmaringen 1995, pp. 179–89.

——, *Balance of Power und Pentarchie: Internationale Beziehungen 1700–1785*, vol. 4 of H. Duchhardt and Franz Knipping, eds, *Handbuch der Geschichte der internationalen Beziehungen*, Paderborn 1997.

Elias, Norbert, *The Count Society*, transl. Edmund Jephcott, Oxford 1983.

——, *The Civilizing Process: The History of Manners and State Formation and Civilization*, transl. Edmund Jephcott, reprint, Cambridge, MA, [1939] 1994.

Elliott, J.H., 'A Europe of Composite Monarchies', *Past and Present*, no. 137, 1992, pp. 48–71.

Engels, Friedrich, *The Origin of the Family, Private Property and the State*, in K. Marx and F. Engels, *Collected Works*, vol. 26, London [1874] 1976.

Ertman, Thomas, *Birth of the Leviathan: Building States and Regimes in Medieval and Early Modern Europe*, Cambridge 1997.

Evergates, Theodore, 'Nobles and Knights in Twelfth-Century France', in Thomas N. Bisson, ed., *Cultures of Power: Lordship, Status, and Process in Twelfth-Century Europe*, Philadelphia 1995, pp. 11–35.

Fenske, Hans, 'Gleichgewicht, Balance', in Otto Brunner, Werner Conze, and Reinhart Koselleck, eds, *Geschichtliche Grundbegriffe: Historisches Lexikon zur politisch-sozialen Sprache in Deutschland*, vol. 2, Stuttgart 1975, pp. 959–96.

Finer, Samuel E., 'State- and Nation-Building in Europe: The Role of the Military', in Charles Tilly, ed., *The Formation of National States in Western Europe*, Princeton, NJ, 1975, pp. 84–163.

Fischer, Markus, 'Feudal Europe, 800–1300: Communal Discourse and Conflictual Practices', *International Organization*, vol. 46, no. 2, 1992, pp. 427–66.

Fletcher, R.A., 'Reconquest and Crusade in Spain, c. 1050–1150', *Transactions of the Royal Historical Society*, 5th series, no. 37, 1987, pp. 31–47.

Flori, Jean, *L'Essor de la Chevalerie: XIe–XIIe siècles*, Geneva 1986.

——, '*L'Eglise et la guerre sainte: De la "Paix de Dieu" à la croisade'*, *Annales E.S.C.*, no. 2, 1992a, pp. 453–66.

——, *La Première Croisade: L'Occident chrétien contre l'Islam*, Paris 1992b.

Fourquin, Guy, 'Le Temps de la croissance', in G. Duby and A. Wallon, eds, *Histoire de la France Rurale. Tome 1: La Formation des campagnes françaises des origines au XIV siècle*, Paris 1975.

Frame, Robin, *The Political Development of the British Isles, 1100–1400*, Oxford 1990.

Frank, Andre Gunder and Barry K. Gills, eds, *The World System: Five Hundred Years or Five Thousand?*, London 1993.

Ganshof, François, *Feudalism*, 3rd rev. edn, transl. Ph. Grierson, London [1952] 1964.

——, *The Middle Ages: A History of International Relations*, 4th rev. edn, transl. Remy Inglis Hall, New York [1953] 1970.

——, 'The Institutional Framework of the Frankish Monarchy: A Survey of its General Characteristics', in Ganshof, *The Carolingians and the Frankish Monarchy: Studies in Carolingian History*, transl. Janet Sondheimer, London 1971a, pp. 86–110.

——, 'The Frankish Monarchy and its External Relations, from Pippin III to Louis the Pious', in Ganshof, *The Carolingians and the Frankish Monarchy: Studies in Carolingian History*, transl. Janet Sondheimer, London 1971b, pp. 162–204.

Geary, Patrick, 'Vivre en conflit dans une France sans état: Typologie des mécanismes de règlement des conflits (1050–1200), *Annales E.S.C.*, no. 41, 1986, pp. 1107–33.

Gerstenberger, Heide, 'Vom Lauf der Zeit: Eine Kritik an Fernand Braudel', *PROKLA*, vol. 67, no. 2, 1987, pp. 119–34.

——, *Die subjektlose Gewalt: Theorie der Entstehung bürgerlicher Staatsgewalt*, Münster 1990.

Giddens, Anthony, *The Constitution of Society: Outline of the Theory of Structuration*, Cambridge 1984.

——, *The Nation-State and Violence: Volume Two of a Contemporary Critique of Historical Materialism*, Cambridge 1985.

Gilpin, Robert, *War and Change in World Politics*, Cambridge 1981.

——, 'The Richness of the Tradition of Political Realism', in R.O. Keohane, ed., *Neorealism and its Critics*, New York 1986, pp. 301–21.

——, *The Political Economy of International Relations*, Princeton, NJ, 1987.

Gintis, Herbert and Samuel Bowles, 'State and Class in European Feudalism', in Charles Bright and Susan Harding, eds, *Statemaking and Social Movements: Essays in History and Theory*, Ann Arbor 1984, pp. 19–51.

Given, James, *State and Society in Medieval Europe: Gwynedd and Languedoc Under Outside Rule*, Ithaca, NY, 1990.

Godelier, Maurice, *Rationality and Irrationality in Economics*, transl. Brian Peirce, New York 1972.

Goetz, Hans-Werner, 'Social and Military Institutions', in R. McKitterick, ed., *The New Cambridge Medieval History, Vol. II, c.700–900*, Cambridge 1995, pp. 451–80.

Goubert, Pierre, *The French Peasantry in the Seventeenth Century*, transl. Ian Patterson, Cambridge [1982] 1986.

Gourevitch, Peter, 'The Second Image Reversed: The International Sources of Domestic Politics, *International Organization*, vol. 32, no. 4, 1978a, pp. 881–911.

——, 'The International System and Regime Formation: A Critical Review of Anderson and Wallerstein', *Comparative Politics*, vol. 10, no. 3, 1978b, pp. 419–38.

Grewe, Wilhelm G., *Epochen der Völkerrechtsgeschichte*, Baden-Baden 1984.

Groh, Dieter, *Kritische Geschichtswissenschaft in emanzipatorischer Absicht: Überlegungen zur Geschichtswissenschaft als Sozialwissenschaft*, Stuttgart 1973.

Gross, Leo, 'The Peace of Westphalia: 1648–1948', *American Journal of International Law*, no. 42, 1948, pp. 20–41.

Gulick, Edward Vose, *Europe's Classical Balance of Power*, New York [1955] 1967.

Habermas, Jürgen, *The Structural Transformation of the Public Sphere: An Inquiry into a Category of Bourgeois Society*, transl. Thomas Burger, London [1965] 1989.

——, *Knowledge and Human Interests*, transl. Jeremy J. Shapiro, Cambridge [1968] 1987.

Haldon, John, *The State and the Tributary Mode of Production*, London 1993.

Hall, Rodney Bruce, *National Collective Identity: Social Constructs and International Systems*, New York 1999.

——, and Friedrich V. Kratochwil, 'Medieval Tales: Neorealist "Science" and the Abuse of History', *International Organization*, vol. 47, no. 3, 1993, pp. 479–91.

Hallam, Elizabeth M., *Capetian France, 987–1328*, London 1980.

Halliday, Fred, *Rethinking International Relations*, London 1994.

——, and Justin Rosenberg, 'Interview with Ken Waltz', *Review of International Studies*, vol. 24, 1998, pp. 371–86.

Halperin, Sandra, *In the Mirror of the Third World: Capitalist Development in Modern Europe*, Ithaca, NY 1997.

Harvey, David, 'The Geopolitics of Capitalism', in Harvey, *Spaces of Capital: Towards a Critical Geography*, New York [1985] 2001, pp. 312–44.

Hatton, Ragnhild M., 'Louis XIV and his Fellow Monarchs', in John C. Rule, ed., *Louis XIV and the Craft of Kingship*, Columbia 1969, pp. 155–95.

Heine, Christian and Benno Teschke, 'Sleeping Beauty and the Dialectical Awakening: On the Potential of Dialectic for International Relations, *Millennium*, vol. 25, no. 2, 1996, pp. 399–423.

——, 'On Dialectic and International Relations: A Reply to Our Critics', *Millennium*, vol. 26, no. 2, 1997, pp. 455–70.

Henshall, Nicholas, *The Myth of Absolutism: Change and Continuity in Early Modern European Monarchy*, London 1992.

——, 'Early Modern Absolutism 1550–1700: Political Reality or Propaganda?', in Ronald G. Asch and Heinz Duchhardt, eds, *Der Absolutismus – ein Mythos? Strukturwandel monarchischer Herrschaft in West- und Mitteleuropa (ca. 1550–1700)*, Cologne 1996, pp. 25–53.

Hexter, Jack , 'Fernand Braudel and the *Monde Braudelien*', *The Journal of Modern History*, vol. 4, 1972, pp. 480–539.

Hilton, Rodney, *Bond Men Made Free: Medieval Peasant Movements and the English Rising of 1381*, London 1973.

——, 'Freedom and Villeinage in England', in Hilton, ed., *Peasants, Knights and Heretics: Studies in Medieval English Social History*, Cambridge [1965] 1976a, pp. 174–91.

——, 'Introduction', in Paul Sweezy, Maurice Dobb et al., *The Transition from Feudalism to Capitalism*, London 1976b, pp. 9–30.

——, 'Feudalism or *Féodalité* and *Seigneurie* in France and England', in Hilton, *Class Conflict and the Crisis of Feudalism: Essays in Medieval Social History*, 2nd rev. edn, London 1990.

Hinrichs, Ernst, 'Merkantilismus in Europa: Konzepte, Ziele, Praxis', in E. Hinrichs ed., *Absolutismus*, Frankfurt/M. [1983] 1986, pp. 344–60.

——, 'Absolute Monarchie und Bürokratie. Bemerkungen über ihre "Unvereinbarkeit" im französischen *Ancien Régime*', in E. Hinrichs, ed., *Ancien Régime und Revolution: Studien zur Verfassungsgeschichte Frankreichs zwischen 1589 und 1789*, Frankfurt/M. 1989, pp. 81–98.

Hinsley, Francis H., *Power and the Pursuit of Peace: Theory and Practice in the History of Relations between States*, Cambridge 1963.

Hintze, Otto, 'The Nature of Feudalism', in F.L. Cheyette, ed., *Lordship and Community in Medieval Europe: Selected Readings*, New York [1929] 1968, pp. 22–31.

——, 'The Formation of States and Constitutional Development: A Study in

History and Politics', in Felix Gilbert, ed., *The Historical Essays of Otto Hintze*, New York 1975a [1902], pp. 159–77.

——, 'Military Organization and the Organization of the State', in Felix Gilbert, ed., *The Historical Essays of Otto Hintze*, New York [1906] 1975b, pp. 180–215.

——, 'The Preconditions of Representative Government in the Context of World History', in Felix Gilbert, ed., *The Historical Essays of Otto Hintze*, New York 1975c, 305–53.

Hobden, Stephen, *International Relations and Historical Sociology*, London 1998.

Hobson, John M., *The State and International Relations*, Cambridge 2000, pp. 174–214.

——, 'What's at stake in 'bringing historical sociology back into international relations'?', in Stephen Hobden and John Hobson (eds.), *Historical Sociology of International Relations*, Cambridge 2002a, pp. 3–41.

——, 'The Two Waves of Weberian Historical Sociology in International Relations', in St. Hobden and J. Hobson (eds.), *Historical Sociology of International Relations*, Cambridge 2002b, pp. 63–83.

Hoffman, Philip T., 'Early Modern France, 1450–1700', in Philip T. Hoffman and Kathryn Norberg, eds, *Fiscal Crises, Liberty, and Representative Government, 1450–1789*, Stanford, CA, 1994, pp. 226–52.

Holsti, Kalevi J., *Peace and War: Armed Conflicts and International Order, 1648–1989*, Cambridge 1991.

Holzgrefe, J.L., 'The Origins of Modern International Relations Theory', *Review of International Studies*, vol. 15, no. 1, 1989, pp. 11–26.

Hoppenbrouwers, Peter and Jan Luiten van Zanden, eds, *Peasants into Farmers? The Transformation of Rural Economy and Society in the Low Countries (Middle Ages-19th Century) in Light of the Brenner Debate*, Turnhout 2001.

Imbusch, Peter, *'Das moderne Weltsystem': Eine Kritik der Weltsystemtheorie Immanuel Wallersteins*, Marburg 1990.

James, Edward, *The Origins of France: From Clovis to the Capetians, 500–1000*, London 1982.

Kaeuper, Richard W., *War, Justice, and Public Order: England and France in the Later Middle Ages*, Oxford 1988.

Kaiser, David, *Politics and War: European Conflict from Phillip II to Hitler*, Cambridge, MA, 1990.

Kandal, Terry R., 'Marx and Engels on International Relations, Revolution, and Counterrevolution', in Michael T. Martin and Terry R. Kandal (eds.), *Studies of Development and Change in the Modern World*, New York 1989, pp. 25–76.

Kant, Immanuel, 'To Perpetual Peace. A Philosophical Sketch', in I. Kant, *Perpetual Peace and Other Essays on Politics, History, and Morals*, transl. Ted Humphrey, Indianapolis, IN, [1795] 1983, pp. 107–39.

Kantorowicz, Ernst, *The King's Two Bodies: A Study in Mediaeval Political Theology*, Princeton, NJ, 1957.

Katz, Claudio J., *From Feudalism to Capitalism: Marxian Theories of Class Struggle and Social Change*, New York 1989.

——, 'Karl Marx on the Transition from Feudalism to Capitalism', *Theory and Society*, vol. 22, 1993, pp. 363–89.

Kerridge, Eric, *The Agricultural Revolution*, London 1967.

Klingenstein, Grete, 'The Meanings of "Austria" and "Austrian" in the Eighteenth Century', in Robert Oresko, G.C. Gibbs, and H.M. Scott, eds, *Royal and Republican Sovereignty in Early Modern Europe*, Cambridge 1997, pp. 423–78.

Kondylis, Panajotis, *Theorie des Krieges. Clausewitz – Marx – Engels – Lenin*, Stuttgart 1988.

Körner, Martin, 'Expenditure', in R. Bonney, ed., *Economic Systems and State Finance*, Oxford 1995a, pp. 393–422.

——, 'Public Credit', in R. Bonney, ed., *Economic Systems and State Finance*, Oxford 1995b, pp. 507–38.

Kosík, Karel, *Dialectics of the Concrete: A Study on Problems of Man and World*, transl. Karel Kovanda, Boston 1976.

Krasner, Stephen D., 'Westphalia and All That', in Judith Goldstein and Robert O. Keohane, eds, *Ideas and Foreign Policy: Beliefs, Institutions, and Political Change*, Ithaca/London 1993, pp. 235–64.

——, 'Compromising Westphalia', *International Security*, vol. 20, no. 3, 1995, pp. 115–51.

——, *Sovereignty: Organized Hypocrisy*, Princeton, NJ, 1999.

Kratochwil, Friedrich, 'On the Notion of "Interest" in International Relations', *International Organization*, vol. 36, no. 1, 1982, pp. 1–30.

——, 'Of Systems, Boundaries, and Territoriality: An Inquiry into the Formation of the State System', *World Politics*, vol. 34, no. 1, 1986, pp. 27–52.

——, *Rules, Norms, and Decisions: On the Conditions of Practical and Legal Reasoning in International Relations and Domestic Affairs*, Cambridge 1989.

——, 'Sovereignty as *Dominium*: Is There a Right of Humanitarian Intervention?', in Gene M. Lyons and Michael Mastanduno, eds, *State Sovereignty and International Intervention*, Baltimore 1995, pp. 21–42.

Krippendorff, Ekkehart, *Staat und Krieg: Die historische Logik politischer Unvernunft*, Frankfurt/M. 1985.

Kuchenbuch, Ludolf, 'Potestas und Utilitas: Ein Versuch über Stand und Perspektiven der Forschung zur Grundherrschaft im 9.–13. Jahrhundert', *Historische Zeitschrift*, no. 265, 1997, pp. 117–46.

Kuhn, Thomas, *The Structure of Scientific Revolutions*, London 1962.

Kula, Witold, *An Economic Theory of the Feudal System: Towards a Model of the Polish Economy, 1500–1800*, transl. Lawrence Garner, London [1962] 1976.

Kunisch, Johannes, *Staatsverfassung und Mächtepolitik. Zur Genese von Staatenkonflikten im Zeitalter des Absolutismus*, Berlin 1979.

——, ed., *Der dynastische Fürstenstaat: Zur Bedeutung von Sukzessionsordnungen für die Entstehung des frühmodernen Staates*, Berlin 1982.

——, 'La Guerre – c'est moi! Zum Problem der Staatenkonflikte im Zeitalter des Absolutismus', *Zeitschrift für Historische Forschung*, vol. 14, no. 1/4, 1987, pp. 407–38.

Lacher, Hannes, *Historicizing the Global: Capitalism, Territoriality, and the International Relations of Modernity*, London: forthcoming.

Ladurie, Emmanuel le Roy, *Les Paysans de Languedoc*, 2 vols, Paris 1966.

——, *The Royal French State, 1460–1610*, transl. Juliet Vale, Oxford [1987] 1994.

Lapid, Yosef and Friedrich V. Kratochwil, eds, *The Return of Culture and Identity in IR Theory*, Boulder, CO, 1996.

Le Patourel, John, 'The Norman Colonization of Britain', in *I Normanni e la loro espansione in Europa nell'alto medioevo: Settimane di Studio del Centro Italiano di Studi sull'Alto Medioevo*, no. 16, Spoleto 1969, pp. 409–38.

——, *The Norman Empire*, Oxford 1976.

Lomax, Derek W., *The Reconquest of Spain*, London 1978.

Luard, Evan, *The Balance of Power: The System of International Relations, 1648–1815*, London 1992.

Lublinskaya, A.D., *French Absolutism: The Crucial Phase 1620–29*, Cambridge 1968.

——, 'The Contemporary Bourgeois Conception of Absolute Monarchy', in Harold Wolpe, ed., *The Articulation of Modes of Production: Essays from 'Economy and Society'*, London [1972] 1980, pp. 161–88.

McKay, Derek and H.M. Scott, *The Rise of the Great Powers, 1648–1815*, London 1983.

McNally, David, *Political Economy and the Rise of Capitalism: A Reinterpretation*, Berkeley, CA, 1988.

Madariaga, Isabel de, 'Tsar into Emperor: The Title of Peter the Great', in Robert Oresko, G.C. Gibbs, and H.M. Scott, eds, *Royal and Republican Sovereignty in Early Modern Europe*, Cambridge 1997, pp. 351–81.

Malettke, Klaus, 'Ludwig XIV. Außenpolitik zwischen Staatsräson, ökonomischen Zwängen und Sozialkonflikten', in Heinz Duchhardt, ed., *Rahmenbedingungen und Handlungsspielräume europäischer Außenpolitik im Zeitalter Ludwigs XIV*, Berlin 1991, pp. 43–72.

Mann, Michael, *The Sources of Social Power: Vol. 1. A History of Power from the Beginning to A.D. 1760*, Cambridge 1986.

——, 'The Autonomous Power of the State: Its Origins, Mechanisms and Results', in Mann, *States, War, and Capitalism: Studies in Political Sociology*, Oxford 1988a, pp. 1–32.

——, 'European Development: Approaching a Historical Explanation', in J. Baechler et al. eds, *Europe and the Rise of Capitalism*, Oxford 1988b.

——, 'State and Society, 1130–1815: An Analysis of English State Financies', in Mann, *States, War and Capitalism: Studies in Political Sociology*, Oxford, 1988c, pp. 73–123.

Marx, Karl, 'Contribution to the Critique of Hegel's Philosophy of Law', in K. Marx and F. Engels, *Collected Works*, vol. 3, New York [1843] 1975, pp. 3–129.

——, and Friedrich Engels, *The German Ideology*, Moscow [1845] 1964.

——, *Grundrisse: Foundations of the Critique of Political Economy*, transl. Martin Nicolaus, London [1858] 1973.

——, 'Moralising Criticism and Critical Morality', in K. Marx and F. Engels, *Collected Works*, vol. 6, London [1847] 1976a.

——, *Capital: A Critique of Political Economy*, vol. 1, transl. Ben Fowkes, London [1867] 1976b.

——, *The Civil War in France*, in K. Marx and F. Engels, *Collected Works*, vol. 22, London [1871] 1976c.

——, *The Poverty of Philosophy*, in K. Marx and F. Engels, *Collected Works*, vol. 6, London [1847] 1976d.

——, *Capital: A Critique of Political Economy*, vol. 3, transl. David Fernbach, London [1894] 1981.

——, 'The Right Divine of the Hohenzollerns', in K. Marx and F. Engels, *Collected Works*, vol. 15, New York [1856] 1986, pp. 151–7.

——, *The Communist Manifesto: A Modern Edition*, London [1848] 1998.

Mattingly, Garrett, *Renaissance Diplomacy*, New York [1955] 1988.

Mayer, Arno J., *The Persistence of the Old Regime: Europe to the Great War*, New York 1981.

Mayer, Theodor, 'Die Ausbildung des modernen deutschen Staates im hohen mittelalter', in Hellmut Kämpf, ed., *Herrschaft und Staat im Mittelalter*, Bad Homburg [1939] 1963, pp. 284–331.

Mearsheimer, John, 'The False Promise of International Institutions', *International Security*, vol. 19, no. 3, 1995, pp. 5–49.

——, *The Tragedy of Great Power Politics*, New York 2001.

Merrington, John, 'Town and Countryside in the Transition to Capitalism', in Paul Sweezy et al. eds, *The Transition from Feudalism to Capitalism*, London 1976, pp. 170–95.

Mettam, Roger, *Power and Faction in Louis XIV's France*, Oxford 1988.

Mitteis, Heinrich, *The State in the Middle Ages: A Comparative Constitutional History of Feudal Europe*, transl. H.F. Orton, Amsterdam [1940] 1975.

Mommsen, Hans, '"Verstehen" und "Idealtypus": Zur Methodologie einer historischen Sozialwissenschaft', in H. Mommsen, *Max Weber: Gesellschaft, Politik und Geschichte*, Frankfurt/M. 1974, pp. 208–32.

——, 'Ideal Type and Pure Type: Two Variants of Max Weber's Ideal-Typical Method', in W. Mommsen, *The Political and Social Theory of Max Weber: Collected Essays*, Cambridge 1989, pp. 121–32.

Mooers, Colin, *The Making of Bourgeois Europe: Absolutism, Revolution, and the Rise of Capitalism in England, France and Germany*, London 1991.

Moraw, Peter, '"Herrschaft" im Mittelalter', in Otto Brunner, Werner Conze, and Reinhard Koselleck, eds, *Geschichtliche Grundbegriffe: Historisches Lexikon zur politisch-sozialen Sprache in Deutschland*, vol. 3, Stuttgart 1982, pp. 5–13.

Morgenthau, Hans J. and Kenneth W. Thompson, *Politics among Nations: The Struggle for Power and Peace*, 6th edn, New York [1948] 1985.

Mousnier, Roland, *The Institutions of France under the Absolute Monarchy, 1598–1789: Society and the State*, vol. I, transl. Brian Pearce, Chicago [1974] 1979.

——, *The Institutions of France under the Absolute Monarchy, 1589–1789: The Organs of the State and Society*, vol. II, transl. Arthur Goldhammer, Chicago [1980] 1984.

Muhlack, Ulrich, 'Absoluter Fürstenstaat und Heeresorganisation in Frankreich im Zeitalter Ludwigs XIV', in Johannes Kunisch, ed., *Staatsverfassung und Heeresverfassung in der europäischen Geschichte der frühen Neuzeit*, Berlin 1988, pp. 249–78.

Münkler, Herfried, *Machiavelli: Die Begründung des politischen Denkens der Neuzeit aus der Krise der Republik Florenz*, Frankfurt/M. 1992.

——, *Im Namen des Staates: Die Begründung der Staatsraison in der frühen Neuzeit*, Frankfurt/M 1987.

Nelson, Janet L., 'Kingship and Royal Government', in R. McKitterick, ed., *The New Cambridge Medieval History, Vol. II, c.700–900*, Cambridge 1995, pp. 383–436.

North, Douglass C., 'Institutions, Transaction Costs, and the Rise of Merchant Empires', in James D. Tracy, *The Political Economy of Merchant Empires: State Power and World Trade 1350–1750*, Cambridge 1991, pp. 22–40.

Oestreich, Gerhard, 'The Constitution of the Holy Roman Empire and the European State System, 1648–1789', in G. Oestreich, *Neostoicism and the Early Modern State*, Cambridge 1982 [1969], pp. 241–57.

Onuf, Nicholas G., *World of Our Making: Rules and Rule in Social Theory and International Relations*, Columbia 1989.

Oresko, Robert, 'The Marriages of the Nieces of Cardinal Mazarin: Public Policy and Private Strategy in Seventeenth-Century Europe', in Rainer Babel, ed., *Frankreich im europäischen Staatensystem der frühen Neuzeit*, Sigmaringen 1995, pp. 109–51.

——, and G.C. Gibbs, and H.M. Scott, eds, *Royal and Republican Sovereignty in Early Modern Europe*, Cambridge 1997.

Ormrod, W.M., 'The West European Monarchies in the Later Middle Ages', in R. Bonney, ed., *Economic Systems and State Finance*, Oxford 1995, pp. 123–60.

——, and János Barta, 'The Feudal Structure and the Beginnings of State Finance', in R. Bonney, ed., *Economic Systems and State Finance*, Oxford 1995, pp. 53–79.

Osiander, Andreas, *The States System of Europe, 1640–1990: Peacemaking and the Conditions of International Stability*, Oxford 1994.

——, 'Before Sovereignty: Society and Politics in Ancien Régime Europe', in Michael Cox, Tim Dunne, and Ken Booth, eds, *Empires, Systems and States: Great Transformations in International Politics*, Cambridge 2001, pp. 119–45.

Overton, Mark, *Agricultural Revolution in England: The Transformation of the Agrarian Economy 1500–1850*, Cambridge 1996.

Parker, David, 'Law, Society and the State in the Thought of Jean Bodin', *History of Political Thought*, vol. 2, no. 2, 1981, pp. 253–85.

——, 'Sovereignty, Absolutism and the Function of the Law in Seventeenth-Century France', *Past and Present*, no. 122, 1989, pp. 36–74.

——, *Class and State in Ancien Régime France: The Road to Modernity?*, London 1996.

Parker, Geoffrey *The Military Revolution: Military Innovation and the Rise of the West, 1500–1800*, Cambridge 1988.

——, and Lesley M. Smith, eds, *The General Crisis of the Seventeenth Century*, London 1978.

Parrott, David, 'A *Prince Souverain* and the French Crown: Charles de Nevers, 1580–1637', in Robert Oresko, G.C. Gibbs, and H.M. Scott, eds, *Royal and Republican Sovereignty in Early Modern Europe*, Cambridge 1997, pp. 149–87.

Philpot, Daniel, *Revolutions in Sovereignty: How Ideas Shaped Modern International Relations*, Princeton, NJ, 2001.

Poggi, Gianfranco, *The Development of the Modern State: A Sociological Introduction*, London 1978.

——, 'Max Weber's Conceptual Portrait of Feudalism, *British Journal of Sociology*, no. 39, 1988, pp. 211–27.

Polanyi, Karl, *The Great Transformation: The Political and Economic Origins of our Times*, Boston [1944] 1957.

Poly, Jean-Pierre and Bournazel, Eric, *The Feudal Transformation, 900–1200*, transl. Caroline Higitt, New York [1980] 1991.

Porchnev, Boris, *Les Soulèvements populaires en France de 1623 à 1648*, Paris 1963.

Postan, Michael M., 'Medieval Agrarian Society in its Prime: England', in Postan, ed., *Cambridge Economic History of Europe*, vol. 1, 2nd edn, *The Agrarian Life of the Middle Ages*, Cambridge 1966, pp. 548–632.

Rabb, Theodore K., *The Struggle for Stability in Early Modern Europe*, New York 1975.

Reinhard, Wolfgang, 'Staatsmacht als Kreditproblem: Zur Struktur und Funktion des frühneuzeitlichen Ämterhandels', *Vierteljahreshefte für Sozial- und Wirtschaftsgeschichte*, vol. 61, no. 3, 1975, pp. 289–319.

——, 'Kriegsstaat – Steuerstaat – Machtstaat', in R. Asch and H. Duchhardt, eds, *Der Absolutismus – ein Mythos? Strukturwandel monarchischer Herrschaft in West- und Mitteleuropa (ca. 1550–1700)*, Cologne 1996a, pp. 277–310.

——, 'Introduction: Power Elites, State Servants, Ruling Classes and the Growth of State Power', in W. Reinhard, ed., *Power Elites and State Building*, Oxford 1996b, pp. 1–18.

——, *Geschichte der Staatsgewalt: Eine Vergleichende Verfassungsgeschichte Europas von den Anfängen bis zur Gegenwart*, Munich 1999.

Repgen, Konrad, 'Der Westfälische Friede und die Ursprünge des europäischen Gleichgewichts', in K. Repgen, *Von der Reformation zur Gegenwart. Beiträge zu Grundfragen der neuzeitlichen Geschichte*, Paderborn 1988, 53–66.

Reus-Smit, Christian, *The Moral Purpose of the State: Culture, Social Identity, and Institutional Rationality in International Relations*, Princeton, NJ, 1999.

Reuter, Timothy, 'Plunder and Tribute in the Carolingian Empire', *Transactions of the Royal Historical Society*, 5th series, no. 35, 1985, pp. 75–94.

——, 'The End of Carolingian Military Expansion', in Peter Godman and Roger Collins, eds, *Charlemagne's Heir. New Perspectives on the Reign of Louis the Pious (814–840)*, Oxford 1995, pp. 391–405.

Robinson, Ian, *The Papacy, 1073–1198: Continuity and Innovation*, Cambridge 1990.

Root, Hilton, *Peasants and King in Burgundy: Agrarian Foundations of French Absolutism*, Berkeley, CA, 1987.

Rosenberg, Justin, *The Empire of Civil Society: A Critique of the Realist Theory of International Relations*, London 1994.

——, 'Isaac Deutscher and the Lost History of International Relations', *New Left Review*, no. 215, 1996, pp. 3–15.

Rösener, Werner, *Agrarwirtschaft, Agrarverfassung, und ländliche Gesellschaft im Mittelalter*, Munich 1992.

Rowen, Herbert, '"L'État, c'est à moi"; Louis XIV and the State', *French Historical Studies*, no. 2, 1961, pp. 83–98.

——, 'Louis XIV and Absolutism', in John C. Rule, ed., *Louis XIV and the Craft of Kingship*, Columbia 1969, pp. 302–16.

——, *The King's State: Proprietary Dynasticism in Early Modern France*, New Brunswick, NJ, 1980.

Ruggie, John Gerard, 'Continuity and Transformation in the World Polity: Toward a Neorealist Synthesis', in Robert O. Keohane, ed., *Neorealism and its Critics*, New York [1983] 1986, pp. 131–57.

——, 'International Structure and International Transformation: Space, Time, and Method', in Ernst-Otto Czempiel and James N. Rosenau, eds, *Global Changes and Theoretical Challenges: Approaches to World Politics for the 1990s*, Lexington, MA, 1989, pp. 21–35.

——, 'Territoriality and Beyond: Problematizing Modernity in International Relations', *International Organization*, vol. 47, no. 1, 1993, pp. 139–74.

——, 'What Makes the World Hang Together? Neo-Utilitarianism and the Social Constructivist Challenge', *International Organization*, vol. 52, no. 4, 1998, pp. 855–85.

Sahlins, Peter, 'Natural Frontiers Revisited: France's Boundaries since the Seventeenth Century', *American Historical Review*, no. 95, 1990, pp. 1423–51.

Salmon, J.H.M., 'Venality of Office and Popular Sedition in Seventeenth-Century France', in Salmon, *Renaissance and Revolt: Essays in the Intellectual and Social History of Early Modern France*, Cambridge [1967] 1987, pp. 191–210.

Sayer, Derek, 'The Critique of Politics and Political Economy: Capitalism, Communism and the State in Marx's Writings of the Mid-1840s', *The Sociological Review*, vol. 33, no. 2, 1985, pp. 221–53.

Schmidt, Alfred, *History and Structure: An Essay on Hegelian-Marxist and Structuralist Theories of History*, transl. Jeffrey Herf, Cambridge, MA, 1981.

Schmoller, Gustav, *The Mercantile System and its Historical Significance: Illustrated*

Chiefly from Prussian History, reprinted 1967 by Augustus M. Kelley Publishers, New York [1884] 1897.

Schroeder, Paul W., 'Did the Vienna Settlement Rest on a Balance of Power?', *American Historical Review*, vol. 97, no. 3, 1992, pp. 683–706.

——, *The Transformation of European Politics, 1763–1848*, Oxford 1994a.

——, 'Historical Reality vs. Neo-realist Theory', *International Security*, vol. 19, no.1, 1994b, pp. 108–48.

Schulze, Winfried, 'Europäische und deutsche Bauernrevolten der frühen Neuzeit: Probleme der vergleichenden Betrachtung', in Schulze, ed., *Europäische Bauernrevolten der frühen Neuzeit*, Frankfurt/M 1982.

——, 'The Emergence and Consolidation of the "Tax State": I. The Sixteenth Century', in R. Bonney, ed., *Economic Systems and State Finance*, Oxford 1995, pp. 261–79.

Schumpeter, Joseph, 'The Crisis of the Tax State', *International Economic Papers*, New York [1918] 1954, vol. 4, pp. 5–38.

Schwarz, Brigide, 'Ämterkäuflichkeit, eine Institution des Absolutismus und ihre mittelalterlichen Wurzeln', in Historisches Seminar der Universität Münster, ed., *Staat und Gesellschaft in Mittelalter und früher Neuzeit: Gedenkschrift für Joachim Leuschner*, Göttingen 1983, pp. 176–96.

Searle, Eleanor, *Predatory Kinship and the Creation of Norman Power: 840–1066*, Berkeley, CA, 1988.

Sheehan, Michael, 'The Development of British Theory and Practice of the Balance of Power before 1714', *History*, vol. 73, no. 237, 1988, pp. 24–37.

——, *The Balance of Power: History and Theory*, London 1996.

Siegelberg, Jens, *Kapitalismus und Krieg: Eine Theorie des Krieges in der Weltgesellschaft*, Münster 1994.

Skocpol, Theda, *States and Social Revolutions: A Comparative Analysis of France, Russia, and China*, Cambridge 1979.

——, 'Wallerstein's World Capitalist System: A Theoretical and Historical Critique', in Skocpol, *Social Revolutions in the Modern World*, Cambridge [1977] 1994, pp. 55–71.

Smith, Julia, '*Fines Imperii*: The Marches', in Rosamond McKitterick, ed., *The New Cambridge Medieval History, c.700–c.900*, vol. 2, Cambridge 1995, pp. 169–89.

Smith, Steve, 'Historical Sociology and International Relations Theory', in St. Hobden and J. Hobson (eds.), *Historical Sociology of International Relations*, Cambridge 2002, pp. 223–43.

Soell, Helmuth, 'Weltmarkt – Revolution – Staatenwelt. Zum Problem einer Theorie internationaler Beziehungen bei Marx und Engels', *Archiv für Internationale Beziehungen*, vol. 12, 1972, pp. 109–84.

Spruyt, Hendrik, *The Sovereign State and its Competitors: An Analysis of Systems Change*, Princeton 1994a.

——, 'Institutional Selection in International Relations: State Anarchy as Order', *International Organization*, vol. 48, no. 4, 1994b, pp. 527–57.

——, 'Historical Sociology and Systems Theory in International Relations', *Review of International Political Economy*, vol. 5, no. 2, 1998, pp. 340–53.

Steiger, Heinhard, 'Der Westfälische Frieden – Grundgesetz für Europa?', in Heinz Duchhardt, ed., *Der Westfälische Friede: Diplomatie, politische Zäsur, Kulturelles Umfeld, Rezeptionsgeschichte*, Munich 1998, pp. 33–80.

Strayer, Joseph, *On the Medieval Origins of the Modern State*, Princeton, NJ, 1970.

Sweezy, Paul, 'A Critique', in *The Transition from Feudalism to Capitalism*, ed. Rodney Hilton, London 1976, pp. 35–56.

——, Maurice Dobb et al., *The Transition from Feudalism to Capitalism*, London 1976.

Symcox, Geoffrey, ed., *War, Diplomacy, and Imperialism, 1618–1763*, London 1974.

Tabacco, Giovanni, *The Struggle for Power in Medieval Italy: Structures of Political Rule*, Cambridge 1989.

Tellenbach, Gerd, 'From the Carolingian Imperial Nobility to the German Estate of Princes', in Th. Reuter, ed., *Medieval Nobility: Studies on the Ruling Classes of France and Germany from the Sixth to the Twelfth Century*, Amsterdam [1943] 1978.

Teschke, Benno, 'The Significance of the Year One Thousand', *Historical Materialism: Research in Critical Marxist Theory*, vol. 1, no. 1, 1997, pp. 196–203.

——, 'Geopolitical Relations in the European Middle Ages: History and Theory', *International Organization*, vol. 52, no.2, 1998, pp. 325–58.

——, 'Geopolitik', in Wolfgang-Fritz Haug, ed., *Historisch-Kritisches Wörterbuch des Marxismus*, vol. 5, Hamburg 2001, pp. 322–34.

——, 'Theorising the Westphalian System of States: International Relations from Absolutism to Capitalism', *European Journal of International Relations*, vol. 8, no. 1, 2002, pp. 5–48.

——, and Christian Heine, 'The Dialectic of Globalisation: A Critique of Social Constructivism', in Mark Rupert and Hazel Smith, eds, *Historical Materialism and Globalization*, London 2002, pp. 165–87.

Tilly Charles, 'Reflections on the History of European State-Making', in Charles Tilly ed., *The Formation of National States in Western Europe*, Princeton, NJ, 1975, pp. 3–83.

——, 'War Making and State Making as Organized Crime', in Peter B. Evans, Dietrich Rueschemeyer, and Theda Skocpol, eds, *Bringing the State Back In*, Cambridge 1985, pp. 169–91.

——, *Coercion, Capital, and European States: AD 990–1992*, Cambridge 1992.

Thomson, Janice E., *Mercenaries, Pirates, and Sovereigns: State-Building and Extraterritorial Violence in Early Medieval Europe*, Princeton, NJ, 1994.

Tracy, James D., *The Rise of Merchant Empires: Long-Distance Trade in the Early Modern World, 1350–1750*, Cambridge 1990.

Van der Pijl, Kees, *Vordenker der Weltpolitik*, Opladen 1996.

——, 'The History of Class Struggle: From Original Accumulation to Neoliberalism', *Monthly Review*, vol. 49. no. 1, 1997, pp. 28–49.

——, Walker, R.B.J., 'History and Structure in the Theory of International', *Millennium: Journal of International Studies*, vol. 18, no. 2, 1989, pp. 163–83.

——, *Transnational Classes and International Relations*, London 1998.

Verhulst, Adriaan, 'Economic Organisation', in R. McKitterick, ed., *The New Cambridge Medieval History, Vol. II, c.700–900*, Cambridge 1995, pp. 481–509.

Vierhaus, Rudolf, 'Absolutismus', in Ernst Hinrichs, ed., *Absolutismus*, Frankfurt/M [1966] 1985, pp. 35–62.

——, *Germany in the Age of Absolutism*, transl. Jonathan B. Knudsen, Cambridge 1988.

Vilar, Pierre, 'Marxist History, A History in the Making: Towards a Dialogue with Althusser', *New Left Review*, no. 80, 1973, pp. 65–106.

Viner, Jacob, 'Power versus Plenty as Objectives of Foreign Policy in the Seventeenth and Eighteenth Centuries', in D.C. Coleman, ed., *Revisions in Mercantilism*, London [1948] 1969, pp. 61–91.

Walker, R.B.J., 'History and Structure in the Theory of International Relations', *Millennium: Journal of International Studies*, vol. 18, no. 2, 1989, pp. 163–83.

Wallerstein, Immanuel, *The Modern World System I: Capitalist Agriculture and the Origins of the European World-Economy in the Sixteenth Century*, New York 1974.

——, 'The Rise and Future Demise of the World Capitalist System: Concepts for Comparative Analysis', in Wallerstein, *The Capitalist World-Economy*, Cambridge 1979, pp. 1–36.

——, *The Modern World-System II: Mercantilism and the Consolidation of the European World-Economy, 1600–1750*, New York 1980.

——, *Historical Capitalism with Capitalist Civilization*, London 1995.

Waltz, Kenneth N., *Man, the State, and War: A Theoretical Analysis*, New York 1959.

——, *Theory of International Politics*, Reading, MA, 1979.

——, 'Reflections on *Theory of International Politics*: A Response to my Critics', in Robert O. Keohane, ed., *Neorealism and its Critics*, New York 1986, pp. 322–45.

——, 'The Origins of War in Neorealist Theory', *Journal of Interdisciplinary History*, vol. 18, 1988, pp. 615–28.

——, 'Realist Thought and Neorealist Theory', *Journal of International Affairs*, vol. 44, 1990, pp. 21–37.

Weber, Hermann, 'Die Bedeutung der Dynastien für die europäische Geschichte in der frühen Neuzeit', *Zeitschrift für Bayerische Landesgeschichte*, vol. 44, 1981, pp. 5–32.

Weber, Max, *General Economic History*, transl. Frank H. Knight, Glencoe, IL, 1927.

——, 'Politics as a Vocation', in *From Max Weber: Essays in Sociology*, transl. and ed. H.H. Gerth and C. Wright Mills, New York [1919] 1946, pp. 77–128.

——, '"Objectivity" in Social Science and Social Policy', in Edward A. Shils and Henry A. Finch, eds, *The Methodology of the Social Sciences*, Glencoe, IL, [1904] 1949a, pp. 49–112.

——, 'The Meaning of "Ethical Neutrality" in Sociology and Economics', in E.A. Shils and H.A. Finch, eds, *The Methodology of the Social Sciences*, Glencoe [1918] 1949b, pp. 1–47.

——, *Economy and Society: An Outline of Interpretive Sociology*, vols. 1 and 2, ed. by G. Roth and C. Wittich, Berkeley [1922] 1968a.

——, 'Über einige Kategorien der verstehenden Soziologie', in M. Weber, *Gesammelte Aufsätze zur Wissenschaftslehre*, 3rd edn, ed. Johannes Winckelmann, Tübingen [1913] 1968b, pp. 427–74.

——, *The Protestant Ethic and the Spirit of Capitalism*, transl. Talcott Parsons, London [1904/5] 1992.

Wendt, Alexander, 'The Agent–Structure Problem in International Relations Theory', *International Organization*, vol. 41, no. 3, 1987, pp. 335–370.

——, 'Anarchy Is What States Make of It: The Social Construction of Power Politics', *International Organization*, vol. 46, no. 2, 1992, pp. 391–425.

——, *Social Theory of International Politics*, Cambridge 1999.

Werner, Karl, ''Missus–Marchio–Comes: Entre l'administration centrale et l'administration locale de l'empire carolingien, in K. Werner and W. Paravicini, eds, *Histoire comparée de l'administration: IVe–XVIIIe siècles*, Munich 1980, pp. 191–239.

Wickham, Chris, 'Historical Materialism, Historical Sociology', *New Left Review*, no. 171, 1988, pp. 63–78.

——, 'Making Europes', *New Left Review*, no. 208, 1994, pp. 133–43.

——, 'Debate: The "Feudal Revolution"', *Past and Present*, no. 155, 1997, pp. 196–208.

Wight, Martin, 'The Balance of Power', in Herbert Butterfield and Martin Wight, eds, *Diplomatic Investigations: Essays in the Theory of International Politics*, London 1966a, pp. 149–75.

——, 'Why Is There No International Theory?', in H. Butterfield and M. Wight, eds, *Diplomatic Investigations: Essays in the Theory of International Politics*, London 1966b, pp. 17–34.

——, 'De Systematibus Civitatum', in Wight, *Systems of States*, Leicester 1977a, pp. 21–45.

——, 'The Origins of Our States-System: Chronological Limits', in Wight, *Systems of States*, Leicester 1977b, pp. 129–53.

——, *Power Politics*, ed. Hedley Bull and Carsten Holbraad, Leicester 1978.

Wohlfeil, Rainer, 'Das Heerwesen im Übergang vom Ritter- zum Söldnerheer', in Johannes Kunisch, ed., *Staatsverfassung und Heeresverfassung in der europäischen Geschichte der frühen Neuzeit*, Berlin 1988, pp. 107–27.

Wood, Ellen Meiksins, *The Pristine Culture of Capitalism: A Historical Essay on Old Regimes and Modern States*, London 1991.

——, 'From Opportunity to Imperative: The History of the Market', *Monthly Review*, vol. 46, no. 3, 1994, pp. 14–40.

——, 'The Separation of the "Economic" and the "Political" in Capitalism', in

Wood, *Democracy against Capitalism: Renewing Historical Materialism*, Cambridge [1981] 1995a, pp. 19–48.

——, 'Rethinking Base and Superstructure', in Wood, *Democracy Against Capitalism: Renewing Historical Materialism*, Cambridge 1995b, pp. 49–75.

——, *Democracy Against Capitalism: Renewing Historical Materialism*, Cambridge 1995c.

——, 'Capitalism, Merchants and Bourgeois Revolution: Reflections on the Brenner Debate and its Sequel', *International Review of Social History*, vol. 41, no. 2, 1996, pp. 209–32

——, *The Origins of Capitalism: A Longer View*, London 2002.

Wolf, Eric R., *Europe and the People without History*, Berkeley, CA, 1982.

Wright, Quincy, *A Study of War*, 2nd edn, Chicago [1942] 1965.

Wrigley, Anthony, 'Urban Growth and Agricultural Change: England and the Continent in the Early Modern Period', *Journal of Interdisciplinary History*, no. 15, 1985, pp. 683–728.

Zech, Reinhold, 'Nationalökonomische Theorien: Merkantilisten, Physiokraten und Klassiker: Die Merkantilisten', in Iring Fetscher and Herfried Münkler, eds, *Pipers Handbuch der politischen Ideen, vol.3, Neuzeit: Von den Konfessionskriegen bis zur Aufklärung*, Munich 1985, pp. 561–79.

Zolberg, Aristide, 'Strategic Interactions and the Formation of Modern States: France and England', *International Social Science Journal*, vol. 32, no. 4, 1980, pp. 687–716.

——, 'Origins of the Modern World: A Missing Link', *World Politics*, vol. 33, no. 2, 1981, pp. 253–81.

Index

Braudel on 131
capitalism and 5
as class relation 56
decline of 2
dynastic 10
as ensemble of lordships 46, 56, 61–2, 67
Marx on 53, 55
medieval 46–7, 61–2, 66, 87–8
modern 53
  emergence of 19–25, 26, 28, 31, 32–3, 40
'organic' 122
permanent war 181
as rational actor 153–5
realist definition of 143
sovereignty of 1–2, 37, 45n, 151–2
tax/office 169–70, 183, 185, 189, 219, 245, 251, 255
territorial 33, 37
war and 118–27
Weber on 37, 134
states-system
European 23, 109–11
feudal 70
modern 32, 117
multiple 14, 265
origin of 19–25, 25, 26, 28, 34, 37, 40–44, 230
as prior to capitalism 264
pre-capitalist 41, 265
under attack today 145
status quo ante bellum 239–40
Stauffers/Hohenstauffens 20
Steiger, Heinhard 238, 243, 244
strategies of reproduction 7, 59
Strayer, Joseph 193n
'structural discontinuity' 39, 41, 43
structuralism 15, 16, 40, 42, 43, 64
structure 30, 48, 56
structure-agent problem 48, 56, 57–69 – *see also* agency
Stuarts 201, 225, 232, 257
subjectivity 29
sublation (*Aufhebung*) 159
surplus 50, 53, 55–6, 60–1, 87, 94, 141–2
Sweden 136, 153, 218, 231
  dominium maris baltici 224
  king of 238, 239
  Westphalian settlement and 239–40, 243–4
Sweezey, Paul 35, 52, 140, 163
Swiss confederation 22, 37
Switzerland 153, 218
Symcox, Geoffrey 238, 247n, 248n
Syria 104
systematic reinvestment in means of production 251
systemic change 17, 26, 28, 30–1, 44, 218, 249
systems change 16–7, 19, 22–4, 32
  denied by Krasner 27

Tabacco, Giovanni 80, 86, 104, 111
tax regime 169
tax state 120
tax/office state 169–70, 183, 185, 189, 219, 245, 251, 255
taxation
  absolutist 21, 36

generalized 33, 120
self- 257–8
socially determined 149n
vs rents 36, 161
teleology 56
Tellenbach, Gerd 91
territoriality
absolutist 37, 264
amorphous 67
bounded 3, 38, 43, 48, 65–6, 84, 209, 211, 232–3
centralized 106
dynastic 37, 91, 230–3, 246
exclusive 1, 30, 32, 36, 65, 72, 230
medieval 28, 59
pre-modern 268
Teschke, Benno 48, 74, 75n, 115n, 247n, 270n
Teutonic Order 102
theocracy 81, 101
theories of history
evolutionary 32–9
materialist 64
stagist 157, 166
theory of social-property relations 7, 47, 118, 249, 262, 272–3
Thessalonica 93
'third hand' 263
'third image' 124
Thirty Years' War 2, 45n, 135, 170, 174, 176, 179, 181, 182, 183, 187, 188, 196n, 239–40, 243
Thomson, Janice 204
Three Orders, doctrine of (trifunctionalism) 103
Tilly, Charles 118, 119, 125, 146n, 147–8n, 193n, 221
totality 30
towns 45n
Tracy, James 212
trade
free 25, 201, 211, 214n
long-distance 96, 204
medieval 111, 163–4
routes 199, 201
wars 202, 210–1
transformation – *see* transition
transition
absolutist to modern international relations 249
geopolitical 38, 46, 47
imperial hierarchy to feudal anarchy 84–6
medieval to modern international relations 38, 43
theories of 40
Transition Debate 163
Treasury Board 253
Treaties of Westphalia – *see under* Westphalia
Treaty of the Pyrenees (1659) 242
Treaty of Utrecht (1713) 3, 232, 233, 234, 258–9
Treaty of Verdun (843) 66, 83
Treaty of Versailles (1919) 126
Treaty of Vienna (1725) 234
Treaty of Vienna, second (1728) 228
treuga dei (truce of god) 69, 103
Triennial Act (1694) 252
Tuscany 148n, 229